W9-AYE-567

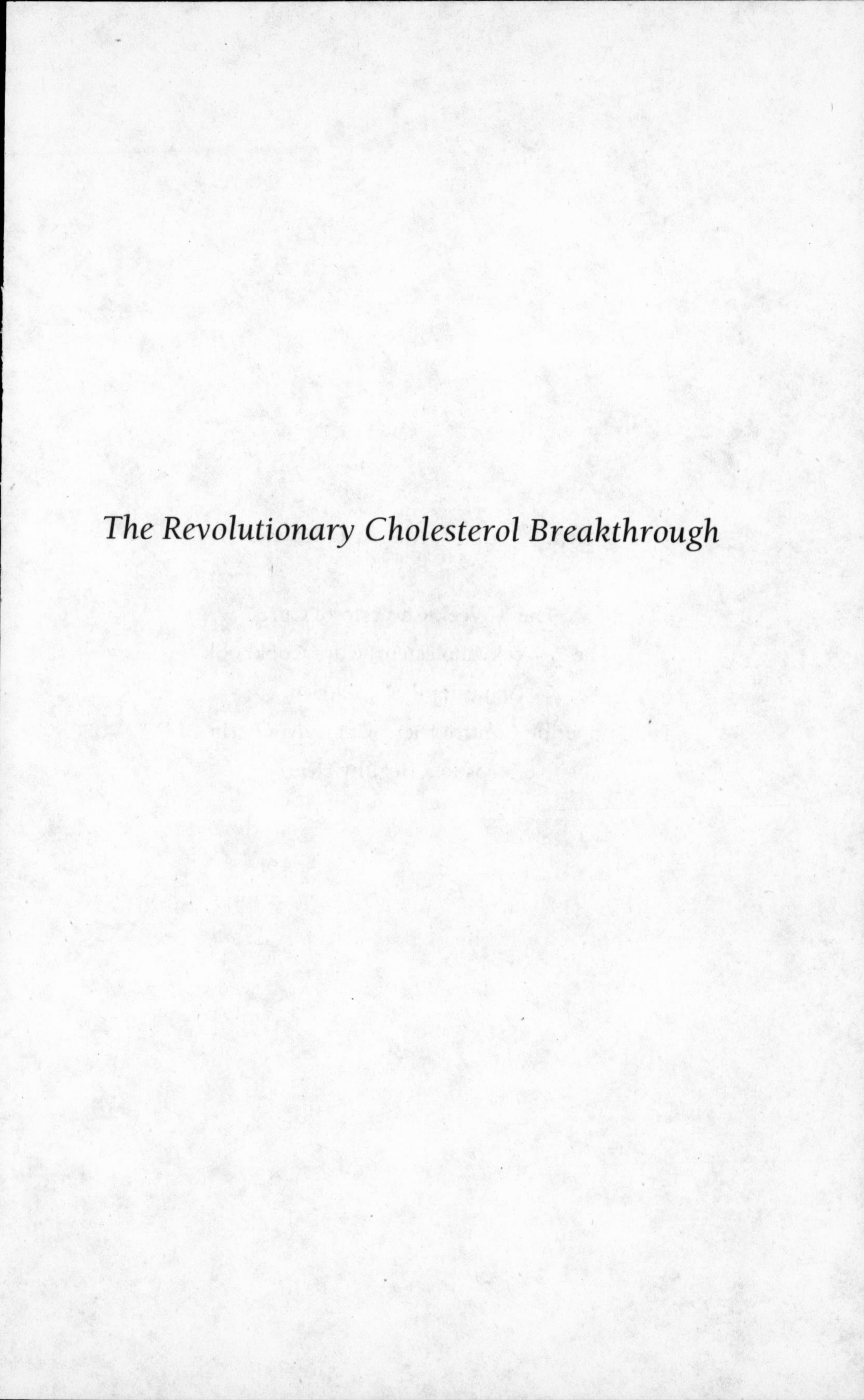

The Revolutionary Cholesterol Breakthrough

Other Books by Robert E. Kowalski

The 8-Week Cholesterol Cure

The 8-Week Cholesterol Cure Cookbook

Cholesterol & Children

The Endocrine Control Diet *(with Calvin Ezrin, M.D.)*

8 Steps to a Healthy Heart

·The·

Revolutionary Cholesterol *Breakthrough*

How to
Eat Everything
You Want
and
Have Your Heart
Thank You
for It

Robert E. Kowalski

·
·
·

ANDREWS AND McMEEL
A UNIVERSAL PRESS SYNDICATE COMPANY
•
Kansas City

The Revolutionary Cholesterol Breakthrough:
How to Eat Everything You Want and Have Your Heart Thank You for It.
Copyright © 1996 by Robert E. Kowalski.
All rights reserved.
Printed in the United States of America.
No part of this book may be used or reproduced in any manner whatsoever
except in the case of reprints in the context of reviews.
For information write to
Andrews and McMeel, a Universal Press Syndicate Company,
4520 Main Street, Kansas City, Missouri 64111.

Library of Congress Cataloging-in-Publication Data

Kowalski, Robert E.
The revolutionary cholesterol breakthrough : how to eat everything you want and have your heart thank you for it / Robert Kowalski.
p. cm.
Includes bibliographical references and index.
ISBN 0-8362-1044-1 (hd)
1. Hypercholesteremia—Prevention. 2. Hypercholesteremia—Diet therapy.
I. Title.
RC632.H83K68 1996
616.1'205—dc20 95-51772
CIP

ATTENTION: SCHOOLS AND BUSINESSES

Andrews and McMeel books are available at quantity discounts
with bulk purchase for educational, business, or sales promotional use.
For information, please write to
Special Sales Department,
Andrews and McMeel,
4520 Main Street, Kansas City, Missouri 64111.

Dedication

For Dawn,
with whom I look forward to enjoying
many hundreds and thousands of delicious meals
together in the years to come.
Here's a toast to dinner
number one million!

Contents

FOREWORD

It is with a great deal of pleasure and enthusiasm that I take on the task of writing this foreword. Bob and I have a long and happy affiliation. Over the years I have always been impressed with the many new ideas and therapies he finds. Sometimes it's variations on his own therapy. Other times it's from scouring the medical literature or from frequently attending postgraduate medical seminars. He has always been very kind in bringing me his latest findings in the field of heart health.

I might digress a moment. When I had my own cardiac concern in the form of a needed coronary bypass operation, the person I consulted was Robert Kowalski. He very succinctly filled me in on what he felt the cardiologist should be doing in my best interest. And he was entirely on the mark. My therapy was extremely successful, thanks largely to Bob's experience and knowledge. I had access to the best cardiologist in southern California, but I turned to Bob for his profound knowledge and understanding.

Who should read Bob's latest book? Who will benefit from it? The answer is simple: all those who want a longer, fuller, healthier life for themselves and for those close to them. This book is like a recipe. Take a number of confusing facts, simmer with clarity, add a pinch of humor, and cut into chapters. Bob has a remarkable style for simplicity and writing understandably. His descriptions are worth the price of admission. His explanations of the pathology of hyperlipidemia, the role of fats and cholesterol in heart health and disease, which is normally extremely complex, is remarkably clear. His chapter on weight loss alone is extremely valuable.

So who would benefit from, or should read, this book? There are very few of us who don't have some type of risk factor, be it blood pressure elevation, hyperlipidemia or high cholesterol, diabetes, obesity, inactivity, stress, or even smoking. These factors coupled with family or genetic problems affect more than 80 percent of the population. Knowledge allows one to make proper choices. The information in Bob's book certainly will improve anyone's knowledge and will offer a reasonable, rational approach to longevity. This book gives everyone a very flexible, workable approach to a problem that almost all of us have in varying degrees.

Even those who read Bob's very popular previous book, *The 8-Week Cholesterol Cure,* will find a vast amount of new knowledge. In this new book, Bob introduces a tremendous number of significant, new concepts regarding heart disease protection and even some variations on old theories. In the section on niacin, his ideas are the point of the lance, both safe and effective. I endorse this therapy wholeheartedly, as does my brother Joseph, a professor of medicine at the University of Minnesota who is doing a good deal of research in the use of niacin preventively. Bob emphasizes the practical and safe ways to utilize the therapy, with some remarkable and valuable new twists.

The chapter on weight loss is essentially a book unto itself. Bob explains a very usable means of manipulating one's diet so that weight loss is easy and effective. This chapter also includes an excellent description of insulin resistance and its links to obesity. Bob's approach is not denial or sacrifice but rather substitution and the use of revolutionary new agents. He gives many alternative choices that make dieting successful and practical for everyone.

As Bob has stressed, he wants to make his program workable and livable. Part of his motivation has been to enable people to eat the foods that they enjoy and to minimize the undesirable effects. His program is extremely successful in this area of his venture. This book actually makes dieting easier by eliminating the mental gymnastics that prior diets outline. His approach is to provide some good generalities that will help you make wise food choices both in the supermarket and in restaurants.

I have to mention Bob's real purpose for writing this book. He really believes that his concepts may help eliminate cardiac disease and vascular disease if his measures are accepted by the population at large. He has sincere humanitarian goals in mind. They key to longevity is the vascular system and in particular the system's pump, the heart. If the measures in Bob's book are followed, there can be no question that one would lead a much fuller and longer life.

I must relate the story of my brother's reaction to my having a triple bypass. In jest, he called me at the hospital on my second day after surgery and said that prior to this, we had no family history of heart disease. Now, he said, "I have another risk factor." Well, he does and I do, and that is more reason than ever for us to enjoy the principles of this treatise. Not only does Bob offer a number of ways to modify our lifestyle, but every concept is also well documented.

I must now reflect on a bit of history. Prior to Bob's first work, I think doctors knew about heart disease risk factors, but they didn't take an active stance with their patients. There was very limited knowledge by the general public regarding the consequences of lifestyle. With the advent of his book, a totally new emphasis was placed on preventive medicine.

The cholesterol problem has been researched in much greater detail since *The 8-Week Cholesterol Cure* came out in 1987. Concepts like HDL, LDL, Lp(a), and others came to the fore and got much respect from the medical community. I don't believe that anyone had ever heard of oat bran prior to that 1987 book. Then it became the rage of the country. This is a credit to Bob's literary talents in the past. Now he has crafted an exceptional work of new principles and ideas and new therapies for eliminating the scourge of heart disease. It will be well worth your while to invest some time in carefully reading this book and following the advice it contains for the sake of your own future health.

Charles M. Keenan Jr., M.D.
Santa Monica, California
November 1995

Acknowledgments

Where does one begin to thank the many people who have enabled this author to complete another book? The list, which spans the years since I became a crusader for heart health, in 1984, must, by limitations of reality, be limited. But I must start, at least in a generic way, by thanking the many doctors, nurses, and other health professionals without whose care I simply wouldn't exist today. Next I must thank my family, all of them, for putting up with my experiments in the kitchen, a work and travel schedule that would have unraveled most families, and the ups and downs that only they have endured with me.

I thank all those who have helped me gather information over the years, culminating in this book. None has been as cooperative and supportive as the now retired Howard Lewis and all his staff at the news division of the American Heart Association.

During my research, literally dozens of highly respected researchers have contributed their time generously for interviews and to answer my questions. I thank all of you.

And a special thanks to everyone who agreed to review the manuscript for accuracy and to add those final touches. Dr. David Kritchevsky of the Wistar Institute in Philadelphia. Dr. David Heber at UCLA. Dr. Gerald Berenson at Tulane University in New Orleans. Dr. Calvin Ezrin at Cedars-Sinai Medical Center in Los Angeles. Dr. Jeff Gero of Success Over Stress in Los Angeles. Dr. Joseph Keenan at the University of Minnesota. His brother Charles Keenan, M.D., Santa Monica, my friend and physician. Jennifer Jensen, R.D., of Santa Monica. Dr. Jack Sternlieb of the Heart Institute of the Desert, and members of his staff, Barbara Crouse, R.D., and Luke Seth, M.S., all of whom reviewed these pages diligently. It's with great pride that I serve as president of the Heart Institute of the Desert Foundation, and as director of lifestyle modification at the Institute in Rancho Mirage, California. Working with all of you has improved my book and has enriched my life.

Before beginning this or any other medical or nutritional regimen, consult your physician to be sure it is appropriate for you.

The information in this book reflects the author's experiences, and is not intended to replace medical advice. Any questions on symptoms, general or specific, should be addressed to your physician.

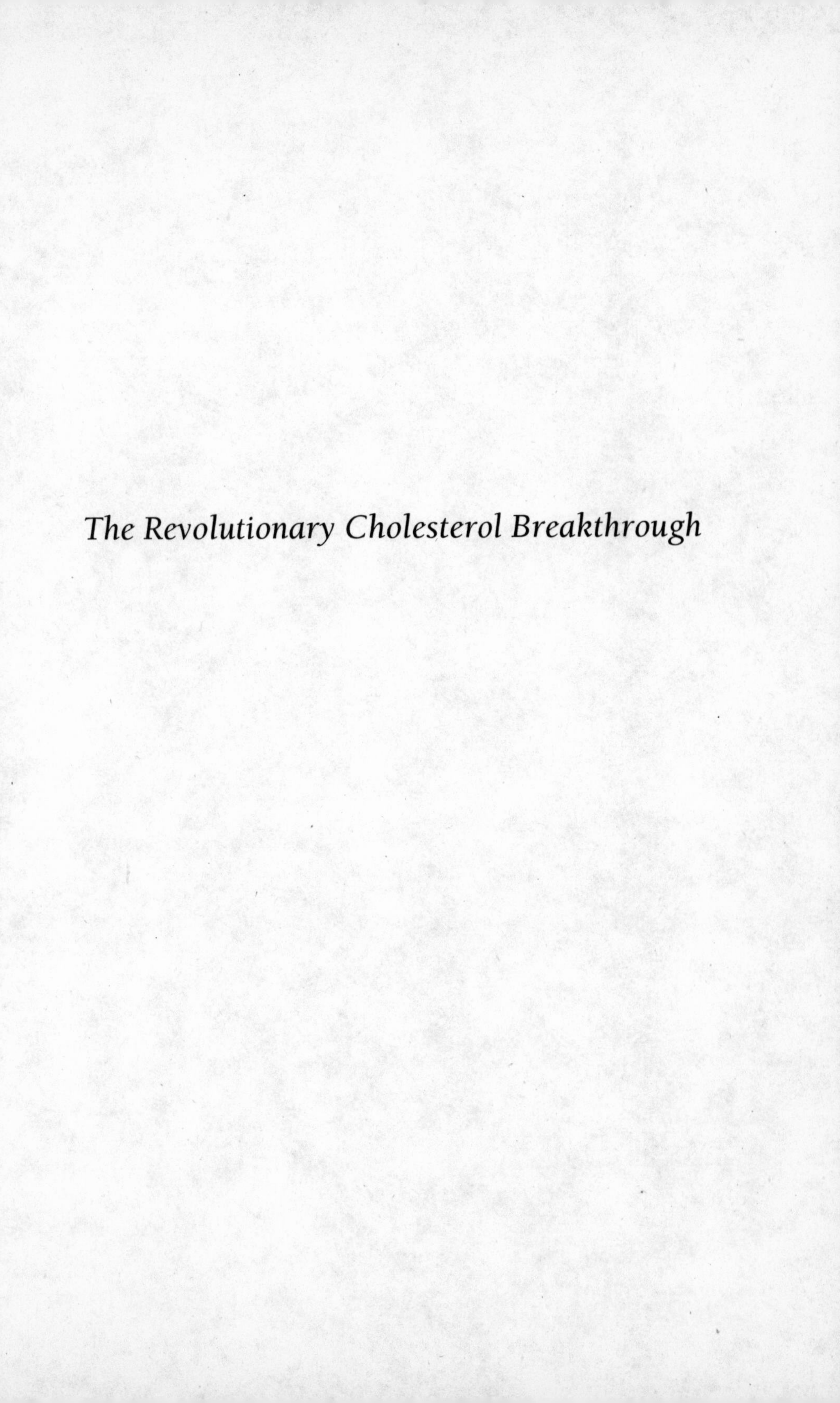

The Revolutionary Cholesterol Breakthrough

Introduction

I celebrated the Fourth of July in 1994 like I'd never done before. The Declaration of Independence had brought America to its revolution, and I'd been fighting—and winning—my own health revolution. You see, it was on that day, ten years prior, that I lay in the hospital recovering from my second coronary bypass surgery at the age of forty-one. A decade later, there I was: free of the risk of heart disease, feeling better than I'd ever felt in my life, and eating a thick, juicy steak!

That's right. I've completely beaten heart disease, controlled my previously high cholesterol level, and I eat steaks. Also sunnyside-up eggs. And lots of pork. Delicious foods I thought I'd have to give up forever. All the while knowing that those foods wouldn't jeopardize my heart.

That day in 1994 I thought back again and again to the events that had led to my life today. I'd had a heart attack and bypass surgery at age thirty-five in 1978. The doctors told me then that I had nothing to worry about, that they had "fixed" my problem. But they were wrong. The disease continued to progress, and a mere six years later, I needed a "re-do," which, owing to potential complications, had five to six times the risk of death as the first operation. I was only forty-one.

Motivated by my little children, whom I refused to leave without a daddy, I swore I'd find some way to be free of heart disease. As a medical writer, with nearly two decades of experience at the time, I gave myself the assignment of researching ways to save my own life. Most notably, I had to find a way to control my elevated cholesterol level.

And I did it! I came up with a plan, as my cardiologist then laughingly referred to it, based on cereal and vitamins. But he wasn't laughing when my laboratory results showed a 40 percent reduction in cholesterol, from 284 to 169, in just eight weeks. Together the two of us demonstrated that the program worked as effectively for others as well. I shared that regimen with the world in 1987 in my book *The 8-Week Cholesterol Cure.*

Ten years after the second bypass, my own cure had become a way of life for me as well as for my entire family. The book had been on the *New York Times* best-seller list for more than two years and was published in thirty-five countries in twenty-three languages. Though initially skeptical, physicians routinely recommended it to their patients. And my files swelled with letters and laboratory results from readers and their doctors telling me of their successes.

Life was good. And even better since I knew that my own doctors had declared me virtually free of the risk of heart disease. The tests I underwent in the intervening years showed abundant flow to my heart through those once-diseased vessels, and the bypass vessels were totally clear. I felt better than I had in my twenties and thirties. Not bad for a guy for whom the medical statistics would have predicted an early death. I had beaten the odds.

But as I contemplated my life that Fourth of July, I realized that my own program had evolved significantly in the past ten years. It was no longer a simple approach of oat bran muffins and a low-fat diet. Researchers had discovered many of the missing links in the development of heart disease, and little by little my program had evolved along with that knowledge. My approach to cholesterol control and heart health was now like comparing a brand-new Mercedes-Benz with a Model T Ford.

For openers, medical investigators had nailed down the role cholesterol plays in heart disease in the arteries. Our view of the clogging of those vessels, and how heart attacks happen, had totally changed. The revolutionary idea that once cholesterol counts come down, and plaques within the arteries stabilize, brings with it the promise of total freedom from the fear of heart attacks. Never have a heart attack! Wow, what a revolutionary concept.

For frosting on the cake, we don't even have to live a life of deprivation, as had been true not many years ago. Not only were new products available in low-fat and nonfat versions but also there were products that could prevent the absorption of fats and cholesterol from the foods we eat. So here I am, free of heart disease risk and eating steaks and eggs.

But outside my own circle of physicians and acquaintances, few people knew about all the changes I'd made over the years. I had been reading the medical literature, attending research conferences regularly, and reporting the progress to the readers of my quarterly *Diet-Heart Newsletter.* I needed to communicate my findings to the millions of men and women whose lives could be dramatically improved by following my new approach. I needed to write a new book, not a mere revision but an entirely new book.

I also needed to correct a number of misconceptions and misunderstandings. Is cholesterol really the culprit? Does diet make any difference? Can some foods provide "good" cholesterol? Should we switch back to butter from margarine? Does red wine really protect the French? Does oat bran work? How about antioxidants? And fish oils? And garlic?

The public is interested in health in general, and heart health in particular, as never before, but the public is confused. Too often people throw up their hands in frustration and head out for the nearest cheeseburger and fries.

To make matters even worse, many people will continue to manufacture high levels of cholesterol despite their best efforts at dietary controls. Their doctors resort to prescription drugs, but those drugs treat only the tip of the iceberg, often leaving people at continued risk owing to factors that such drugs cannot change.

I've always believed in getting to the roots of problems in order to find their solutions. When it comes to fighting heart disease, my original motivation remains the same: to save my own life. This book, then, is my opportunity to share the collected findings of the past ten years. Quite literally, my own life was on the line. I didn't want to settle for what passed as a blanket recommendation for the entire population, given out by those who often see lives in terms of statistical numbers. I wanted the very best that science and medicine had to offer, and so should you!

Here's a sampling of what you'll learn in the coming pages.

- Yes, a low-fat diet is important but in and of itself probably won't be sufficient to ensure heart health. The recommendations of the American Heart Association (AHA) and others to cut fat back to 30 percent of total calories might be a good start for the nation as a whole, but fat reduction alone won't do much to help those who need it most. Don't be misled!
- There are foods and products that can enable you to slash your fat intake by a full 50 percent as compared with the average consumption. Yet you'll continue to enjoy all the typical family favorites that Americans love.
- Critics contend that since many people have heart attacks when their cholesterol levels are quite normal, the whole concept of cholesterol reduction is pointless. We now know that the individual components of cholesterol are far more important than the total number. This program takes care of all those components.
- The combination of low levels of the good cholesterol, HDL, along with slightly elevated amounts of triglycerides is often a more accurate predictor of heart disease than total cholesterol or even the bad LDL cholesterol. An inexpensive vitamin can raise HDLs to healthier levels.

• A simple blood test can detect levels of a blood fat known as lipoprotein (a), usually abbreviated as Lp(a) and pronounced "el-pee-little-a," which can predict who will have a heart attack even if there are no other risk factors. Researchers have known about Lp(a) for a few years, but the information has not trickled down to the practicing physicians and their patients.

Will dietary changes, even the most radical ones, influence Lp(a) levels? Unfortunately, no. How about those expensive prescription drugs for cholesterol reduction? No, those have no effect either. The best solution is a simple one: an inexpensive daily dose of vitamins.

• Prescription, cholesterol-lowering drugs can be very effective, but they work even better when combined with the elements of this revolutionary program. In fact, most people won't even need these drugs. Considering their very high cost and the fact that heart disease is an equal-opportunity killer, money should not be a factor in prevention.

• It has been estimated that up to 80 percent of all physicians are currently taking antioxidants to protect themselves against heart disease. They are very aware of the compelling data demonstrating the benefits to heart health. Yet those same doctors fail to recommend these supplements for their patients. You need the details regarding both dietary sources of antioxidants (which will provide protective substances not found in pills) and supplements.

• One piece of flawed research, much ballyhooed by the media, destroyed the public's confidence in oat bran. That erroneous information has subsequently been put into proper perspective in the medical literature. Moreover, we now have a "next generation" of products that concentrates the potential of the soluble fiber, which has the cholesterol-reducing capability. One such product has been proven to slash levels of the bad LDL cholesterol an average of 25 percent. You can't find it in your health food store, but I'll tell you how you can get it.

• Food choices in the supermarket allow you to cut way back on fat and cholesterol. But an enjoyable diet will still contain a few of those two culprits. A virtually fat-free diet is mighty boring. Fortunately, today a few new products can literally block your body from absorbing the fat and the cholesterol from the foods you eat.

• It all comes down to the numbers. Depending on the results of your cholesterol test, you'll know just how much improvement you have to make. (We'll talk later about testing in the laboratory as well as in your own home.)

Then you'll learn to tailor a program that will achieve the improvement you seek. You'll need to know (1) how many grams of fat you should have in your foods; (2) how many grams of fat and milligrams of cholesterol you can block with the new products now on the market; (3) how much cholesterol can be removed from your blood by way of soluble fibers; (4) what dosage of antioxidants of all sorts will prevent the bad LDL cholesterol from doing its damage; (5) how much exercise will raise the levels of your good cholesterol, lower those of triglycerides, and help burn the calories you eat more efficiently; and (6) how much of the special B vitamin you'll need to control all of your body's production of good and bad cholesterol components. Other B vitamins will eliminate completely the risk posed by elevations of a particular amino acid in the blood that is responsible for 10 percent of heart attacks.

But I don't want you to simply follow a program blindly. You should have a complete understanding of just how that program works and why. That's why I've structured this book into four parts.

In the first part I provide the basis for the program itself. Perhaps for the first time, you'll have a solid grasp of the total cholesterol/fat/saturated fat picture and how those and other factors have an impact on your health. In the process, I'll clear up many misunderstandings about testing, dietary influences, and just how your body works.

The chapters in part 2 outline the program itself. Limiting fat consumption without deprivation. Blocking the absorption of fat and cholesterol in the foods you eat so they can't do your body harm. Eliminating cholesterol from the bloodstream by way of potent soluble fibers. How to take antioxidants so that the bad LDL cholesterol can't clog your arteries. And how to take a unique combination of the vitamin niacin to control your body's manufacture of both good and bad components in the cholesterol/lipid profile. In each chapter, you'll learn just how the numbers work for you: Do this, expect that.

Finally, in part 2 we'll put it all together as one, unified program including dietary measures, supplements, vitamins, exercise, weight control, and stress control.

In part 3, I address the many issues that have caused so much confusion and controversy regarding a heart-healthy lifestyle. Does garlic really work? Is alcohol good for the heart, and if so, is one kind better than another? Will too much iron in the diet lead to problems? What about coffee and tea? And salt? And sugar? I'm sure many of your questions will be answered.

I've devoted part 4 of the book to the subject that's near and dear to my own heart: food! If you could see the way my family and I eat every day, you'd never know we were doing anything different from any other American family. We enjoy meatloaf, mashed potatoes, and gravy. Short ribs. Pot roast. Tacos and burritos. Grilled cheese sandwiches. Macaroni and cheese dinners. Even pork spareribs and T-bone steaks.

The bottom line is that I love food! I don't just like it, I feel passionate about every mouthful. I cheer for cheeseburgers. I prefer potato chips over carrot sticks. I lust for lasagna, and I salivate for hot fudge sundaes. Food is truly a blessing and a joy of life and living.

During the 1980s, there were all sorts of foods that I could no longer eat. I gave them up, but I sure did miss them. I kept searching for ways that I could, so to speak, have my cake and eat it, too.

I've made a hobby out of figuring out and discovering ways to eat what I want to eat—not what some dietitian tells me I should eat—and still keep my heart happy. As I've given lectures and presentations all over the country during the past few years since my books launched me into coronary celebrity, audiences have drooled as I've detailed my menus and explained how I achieve the perfect balance between fun and flavor, between heart and health. "Is that information all in your books?" they'd ask. Unfortunately, until now the answer was no.

A healthy diet must be for life, not for just a few weeks or months. I'll show you how you can eat all your favorites and still keep your fat intake lower than you thought possible without feeling any deprivation at all.

MY PROMISE TO YOU

I'm not a doctor. I am a medical journalist, but I feel that I can help you in many ways. I fervently believe that Providence has led me down the path to near death and then brought me back to spectacularly good health for a reason. That reason is to share with you the information it has taken me ten years to accumulate.

It seems, in retrospect, that I have spent my whole life preparing to write this book. My love of food and cooking. My health problems. My training in science and journalism. My nearly three decades of writing exclusively about health. And probably most important, my passionate love of life and living it robustly as one can do only when enjoying exuberant wellness.

If I could be granted one supernatural power, I would ask for the ability to have you "step into my moccasins" for a day to experience what it feels like to be in vibrant good health. Most people know what it's like to be sick, to be ill, and conversely, to be not sick. But very few know the feeling of being well, of being so filled with energy that it almost makes you feel as though you're ready to burst!

So here's my promise to you. I can't, of course, let you step into my skin for the day, but I can tell you all the steps I've learned to take to achieve that state of wellness. Not just avoiding heart disease, but feeling terrific. Read the book. Take those steps. Follow the program. Soon you'll start to feel better than you ever have.

Some of your improvement will be measurable. Your levels of bad cholesterol, triglycerides, and that new risk factor Lp(a) will drop while your good HDLs will go up. Your weight will come down with less effort than you thought possible. Your blood pressure will come down. Your stamina and physical capabilities will increase.

Other improvements will be more subtle, but just as real. You'll fall asleep faster, sleep better, and awaken more rested and ready to face the day. You'll be more productive at your work and have more energy. You won't experience those midafternoon slumps when you yawn and feel like quitting. You'll enjoy recreational activities more and find you do better at them. Even your sex life will improve! You'll feel better about yourself. Very likely, you'll become an advocate, if not a zealot, of this lifestyle, wanting to share it with your family and friends.

Most amazingly, you'll eat all the foods you love!

Real eggs! Not those substitutes but real eggs with their delicious, golden yolks. And not a bit of the cholesterol will get into your bloodstream, thanks to the blockers I'll tell you about.

Real beef! Steaks, roasts, ribs, all your favorite cuts. Rare, juicy, real beef just the way you love it but without the fat.

Imagine enjoying those previously forbidden treats and blocking the absorption of their fats and cholesterol. You literally remove the fat and cholesterol of foods after you've eaten them! That's never been possible before, but it is now.

Meanwhile your cholesterol will actually drop to normal, and as that happens, the risk of heart disease and the fear of heart attack drop to practically zero. For the first time ever, we have dramatic proof that practically anyone can eradicate the risk of heart disease—effectively, easily, and permanently. You can stabilize the factors that precipitate heart disease. Doctors have learned exactly what causes a heart attack and how to stop it. So don't wait. Start now!

Welcome to the revolution!

PART I

Cholesterol, Fat, and Your Heart

•

•

•

· 1 ·

CHOLESTEROL: *Guilty as Charged*

Probably no single word in science or medicine has caused as much controversy and confusion as cholesterol. But when all the smoke clears, one thing is certain: Those with an elevated level of cholesterol in their bloodstreams are at increased risk of heart disease and of suffering a heart attack. The flip side of that coin is equally clear: When cholesterol levels are low, the risk of that disease practically disappears.

There can be no argument about those facts. Period. When a group of people are tracked over a period of time, those with the elevated cholesterol levels develop heart disease. The higher the levels, the greater the risk. Conversely, those who have low cholesterol counts rarely if ever encounter this killer.

Not only does excessive cholesterol in the blood cause the disease to develop, bringing those levels down to normal results in the disease ceasing to progress, and in many cases, to go away. Reversing heart disease depends directly on getting the cholesterol out of your bloodstream.

Heart disease begins in childhood, continues through life, and far too often prematurely ends life. Every year, 1.5 million American men and women have a bomb go off in their hearts. Five hundred thousand die immediately. The other million typically succumb some time later. That bomb is a heart attack, and its explosive element is cholesterol. To defuse that bomb for yourself, you'll want to lower your cholesterol level starting today and keep it low for the rest of your life.

It's the cholesterol in your blood that does the damage, not necessarily the cholesterol in the diet. While there may be controversy regarding that dietary link, no one questions the role of cholesterol in the arteries. But just what is the stuff?

THE CHOLESTEROL PROFILE

Cholesterol is one member of a large family of chemicals called sterols that are found in both animal and plant tissues. The isolated substance is whitish-yellow without odor and with a slightly waxy feel. Insoluble in water, cholesterol must be ferried through the bloodstream courtesy of other molecules of fat and protein called lipoproteins. More than cholesterol itself, it is the cholesterol/lipoprotein complex and its variations that pose the risk of heart disease.

In an ideal situation, the liver produces cholesterol that is then bound by a lipoprotein molecule, shuttled through the body to carry out its vital functions, and then brought back to the liver for proper disposal. The lipoprotein molecules vary by size and density, hence the names high density lipoprotein and low density lipoprotein, typically abbreviated HDL and LDL. LDL carries cholesterol out from the liver through the bloodstream, and HDL brings it back. Scientists refer to this as a "reverse transport system."

The problem occurs when there's too much LDL-bound cholesterol and not enough HDL to haul the cholesterol back to the liver. As a result, the LDL-bound cholesterol builds up in the bloodstream where it can do its damage to the lining of arteries. We're concerned mostly about blockage in the arteries that supply blood to the heart muscle, but the disease process also occurs elsewhere, clogging arteries in the abdomen, the legs, and even in the penis where the result can be impotence. Within recent years we've learned that LDL cholesterol is most likely to do its damage when the molecules are small and dense and when they are oxidized. More about that later.

Scientists have focused a lot of their efforts on the process of arterial clogging, hoping that by understanding that process, they can work on ways to prevent, treat, or even reverse it. Contrary to popularly held perceptions, the blockage does not occur like a lump on the lining of the artery, but rather under that lining.

Blockage is referred to as a plaque, in the same way we form plaque on our teeth, as a composite of materials including cholesterol. The result is a bulge inside the artery that interferes with bloodflow. That bulge is termed an "atheroma," while the concommitant hardening of the artery is "sclerotic." Hence the name of the disease, atherosclerosis.

Atheroma comes to us from the Greek, meaning a tumor formed of a "gruel" of components. We're not sure what exactly precipitates the formation of the plaque. It may be an injury to the lining of the artery and the body's subsequent effort to heal that damage. We do know that types of white blood cells called macrophages and monocytes arrive at the site and develop into forms termed "foam cells." LDL brings in cholesterol that is mixed into the gruel, much as a construction worker makes concrete to build a wall. At first the plaque is soft and loose but eventually hardens as calcium enters the mix. Over time, the size of the plaque and the blockage of bloodflow increase. We'll look at how rupture of the plaque, rather than growth of that plaque, results in heart attacks on page 18. But now, back to the profile.

Research has shown us that the ratio of total cholesterol or LDL cholesterol to HDL cholesterol is more predictive of heart disease than total cholesterol itself. That information should be part of a cholesterol test, along with a measurement of another blood fat, or lipid, known as triglyceride, which is used by the body as energy from food consumed. Until rather recently, doctors weren't too concerned about a small elevation in triglycerides. Today we know that even modest increases above normal, especially when combined with low HDL counts, can indicate future problems.

Taking the Test

The only way to get a complete analysis of your total, LDL, HDL, ratio, and triglycerides—the lipid profile—is through your doctor's office or at a clinical laboratory to which he or she refers you. To get an accurate reading, you'll need to fast for twelve to fourteen hours prior to the test. Fasting means not only no food but also no beverages with any nutrient value, including sugar. Only water, tea, or black coffee will not interfere with the results. The foods and beverages you consume just before the test don't influence the cholesterol measurements, only the triglyceride levels. Test results are usually back within twenty-four hours. Armed with the information I'm about to provide, you can interpret the readings along with your doctor. Find out what the exact numbers are; don't settle for "everything's fine." Take notes on the specific counts and keep an ongoing record in your files for future reference.

Total cholesterol is measured in milligrams per deciliter (mg/dl) in the United States. Virtually everywhere else the designation is in millimoles per liter (mmol/l). (To convert mg/dl to mmol/l, divide by 38.67.) The AHA and the National Cholesterol Education Program (NCEP), which is part of the National Institutes of Health, recommend that for the entire population adult readings should be no higher than 200 mg/dl. Levels between 200 and 239 are considered borderline high, and those 240 and above are high. The AHA in 1994 revised its recommendations for those with a history of heart disease and advised keeping levels to less than 180 to prevent progression. It would seem logical to extend that recommendation to everyone who wants to prevent future heart problems. My own recommendation is to shoot for a target range of 160 to 180, ideally at the bottom end of that range. That's where mine is. For convenience, and to remain more conversational, for the most part I've dropped the "mg/dl" designation and use only the number throughout this book.

LDL cholesterol, termed "bad" cholesterol, should be no more than 130 mg/dl according to NCEP and AHA. For those with a prior history of cardiac events or demonstrated disease, they drop that number to 100. Again, I think that number is more prudent for the entire population, especially if other risk factors are present.

HDL cholesterol, the protective "good" cholesterol, should be at least 40 mg/dl for women and 35 mg/dl for men. The resulting ratio of total cholesterol to HDL cholesterol, sometimes referred to as the risk ratio, should be no higher than 4.5 for women and 4.0 for men. For example, a total cholesterol of 200 and an HDL of 50 gives a ratio of 4.0.

Triglycerides have a normal range of 50 to 150 mg/dl. (To convert to mmol/l divide by 88.5.) Doctors previously were concerned only about elevations beyond 500, which were associated with pancreatitis that can lead to serious abdominal emergency and eventual deficiency in the ability of the pancreas to function. Today's research indicates that maintaining a normal range is an important aspect of a heart-healthy lipid profile, especially if HDL levels are lower than desired.

In my previous books, I published charts showing cholesterol and other lipid values for both men and women at increasing ages. I've not done so in this book simply because today I believe that those lipids shouldn't change beyond seventeen years of age. Risk is risk, and there's no point in providing excuses. Those with a total cholesterol level beyond 180, an LDL greater than 100 or so, an HDL less than 40, or a triglyceride count of more than 200 are at increased risk of heart disease regardless of sex or age. Period. The degree of risk varies through the years, but it is risk nonetheless. Obviously, a young man with a total cholesterol level of 230 at age twenty-four is not in immediate danger of having a heart attack. But it's likely that the disease is developing in his unsuspecting arteries. Statistically speaking, a woman with a cholesterol of 250 at age seventy is at less risk than a fifty-five-year-old woman. But that risk is still greater than if her cholesterol were under 200. I won't belabor the point by listing all the supportive medical literature, but it's all there.

As I've stated previously, risk owing to elevated cholesterol counts is greater when other risk factors exist at the same time. But the fact is that few adults lack cardiovascular risk factors. The 1992 Behavioral Risk Factor Surveillance

System polled ninety thousand Americans over the age of seventeen, asking about six factors for heart disease: smoking, physical inactivity, excess weight, high blood pressure, elevated cholesterol, and diabetes. Only 18 percent reported having none of the six risk factors; 35 percent had one; 29 percent reported two; 13 percent had three; and 5 percent indicated four to six.

If you have your cholesterol level checked and the doctor reports a total of somewhere in the range of 160 to 180, no lower than a 40 HDL, and a triglyceride count of less than 200, congratulations. This means your lipid profile shows no present risk. If you're aware of other risk factors, by all means work at reducing them. For example, you might need to lose some weight or do more exercise or quit smoking. But there's no reason to do anything particularly different about your diet. As we'll see in chapters 2 and 7, there's certainly no reason not to limit the eggs you want, not to limit yourself to four per week. Also, fat intake should correspond to caloric needs rather than to the desire to prevent heart disease. Again: Diet and cholesterol elevation is not a cause-and-effect affair. This doesn't mean, of course, that just because you have a normal cholesterol level that you can or should take this as a license to eat gobs of fat, especially saturated fat, with impunity. There are many other health reasons to moderate fat intake.

Now what if your cholesterol level hovers somewhere at the 200 count? If you take inventory and find that you have no other risk factors, especially that of family history, then you most likely have nothing to be concerned about. Be sure to have another lipid profile done in at least five years' time. If one or more risk factors loom, however, you'd be well advised to get that count down to the 160 to 180 range. As you will read, that's easier to do today, with the recommendations in this book, than ever before.

If your total cholesterol is in excess of 200, there's little question that you are at high risk. You'll also want to take any other risk factors into consideration.

Small elevations of cholesterol over a longer period of time are equal in risk to greater elevations during a lesser time period. Twice the risk of coronary heart disease at thirty-five years is still quite small for most people since risk is slight at that age; but that risk is significantly higher for the person at age seventy. There is never a time in life, either too young or too old, when elevations of cholesterol do not pose a risk, according to Dr. William Kannel of the Framingham Heart Study.

Cholesterol levels fluctuate, so it's best to take the average of two or even three tests over time. Things affecting the count include the season of the year, emotional stresses, colds and flu, women's menstrual periods, and normal day-to-day swings. If a test comes in quite low, it's unlikely that such fluctuations would be sufficient to warrant another test. The same holds if the results are high, but for findings in the midrange, routine variances might be enough to swing a decision from "do nothing" to "make significant lifestyle changes" and vice versa.

The new home cholesterol test kits are remarkably accurate but test only for total cholesterol. You read the results like a thermometer. Home testing should not be a substitute for initial analysis in the doctor's office or laboratory. The kits are handy, however, to let you know how you're doing from time to time. For example, you might want to know how a vacation splurge might have affected your count. Since the HDL level is unlikely to change significantly from test to test, monitoring total cholesterol provides a good overview.

I use the home tests regularly as I experiment with various approaches. They were enormously useful when I began testing the concepts of blocking fat and cholesterol absorption described in this book. My family and I would take our cholesterol counts, then do our dietary experiments, and remeasure to see how we did. As you'll read, we did beautifully!

The CholesTrak cholesterol testing kit consists of a little cassette that reads the cholesterol in a few drops of blood much like a thermometer. Prick your finger with the device supplied, follow the directions in the kit, and fifteen minutes later you'll have your numbers.

The CholesTrak's accuracy has been demonstrated in a number of clinical studies. To see for myself, I used the kits on the days I went in for cholesterol measurements in my doctor's office. CholesTrak's numbers were always right on target.

The kit costs no more than what you'd pay for a laboratory test, and you have the convenience of doing it in your own home, whenever you want. Of course, since you're not measuring triglycerides, there's no need for fasting.

CholesTrak is available in most drugstores and pharmacies. You can also order directly from the company for delivery to your home. Discounts are available for quantity purchases. Call (800) 927-7776.

IMPROVING YOUR LIPID PROFILE

The program and suggestions provided in this book will enable you to make significant improvements in all aspects of your lipid profile in a relatively short period of time and without radical lifestyle changes. It's never been easier to do.

But why bother? One of the world's leading heart disease researchers put it quite simply. According to Dr. Lars Wilhelmsen of Gotenburg University in Sweden, of 100 percent of heart attacks, 80 to 90 percent can be explained by the presence of high cholesterol levels. The remaining percentage is the combined result of other risk factors that are also considered in this book, things you probably have never heard of but that have put you in jeopardy—until now!

If you have an elevated cholesterol level, you are at greater risk of developing heart disease or having a heart attack. Conversely, by lowering that level you will slash or even eliminate that risk. The data proving this to be true is overwhelming for both men and women.

- Research at Stanford University published in 1994 showed that reducing risk factors prevented the development of additional blockages in men and women diagnosed with heart disease.
- British scientists combined and reviewed the results of ten major studies and found that even modest improvements in cholesterol readings pay big dividends. Looking at the results for nearly a half million men and women, the reductions in risk from just a 10 percent drop in total cholesterol led to declines in the incidence of heart disease of 54 percent at age forty, 39 percent at age fifty, 27 percent at age sixty, 20 percent at age seventy, and 19 percent at age eighty. The data were published in the *British Medical Journal* in 1994.
- That same year, U.S. scientists at the University of California at Berkeley also analyzed ten previously conducted studies. They concluded that aggressively lowering cholesterol counts resulted in fewer heart attacks and even regression of the disease.
- The benefits of cholesterol reduction are linear. The closer you get to that ideal range of 160 to 180, along with normalized LDL and HDL readings, the greater the payoff. Owing to the limitations of the methods of intervention in current studies done, cholesterol reductions have been small to moderate. Even so, vast improvements were noted. By bringing your lipid profile to normal, you can wipe heart disease out of your future. How quickly will that happen? While it's taken a lifetime to develop the heart disease that currently blocks your arteries, recent data strongly suggest that in just six months to two years risk can be virtually eliminated.

Let's look at that statement one piece at a time to see just how revolutionary the promise truly is. First, we know that heart disease develops from childhood. Autopsies done on soldiers during the Korean and Vietnam Wars, as well as on children as young as ten and twelve years old examined over a period of time during the Bogalusa Heart Study in Louisiana, show the beginnings of the disease. The higher the levels of cholesterol during life, the greater the degree of heart disease found after death. Horribly simple and direct evidence.

Second, blockages in the form of atherosclerotic plaques continue to develop and grow as long as excessive cholesterol remains in the bloodstream. Some of the most exciting research in heart disease during the past few years has taken place at the microscopic level. New information takes the arcane concepts of stabilized plaque and healthy endothelium from the laboratory into the practical arena. Those concepts explain how heart disease develops and why heart attacks happen.

Forget the image of arterial clogging likened to old plumbing getting blocked by mineral deposits. Rather, picture a sort of tumor forming under the innermost lining of the artery, the endothelial cells comprising the intima. Those tumors start at a very early age, probably the result of routine microscopic injuries throughout the arterial system. White blood cells known as phagocytes and monocytes enter the site in an effort to mend the injury. They next turn into a matrix of what are termed foam cells that attract cholesterol from the bloodstream. If there isn't much cholesterol in the blood, the tumor grows very little or not at all. However, when LDL cholesterol, especially the oxidized form, abounds, the tumor grows and grows, gradually limiting blood flow.

New, relatively small, cholesterol-rich tumors, called atheromas, are quite soft, have a fragile cap, and are prone to rupture. Older atheromas become hardened with smooth muscle tissue and calcium and are less likely to break open. A rupturing atheroma produces a blood clot that is released into the bloodstream. If arterial blockage prevents its travel and eventual reabsorption, blood flow to the muscle of the heart stops and this event is a heart attack or myocardial infarction (MI).

Picture the lumen of the artery—the hole in the doughnut, if you will—starting out in life nice and clear, but eventually becoming narrowed here and there by new and old plaque formations pushing out from the artery's lining. Ironically, older blockages or stenoses aren't as dangerous because the body compensates for the compromised blood flow by creating collateral arteries, natural bypasses that bring blood to the heart's muscular wall. The more exercise one does and the less one smokes, the more this collateral circulation develops. So even when the artery might be completely blocked off at some point, those collateral arteries prevent a problem.

While the older, larger, more solid atheromas are less likely to rupture, their narrowing of the lumen of the artery results in reduced flow and increased risk that a clot will become lodged when one of the smaller plaques ruptures. That rupture, it turns out, can be precipitated by shear force of the blood rushing through the artery, emotional stress, high blood pressure, or physical exertion in individuals who are in poor physical condition. Thus the presence of large blockages serves as a marker, when seen in an angiogram or detected by an exercise stress test, that numerous smaller atheromas exist and place the patient in jeopardy.

All this damage takes place over a lifetime. Cholesterol is brought to the site of the atheroma via LDL and taken away by way of the HDL. That's why we want more of the latter and less of the former. Smoking leads to further narrowing of the arteries, reduced HDL counts, and stiffening of the endothelium, that cellular lining of the arteries. The natural history of heart disease is to progressively develop more and larger plaques that eventually cause a heart attack.

In the old days, doctors saw heart disease as a progressive, chronic, ultimately terminal disease. That is to say, you get worse and then you die. But that was then, and this is now!

For one thing, physical exertion no longer need be a precipitating factor in heart attacks. Those in good physical condition needn't fear even the most strenuous activity, even including a "cardiac killer" such as snow shoveling. You'll have the protection conferred by physical fitness by reading and following the suggestions in chapter 10. Similarly, we can control blood pressure with lifestyle modifications, and when necessary in severe cases, with medications. Relaxation techniques can also help relieve periods of emotional stress.

But what about the underlying causes of those heart attacks? Well, one such cause is the amino acid homocysteine, excessive amounts of which in the blood lead to scarring of the artery and thus formation of another plaque, as well as precipitating the rupture of the atheroma. Fortunately, as you'll see in more detail in chapter 5, the cure is simply a daily intake of B vitamins through diet and supplementation. In that chapter, we'll also cover a newly discovered risk factor called lipoprotein (a), which can also be controlled by simple vitamin supplementation.

You'll want to haul as much cholesterol out of those plaques as possible. Do that by slashing the amount of cholesterol floating around in your bloodstream and getting socked into those arteries by LDL molecules and by increasing HDL levels as much as possible through the means discussed in this book.

Oxidized LDL packs the cholesterol into those plaques far more than when LDL is protected by antioxidants. You'll get lots of details and specific recommendations in chapter 8 but for now note that an article in the June 21, 1995, issue of the *Journal of the American Medical Association* reports that antioxidant intake reduces progression of the disease in terms of plaque development in patients previously studied in regard to cholesterol lowering. Yes, those whose levels dropped fared far better than those whose cholesterol counts stayed up. But those also taking at least 100 IUs (international units) of vitamin E did the best of all.

For years we've been hearing about studies that show regression of heart disease when cholesterol levels fall. Even more important, in a practical sense, is the vastly decreased incidence of heart attacks and deaths for those with reduced counts. In fact, decreased risk is typical even when doctors haven't seen any regression. Now we know why.

Dr. Valentin Fuster of Mt. Sinai Medical Center in New York says reducing risk is a matter of stabilizing those soft, rupture-prone plaques and healing the endothelium. Both those changes occur, he says, in a linear fashion as total and LDL cholesterol levels, along with homocysteine and Lp(a) counts, fall. Shoot for a goal of an LDL count no more than 100 and the total cholesterol into a range under 180, ideally around 160. Dr. Fuster also advocates aggressive treatment to raise dangerously low HDL levels. Once the lipid profile improves, the healing begins, and he believes that within six months to two years, the individual is completely out of the woods. Dr. Fuster's research has been published serially in *Circulation,* and he presented an outstanding overview at the 2nd International Heart Health Conference in Barcelona, Spain, in May 1995.

That presentation was electrifying. I attended along with two physician colleagues who are friends, and we left smiling from ear to ear. The data were a validation of everything we've been doing and recommending to eradicate heart disease. In fact, another speaker, Dr. John Farquhar of Stanford University, stated unequivocally that heart disease today is largely preventable. Think of that: a world with no heart attacks!

Then in late 1995 at the annual meeting of the AHA we got the definitive, no-doubt-about-it proof of how lowering cholesterol levels can save lives. The West of Scotland Study, headed by Dr. James Shepherd, looked at sixty-six hundred men aged forty-five to sixty-four for five years. All were identified as having an LDL cholesterol more than 155, and the average total cholesterol was 272. None had had a heart attack or had been diagnosed as having heart disease. All received information on low-fat diets, and half received a single,

40-mg dose of the cholesterol-lowering drug pravastatin (Pravachol). Treated men had a drop of 20 percent in total cholesterol, 26 percent in LDL, 12 percent in triglycerides, and a 5 percent increase in HDL. Diet alone didn't get the job done.

Here's the payoff: Those with lowered cholesterol counts experienced 31 percent fewer cardiac events including heart attacks, 28 percent fewer heart attack deaths, 37 percent fewer bypass surgeries, and 22 percent less total mortality. There was no increase in noncardiovascular deaths such as suicide, accidents, or cancer.

This is the first study to definitively prove the effectiveness of cholesterol reduction for primary prevention, that is, to treat those who have no present disease. Previous studies had not achieved a sufficient cholesterol reduction to result in significant benefits.

Importantly, those benefits were noted as early as after just six months of cholesterol lowering. This study was the proof of the pudding and should once and for all silence the critics who have held out that cholesterol reduction offers no benefits.

While the drug pravastatin was credited for cholesterol lowering, authorities concur it was the reduction itself, not the drug, that was responsible for the benefits. Any approach to getting the numbers down would be expected to have the same payoff, and the revolutionary cholesterol breakthrough detailed in this book will get your numbers down safely and effectively without the use of those expensive medications.

Every time you follow one recommendation or another in this book, visualize your arteries becoming more elastic, their endothelium healed or healing, and your plaques being drained of their cholesterol and becoming stabilized. That's revolutionary. Never before have such promises been possible.

HOW DANGEROUS IS CHOLESTEROL REDUCTION?

The *New York Times* published a story that scared the bejesus out of millions; it warned readers that lowering cholesterol levels could be life threatening. The author cited a threefold increase in suicides but failed to note that there were just six cases in the thousands of men and women studied. The doubling of accidental deaths doesn't sound as dramatic when one considers that there were just four, again out of several thousand persons studied. Probably merely statistical coincidences. But to be absolutely certain that cholesterol reduction is indeed safe as well as effective, a number of careful studies have been undertaken by a number of researchers.

Does a lowered cholesterol level increase the risk of cancer? The first observation that cancer patients had lower cholesterol counts than healthy men and women caused alarm. Closer analysis revealed that cancer itself leads to cholesterol reductions as the diseased cells metabolize more of it than normal cells. It is a matter of which comes first, the chicken or the egg. In this case, the cancer occurs first, then cholesterol levels drop.

Other analyses show that other lifestyle habits are more likely the culprit. Cigarette smokers are more prone to lung cancer, regardless of cholesterol level. Heavy drinkers will develop more liver cancer.

Moreover, concern over very low cholesterol levels is really moot. There's no reason for anyone to lower his or her level beyond 150 in an effort to prevent heart disease. It's really a matter of diminishing returns after reaching the heart-healthy range of 160 to 180. So why worry about dangers associated with numbers like 115 or 120?

More to the point, we know that heart disease is the nation's number one killer of both men and women. And we know that lowered cholesterol counts slash that risk. The benefits are overwhelming. The risks are nil.

IT'S YOUR CHOICE

Some skeptics still thumb their noses at the "diet-heart connection." They point to flaws in studies. They note that those who attempt cholesterol modifications through dietary changes don't see improvements. They question whether the entire population should change its eating habits.

Frequently those criticisms have a nugget of truth. It all comes down to two things that even the most strident critics won't argue about. First, people with elevated cholesterol levels, especially those with additional risk factors, face a greater risk of developing heart disease and having heart attacks. Second, reducing those levels to where they should be will prevent the progression of disease, often result in regression, and vastly improve the odds against having a cardiac event.

As to that first point, only a test will tell who will really benefit from cholesterol reduction, including any dietary changes and other efforts. If it ain't broke, don't fix it. Only those with a problem will benefit from a solution.

Blanket recommendations for the entire population, even if the vast majority might benefit, aren't completely logical. If your cholesterol level is under 180, enjoy that cheeseburger with no guilt and remember me when you toast with your chocolate malt.

Regarding the second point: You just won't succeed simply by following a diet that doesn't get the job done. A slight cholesterol reduction might look good on paper when statistically analyzing results for an entire population or group, but it doesn't get you, individually and personally, out of the woods. I have no doubt that a small reduction will produce a small statistical improvement in odds. But you want better than that. You want to completely stack the deck in your favor. You'll do that by getting your cholesterol down to less than 180. This program will let you do just that.

Of course, you'll want to consider the other risk factors as well. Heart disease is a "polygenic" disorder; it is caused by a large number of risk factors, all of which intensify the effect of cholesterol.

High blood pressure, cigarette smoking, emotional stress, diabetes, obesity, family history, and a number of recently discovered risk factors paint the entire heart disease picture. It's interesting to note that the heavy-smoking Japanese suffer little heart disease while living in Japan and eating a traditional diet. However, when they come to America, eat a high-saturated-fat diet, and have their cholesterol levels soar, they develop that disease. Some of them. Not all.

Which brings up the question of whether to treat individuals or the entire population. The AHA and others have taken the population approach. They base their arguments and recommendations on statistics. If everyone cut back on fat, cholesterol, and sodium, they say, the average cholesterol level and blood pressure measurement would fall in the population as a whole and the number of heart attacks and strokes would decline. True. But true only because within that population are those who are actually at risk; they are the only ones to benefit. While on average, one person within that population gains a couple of months of life, some gain a day because they were never at risk to begin with; others may gain decades because they were at tremendous risk.

Scientific facts cannot be denied. About 80 percent of the cholesterol present in everyone's bloodstream was produced by the person's own body by way of the liver. Only 20 percent results from the person's dietary habits. Perversely, those at risk owing to elevated cholesterol levels will achieve, on average, only 5 to 6 percent reductions by following the typical dietary recommendations. I think it's important to realize that it's not necessarily your fault that you have a high cholesterol count—if you actually do. It's a matter of genetics. Some people simply produce more cholesterol than others do and are less efficient in terms of the body's elimination of cholesterol from the bloodstream.

Ironically, cholesterol itself is absolutely vital to life. That's no doubt why the body produces its own supply—so that no matter what we eat or what we don't eat, we'll have enough to satisfy certain basic needs. Cholesterol is essential for the manufacture of sex and adrenal hormones, bile used for digestion of fats, and protective sheaths around nerve fibers. We couldn't live without the stuff. But more is not better.

When we're genetically programmed to produce excessive amounts, and then throw fuel on the fire by consuming a diet high in saturated fat, cholesterol builds up in the bloodstream and eventually clogs the arteries. Those blessed by nature with low counts and those who actively work to bring cholesterol levels down don't have that problem.

By looking at the data gathered over the decades in Framingham, we can see that people with cholesterol counts of 155 or less seldom if ever have heart attacks. Other research done at Northwestern University reveals a healthy range of 160 to 180 in which heart disease is rare; other risk factors come into play for those having heart attacks with lifelong cholesterol levels in this range. When counts inch above the 180 mark, heart attack incidence begins to rise, slowly but perceptibly. Levels over 200 are marked with a significant increase in heart disease risk. That risk is linear, but it is worth noting that most heart attack victims have counts of about 220 to 230—far lower than most physicians would get concerned about based on recommendations currently coming from the AHA.

The astute reader will conclude that the logical goal is to keep cholesterol levels under 180. So why do we hear so often that 200 is safe and that only counts of 239 or more place one at high risk? Again we come to the AHA's reliance on the population approach. Certainly researchers are aware of the same medical literature that others and I have read. In fact, they themselves shoot for the more prudent numbers.

They justify their recommendations in a number of ways. First, as previously explained, if the average cholesterol level for the population drops just a little bit, there will be fewer heart attacks. Some lives will be saved, and that's better than none, they say. Second, they feel it's too difficult to educate the entire public on the nuances involving cholesterol and its variations along with all the other risk factors; people just won't understand, they say. And third, not everyone would be willing to do what it might take to bring cholesterol levels down to where they pose no risk. That's because the AHA has put so much faith in the ability of diet alone to do the trick. But diet alone simply won't work for most people.

Yes, what you eat does influence cholesterol levels, especially if you happen to be genetically prone to elevations because your liver makes too much and your body doesn't clear out the excess. But the 30 percent–fat diet recommended by the AHA won't do the job for the majority of those with levels that place them at risk. Conversely, the kind of radical lifestyle modifications that might result in adequate control are not very practical. Not everyone is willing—or should be willing—to abandon restaurants, avoid eating with friends and relatives, and consume only foods best suited to a rabbit warren. Moreover, there are subfractions of cholesterol as well as other risk factors that must be taken into consideration.

But fear not, you're reading the book that will both educate you and enable you to virtually eliminate the risks of heart disease associated with cholesterol and other considerations. You'll be empowered to use the tools and techniques that will achieve total control without deprivation.

· 2 ·

EGGS, CHOLESTEROL, AND YOU: *Unscrambling the Facts*

Eating a lot of dietary cholesterol from such foods as egg yolks will raise the cholesterol levels in your blood. Or maybe not. Confused? Try this. Cutting back on dietary cholesterol will lower cholesterol levels in your blood. Or maybe not. Totally confused? Let's see if we can sort this mess out.

Chemically, the cholesterol in food is no different from the cholesterol in your blood and throughout your body. Since there is no doubt that elevated levels of cholesterol in the blood pose a risk for heart disease, it makes sense to get them down low. And common sense would dictate that the place to start is with the cholesterol in the diet. For quite a few years, that's what scientists believed. But a nasty fact got in the way of this lovely theory. When people did restrict dietary cholesterol, levels of cholesterol in the blood did not always go down.

Then researchers learned that dietary fat, especially saturated fat, was far more influential than dietary cholesterol. However, the authorities continued to recommend restricting cholesterol in the diet as well, as part of a total cholesterol-lowering program. But are those recommendations valid?

Well, we do know that saturated fat is *the* most important dietary component to restrict. In fact, if you don't do that, first and foremost, limiting dietary cholesterol won't make much difference at all.

A study in the *American Journal of Clinical Nutrition* showed just that in 1992. Researchers found that blood levels of cholesterol do not fall when saturated fat is not reduced, regardless of restriction of dietary cholesterol.

On the other hand, when one limits saturated fat *and* cholesterol, cholesterol levels in the blood do come down. That has been demonstrated in both men and women with high levels of total and LDL cholesterol. In fact, two rather famous cholesterol researchers attached their names to formulas predicting cholesterol improvements. The Keyes equation and the Hegstead equation, developed by Ancel Keyes of the University of Minnesota and Mark Hegstead of Harvard University, quite accurately anticipate cholesterol reductions in the blood when one restricts total fat, saturated fat, and cholesterol.

The equations really apply primarily to people who have a cholesterol problem, as compared to those with numbers in the normal range. In 1994, researchers at Bowman Gray School of Medicine in North Carolina showed that a particular gene largely determines whether dietary cholesterol influences cholesterol in the blood. They worked with twenty-three medical students who were fed either restricted cholesterol amounts or a diet rich in cholesterol coming from four eggs daily. For those lucky enough to have the right gene pattern, LDL cholesterol hardly rose at all, even with the four eggs a day. But those with the more typical gene showed a very significant LDL elevation.

The North Carolina researchers estimate that the favorable gene occurs in about 12 to 15 percent of the population of the United States. Those lucky individuals can eat all the cholesterol they want, and levels of cholesterol in their blood will remain at about the same levels.

In 1995, researchers at Columbia University in New York found similar results when they gave as many as four eggs daily to thirteen women ages twenty-one to twenty-five. Cholesterol levels in the blood just did not go up as much as would be expected.

Now, before you dust off your egg poacher, keep in mind that those who are not affected by dietary cholesterol in eggs and other foods either have normal blood cholesterol levels to begin with and/or have the gene pattern that enables them to consume those yolks with impunity. Some statistics put this into perspective.

First, about half the American population of both men and women will eventually succumb to heart disease. Second, about half the people in the United States have a higher-than-optimal level of blood cholesterol along with other risk factors. Third, those who do die of heart attack have arteries clogged with plaques composed largely of cholesterol. Fourth, the vast majority of those victims also had elevated cholesterol levels when they were alive. Fifth, those whose cholesterol levels are in the 150 range are virtually never victims of heart disease. Sixth, heart attack victims with cholesterol levels under 200 are now known to have other lipid abnormalities that put them at risk.

What all that means is that about half of us have a problem and half of us do not. Half of us can eat egg yolks till we're sick of 'em, and half of us cannot. The gene contributes to part of that half but obviously not to all.

The AHA came up with a recommendation to limit egg yolks to no more than four per week. That number was based on dietary estimates of other foods such that the total cholesterol consumed, on average, would be less than 300 milligrams daily. That's the recommendation for the general population. But some people need even more restriction and should not even look at an egg yolk. Others, as we've seen, can eat many more than four.

How can you tell if you are, as the scientists call it, cholesterol sensitive? Eventually there will probably be a test we can all take so that our dietary needs can be more precisely tailored. But no such test currently exists. So it comes down to a matter of trial and error.

Eggs didn't raise cholesterol levels for individuals who had elevated counts but who had normal triglycerides in a study done at the University of Washington in Seattle in 1995. In fact, those consuming two eggs daily for a full month not only saw no increase in cholesterol but also found their HDL levels rose from 48 to 52 on average. Conversely, those with what is termed "combined hyperlipidemia," with elevations of both total and LDL cholesterol as well as triglycerides, who ate that many eggs saw their triglycerides go from 238 to 250 and their LDLs go from 149 to 162. All subjects were on an otherwise low-fat diet. The bottom line here is that if your problem is just cholesterol, not the other lipids, eggs may not matter that much.

If your cholesterol has tested out on the high side, you can be sure it's been that way all your life. That tendency shows up from the moment of birth. In fact, doctors can even check the blood in the umbilical cord before birth: If that cholesterol level is elevated in the blood, the disease progresses from childhood on through adulthood.

If you have an elevated cholesterol level, with or without elevations in the other lipids, it behooves you in the strongest possible terms to get your numbers down. We know for sure that the place to start is with saturated fat, and this book is filled with other recommendations as well. Does dietary cholesterol influence your blood cholesterol? Probably so. Maybe not, but probably so. Maybe you're sensitive only to saturated fat and not cholesterol. And maybe not.

So here comes the trial-and-error part. If you really want to do so, you can determine whether you are cholesterol sensitive. The first step is to get your blood cholesterol down to normal. Do so by following a low-fat, low-cholesterol diet and the other recommendations in my program. Make sure that the count stays low for a period of time, as shown by repeated cholesterol tests. Then challenge yourself by eating a few extra eggs weekly for two or three weeks, perhaps a month. The next cholesterol test will tell you whether those yolks made a difference. Based on the research done so far, it's most likely that you will be sensitive and that your cholesterol will go up when you eat those eggs. Then again, you may be one of the lucky ones. No one knows.

You may decide that the whole issue is moot after reading about the wonderful effectiveness of phytosterols to block the absorption of cholesterol in the diet. It's all in chapter 7. Whether you're sensitive or not, you'll be able to enjoy those eggs again whenever you want.

· 3 ·

Fats in the Fire

Fat tastes good, and added fats make other foods taste better. If that weren't true, no one would make a big deal about reducing the amount in the diet. Despite all the bad things you've read and heard about them, we need at least some fat to stay healthy.

On the positive side of the ledger, fats carry the fat-soluble vitamins including vitamin E, vitamin A and its precursor beta-carotene, and vitamin K, which assists the blood-clotting process. Fat also provides a concentrated source of energy and keeps many tissues of the body healthy. Too little fat in the diet can lead to dry, scaly skin; diminished growth and tissue replacement; and reproductive problems. An absolute minimum of 5 percent of total calories must come from fat to prevent such problems, which collectively is referred to as essential fatty acid deficiency.

On the other side of that ledger, we now know that too much fat poses a number of health problems. That's particularly true for certain kinds of fat. Saturated fats have been implicated in elevated cholesterol levels and the resulting increases in risk of heart disease and have been linked to a number of cancers. Excess of total fat leads to obesity, hypertension, and diabetes.

Paradoxically, some people in the world appear to eat vast quantities of fat without problems. Eskimos get most of their calories from marine mammals and fish rich in fat, and Greeks often eat far more total fat than even Americans. Nevertheless, both Eskimos and Greeks have low rates of heart disease. However, all that fat still adds up calorically, and those people are often obese.

Scientists have been tinkering with facts and oils for decades in both animals and people, trying to come up with healthy recommendations. Despite the vast amount of data accumulated, the public for the most part remains terribly confused. Owing to the philosophy of many health authorities that the public cannot be expected to understand complex issues, the attitude held by many is that all fat is bad and that the only foods worth purchasing must be reduced fat or fat free.

When it comes to fat, we have thrown the proverbial baby out with the bathwater. I have spoken with dozens of men and women who smile and brag that they eat "practically no fat at all." Best-selling books ill advise people to add no fat to the foods they prepare. And the joy of eating gets thrown out with the fat. For nothing. All pain, no gain.

By reading and understanding this chapter, you will be able to grasp the subtleties that many authorities appear to think you're too ignorant to understand. Your reward will be not only improved health but also a much tastier diet! Let's start with the basics.

TAKING FATS APART

All fats are composed of chains of carbon atoms. Some carbon atoms are linked with hydrogen atoms, and some are linked with a carboxyl molecule (COOH) at one end and a methyl group (CH_3) at the other. Of all that chemistry, the important parts are how many carbon atoms a particular fatty acid has and how many spaces are left without hydrogen atoms. These components of fats are fatty acids.

If all the carbon atoms are linked with hydrogen atoms and no spaces are left, the fatty acid is said to be saturated. If a space is left open that could be occupied by a hydrogen atom, that fatty acid is monounsaturated. If many such unoccupied spaces exist on the molecule, the fatty acid is polyunsaturated.

All fats are a medley of saturated fatty acids (SFAs), monounsaturated fatty acids (MUFAs or monos), and polyunsaturated fatty acids (PUFAs or polys). However, the percentages of these fatty acids varies enormously, and it is the differences that indicate healthfulness. For the most part, foods rich in saturated fats tend to be solid or semisolid at room temperature, while those rich in unsaturated fatty acids are liquid.

Take a look at the chart on page 37 to see the spectrum of fatty acid compositions of fats and oils. Even the healthful olive oil has some saturated fat, while butter and lard have some polys and monos.

Now the plot thickens. Not all saturated fatty acids are equally bad. Their compositions vary considerably, notably in the number of carbon atoms in their chains. Some raise cholesterol levels in the blood far more than others; some appear to have little effect on cholesterol counts at all. For example, myristic acid, found in coconut oil and butterfat, is a real artery clogger, and both of those foods contain other cholesterol-raising fatty acids as well. But stearic acid, found in a variety of fatty foods including beef and chocolate, appears to be neutral, having little or no effect at all.

The problem, of course, is that we can't pick and choose our fatty acids. The same chocolate bar with stearic acid comes with a complement of those nasty SFAs as well. At least that's the case today; tomorrow's food scientists may offer specially engineered foods with hand-picked fatty acids.

THE EFFECTS OF FATS ON HEALTH

When the link between diet and heart disease came into focus in the 1960s and 1970s, dietary cholesterol was targeted as the bad guy. It made simplistic sense. Cholesterol in food is chemically the same as cholesterol in the blood and in clogged arteries, so logic would have one conclude that reducing cholesterol in the diet is the prudent thing to do.

It was much later that scientists learned that saturated fat is the real villain. For many people, dietary cholesterol makes little or no difference.

If one replaced foods rich in SFAs with those high in PUFAs, cholesterol levels fell. Even if one changed the ratio of SFAs and PUFAs in the diet by adding quantities of PUFA-rich corn oil, those cholesterol counts fell. So the big push from the American Heart Association, with a nice assist from the corn oil industry, was for the American public to increase its consumption of corn oil and other oils high in PUFAs.

But there was a fly in that ointment, or oil. We had little experience with diets high in PUFAs, since no previous cultures consumed those oils. The long-term effects of shifting fat intakes were unknown, and then some later laboratory findings came along. The reports showed that rodents fed diets high in PUFAs developed far more cancers than anticipated. And low-fat diets enriched with PUFAs lowered levels of the protective HDL as well as the total and LDL cholesterol. More recently, researchers have shown that PUFAs contribute to the oxidation of LDL, making the development of plaques in arterial walls more likely.

Then in the 1980s, olive oil came into vogue owing to its high content of MUFAs and the fact that Mediterranean peoples, including the Greeks, had been consuming it in large quantities and staying very healthy, thank you. Moreover, MUFAs appeared to have far less effect on HDL than PUFAs. So where do we stand today?

Now that the dust has settled and a number of studies have looked at the issue, it seems that both PUFAs and MUFAs lower cholesterol equally well. When used to replace SFAs in the diet, either results in cholesterol reductions of 25 mg/dl on average. That was the case when Stanford University researchers pooled the data from fourteen clinical trials reported between 1983 and 1994. But those investigators saw no statistically significant difference in the effect on HDL. The conclusion from studying those data would be that either corn oil or olive oil would be equally healthy choices.

But there's more. In a collaborative effort, researchers in Spain and at Tufts University compared diets rich in MUFAs and PUFAs with regard to the degree of oxidation of LDL cholesterol in the blood. They found that those consuming PUFA-rich diets had more oxidation than those on MUFA-rich diets. That's probably because corn oil and other PUFA-rich oils turn rancid more easily, which means they are themselves more oxidized and they carry the potential to oxidize LDL into the bloodstream. But don't toss out your bottles of corn oil just yet. You can largely prevent that oxidation by squeezing a gelatin capsule or two of vitamin E into the oil when you bring it home from the supermarket.

Speaking of vitamin E, doctors at the University of California at San Diego wanted to know if it would protect against the oxidation of the worst of the LDL cholesterol, the so-called small, dense LDL. (See details on this type of LDL on page 54.) They found that while vitamin E did a fine job as an antioxidant for most types of LDL, it was effective on small, dense LDL only when the diet included monounsaturated fats. Moreover, MUFAs alone provided some protection, while vitamin E alone did not. The best approach, though, was the combination of vitamin E and a diet rich in MUFAs.

OILS ON THE SHOPPING LIST

What can we conclude from all this? Let's review. SFAs raise cholesterol levels in the blood, increasing the risk of heart disease. Both PUFAs and MUFAs lower those levels when used to replace SFAs. MUFAs seem to have some distinct advantages over PUFAs. Mediterranean peoples have enjoyed a diet rich in MUFAs for centuries and have one of the world's lowest rates of heart disease. Asian peoples have prepared their foods with a number of oils, including peanut and sesame, for hundreds of years with similar good health.

The logical conclusion, then, would be to reduce SFAs as much as possible while enjoying PUFAs and MUFAs, especially the latter, in reasonable moderation. By that I mean not eating so much of those fats that they make you fat, since that's not very healthy either.

In terms of protection against heart disease, there is no logical reason to severely limit consumption of total fat other than to keep caloric intake down, as long as one restricts saturated fat as much as reasonably possible. Why, then, you might ask, not completely eliminate saturated fats? First, that's not really possible, since all fats contain at least some SFAs. Second, the enjoyment of food should not be denied.

Many of those who wag angry fingers at us really don't like food, much less love it. They see food, quite literally, as a necessary evil, fuel for the engine and nothing more. Moreover, they fear that people will not make adequate lifestyle modifications unless everything is painted in black and white.

This will sound like heresy to some, but when eating a Mediterranean meal rich in olive oil, I sprinkle on a bit of feta cheese for its wonderful flavor. A bit of crumbled blue cheese on a salad of sliced tomatoes, fresh basil, and olive oil makes the dish sing. Yes, cheese has a lot of SFAs. But looking at the total fat intake for that given meal and for the entire day, the percentage of SFAs is still extremely low in my diet. I'll go into far more detail in the chapters on foods at the end of this book. But now back to those oils. Which ones should you put in your kitchen and in your diet?

In my house, two oils tie for first-place honors. Olive oil is rich in monos, is delicious, and has a number of uses. I use it to sauté garlic, to toss with a salad, or on the table to dip bread instead of using butter or margarine. (To cut the calories, I'll mix olive oil with balsamic vinegar.) Canola oil is our all-around cooking oil. Also rich in monos, it is particularly low in SFAs.

Canola oil has another distinction, shared by no other oils. It has more alpha-linolenic acid than all the rest. That fatty acid may help lower the risk of stroke. Researchers at the University of California at San Francisco found in 1995 that individuals with the highest levels of alpha-linolenic acid had the least incidence of stroke. Soybean oil is the second-richest source.

Personally, I don't use corn oil or the other PUFA oils very much. It's not that I think they're unhealthful, but rather, olive and canola are better choices. If you do like one of the oils in this class, be sure to prevent oxidation by adding a few drops of vitamin E by piercing and squeezing a gelatin capsule.

But our shelf has a number of other oils as well as olive and canola. Peanut oil works particularly well in stir-frying and imparts a delicious flavor. I'll also add a splash of sesame oil for a flavor boost. Mixed fifty-fifty with raspberry vinegar, walnut oil makes a wonderful salad dressing. It also contains quite a bit of the stroke-preventing alpha-linolenic acid.

We use all our oils in moderation, mainly to limit our total calories. As such, my indispensable kitchen companion is a can of butter-flavor cooking oil spray. Scarcely a day goes by that I don't use it in one way or another. You'll find plenty of examples of that in my recipes.

FATS WITH A FUTURE

Two cooking oils that show tremendous preliminary promise of health benefits are grapeseed oil and rice bran oil. Grapeseed oil is as common in Australia as corn oil is here; you'll find it in some specialty and health food stores, and you can order grapeseed oil by calling the Lifestyle mail order company at (800) 858-7477. Rice bran oil is a principal cooking and deep-frying oil in Japan and elsewhere in Asia. Not found in most supermarkets, you can locate rice bran oil in specialty and health food stores or by calling Ener-G Foods at (800) 331-5222.

Why go out of your way to find and use these two exotic oils? Because early research indicates potential health benefits for both.

Dr. David Nash, a cardiologist at the State University of New York in Syracuse, started the interest in grapeseed oil with his 1991 report in the *Journal of Arteriosclerosis* that in just two weeks the oil raised HDL levels by more than 13 percent. A second article, in the 1994 *Journal of the American College of Cardiology,* confirmed Dr. Nash's findings. Participants in the study used one ounce daily, replacing other oils in the diet.

Grapeseed oil has a very high smoke point (485°F) and makes high-heat cooking a breeze. Its high level of vitamin E means you won't have a problem with rancidity; it can sit on a shelf for a couple of years without oxidizing.

The champion of rice bran oil is Dr. Robert Nicolosi of the University of Massachusetts at Lowell. When fed to monkeys, rice bran oil brought cholesterol levels down by 20 to 30 percent without decreasing HDL counts. Dr. Nicolosi believes that the so-called unsaponifiable oils in rice bran and its oil are responsible for the cholesterol-lowering effect.

PROCESSED FOODS, FAST FOODS, AND THEIR FATS

If Americans were to eliminate most processed foods and fast foods, they could enjoy all the oils they wanted and be much healthier. Certainly there are some notable healthy exceptions, but they are just that: exceptions to the rule.

Sure they're convenient, but you pay a high price for most processed, high-fat foods. Obviously, I'm not talking about canned peas or the low-fat frozen dinners and entrées. Read some of the labels on the foods in the supermarket. Not only are the fat contents high, but the type of fat itself poses health risks.

The issue of trans fatty acids is so important that I've devoted an entire chapter to it starting on page 187. Manufacturers start with perfectly good oil and transform it into a type that has all the cholesterol-raising abilities of saturated fat. In fact, Dr. David Kritchevsky of the Wistar Institute in Philadelphia feels that trans fatty acids should be considered the equivalent of SFAs. Processed foods have lots of those trans fatty acids parading as innocent soybean or cottonseed oil.

Let's examine the cottonseed oil in processed foods a little more closely. To begin with, this is one of the worst of the vegetable oils, with 27 percent SFAs. Hydrogenation converts at least 50 percent of an oil's PUFAs and converts them to saturated and trans fatty acids. For cottonseed oil that's 50 percent of 54 percent, adding another 27 percent to the original 27 percent for a total of 54 percent SFAs or trans fats. That's worse than lard!

Cottonseed oil is sneaking into the American diet in other ways as well. The next time you're in a Chinese restaurant, ask what kind of oil they use for stir-frying. Don't be surprised when they say cottonseed rather than the traditional peanut oil. It's cheaper.

When it comes to deep-fried foods at your local fast-food outlet, ignorance seems to be bliss. Sure, most places no longer use beef suet for their french fries. Instead, the tubs are filled with hydrogenated oils that are used over and over again, creating more trans fats with each reheating. Do I ever have a serving of fries? Sure. Once in a while, because, doggone it, they taste good! But that's a rare treat, no more than once or twice a month.

Some issues in the arena of heart disease remain cloudy. But we know for certain that both saturated fats and trans fats raise the bad LDL cholesterol levels in blood. Conversely, we know that reducing the amounts of those fats we eat will bring LDL counts down. Happily, we know that monounsaturated and polyunsaturated fats do not raise cholesterol levels when enjoyed in moderation. However, if we go beyond that moderation, cholesterol levels will rise, if for no other mechanism than weight gain because the fats and oils—all of them—are rich in calories. Moderation is the key.

One might rightly ask, If Greeks and Italians and other Mediterraneans enjoy large amounts of olive oil and are virtually free of heart disease, why practice moderation? Indeed, stories are told of Mediterranean shepherds actually drinking a glass of olive oil for their morning breakfast and drenching pieces of bread with it during meals. But it's also true that their cholesterol levels rise as a result, often averaging as high as 250 as was determined in an ongoing project called the Seven Countries Study.

Obviously, something else operates to keep those people healthy despite cholesterol levels that put Americans at high risk. Some authorities believe it might be the very low content of saturated fat in the diet or the heavy consumption of fruits and vegetables along with wine as a beverage. Perhaps the antioxidants and other substances in the heavily vegetarian diet prevents the cholesterol from oxidizing in the blood, thus keeping it from clogging the arteries.

In any case, it's a good idea to hedge your bet when it comes to olive oil and other healthful oils. Again, moderation. Keep total fat down to reasonable levels, since total fat intake is second only to saturated fat in its tendency to raise cholesterol levels in the blood.

COMPARISON OF DIETARY FATS AND OILS

TYPE	SATURATED FATTY ACIDS (% OF TOTAL)*	MONOUNSATURATED FATTY ACIDS (% OF TOTAL)*	POLYUNSATUARTED FATTY ACIDS (% OF TOTAL)*
Canola oil	6	62	32
Walnut oil	9	23	64
Safflower oil	10	13	77
Sunflower oil	11	20	69
Corn oil	13	25	62
Olive oil	14	77	9
Soybean oil	15	24	61
Peanut oil	18	49	33
Margarine (tub)	18	47	31
Sesame oil	20	39	41
Cottonseed oil	27	19	54
Tuna fat	27	26	21
Chicken fat	30	45	11
Margarine (stick)	31	47	22
Shortening (can)	31	51	14
Lard	40	45	11
Mutton fat	47	41	8
Palm oil	49	37	9
Beef fat	50	42	4
Butterfat	62	29	4
Palm kernel oil	81	11	2
Coconut oil	86	6	2

*PERCENTAGES ARE AVERAGED AND THUS MAY NOT TOTAL EXACTLY 100 PERCENT.

Part II

Putting the Program Together

.

.

.

· 4 ·

Good Food: *The Cornerstone of Good Health*

Years ago someone came up with the notion that "you are what you eat." Today that's been modified to "you are as healthy as what you eat." Dietary practices have a direct connection with practically every degenerative disease including diabetes, hypertension, and cancer as well as heart disease.

While it's true that our bodies produce the vast majority of the cholesterol in our bloodstreams, we can still control it to a great extent by wisely choosing the foods we eat. Paradoxically, while dietary modifications result in only small percentages of cholesterol improvement when undertaken alone, those same changes synergize the effects of other efforts. For example, those taking prescription cholesterol-lowering drugs have vastly better success when they also limit the amount of fat they consume. Conversely, failure to lower fat intake can undermine such efforts.

Moreover, there's no question that fat packs more calories than any other dietary component. Cut back on fat consumption and you're virtually assured of weight loss.

In this part of the book, I'm going to introduce you to two absolutely revolutionary substances. One blocks the absorption of fat, and the other blocks the absorption of cholesterol. These products will allow you to enjoy foods that have long been on the forbidden list for heart-healthy people.

In other chapters in part 2, you'll learn about soluble fibers that can help remove excess cholesterol from the bloodstream. Then there are vitamins that will defeat newly identified risk factors for heart disease and antioxidants that offer special protection.

But the starting point is the diet, the foods we eat and enjoy every day. Food should be the cornerstone of any healthy lifestyle, but there's no reason for it to be the millstone around our necks. There are those whose philosophy can be summarized by saying, "If it tastes good, spit it out." That's absolute nonsense. Food was meant to be enjoyed, and there are hundreds of absolutely delicious foods that are naturally low in fat and cholesterol. There's no reason not to enjoy them to the fullest.

Today, the availability of wonderful low-fat and nonfat foods in supermarkets is revolutionary in its own right. If you had told me ten years ago that I'd be eating hot fudge sundaes for dessert following a dinner of steak and baked potato with sour cream, I'd have called you nuts. In 1984 only strict dietary compliance would do the trick. No food could possibly tempt me to forgo my quest for total, vibrant health.

But today I can have it all, and so can you. In part 4 of the book I'd like to take you shopping for some wonderful foods. It's as close as I can get to personally walking down supermarket aisles with you and your shopping list. Then I'll share with you the ways my family and I enjoy all the dishes most Americans enjoy. Not tofu and bean sprouts but meatloaf with mashed potatoes and gravy, rare steaks and roasts, tacos and burritos, grilled cheese sandwiches, and on and on. The Kowalski family loves food, and we'll invite you into the kitchen for breakfast, lunch, and dinner as well as to a variety of restaurants where you can dine like royalty and have your heart thank you for it!

As I detailed in part 1, the biggest dietary offender is saturated fat. Control that one factor, and you can pretty much forget about cholesterol and, to a certain extent, even total fat in the diet. Cholesterol is found only in animal foods; no plant foods have any at all. As you graduate to lower fat and even nonfat animal foods, you automatically slash your cholesterol intake. In addition, you can block the absorption of the cholesterol in eggs and other cholesterol-rich foods with phytosterols. Really, there's not even much point in reading the cholesterol information on the Nutrition Facts label on foods in the supermarket.

But what about total fat? Much of the fat in the foods we enjoy—and which have been enjoyed in good health for centuries—has no direct effect on cholesterol levels in the blood. The monounsaturated fats in olive oil, canola oil, avocados, and cashews and other nuts are considered "neutral" in their effect on cholesterol. Enjoyed in moderation, no problem. But when total fat intake is excessive, even the healthiest fats and oils can raise cholesterol levels.

You can forget about paying any attention at all to certain fats. Salmon, for example, is one of the fattiest of fish and one of the most delicious! Happily, its fat is good for you—rich in the omega-3 fatty acids that have kept the Eskimos healthy for generations. Don't even bother to count those fat grams. Oat bran has two grams of fat per ounce, but you sure wouldn't want to restrict your use of that cholesterol-lowering cereal because of the fat! The same holds for barley and all other grains. Think of those foods as free of fat; don't even think about the fat.

As a practical matter, limiting the total day's fat intake comes down to limiting calories. Dipping your bread into a little saucer of olive oil offers a healthier alternative to slathering it with butter, but at 120 calories per table-spoon, the calories can add up quickly. Total fat intake can also contribute to the cholesterol levels in the blood, especially for hypersensitive individuals, although not nearly as much as saturated and trans fats. But total fat does count.

So how much fat is enough? The average American diet contains 36 percent of calories taken as fat. The AHA has long recommended a healthier intake of 30 percent fat. At the other end of the spectrum, some individuals, including Pritikin and Ornish, have advocated a diet of less than 10 percent fat. That's simply unpalatable; there's no need to be a martyr. Since 1985 I've been suggesting a 20 percent–fat diet as the perfect compromise, and a number of authorities including the American Health Foundation concur.

The 20 percent–fat diet, especially when part of a total heart-health program such as mine, really produces results in terms of both cholesterol and weight control. You just can't argue with success, and hundreds of thousands of men and women have succeeded beautifully with this approach.

Remarkably, as part of my revolutionary new program, a 20 percent–fat diet is actually easy to achieve. First of all, as discussed above, don't even bother to count the fat from shellfish, fish, and grains. Next, if you burn some extra energy, let's say during a day's heavy gardening, garage cleaning, or cross-country skiing, indulge in extra fat from olive oil and the other sources of monounsaturated fatty acids in the same way you'd allow yourself an extra serving of potatoes or slice of bread. You don't count those extra fat grams into the 20 percent! Third, the use of products to block fat absorption can accommodate a lot of fat over and above the 20 percent level so that it just doesn't count! And finally, as we'll see in the coming chapters, foods in supermarkets and restaurants eliminate much of the fat we used to worry about. It's never been easier!

The 20 percent–fat concept really becomes a starting point, helping us put fat into proper perspective. But what does it really mean? Do we pay attention to teaspoons of fat, as one organization would have us believe? Of course not. No foods are labeled in teaspoons of fat. In fact, no foods are listed as 20 percent as fat either! Moreover, since some foods are 100 percent fat (oils) and others are virtually zero fat (fruits and vegetables), calculating the fat content of individual foods is folly. The only thing that matters is the total amount of fat consumed over the course of the day, the week, and the month. One food high, another low. One day high, another low. All in moderation.

The most convenient way to get a handle on this, especially for our individual needs, is to be aware of grams of fat. Note that I say be aware of, not count slavishly. Do you know exactly how many calories you ate today or yesterday? Of course not. But you do know which foods are rich in calories and which are low; you've learned that by experience over the years. And you do know whether the calories you're consuming allow you to maintain healthy weight. If you gain, you cut back on those foods you know to be high in calories. With just the slightest effort, you'll develop that same awareness of the grams of fat in certain foods, and you'll apply that awareness to food decisions in your own situation.

For a 150-pound person who is moderately active, a 20 percent–fat diet means about fifty grams of fat daily. With all the labels on foods in the supermarket and the information I'll provide in the coming chapters, it's easy to shoot for those fifty grams daily, give or take. So how do we come up with that figure?

That moderately active 150-pound person needs about fifteen calories per pound daily to maintain weight, to neither lose nor gain. The more you weigh, the more calories you need. The more active you are, the more calories you can burn. On average, though, most of us getting exercise at least three days a week, and hopefully more than that, can accommodate fifteen calories to maintain each pound of weight. That 150-pound person will thus burn 2,250 calories daily (150 pounds multiplied by fifteen calories).

Since we want no more than 20 percent of those calories to come from fat, we do the simple calculation to come up with 450 calories from fat (2,250 divided by 20 percent).

Fat provides nine calories per gram. So those 450 fat calories will come from fifty grams of fat (450 calories divided by nine). That's all there is to it. Fifty fat grams for a 150-pound person.

If you weighed 110 pounds you'd need thirty-seven grams of fat. If you weighed 190 pounds you'd calculate sixty-three grams. And so on. The chart on page 47 saves you the effort of doing your own number-crunching; it shows fat-gram allowances for persons of varying healthy weights and levels of activity. Keep your personal allowance in mind as you read through the following chapters, and you'll see just how easy it'll be to stay on target.

But what about that all-important saturated fat? Of the total amount of fat we consume, the goal on a practical level is to include as little saturated fat as possible. The healthiest ideal would be to concentrate those fat grams on monounsaturated and polyunsaturated fats, with no more than a third coming from the saturates. Avoid the tropical oils: coconut, palm, and palm kernel. Choose low-fat or nonfat dairy foods. Select the leanest cuts of meats. Opt for oils lowest in saturated fats. Buy soft margarine instead of butter or stick margarine. In recipes replace the saturated fats with unsaturated fats. That's all there is to it. No need to concentrate on specific numbers of grams.

Don't be confused, and don't be discouraged. As you read through the coming pages, the total picture will become completely clear to you. Promise.

To be honest, I can't remember the last time I bothered to count my fat grams for the day. I just pick the foods that don't pose the problems. But when I do want a bit more fat, I make it olive oil or avocados or a handful of nuts. And when I enjoy some cheese or a doughnut or a Butterfinger candy bar, I cancel out the fat with a product that blocks the absorption of much of that fat. Nothing to it.

REPLACING FAT WITH PROTEIN

We all know that fat, especially saturated fat, contributes to a high cholesterol level in the blood, resulting in clogged arteries. The question that remains is, What does one use to replace the fat, recognizing that calories come from only three sources: fat, carbohydrates, and protein? Most authorities have suggested a high-carbohydrate approach, but that approach has its limitations, since excessive carbohydrates raise triglycerides, lower HDLs, and sometimes lead to weight gain. That leaves us with protein.

Dr. Bernard Wolfe of the University of Western Ontario in Canada suggests that a heart-healthy diet should emphasize protein rather than focusing exclusively on carbohydrates. He notes in an article in the October 1995 issue of the *Canadian Journal of Cardiology* that the Masai tribe of Africa has a very low cholesterol level, averaging 130, and virtually no heart disease. Yet these people consume a diet in which protein provides about one-third of calories.

Some have questioned the safety of relatively high amounts of protein in the diet. Dr. Wolfe points out that studies indicate that such diets are safe, in terms of the point of concern, that is, the "stress" on the kidney that processes protein wastes. In a study comparing a high-protein diet with a low-protein vegetarian diet, there was no difference in kidney function.

In his own study, Dr. Wolf looked at substituting protein for carbohydrate and the effect of that substitution on lipid levels. Fat intake remained constant at 24 percent of calories. In one diet, carbohydrate was at 65 percent with 11 percent of calories from protein. In the other diet, protein was increased to 23 percent of calories with 53 percent as carbohydrate.

In the higher protein diet, total cholesterol was lower by 6 percent. Triglycerides in the high-protein group were 150, compared with 212 for the low-protein group. In addition, HDL levels, rather than falling as with high-carbohydrate diets, actually rose significantly for those enjoying the high-protein diet. The bottom line: Using low-fat fish, poultry, meat, and dairy foods in a heart-healthy program is as safe and is probably more effective than a vegetarian approach. And a whole lot more appetizing!

Nature designed food to taste good so all God's creatures would eat plenty of it. Throughout history people have included food as part of their culture, and rightly so; we give thanks when we partake of that food. Food is a joy, a gift, a true blessing. And now food is part of the healthy revolution that can eradicate heart disease in the twenty-first century. But don't wait till then. Start today!

DAILY FAT-GRAM ALLOWANCE

WEIGHT (LBS)	SLIGHTLY ACTIVE PERSON (1)	MODERATELY ACTIVE PERSON (2)	HIGHLY ACTIVE PERSON (3)
110	32	37	42
115	33	38	43
120	35	40	45
125	36	42	47
130	38	43	49
135	39	45	51
140	40	47	53
145	42	48	55
150	43	50	57
155	45	52	59
160	46	53	60
165	48	55	62
170	49	57	64
175	51	58	66
180	52	60	68
185	53	62	70
190	55	63	72
195	56	65	74
200	58	67	76

(1) Based on 13 calories per day required to maintain 1 pound of weight.
(2) Based on 15 calories per day required to maintain 1 pound of weight.
(3) Based on 17 calories per day required to maintain 1 pound of weight.

Examples:

1) Weight	110
Slightly active person—daily calories	13
Total calories required per day	1,430
2) Allowable calories from fat	0.20
Total allowable fat calories	288
3) Divide fat calories to get fat grams	9
Total allowable fat grams per day	31.78
Rounded amount	32

· 5 ·

Meet and Defeat the Newest Bad Guys

For many years the cholesterol critics have carped that if elevated cholesterol levels were truly the culprit, then everyone whose counts are up would get heart disease, and conversely, everyone having a heart attack would exhibit high cholesterol. But that's not the case. About 20 percent of those having an MI have perfectly normal levels. And not everyone with high cholesterol measurements goes on to develop heart disease.

It turns out that some important pieces of the puzzle have been missing. Those pieces fill in the gaps of previous explanations of and efforts to prevent heart disease. Together with what we've known about risk factors for quite some time, the newest bad guys offer us an opportunity to protect ourselves from the western world's number one killer of men and women.

Do elevated cholesterol levels, high blood pressure, and cigarette smoking still factor in as risks? Absolutely so, as seen in the vast majority of those who do succumb to that disease. And certainly the elimination of those risk factors offers tremendous success in both primary and secondary prevention efforts. Recognizing and eliminating the newly researched factors now fine-tunes our protection, providing the opportunity for practically everyone to remove not only the potential but also the possibility of having heart disease.

Think of the enormity of that statement. You and I have the unprecedented ability to render ourselves invincible from the onslaughts of the enemy that claims the lives of nearly one out of every two men and women. It's like walking through a battlefield with the sure and certain knowledge that no bullet, bomb, or blast can harm us. What an incredible talisman!

So, who and what are these newest enemies, and how do we defeat them? Six previously missing pieces complete the puzzle. They are (1) homocysteine, (2) lipoprotein(a), (3) small, dense LDL, (4) fibrinogen, (5) unbalanced lipid ratios, and (6) slight triglyceride elevations in the presence of HDL depressions. Never heard of such things? Most people, even most practicing physicians, have not. By the end of this chapter, you'll know not only what all these things are and mean but also how to eliminate them as risks.

HOMOCYSTEINE

Amino acids are the building blocks of proteins and of tissues of our bodies, essential for growth and maintenance. But when one of these amino acids, homocysteine, isn't properly metabolized and excessive amounts build up in the bloodstream, the risk of cardiovascular disease, including heart attacks and strokes, soars.

The first person to associate homocysteine with heart disease did so more than a quarter of a century ago. Dr. Kilmer McCulley noted in the medical literature that an infant with a genetic metabolic problem that led to a rise in homocysteine in the blood had severe atherosclerosis when an autopsy was done after the child's death. Since that time, more than twenty studies have confirmed the link between homocysteine and heart disease.

Assuming that one has a normal metabolism for breaking down amino acids and properly utilizing them, the body requires adequate supplies of three B vitamins: folic acid, B_6, and B_{12}. Consuming too little of these nutrients causes homocysteine to build up in the blood. Men more frequently exhibit elevated levels, but the condition afflicts both sexes. Certainly there is a genetic component that determines just how efficiently one breaks down the amino acid, but the principal problem appears to be dietary insufficiencies if not deficiencies. And as we age homocysteine levels tend to climb. Nearly one-third of all patients followed in the long-term Framingham Heart Study who were over the age of sixty-seven had a high level of the substance in the blood.

The study that really blew the lid off this issue involved 271 male physicians participating in a long-term health project. Men whose homocysteine levels were in the highest 5 percent had more than three times the risk of having a heart attack, even after eliminating all other risk factors. Pooling the data from all recent investigations indicates that homocysteine concentrations are about 30 percent higher than normal in people who develop heart disease.

Similar data show that homocysteine also puts men and women at vastly increased risk of stroke, and European research leads to the same conclusion. In a 1995 editorial in the *New England Journal of Medicine,* two homocysteine researchers state unequivocally that elevated homocysteine levels present a cause-and-effect relationship with heart disease. In fact, when baboons were infused with homocysteine for just three months, atherosclerotic plaques developed.

High levels of homocysteine lead to trouble in a number of ways. Damage is done to the endothelium lining of the arteries, leading to the formation of plaques. Homocysteine stimulates the proliferation of smooth muscle cells, causing the plaques to grow. And the stuff is frequently responsible for the rupture of plaques and the subsequent release of the blood clot, which precipitates the heart attack.

How bad are elevated homocysteine levels? Worse than previously thought. Researchers reporting from the Cleveland Clinic in the journal *Circulation* in November 1995 said that individuals with high levels had almost five times the risk of developing coronary artery disease. Utah investigators wrote in *Arteriosclerosis, Thrombosis, and Vascular Biology* in September 1995 that those with the highest levels of homocysteine had up to fourteen times the risk as those with the lowest counts.

Homocysteine is a metabolic product of another amino acid, methionine. Fortunately, sufficient amounts of the B vitamins folic acid, B_6, and B_{12} reduce the blood levels of homocysteine back to methionine, thus cutting risk. The Utah scientists found that the higher the concentrations of folic acid, the lower the homocysteine. Both men and women are at increased risk when homocysteine levels rise.

How much does homocysteine contribute to the nation's heart disease problem? Reviewing thirty-eight separate studies, Seattle researchers reported in the October 1995 issue of the *Journal of the American Medical Association* that up to 10 percent of all heart disease can be traced to homocysteine elevations. The University of Washington investigators concluded that reducing homocysteine elevations with folic acid "promises to prevent arteriosclerotic vascular disease."

Interest in homocysteine extends around the world. A Norwegian study published in the November 15, 1995, *Journal of the American Medical Association* linked high levels with other, well-established risk factors. In other words, smokers had higher levels of homocysteine than nonsmokers; those with high cholesterol levels had higher homocysteine levels as well; older people had higher counts; and sedentary individuals had higher homocysteine elevations than those who were physically active. Just why that was so, the researchers didn't know. Obviously, we want to reduce all our risk factors as much as possible, and this study provides one more motivation.

Measuring homocysteine levels is not routine practice, although the test is not limited to certain centers of research. It is possible for you to get tested through your doctor's office; he would send the sample to an appropriate laboratory. Reading the results is the trickier part. Homocysteine is measured in micromoles per liter; ten is in the "normal" range, while higher levels of, say, fourteen have been associated with heart disease.

The University of Washington researchers wrote that increased folic acid intake of approximately two hundred micrograms daily reduces homocysteine by about four micromoles/liter. That has been the recommended RDA recently, but it represents a reduction instituted in 1989 from previously recommended daily intakes of four hundred micrograms/day. Many are now saying that the recommendation should be returned to those higher levels.

But it's not just folic acid. The Cleveland Clinic investigators reported an "independent increased risk of coronary disease" in patients with vitamin B_6 deficiency. Such low levels were noted in 10 percent of patients entering the clinic with heart disease but only in 2 percent of individuals acting as "controls" who did not have the disease. Vitamin B_{12} also enters the total equation.

This whole area of investigation becomes philosophically interesting. We know that sufficient amounts of folic acid, vitamin B_6, and vitamin B_{12} will lower homocysteine levels to where they pose no risk. Obviously, taking those vitamins at the low levels at which they are effective poses no risk and has other potential benefits, not the least of which is protection from anemia for those not consuming much meat and from the birth defect spina bifida in women of reproductive age. So why even bother to have homocysteine levels measured? Just take the B-vitamin supplements, and the problem, if it ever existed for you, is gone.

Start with the diet. Make sure that you eat lots of fruits and vegetables, which are excellent sources of folic acid. The same goes for beans and lentils of all sorts. But those of us who have cut back on animal foods miss some vitamin B_6 and B_{12}. To make absolutely sure that you're getting enough B vitamins to completely eliminate the risk factor of elevated homocysteine levels, supplementation is the way to go: folic acid (400 micrograms), B_6 (2 milligrams), and B_{12} (6 milligrams). You'll find those amounts and more in typical B-vitamin supplements. The supplement I take is called Endur-B Complex, made by Endurance Products in Oregon. The quality is high and the price is very reasonable. If interested, you can receive an order form by calling (800) 438-2532.

EVEN IF YOU BELIEVE YOUR DIET IS VIRTUALLY PERFECT AND THAT YOU'RE GETTING PLENTY OF B VITAMINS, I RECOMMEND A DAILY SUPPLEMENT TO GUARANTEE FREEDOM FROM THE THREAT OF AN ELEVATED HOMOCYSTEINE LEVEL. REMEMBER: HOMOCYSTEINE KILLS.

LIPOPROTEIN(A)

Next on the list of bad guys to eliminate is a lipid floating around in your bloodstream that goes by the name of lipoprotein(a), typically abbreviated as Lp(a) and pronounced "el-pee-little-a." Never heard of it? Probably neither has your doctor, even if he keeps up with the medical literature rather faithfully. This substance just hasn't gotten the attention it deserves.

Lp(a) is a variant of the more well-known bad cholesterol LDL. Chemically it is like LDL with an extra protein molecule. Our genes largely determine how much of the stuff will be found in the bloodstream. Those individuals with elevated levels produce more and break it down and dispose of it less efficiently. Diseases of the kidney and diabetes tend to be associated with high Lp(a) counts. That may be one reason those particular patients have significantly greater risk of heart disease. Postmenopausal women have higher levels, as do heavy drinkers. About one-third of all men and women have an elevated level of Lp(a). Diet appears to have virtually no effect; what you eat doesn't make it worse, and attempts at diet don't make it better. None of the prescription cholesterol-lowering drugs have any impact.

The research data pointing to Lp(a) elevations as an independent risk factor for heart disease have been building for the past few years. Tufts University investigators found high Lp(a) in 42 percent of patients with premature heart disease. At the University of Virginia, doctors noted that patients suffering reblockage of arteries after balloon angioplasty had significantly higher counts of Lp(a). Looking at consecutive patients having an angiogram, physicians at Auvergne University in France found that more than 50 percent of men and 60 percent of women who showed the presence of blockage in the arteries had elevated Lp(a). At the University of Cincinatti, tests revealed higher than normal Lp(a) in children whose parents suffered an early heart attack. Analysis of data from the Lipid Research Clinics Coronary Primary Prevention Trial, which involved nearly four thousand middle-aged white men, showed a significantly higher Lp(a) count in those who developed heart disease and experienced a heart attack than in those who did not.

In every single one of those studies, Lp(a) remained a strong predictor of heart disease after statistically eliminating the effects of other risk factors including smoking, high blood pressure, age, diabetes, and other lipid abnormalities. The conclusion that has been stated at the bottom of report after report is the same: Lp(a) is a strong, independent risk factor in the development of heart disease.

Lp(a) kills in a number of ways. It contributes to the formation of plaque, partly by short-circuiting the substance that normally inhibits proliferation of smooth muscle fibers. It gets in the way of normal dissolving of blood clots, a process termed "fibrinolysis," by reducing the formation of a substance called plasmin. And Lp(a) precipitates the rupture of plaques, leading to clot formation and heart attacks.

Unfortunately, doctors don't typically test patients for Lp(a) elevations, but that test is particularly important in cases of family history of premature heart attacks and death. Excuses given usually include the fact that testing for Lp(a) is rather difficult and expensive to do. I think that's a smoke screen.

In reality, most practicing physicians simply have never heard of Lp(a), don't know what normal or abnormal levels are, and wouldn't know how to treat elevations if revealed. Why? As mentioned earlier, none of the prescribed anticholesterol drugs have any effect on Lp(a). If they did, an army of pharmaceutical company salesmen would be trooping into doctors' offices touting the ability of their drugs to reduce this major risk factor. Simply enough, no one is getting the word out to doctors on the dangers and treatment for this cardiovascular threat. It's one of those little details that happens to fall between the cracks. Except that this little detail kills.

Levels of Lp(a) from one person to another vary tremendously, from a low of 1.0 mg/dl (0.03 mmol/l) to 210 mg/dl (5.25 mmol/l). In the case of the doctors participating in the Physicians Health Study, those with heart disease averaged 23.7 mg/dl (0.59 mmol/l), while healthy individuals had an average of 19.5 mg/dl (0.49 mmol/l). Many more with heart disease had values above 30.0 mg/dl (0.75 mmol/l). In a similar study in Sweden, those with an Lp(a) measurement greater than 36.5 mg/dl (0.91 mmol/l) were twice as likely to develop heart disease. The risk presented by Lp(a) appears to be linear; the higher the level, the greater the risk. Especially if you have a family history of heart disease or if you have already been diagnosed as having it, you'll want to have your Lp(a) measured.

Then it's a question of just what to do about an elevated count. Neither diet changes nor prescription drugs lower Lp(a). Suggestions that high doses of vitamin C work have proven worthless in research done with Framingham Study patients.

We know that postmenopausal women are at greater risk of heart disease than younger women, and it turns out that postmenopausal women also have higher levels of Lp(a). That may partly explain why heart disease risk rises after menopause. Fortunately, hormone replacement therapy (HRT) results in significant Lp(a) reductions and has been proven to slash the risk of heart disease. If you or a loved one is at that stage of life, please discuss the matter of HRT with your doctor to evaluate and balance the risks and benefits.

Smokers are also at greater risk of heart disease, and one reason may be that their Lp(a) levels are higher. That was especially true in a survey done at Johns Hopkins with both black and white men. The researchers concluded that Lp(a) was strongly influenced by smoking, particularly for the black population. One more reason to quit.

The only proven Lp(a) fighter is the vitamin niacin taken in larger than normally supplemented levels. In a report from the National Institutes of Health published in the *Journal of the American Medical Association* in February 1992, niacin was called "the best pharmacologic option for treating elevated plasma levels of Lp(a)." Happily, the same dosages of niacin that lower Lp(a) levels do the same for total cholesterol, LDL cholesterol, and triglycerides while often dramatically raising protective levels of HDL. For details on this heart-saving vitamin, see chapter 9.

Speaking at the annual meeting of the American College of Cardiology in 1995, researchers from the University of Washington had good news and bad news. The bad news first. In men studied for more than 2.5 years, the degree of progression of heart disease and the incidence of cardiac events, including heart attacks, were significantly worse in those whose Lp(a) counts were high. But the good news was that the influence of Lp(a) was eliminated by substantially lowering LDL cholesterol.

SMALL, DENSE LDL

Niacin also comes to the rescue in correcting a condition only recently found to be associated with heart disease risk. Those whose LDL particles are small and dense are more likely to develop heart disease than individuals whose particles are larger and less dense. New research presented by University of California (Berkeley) investigators in 1994 indicated that those with the smallest particles are at three times the risk as those with the largest particles.

Other work from the same campus but from a different laboratory posed the solution. Dr. Robert Superko found that a daily dosage of 1,500 milligrams of niacin resulted in a significant increase in LDL particle diameter.

Prevalence of small, dense LDL particles is typically associated with a concurrent elevation in triglycerides, and the two factors, particularly when combined with a lowered HDL level, raise your risk of developing heart disease. Remarkably, as noted in chapter 9, niacin corrects all three.

FIBRINOGEN

Fibrin is a protein found in the bloodstream that forms the essential portion of the blood clot. Levels of fibrin, which are correlated with the degree of clotting an individual exhibits, are determined by a precursor called fibrinogen. Obviously, the ability to form blood clots is essential to life; otherwise, we'd bleed to death from the slightest injury. But too much of a good thing can be bad, and that's the case with fibrinogen.

Several studies have confirmed the link between high fibrinogen levels and the development of heart disease and precipitation of heart attacks. Workers at Tufts University found elevated fibrinogen in 70 percent of all cases of heart disease they studied. French investigators reported in *Circulation* that patients with elevated fibrinogen levels were far more likely to suffer reblockage of arteries following balloon angioplasty. Those attending the 2nd International Heart Health Conference in Barcelona, Spain, in 1995 unanimously concurred that too much fibrinogen places one at risk over and above that posed by the more traditional factors, such as elevated cholesterol levels and smoking.

Once again, the test to measure fibrinogen levels in the blood is not typically performed. Certainly, I would not recommend that everyone learn his or her fibrinogen status, but for those with a family history or a current diagnosis of heart disease, every piece of the puzzle can be critical. Levels of fibrinogen higher than 300 mg/dl definitely stack the deck against you.

The body has a built-in system of checks and balances in all physiologic functions, and blood clotting is no exception. To counter the clot-encouraging action of fibrinogen, we have the clot-dissolving function of plasminogen. The latter is triggered by tissue plasminogen activator (TPA), the same stuff that doctors inject into the arteries of heart attack victims to dissolve the clot blocking the flow of blood and causing the MI. The process of dissolution of those clots is called fibrinolysis. So how can we assist that process of checks and balances to assure an adequate supply of TPA and plasminogen to allow for healthy fibrinolysis?

One part of the effective approach calls for the moderate intake of alcohol. As detailed on page 210, alcohol has long been associated with longevity and protection against heart disease. It turns out that alcohol favors fibrinolysis. Researchers in Glascow found that alcohol intake was related to increased levels of TPA in both sexes. Their findings have been confirmed by many others.

In addition to improving the lipid profile, the vitamin niacin appears to have a heart-saving function of improving fibrinolysis. More about that in chapter 9.

Today most physicians and health authorities concur in the recommendation that daily or every-other-day doses of aspirin provide tremendous protection against heart attacks for both men and women, particularly those at increased risk. The only question involves the ideal dosage. There's no consensus as to whether the dosage should be a baby aspirin or a full-strength 325-mg tablet. Talk with your doctor about that. How does aspirin protect against future heart attacks? It increases the body's fibrinolysis and provides an anticlotting action.

The Eskimos of Greenland have long benefited from the anticlotting properties of their diet. The fat of marine animals, from seals to whales to salmon, is rich in the omega-3 fatty acids that facilitate fibrinolysis. Increased fibrinolysis may be the reason why these people suffer virtually no heart disease. Salmon for dinner tonight sounds mighty delicious.

UNBALANCED LIPID RATIOS

You say a friend of yours had a heart attack despite having a perfectly acceptable cholesterol level and following a heart-healthy lifestyle of low-fat diet and plenty of exercise? Maybe the doctors didn't look closely enough at his or her lipid ratios. We covered this aspect a bit in the last chapter, and the concept bears repeating and clarifying. The predictive ability of the ratio of total cholesterol divided by HDL is now generally recognized to be greater than that of either factor alone. The most recent guidelines published by the NCEP strongly advocate the inclusion of this critical bit of information in making recommendations for patients.

For women, that ratio should be no higher than 4.0. One can attain that number in a variety of ways. A total cholesterol (TC) of 200 and an HDL of 50 gives you a ratio of 4.0. So does 240 TC and 60 HDL. For men, the ratio should be no higher than 4.5. A TC of 220—not typically considered to be alarming—with an HDL of 30 equates to a ratio of 7.3 and puts that person at distinct risk.

Sometimes the ratio of LDL to HDL is used instead. For both men and women, the resulting number should be less than 3.0. However, the LDL/HDL ratio is not as accurate a predictor as using TC. LDL is most typically not measured directly. Rather, it is calculated by subtracting the HDL plus the triglycerides divided by five from the total cholesterol.

For example, 240 TC minus 40 HDL minus 250 triglyceride divided by five equals an LDL of 150: (240 - 40 - 250/5 = 150). However, if the triglyceride count was a healthier 150, the equation and LDL calculation would change considerably: (240 - 40 - 150/5 = 180). Thus the presence of a less desirable, higher triglyceride can actually result in an LDL calculation that appears to be healthier.

Direct measurements of LDL will become more available in the future, making the LDL/HDL ratio more valid. Until then, however, the TC/HDL ratio is the better predictor.

For many women, learning the TC/HDL ratio can eliminate the need for taking cholesterol-lowering drugs. It is an unfortunate reality that doctors sometimes prescribe such drugs for female patients whose cholesterol counts have not come down after dietary efforts. But a look at the TC/HDL ratio could reveal that medication isn't indicated. Let's consider the case of a woman with a TC of 260. After months of watching her diet, her TC comes down only to 250 and the physician prescribes an expensive drug that calls for routine monitoring for the rest of her life. But it turns out that her HDL is 80, giving her a ratio of about 3.0, actually lower than the 4.0 we'd like to see for women.

Now how can we improve our ratios if we're not as fortunate as that woman? Obviously, we need to work at both sides of the ratio. HDL levels are, for the most part, genetically determined. Diet has virtually nothing to do with whether they are high or low, and counts vary very little from day to day, month to month, year to year.

We can do a number of things to tip the balance in our favor by increasing the levels of HDL in our bloodstream to shuttle cholesterol back to the liver to be properly disposed of. Here's a checklist of what's been shown to work:

- Quit smoking cigarettes. Smoking definitely reduces HDL levels. 'Nuff said about that.
- Attain healthy body weight. Obese individuals tend to have lower HDL counts.
- Drink in moderation. Unless there are reasons not to, and if you

enjoy it, drinking in moderation raises levels of protective HDL. Details in chapter 20.

- Do plenty of aerobic exercise. There appears to be a linear relationship between exercise and HDL levels, with competitive athletes enjoying the highest counts. You probably won't become a marathon runner, but the more rigorous and regular your workouts, the better.
- Consider some outside help. If HDL levels drop below 35 mg/dl, you're at significantly increased risk. The prescription cholesterol-lowering drug Lopid (gemfibrozil) raises HDL levels appreciably. In fact, increased HDL levels may be the principal reason for the success of a study done in Finland with that drug. But the vitamin niacin is even more effective in raising HDL measurements.

Let me clarify a confusing point that comes up over and over as I make presentations around the country and answer mail from readers. There is no food you can eat to get "good cholesterol." HDL is a lipoprotein molecule that shuttles cholesterol around in the bloodstream. Cholesterol in food has nothing to do with these lipoproteins, either good or bad.

And now for the other side of the equation. You can improve your TC/HDL ratio immensely without changing your HDL one iota by reducing the level of total cholesterol. Certainly that's the main thrust of this entire book and program. In fact, if the total cholesterol level drops low enough, say under 160, then the importance of HDL becomes less important. When scientists measure the lipids of various populations that suffer practically no heart disease, they often find that along with remarkably low total cholesterol levels in the range of 120 to 130, HDLs are also very low.

There is one perverse aspect of dietary efforts at lowering cholesterol levels that should be stated and understood. As the total cholesterol falls, typically HDL counts go down also. Most of the time the ratio will improve, but that's not always the case. To ensure an improved ratio as part of the lipid profile, keep a few points in mind.

- A very-low-fat diet tends to drive down HDLs and LDLs simultaneously. Enjoying a moderate amount of olive oil makes for a more palatable diet but also maintains HDL counts. Greeks, Italians, and other Mediterranean peoples have savored a diet rich in olive oil for centuries. We can learn much from them.
- If your ratio is good to begin with, dietary changes may yield nega-

tive results. Women, in particular, frequently see their HDLs fall more dramatically than their TCs, resulting in adversely affected ratios. Unless you have a very high total cholesterol level to begin with, or have been diagnosed with heart disease, dietary modifications other than to maintain a healthy weight probably aren't warranted.

- Initial dietary efforts often bring HDLs down but only on a temporary basis. Keep at it, and you'll probably see the HDLs go back up while the total stays down.
- Be sure to get plenty of vigorous aerobic exercise during your efforts to reduce the fat and cholesterol content of your diet. Exercise will offset the tendency for HDLs to drop.
- When total cholesterol and LDL come down favorably, but HDL declines offset the benefits as seen in your ratios, it may be wise to consider including some niacin in your regimen. Talk with your doctor about this and read all about it in chapter 9.

HIGH TRIGLYCERIDES AND LOW HDLS: A NASTY COMBINATION

Right up until the early 1990s, doctors paid almost no attention to triglyceride levels. The normal range is from 50 to 150, but slight elevations were shrugged off, even when counts came in over 200. Physicians were concerned only when triglycerides went over 500 or 600, posing a hazard from pancreatitis.

But closer scrutiny of the data changed all that. The analysis of lipid profiles from those suffering heart attacks showed a distinct correlation between the disease and the combination of low HDLs with even moderately elevated triglycerides. Finally the evidence became overwhelming, and a report was issued by the NCEP through the National Institutes of Health warning doctors about this deadly duo. It's too bad that not every physician paid attention to the guidelines.

Dr. Anthony Gotto of Baylor University and Methodist Hospital in Houston was the author of the report. He adamantly states the danger of the combination and proclaims it to be an independent risk factor above and beyond all individual aspects of the lipid profile.

Fortunately, there are efficient ways of dealing with the problem. We've already examined approaches to raising HDLs. Triglycerides are, actually, a bit easier to control. Excessive amounts of sugars and alcohol can drive counts up. Often first-time cholesterol watchers eschew fats in favor of sugar-laden treats, and their triglycerides go way up. Moderation, not elimination, is the watchword. Obesity frequently results in high triglycerides; attaining a healthy weight routinely lowers triglycerides. Exercise burns off excessive triglycerides, which are the body's storage units of energy. And, if all else fails, the use of either Lopid or niacin can bring those triglycerides tumbling down to normal in short order. As you'll read in chapter 9, the immediate-release form of niacin is far more efficient for triglyceride control than sustained-release types.

WHAT'S MORE IMPORTANT?

For most people, in most instances, the big three risk factors—elevated cholesterol levels, high blood pressure, and smoking—largely determine their potential for developing heart disease. Despite the information regarding the new bad guys covered in this chapter, our emphasis shouldn't really shift. It would be ridiculous to take a few B vitamins to control homocysteine levels while ignoring one's other risk factors. When it comes to heart health, we should want 100 percent protection. Filling in the pieces of the puzzle now allows us to get just that.

· 6 ·

THE SOLUBLE SOLUTION

"Don't eat this, don't eat that." Dietary advice tends to be negative. Instead, I prefer to focus on what I should eat. While some foods do raise cholesterol levels in the blood, many others actively lower them. Let's put more emphasis on these.

As I write this chapter, I'm surrounded by stacks of scientific articles documenting the effectiveness of foods and supplements rich in soluble fibers. *There's no question about it: Soluble fibers effectively lower cholesterol.* And we're not limited to just one or two choices any more. New ones are better than ever—we've come a long way since oat bran muffins!

We often hear that Americans should increase their fiber consumption. Authorities recommend thirty-five grams of fiber daily, combining both soluble and insoluble fiber. Soluble fiber dissolves in water, while insoluble fiber does not. Some foods are particularly rich in one, while others contribute primarily the other. Wheat and most fruits and vegetables are principally known for insoluble fiber. I'll detail all the foods and supplements to seek out for soluble fiber in this chapter.

We need a balance of both fiber types daily. Insoluble fibers keep the gastrointestinal tract healthy and speed up the passage of food through the gut. Soluble fibers, on the other hand, form a gel when dissolved in water and pass slowly through the GI tract.

Both fiber types prevent constipation, but soluble fibers must be taken with plenty of water and other fluids in order to be effective. Ironically, those soluble fibers can actually be constipating if one does not consume sufficient water. That's even true for products such as Metamucil, which contains psyllium and is sold primarily to promote regularity.

I introduced the concept of soluble fibers and their protection against heart disease to the world way back in 1987 in *The 8-Week Cholesterol Cure.* That's the book that popularized oat bran, one of the best sources of soluble fiber. Back then, oat bran became ubiquitous, and manufacturers began to put it into all sorts of food products. Many health authorities applauded the improvement in the American diet.

Then the mass media got wind of a tragically flawed research study that concluded erroneously that oat bran did not work. Bear in mind that at that time oat bran had become a sort of cultural icon, something that everyone knew about and respected. The media love to be iconoclastic. Stand-up comedians reveled in the new material. The popularity of oat bran declined precipitously. We'll examine that study in detail a little later. For now, suffice it to say that oat bran—and all the other foods rich in soluble fibers—really does work.

In fact, a number of studies have shown exactly how soluble fibers (SF) do their cholesterol-lowering trick. Essentially, the mechanism comes down to preventing the body from efficiently recycling cholesterol in the liver and shunting it out through the bowel movement.

Cholesterol is critically important to the body, and it is guarded like treasure. It is a major ingredient in making bile acids, which are needed for fat digestion. Unused bile acids are sent back to the liver for recycling so the body does not have to turn to its cholesterol reserves. That's where the SF comes into play.

Soluble fibers are bile sequestering agents. They bind onto and hold bile acids as they pass through the gastric tract like a gelatinous glacier. Those sequestered bile acids are then eliminated in the bowel movement. As a result, the body has to make more bile acids, and to do so it uses cholesterol that would otherwise pile up in the bloodstream and ultimately clog our arteries. Over a period of time, a matter of weeks, the cholesterol count in the blood goes down.

Now, if all that is true, then we should be able to measure an increased amount of bile acids in the bowel movement. Though not a particularly pleasant task, I would imagine, a number of researchers have done just that. In 1991 researchers published in the *Journal of the American Medical Association* a report that beta-glucan, the soluble fiber found in oat bran, lowered cholesterol levels and increased fecal excretion of bile acids. In 1992, Swedish doctors examined the fecal elimination of patients with ileostomies who consumed oat bran. Such patients must empty their ostomy bags daily, and their contents showed an increased amount of bile acids. And in 1994, investigators from the University of Wisconsin and Purdue University published definitive evidence of this effect of soluble fibers.

Soluble fiber may also have a second mechanism of action. It is fermented in the colon to form a particular form of fatty acids that are absorbed by the portal vein in the abdomen and are then transported directly to the liver where they inhibit cholesterol synthesis.

Soluble fiber also helps us control weight in two ways. First, SF stabilizes the level of sugars in the bloodstream; consequently, blood sugar doesn't drop as quickly, and one doesn't get hungry for quite a while after a SF-rich meal. Second, SF promotes a feeling of satisfaction, termed satiety, owing to the slow movement of the gel formed by SF with water while going through the digestive system.

Okay, SF works. But how much can we realistically expect from this single element in a heart-smarter lifestyle? Studies from all over the world, working with a wide variety of foods and supplements, have shown cholesterol reductions of as low as 3 percent to as much as 25 percent. More typically, drops are in the 9 to 11 percent range.

Both total cholesterol and LDL cholesterol come down when soluble fibers are added to the diet. But it's critical to note that the levels of protective HDL cholesterol do not drop. Now that's quite different from the effects of a commonly advocated low-fat diet, which inevitably results in a significant HDL decline. By keeping the HDL up and getting the TC and LDL down, a low-fat diet with added SF is much more effective in improving the vital risk ratio of TC/HDL and LDL/HDL than a standard low-fat diet. (See page 14 for more about the risk ratios.) Moreover, you'll find it a whole lot easier to add something to the diet rather than to restrict that diet. There's even research at Syracuse University proving that to be true.

Our choice of foods and supplements rich in SF has grown significantly since I started baking oat bran muffins in 1984. Variety is the spice of life, and mixing those choices makes success a certainty.

I could fill the entire book with a recitation of the dozens if not hundreds of research studies that have unequivocally proven the effectiveness of SF in cholesterol reduction. Instead, I'll give you just a sampling of data about all the potential fibers you might want to try. Since oat bran was the first to show benefits, let's start there.

YES, VIRGINIA, OAT BRAN REALLY DOES WORK!

Back in 1963, Dutch researchers first noted an 11 percent TC decrease in patients consuming an enormous amount of oatmeal—almost five ounces daily—for three weeks. However, no one knew it was the bran portion of the oat that did the trick. That finding is credited to Dr. James Anderson at the University of Kentucky.

In the early 1980s, Dr. Anderson was interested in the ability of certain cereals to control glucose levels in diabetic patients. Wondering which cereal might work best, he systematically fed patients one at a time for periods of time. Ultimately, oatmeal became the star blood sugar stabilizer, and rather coincidentally, the researchers noted that cholesterol levels fell as well. Now what was it about oatmeal that did that? Dr. Anderson identified oat bran's soluble fiber, beta-glucan, as the magic ingredient. From that point forward, most research has concentrated on the bran rather than on the oatmeal. It takes two to three times as much oatmeal to do the job of the same amount of oat bran.

Since the days of those early research findings, the data have continued to pile up. Here's a sampling of studies from around the world.

- In 1991, Dr. Anderson saw a 12.8 percent drop in TC and a 12.1 percent fall in LDL after twenty-one days of consuming 110 grams of oat bran daily. That year New Zealand researchers found an 11.6 percent TC decline with a rise of 10.3 percent in HDL in individuals after four weeks of eating forty-four grams of oat bran baked into bread eaten daily. And at Northwestern University in Chicago, noted nutrition researcher Dr. Linda Van Horn demonstrated a 6.25 percent drop in TC and 9.2 percent lower LDL after eight weeks of consuming fifty-six grams of instant oats. (There are twenty-eight grams in an ounce.)
- Ready-to-eat cold oat bran cereal also works. Anderson found a 5.4 percent drop in TC and 12.1 percent decline in LDL after twenty-one days of eating fifty-six grams, the serving size listed on the box. That's just two ounces. Researchers saw a more impressive 14.9 percent fall in TC with the same amount eaten by participants in the famed Framingham Heart Study in Massachusetts.
- German researchers in 1992 found that sixty grams of oat bran daily brought TC down by 9.7 percent in just three weeks. Australians that same year reported a 5.7 percent decline in LDL and a 7.5 percent improvement in the LDL/HDL ratio in subjects consuming sixty grams of oat bran as muffins.
- And the positive findings continue to come in. In 1993 a Louisiana State University study showed a 10 percent reduction in TC with a 13.5 percent fall in LDL in three weeks of eating one hundred grams of oat bran. That same amount achieved an 8.2 percent decline in TC and a 9.9 percent drop in LDL, as reported in the *Journal of the American Dietetic Association* in 1994.

Good research has been published by outstanding investigators from all over the globe in very well respected scientific and medical journals. So where did the idea that oat bran doesn't work come from?

On January 18, 1990, an article in the *New England Journal of Medicine* proclaimed that oat bran did not lower cholesterol levels any better than Cream of Wheat, a cereal with virtually no fiber whatsoever. The conclusion was based on a study done with twenty women whose initial cholesterol levels were perfectly normal, averaging 186. After eating either oat bran or Cream of Wheat for six weeks, both groups' levels averaged 172. Thus, the Harvard research group stated unequivocally, the oat bran was no better than any other cereal, and cholesterol reductions were probably owing to replacement of other, fattier foods rather than any special quality of oat bran.

Normally nothing much would have come of a little study with no particular consequence. But it happened that the senior author, Dr. Frank Sacks, also served, and still serves, on the board of the Center for Science in the Public Interest (CSPI), a rather radical advocacy group in Washington, D.C. CSPI, in turn, had been embroiled in arguments with Quaker Oats for months. And with the enormous media resources and clout at its disposal, CSPI joined hands with Sacks for a virtual media blitz. Within days, the "cereal killers" had done their job, and oat bran's reputation was destroyed. For whatever their political purposes, Sacks and CSPI undermined public confidence in oat bran. What was even worse, the public concluded that even the scientists were confused, and the national interest in heart health in general declined terribly.

In reality, that Harvard study was horribly flawed, a conclusion that was eventually agreed to by virtually the entire scientific and medical community. Unfortunately, newspaper and TV reporters typically do not have the expertise to read original papers. They put their faith in statements and news releases from organizations that have prestige, such as Harvard University and the *New England Journal of Medicine* and ignored the dozens of studies demonstrating the efficacy of soluble fiber in general and oat bran in particular.

The story of the cereal killers has become a classic. As recently as late 1994, students at the Wistar Institute in Philadelphia studied the episode in a seminar dealing with science, politics, and public policy. Even undergraduate students were able to poke holes in the flawed study and wondered how it all could have happened.

What was wrong with the Harvard study?

- Conclusions were based on a group of uniformly healthy women with perfectly normal cholesterol levels to begin with. What about men? What about people with elevated cholesterols? Even aspirin won't work if one doesn't have a headache to begin with. And those twenty women were health professionals with exemplary lifestyles.

- The authors claimed that everything was equal in both the oat bran (OB) and Cream of Wheat (CW) groups, but a closer look at the data shows that claim isn't true. The OB group consumed a diet in which 35 percent of the calories came from fat while the CW group's diet contained only 30 percent fat. In truth, it was remarkable that oat bran consumption would allow all those extra grams of fat to be enjoyed while keeping cholesterol levels low!
- The authors also claimed that there were no differences in cholesterol levels between the OB and CW groups. But that was true only for total cholesterol. Eating the low-fat, high-carbohydrate diet, the CW group experienced a decline in HDL from an average of 54 down to 50.9. Conversely, the OB group had a slight increase from the initial average of 54 to 54.2 for HDL readings.
- That difference in HDLs translates to a distinct improvement in the risk ratio of TC to HDL for the OB group. The CW group's risk was worsened.

My anger at the researchers and whatever their motives were isn't a matter of sour grapes. Sure, I was the man who personally introduced oat bran to the world. But my intentions are far beyond merely selling books. I fight a very personal fight against heart disease, and I have come to view that disease as The Enemy to be fought and defeated, not only for myself but for all others as well. I feel pain when I see someone smoking a cigarette or not exercising or not caring about the foods he or she eats. That research and its subsequent publicity hurt people and undermined their health, and those researchers and those assisting them with their public lies are responsible for that harm.

Actually, there is a lot of anger in the scientific community about the oat bran fiasco. After a study published in autumn 1992 in the *Journal of the American Medical Association* unequivocally showed the benefits of oat bran, a subsequent letter to the editor bemoaned the fact that the "exhaustive analysis did not receive the same media blitz . . . as that accompanying the flawed study." Dr. Roger Brumback, of the University of Oklahoma Health Sciences Center, wrote that "it only takes one negative story to undo much of this effort (to show the benefits of oat bran)."

Even more ironic is the fact that even the senior author of the flawed study, Dr. Frank Sacks, had become convinced of oat bran's effectiveness by 1992, according to the CSPI publication *Nutrition Action Healthletter.* In an article in the September 1994 issue, CSPI grudgingly admitted that oat bran lowers cholesterol. Of course, CSPI didn't bother to repeat its original media blitz or admit its mistakes and apologize to the public.

On the bright side, millions of people still do eat oat bran regularly and other foods rich in soluble fiber as well. Years later, I continue to receive letters from people telling me of their terrific successes in cholesterol reduction. Many of those writers have done nothing more than cutting back on fat and adding that soluble fiber and have avoided the need for prescription medications entirely. And test have shown that my own heart's health remains excellent.

Back in 1984 when I started my search for ways to improve my cholesterol level—and save my own life—the emphasis was on oat bran. I tried eating it as hot cereal, but found that far from a gourmet treat. So I developed recipes for oat bran muffins. And later the ready-to-eat (RTE) oat bran cereal came on the market. I continue to enjoy that RTE cereal regularly. You can find it marketed in a red box as Quaker Oat Bran High Oat Bran Fiber Cereal. If you can't find it readily, call the company at (800) 570-8718. It's worth the effort.

But don't limit yourself to oat bran by any means. In fact, that can lead to boredom. Almost no one can eat the same food every day, day in and day out, for the rest of one's life. I definitely recommend the widest possible variety when it comes to soluble fiber. And today we have the research to document the effectiveness of a wide variety of foods and supplements.

BEANS, BEANS, GOOD FOR YOUR HEART

Probably the easiest way to get soluble fiber—and lots of insoluble fiber as well—into your diet regularly is by eating a variety of dried beans and peas. Research studies have shown that a cup of beans provides the cholesterol-lowering effect of a half cup of oat bran. And, as with oat bran, studies have demonstrated cholesterol reductions of anywhere from 3 percent to 10 percent and more. Importantly, only the bad LDL goes down, leaving the protective HDL levels intact, thus improving the risk ratio significantly. Of all the dried beans and peas, one of the richest sources of soluble fiber is the black-eyed pea. Try them out of a can, drained and rinsed, or prepared from scratch. For a real treat, look for fresh black-eyed peas in your supermarket's produce section. All you have to do is simmer the peas in water for about fifteen minutes. Serve with a drizzle of extra-virgin olive oil, and you'll experience one more example of the ultrahealthy Mediterranean diet.

Think about the variety: pinto beans in chili, white beans in soups, refried beans, black beans with roasted chicken Cuban style, red beans with cajun cooking, kidney beans in minestrone, three-bean salads, and garbanzo beans (chick peas) mashed into hummus, that staple of Middle Eastern eating—the list goes on and on.

Concerned about the potential gas from beans? First, don't cook the beans in the same water they soaked in. Second, consider trying Beano when you eat beans. That product is very effective in preventing the formation of gas from undigested beans fermenting in the digestive tract.

Like oat bran, beans really work. Dr. James Anderson at the University of Kentucky has studied them extensively. In one study, he found that a daily cup of pork and beans from which the pork had been removed (you could choose vegetarian-style baked beans) cut cholesterol levels by 13 percent. The men in his study made no other dietary changes, continuing to eat a standard, 38 percent–fat diet. Dr. Anderson believes that while canned beans are good, dried beans appear to be better. His study with the latter produced a 19 percent reduction in cholesterol levels.

BARLEY'S GOOD, THAT'S NO BLARNEY

Once upon a time, barley was a staple grain in the American diet. It's really too bad that consumption has declined, since barley has always been an excellent source of good nutrition and fiber. In a paper delivered at the 2nd International Conference on Heart Health in May 1995, Dr. Joseph Keenan reported that pearl barley effectively lowers cholesterol levels, thanks to the content of soluble fibers. In his study at the University of Minnesota, Dr. Keenan fed seventy-five men and women with elevated cholesterol levels a low-fat diet for four weeks. That diet produced a cholesterol reduction from 245 to 234. Then he added four muffins daily made from barley. Levels fell by another 10 mg/dl.

While ordinary barley does, indeed, offer a modicum of cholesterol-lowering benefit, a newly developed strain of the grain does far more. The so-called waxy hull-less barley contains two to three times as much of the soluble fiber beta-glucan (the same found in oat bran) as normal barley. Moreover, the new barley is rich in a chemical cousin of vitamin E (*d*-alpha-tocotrienol), which works in the liver to actually inhibit cholesterol manufacture. Barley gives you a double health whammy!

NuWorld Nutrition in Fargo, North Dakota, produces the new barley in a form that can be made into a very satisfying hot cereal and used recipes for baking such goodies as cookies, muffins, and pancakes. Currently it's available only through mail order, but unlike other mail-order products this one is quite inexpensive. You can call NuWorld at (800) 950-3188 to place an order.

The waxy hull-less barley has been extensively studied at Montana State University and North Dakota State University. You can incorporate it into your diet in a number of ways beyond just making a tasty hot cereal.

- Replace all of the flour in muffin recipes with barley cereal. For a lighter, cakelike muffin, add one-fourth cup of flour.
- Prepare quick breads by replacing up to one-half of the flour with barley cereal.
- Replace up to one-fourth of the flour in biscuit recipes, coffee cakes, and yeast breads and up to one-half of the flour in cookie recipes with barley cereal.

This product is not available in supermarkets, and few people have heard of it, even in the research community. But, boy, does it ever work! Even if you eat the barley cereal only two or three times a week, you'll notice the difference in your regularity. And as part of the total cholesterol-lowering program, you'll see significant lipid improvements.

BRAN, BRAN, SEEDS, AND PECTIN

We know all about oat bran; now it turns out that other types of bran have similar cholesterol-controlling capabilities. Both corn bran and rice bran have racked up data demonstrating their effectiveness. In 1993, for example, researchers from Louisiana State University in Baton Rouge published their findings that rice bran was as effective as oat bran in controlling cholesterol levels.

Neither type of bran, however, attained the popularity of oat bran, and you might have some difficulty locating either one. Look first in health food stores—the type that sells food, not just pills and powders. If you can't find these alternative brans, you can order them by phone for home delivery. Call Ener-G Foods at (800) 331-5222. If you live in the state of Washington, the number is (800) 325-9788.

While you're in the health food stores looking for bran, you might come across flax seed, which also has a cholesterol-lowering characteristic. As reported in the *Journal of the American College of Nutrition,* eating flax seed baked into six slices of bread daily for two months yielded a 10 percent cholesterol reduction. Additionally, flax seed is a good source of the omega-3 fatty acids that are also found in fish. So, if you want the anticlotting benefits of fish oil without eating the fish, flax seed might be for you.

Next we come to pectin, another type of soluble fiber. Maybe the reason an apple a day keeps the doctor away is that apples contain a small amount of pectin. A richer source of apple fiber can be found in a product named, aptly enough, Tastee Apple Fiber. While apple pectin does not appear to have as strong a cholesterol-lowering effect as oat or rice bran, it is a nice change of pace. The Tastee product bakes up into really delicious cookies and cakes, replacing half the normal amount of flour in a recipe. Tastee Apple Fiber can be ordered directly from the company at (800) 262-7753.

ANOTHER REASON TO EAT FRUITS AND VEGETABLES

I have my serious doubts that vegetarians tend to be healthier because they avoid meat. If that were the case, the lacto-ovo-vegetarians who also enjoy dairy products and eggs wouldn't share the benefits. Rather than avoiding this food or that, I think vegetarians have a lower rate of heart disease and other degenerative diseases because they eat a lot of fruits and vegetables.

Throughout this book you'll read about the advantages of fruits and vegetables. They're a source of antioxidants. They contain flavonoids. In addition, they probably have beneficial chemicals scientists have yet to identify, and they deserve a mention in this chapter because many are an excellent source of soluble—as well as insoluble—fiber. Take another look at the chart on page 82.

But don't just read and nod your head in agreement. Make a decision to consciously increase your daily intake. Figs and prunes are the real winners in the soluble fiber showdown. Why not have them readily available for munching when watching TV? Keep some single-serve packets in the glove compartment of the car and in your office desk drawer for when you need a snack in a hurry. Take them along on a bike ride or when you're out hiking. Or fishing. Or golfing.

According to Dr. Anderson, not all the soluble fibers are equally effective, and some may not lower the levels of cholesterol at all. String beans, for example aren't very effective, and as we've seen, apple pectin isn't as potent as oat's beta-glucan fiber. But all contribute to the total intake of both types of fiber we all need.

Moreover, a combination of the different types of fiber achieved by eating a wide variety of fruits and vegetables regularly may be particularly effective. Each has its distinctive profile of nutrients. Medical research has shown that combinations of different agents meant to achieve the same effect are often more effective than merely increasing the dosage of a single substance. Certainly that's true for the prescription-only, cholesterol-lowering drugs.

SUPER-POTENT SUPPLEMENTAL SOLUTIONS

Okay, it's not always possible to whip up a batch of muffins or a bowl of bean soup. And what about those times when you really want a meal that just happens to be relatively low in fiber? Like an omelette with white toast for breakfast, for example, or even a bowl of that notorious virtually fiber-free Cream of Wheat. Or when you're traveling and not paying a whole lot of attention to grams of fiber. Those are the times to reach for one of the supplements that are particularly wonderful sources of soluble fiber. Truth be told, they're a more reliable source, since you know just how many grams of fiber you'll get in any given dose. And those supplements have been proven without question to dramatically whack cholesterol counts.

THERE'S NOTHING SILLY ABOUT PSYLLIUM

That's the active ingredient in Metamucil and other brands of products marketed to maintain bowel movement regularity. Some breakfast cereals also list psyllium as an ingredient, boosting their fiber content. The good news is that psyllium provides a very efficient, effective method of cholesterol control.

In one of the early studies with this fiber, Dr. James Anderson gave participants 3.4 grams of psyllium three times daily with meals. That's the amount found in one rounded teaspoonful, which is mixed with water or juice. Twenty-six men followed the program, which included no changes in diet whatever, for eight weeks. Total cholesterol levels fell by nearly 15 percent, and LDL counts came down about 20 percent. Dr. Anderson noted that cholesterol measurements improved throughout that time period, reaching the peak at eight weeks.

Not all studies have achieved such excellent results. Reporting in the *Annals of Internal Medicine,* Dr. D.L. Sprecher and his associates found reductions of about 6 percent after giving participants 5.1 grams of psyllium twice daily for eight weeks. Other investigations have turned up reductions from 6 to 10 percent.

Psyllium-containing breakfast cereals have also been studied. Dr. Anderson saw an 8.4 percent decline in total cholesterol after six weeks of a daily diet including four ounces of cereal. Reductions continued in subsequent weeks, with one subject enjoying a cholesterol decline of more than 20 percent.

Why are there such differences in results? First, Dr. Anderson's research is done in metabolic wards of hospitals where every last ounce of food is observed and measured. Other investigations rely on free-living populations who may not strictly adhere to the dietary regimen in question. Your results, of course, will depend on just how religiously you decide to follow the program. Just buying a canister of psyllium and putting it on the back shelf won't do you much good at all.

Another reason for variance in success with psyllium comes down to when it is taken. An important report in the *American Journal of Clinical Nutrition* in 1994 proved what many of us had suspected for some time. When psyllium was taken with meals, participants had a reduction of total and LDL cholesterol of 8 and 11 percent, respectively. But when the psyllium was consumed between meals, there was no difference in cholesterol counts from the control group receiving a placebo.

Finally, the duration of the studies has varied enormously. One sees a positive result within two to three weeks, but the decline in cholesterol continues in subsequent weeks and even months.

If you decide that psyllium should be a part of your program, take it regularly with meals. One rounded teaspoonful with any fluid three times daily is better than taking one tablespoonful once a day, even though the total amount is the same. Always wash it down with an extra glass of water for greatest effectiveness. Remember that psyllium is water soluble, and it takes water to produce the desired effect. Give yourself plenty of time to determine effectiveness in your own case; you can expect more reduction after two months than after just two weeks.

Finally, don't be fooled by advertisements for non-psyllium-based, look-alike products. Citrucel, for example, compares itself directly with Metamucil, citing its superior solubility, taste, and texture. Although both Metamucil and Citrucel are high-fiber supplements that promote regularity, Citrucel contains methylcellulose, not psyllium, and has absolutely no effect on cholesterol reduction. Read the labels.

GUAR: THE GUM YOU DON'T CHEW

You'll find guar gum listed on many fat-reduced foods, such as yogurt and custards. This additive provides thickening and texture to replace the missing fat. You might also see a list of other foreign-sounding ingredients, including xanthan gum and carrageenan. All these are soluble fibers, which, rather than being harmful, are actually quite beneficial.

Guar gum comes from the cluster bean plant that grows in arid regions such as India, Pakistan, and parts of the U.S. Southwest. As with both oat bran's beta-glucan and psyllium, this soluble fiber forms a gel when it comes into contact with water. When it comes to cholesterol reductions, it's one of the best agents.

Data have been collected all over the world showing the benefits of guar gum. The principal researcher in the United States has been Dr. John Farquhar of Stanford University. His results have been uniformly positive.

In a typical study, fifteen grams of guar gum were consumed in three doses with meals. Each dose, about a teaspoonful, was mixed with water or juice. After three weeks, average cholesterol levels came down from 244 to 218. HDL levels were not affected, thus greatly improving the risk ratios. It would be expected that improvement would continue in subsequent weeks and months, based on similar research results.

Guar gum has certain advantages over oat bran and other foods. First, you know exactly how many grams of fiber you're getting. As with all foods, fiber content varies from brand to brand and crop to crop. Second, as with psyllium, one needn't do any special preparations or planning. Either can be consumed with any meal. The recommended dosage is one teaspoonful (5 grams) three times daily.

Like oat bran, guar gum experienced some bad publicity. A few individuals taking it as capsules didn't drink enough water to wash these capsules all the way down, and the capsules stuck in their throats. The obvious solution would have been to warn consumers to be certain to drink plenty of water, as they should do with any soluble fiber. Instead, the capsules were taken off the market entirely. Now only the powdered guar gum is available. One reliable maker is Twin Labs; you can find their products in most health food stores. If you can't locate the guar gum, you can call the company at (516) 467-3140 in Ronkonkoma, New York, to learn where guar gum is sold in your area. You can also order it from Ener-G Foods at (800) 331-5222.

Experiment a bit. Mix the guar gum with various juices to see what you like best. Try making what I call an "orange guarius," which is a frothy mixture of orange juice, one teaspoon of guar gum, one egg white, and one tablespoonful of honey blended together with ice chips. It's actually delicious. Or take advantage of guar gum's thickening properties to concoct shakes and smoothies. Add one teaspoonful to chocolate milk, and you have a thick shake.

A LITTLE OF THIS, A DAB OF THAT

Walking down the aisles of the health food store you might see products that contain a combination of two, three, or more types of soluble fiber. Do they work? Absolutely. Let's look at two examples.

Researchers tested a product made by the Shaklee company that consisted of psyllium, pectin, guar gum, and locust bean gum. Subjects consumed a five-gram dose three times daily and experienced a 10 percent decrease in total cholesterol and a 14 percent drop in LDL. The researchers published their results in 1993 in the *Journal of the American College of Nutrition.*

A blue-ribbon group of researchers at the University of Minnesota looked at another fiber supplement product in 1994. During a fifteen-week period, participants took either ten or twenty grams daily. The smaller dose produced a 6 percent drop in total cholesterol and an 8 percent fall in LDL. Interestingly, the larger dose yielded a *smaller* improvement: Total cholesterol was down 5 percent and LDL declined just over 7 percent. We'll look at that paradox a bit later.

Yes, combinations of different soluble fibers do work, but you can expect to pay significantly more per gram for fibers purchased this way.

BUT NOT ALL SOLUBLE FIBERS ARE CREATED EQUAL

I've already noted that methylcellulose found in Citrucel may keep you regular but won't cut cholesterol. And unfortunately, not all soluble fibers produce that effect. When studying the Shaklee product, for example, researchers used acacia gum as the placebo. As expected, that fiber did not affect cholesterol levels one bit. Another soluble fiber loser is tragacanth gum. Perhaps, it has been speculated, viscosity is the critical factor. Those fibers known to lower cholesterol are much more viscous than those that don't. That is to say, they create a thicker gel when mixed with water. Fortunately, I've not found any products that include acacia or tragacanth gums in formulas intended for cholesterol control.

IN THE MOOD FOR SOME GRAPEFRUIT RINDS?

A few years ago a researcher at the University of Florida got a lot of publicity when he found that pectin derived from grapefruit rinds had a powerful cholesterol-lowering effect. Of course, not too many people started eating grapefruit rinds!

Dr. James Cerda continued his research and found some truly amazing results with the swine he used as experimental animals because their hearts and blood vessels are so similar to ours. When they were fed a high-fat diet, those pigs developed severe atherosclerosis. The research included directly examining the insides of the pigs' aortas and arteries after they were slaughtered, which would be impossible to do with humans. Not many humans will volunteer for that!

Then they conducted what could eventually be a milestone research project. Dr. Cerda and his associates fed the artery-clogged swine a diet supplemented with either grapefruit pectin or cellulose as the placebo. You'll recall that cellulose does not have the heart-protecting qualities of other fibers. The results were nothing short of amazing.

After consuming the fiber for 270 days, pigs getting pectin had coronary arteries with 24 percent blockages, while those getting the cellulose had 45 percent clogging. All the pigs had been eating a very high-fat diet all along, and their cholesterol levels had soared. Looking at the pigs' aortas, the main vessel leaving the heart, Dr. Cerda found one-third the blockage in those getting pectin as compared with the placebo group.

Does pectin, and perhaps other soluble fibers as well, retard the development of atherosclerosis or maybe even reverse it in humans as well as swine? On the pessimistic side, this was an animal trial, and no similar studies have been done with humans. Optimistically, however, the pig's cardiovascular system is remarkably similar to ours, and swine have been used for decades to predict what dietary influences might mean for us. Most typically, findings in swine have turned out to be similar in human studies.

Based on the success of his research, Dr. Cerda and his associates developed a fiber supplement product called Pro-Fibe, which combines grapefruit pectin with that other proven soluble fiber guar gum. They also added some protein that makes the product more easily dissolved in water or other fluids. One scoop of Pro-Fibe provides five grams of fiber, and the recommended dosage is three scoops daily. One would expect it to be most effective, as is true for other fibers, when taken with meals rather than in between. Pro-Fibe can be incorporated into a number of cooking and baking recipes. I've mixed a scoop into a bowl of Cream of Wheat, for example, turning this otherwise fiber-free cereal into a high-fiber breakfast.

Unpublished data from Dr. Cerda's laboratories indicate significant cholesterol reductions as well. This time it was with humans. After thirty days of consuming three doses of Pro-Fibe daily, total cholesterol levels fell by 17 percent and LDL came down 25 percent on average.

Want to try some Pro-Fibe in your heart-smarter program? Order it directly from the company in Florida by calling (800) 756-3999.

THE EASIEST WAY TO INCREASE FIBER

Psyllium, guar, pectin, and the Pro-Fibe combination product all work, but the downside is taking them. All produce a thick, sludgy fluid when mixed with water or juice. Fortunately there's another way to ingest them that's a lot easier and tastier. A small company in Oklahoma named after the owner's wife produces what they accurately call 100% Soluble Fiber or SF-100. Manufactured in extreme secrecy to protect its exclusivity, SF-100 is a plant-derived powder that dissolves completely in water or other fluids. Because of that 100 percent dissolution, there's no thickening and it remains clear and drinkable even after hours. Try that with Metamucil, and you'd have a glass of goo.

The Nanci Company sells SF-100 as Fruity Fiber in orange and fruit punch flavors. It comes in individual packets or canisters and, especially when compared with any other fiber supplements, actually tastes good, rather like Tang or Hawaiian Punch. Each packet or one-teaspoon serving contains two grams of soluble fiber. You can also get SF-100 in its pure form, which you can mix with any beverage. Now you can have high-fiber juice, fruit nectar, or even soda pop. Stir it into milk and turn any cereal into a high-fiber breakfast. Each packet contains a whopping six grams of soluble fiber.

SF-100 offers the easiest way to boost your soluble fiber intake daily, whether at home, in the office, or while traveling. Nanci also makes shakes that are ideal for use in weight control as meal replacements. But do these products really work?

Nanci's SF-100 was tested at the University of Texas Health Science Center in San Antonio. Two groups received the fiber by way of Nanci shakes. One group got a total of fourteen grams of soluble fiber, and the other received seven grams. Both used the shakes as daily meal replacements. Neither made any other dietary or exercise changes in their lives.

After six weeks, the group drinking two shakes containing seven grams of fiber daily experienced a reduction in total cholesterol of 6.2 percent; their LDLs fell by 8.15 percent. Those drinking two shakes daily with a total of fourteen grams of fiber had a 9.68 percent drop in total cholesterol and 12.17 percent drop in LDLs.

When the company wanted to introduce its products in Mexico, the government there required its own clinical trials. Physicians at the University Hospital in Mexico City found similar cholesterol reductions in those taking the Nanci soluble fiber products.

You can order SF-100 soluble fiber as Fruity Fiber drinks, the pure SF-100 to be mixed with a beverage of your choice, or as shakes. For more information or to place an order, call (800) 985-2582 or write to P.O. Box 700867, Tulsa, OK, 74170.

MORE IS NOT BETTER

There's no question that most Americans need more fiber in their diets and that soluble fiber in particular can lower cholesterol levels. But how much is enough? Can one get too much fiber?

The average fiber consumption in the United States is about ten grams or less daily. That number includes both soluble and insoluble types. Authorities feel that consumption should be closer to thirty-five grams a day. For many people, that's quite a stretch. Meats of all sorts, dairy foods, fats and oils, and the majority of processed and fast foods contain absolutely no fiber at all. None. Nada. Zip. The only foods with fiber are grains, fruits, and vegetables, and since a good many people eat few to none of these foods, their total fiber intake is close to zero. Sad but true.

Especially if you're currently consuming very little fiber, you'll want to increase your intake gradually. Going from zero fiber to four oat bran muffins a day back in the 1980s when my book came out caused a lot of gas! Start with a small bowl of cereal. Maybe next day a side dish of beans. Little by little you can work up to the totals I'll recommend shortly. This is a decision you'll want to stick with for life, so you don't want any unpleasant experiences of gassiness, bloating, or other forms of gastric distress.

I know I've mentioned this before, but it bears repeating: Drink plenty of water throughout the day. Soluble fibers soak up water like a sponge, and you'll need plenty to form the gel that will bind the bile acids and move them out with your bowel movement. Too little water can lead to constipation.

When soluble fibers first caught the attention of the scientific and medical communities, some nutritionists were concerned about the potential of those fibers to interfere with proper absorption of minerals. Those worries were intensified by early research in animals and then in humans showing declined absorption of calcium and other minerals when soluble fibers were introduced to the diet. But subsequent studies showed this decline to be a temporary condition; the body soon adapts to the fiber, and mineral absorption quickly returns to normal. To be extra cautious at the start of this program, you might want to take any mineral supplements during meals when you're not consuming fiber-containing foods or supplements. Again, that concern applies only to the first two or three months of increased intake of soluble fibers.

But by all means you won't want to limit your efforts to increasing only soluble fiber. There are distinct health benefits you'll want to derive from balancing your diet with both soluble and insoluble fibers. Again, wheat and most other whole grains, fruits, and vegetables are good sources of insoluble fiber.

In the 1980s, everyone assumed that since soluble fiber reduced cholesterol levels in the blood, the more one ate, the lower the levels would go. When Dr. Joseph Keenan of the University of Minnesota did what is known as a meta analysis, combining the data of dozens of studies to look at them as one, he concluded that the benefits were linear. That is to say, more is better.

But it now appears that while a certain threshold of intake must be achieved to see the greatest effect, after reaching that threshold, cholesterol reduction becomes a matter of diminishing returns. In fact, consuming more soluble fiber may actually cause poorer results than consuming less fiber, which appears to be the case whether considering foods such as oat bran or fiber supplements.

In 1991 Chicago researchers reported data in the *Journal of the American Medical Association* comparing the effects of consuming 84 grams of oatmeal, 56 grams of oat bran, and 84 grams of oat bran. Oatmeal contains less soluble fiber than oat bran; it takes about three bowls to get the same amount as found in two bowls of bran. Predictably, then, the oatmeal reduced LDL cholesterol by about 10 percent while the smaller amount of oat bran brought it down by nearly 16 percent. Now you'd expect even better results from the larger amount of oat bran. Not so! With 84 grams, LDL fell by 11.5 percent. Thus the optimum amount appeared to be 56 grams of oat bran, just two ounces. While success has varied significantly in terms of cholesterol reduction, anywhere from 4 to 21 percent reductions (typically 6 to 10 percent), other studies have confirmed that less is more when it comes to oat bran. That certainly takes the wind out of the sails of those who had previously said that it would take enough oat bran "to choke a horse" to see cholesterol benefits.

The same seems to be true for supplements. For example, in the *New England Journal of Medicine* in 1994, doctors with stellar reputations in cholesterol research reported their findings comparing ten- and twenty-gram doses of a supplement containing a combination of fibers including guar gum and pectin as well as some insoluble fiber. The two soluble fibers totaled 7.5 grams of the ten-gram dosage and fifteen grams in the twenty-gram regimen. The ten-gram dosage resulted in reductions of 5.8 percent in total cholesterol and 8.1 percent in LDL, but the twenty-gram dosage produced only 4.9 percent declines in total cholesterol and 7.3 percent falls in LDL. Why take twice as much to get lesser results?

It's amazing to think that moderation in things that are "good" for you is as prudent as in things that are "bad" for you!

One question that has never been researched is how a combination of a wide variety of foods, including a number of types of both soluble and insoluble fibers, might influence cholesterol levels. Researchers have combined fiber supplements such as guar gum and pectin, and they have compared foods such as oat bran and beans. But the real question might be whether the whole will equal more than the sum of its parts if one were to seek a variety of fiber-rich foods and supplements.

I think that would be the case if anyone were to invest the millions of dollars such a comprehensive study would cost. Oat bran, for example, appears to work because of its beta-glucan, a distinctive type of soluble fiber. Psyllium fiber is quite different, but it also works. And so do pectin, guar gum, figs, prunes, barley, and rice bran. Yet each has its distinctive chemical profile, and each lowers cholesterol because of its particular composition.

Now we know that when doctors combine two or more cholesterol-lowering drugs, they get more response than when they simply use more of one or another. There appears to be a synergistic action. And, when it comes to these drugs, each has its own mechanism of action. Literally dozens of articles have been published over the past few years demonstrating the efficacy of such combination therapy.

Perhaps combining the fiber-rich foods and supplements might achieve similar synergy. I don't know that synergy would occur for certain in the strict scientific sense because a definitive study has never been done. However, I can offer a lot of testimonial or anecdotal evidence, including my own case history and those of hundreds of readers who have written to me over the past decade. Making the effort to seek out a wide variety of foods and supplements rich in soluble fibers appears to be the thing to do. Again, look at the chart on page 82. I can honestly say that scarcely a day has gone by since 1984 that I haven't had at least one source of soluble fiber, and usually I have more.

It may be that eating twice the amount of oat bran might actually impede the cholesterol reduction achieved by enjoying half that amount. Instead, include other fiber-rich foods in your diet. What about enjoying a bowl of minestrone soup with its beans before a serving of pasta? Or red beans and rice for lunch? Consider a serving of one of those supplements—Pro-Fibe, psyllium, guar gum—with an evening meal or a breakfast that would otherwise be fiber-poor. That's the approach that I have personally been taking for years, and my cholesterol has remained comfortably in the safety zone.

Will everyone see a cholesterol reduction by including soluble fibers in their diet? It appears that people with the highest cholesterol elevations to begin with will have the largest responses. If counts are normal at the start, one should not expect a lot of change. Although some studies have shown a nice response even without dietary improvements, others have demonstrated the need to cut back on fat in general, and saturated fat in particular, for the fiber to have its impact. Does that mean that the effect is from the fat reduction rather than from the addition of fiber? Not at all. Individuals reducing fat intake along with fiber in the diet have a much greater cholesterol reduction than those simply limiting fat.

Conversely, adding fiber rather than just worrying about subtracting this food or that is a lot easier than undertaking a life of total deprivation, such as becoming a complete vegetarian. The heart-smarter approach is to take a lot of little steps that all add up to an incredible journey!

Soluble fiber has been a part of my personal program since 1984. Certainly I've reaped the benefits of cholesterol control, which in turn, has kept my arteries clear and flowing and my risk of heart disease virtually zero. But increased fiber is essential for good health in general, and my own health is spectacular. Let me share a wonderful little story.

In October 1995, I finally got around to doing what all of us should do when we reach the age of fifty. I had a sigmoidoscopy, a test to examine the inside of the colon to detect any cancers, polyps, or precancerous states. A sigmoidoscopy is not something anyone looks forward to, and I'd put it off for a while. The doctor had no idea who I was as he probed my insides. When he concluded the test he said, "I don't know what you've been doing, but you have the insides of a forty-year-old." I was fifty-three at the time. I then introduced myself and explained my interest in a high-fiber diet. He grinned ear to ear and said that I was a walking advertisement of how one can protect against cancer as well as heart disease, that I was free of any signs of age-related deterioration, polyps, or precancerous conditions. Certainly that experience was a terrific "fringe benefit."

In February 1996, the *Journal of the American Medical Association* published the ultimate valentine for all of us who eat a high-fiber diet. A long-term study involving thousands of men and women showed that diets high in fiber, those containing about thirty grams daily, slashed the risk of heart disease by 40 percent. Each gram produced up to a 2 percent decline in risk. Commenting on the study, Dr. Ronald Kraus of the University of California said that a high-fiber diet might even be more important in preventing heart disease than a diet low in fat, although it would be better to have both, of course. The study in question looked at *all* dietary fiber, both soluble and insoluble, pointing once again to the urgent need to make a real effort to increase the amount of fiber eaten daily by way of fruits, vegetables, cereals, and whole-grain breads.

As I've detailed in this chapter, there are a lot of ways to increase the fiber content of your diet every day. Personally I begin most mornings with a bowl of Quaker ready-to-eat oat bran cereal with sliced banana and skim milk. Lunch might be a sandwich made with whole-wheat bread. At dinner I often choose a side dish of beans of some sort or some bean soup. Or it might be barley. Two or three times a day I'll drink some of the Nanci SF-100 fiber mixed with juice; I think these are the best of the commercial fiber supplement products. Dr. Anderson of fiber fame agrees with me that combining these many types of fibers daily almost certainly is better than taking just one fiber source in larger amounts. And, of course, I enjoy plenty of fruits and vegetables throughout the day as snacks and at meals, and I make my sandwiches with whole-grain breads to complete the total fiber factor. What can I tell you? It's worked for me, and I'm sure it'll work for you. It's the soluble solution!

FINDING THE FIBER IN FOODS

SOURCE	GRAMS TOTAL FIBER (PER 3 1/2 OZ)	GRAMS SOLUBLE FIBER (PER 3 1/2 OZ)
CEREALS		
All Bran	30.8	5.1
Barley (regular, pearled)	14.0	3.5
Barley (waxy, hull-less)	18.0	6.5
Bran Buds	36.0	10.0
Cheerios	9.1	4.2
Cream of Wheat (uncooked)	3.8	1.6
Fiber One	42.4	3.0
Oat Bran (uncooked)	14.4	7.2
Oat Bran (cold cereal)	10.3	5.2
Oat Bran Crunch (Kolln)	16.4	9.3
Oat Meal (uncooked)	9.5	4.9
Raisin Bran	13.5	2.4
Rice Krispies	1.2	0.3
Shredded Wheat	12.5	1.6
Wheaties	8.3	2.4
FRUIT		
Apple	2.0	0.6
Apricots (dried)	7.9	4.4
Banana	1.9	0.6
Dates (dried)	4.4	1.2
Figs (dried)	8.2	4.0
Orange	2.0	1.0
Pear	3.5	1.3
Prunes (dried)	6.6	3.8
Raisins (dried)	2.3	1.1
VEGETABLES		
Asparagus	2.0	0.8
Beets	2.6	1.2
Broccoli	3.1	1.5
Brussels Sprouts	5.7	3.0
Carrots	3.2	1.5
Cauliflower	1.8	0.9
Corn	2.9	0.5
Potato (sweet)	2.5	1.1
Potato (white w/skin)	2.0	1.0
Spinach (cooked)	1.8	0.6

FINDING THE FIBER IN FOODS

SOURCE	GRAMS TOTAL FIBER (PER 3 1/2 OZ)	GRAMS SOLUBLE FIBER (PER 3 1/2 OZ)
DRIED BEANS & PEAS		
Black Beans (cooked)	7.1	2.8
Black-Eyed Peas (canned)	3.9	0.4
Butter Beans (cooked)	7.3	2.9
Chick Peas (cooked)	5.3	1.6
Kidney Beans (canned)	6.2	1.6
Pinto Beans (cooked)	6.9	2.2
Pork & Beans (canned)	4.2	2.0
Split Peas (cooked)	3.2	1.1
NUTS		
Almonds	8.8	1.1
Peanut Butter	6.1	1.6
Sesame Seeds	9.1	1.9
Sunflower Seeds	6.1	2.1
Walnuts	4.2	1.5
SUPPLEMENTS		
Citucel (1 tbsp)	2.0	2.0
Citrus Pectin (1 tbsp)	5.5	5.5
Flax Fiber (2 tbsp)	5.7	2.2
Metamucil (1 tsp)	2.7	2.1
Metamucil, Sugar Free (1 tsp)	3.0	2.6
ProFibe (1 scoop)	5.0	5.0

Excerpted by permission from *Plant Fiber in Foods* by James W. Anderson, M.D., HCF Nutrition Research Foundation, Lexington, KY. 1990. And other sources.

· 7 ·

Blocking Fat and Cholesterol Absorption

How much do you really like food? I mean, really savor the flavors and the aromas. I happen to love food. I look forward to dinner, whether at home or in restaurants. I remember special meals eaten at special occasions or on vacations. Eating is a joy of life for me. But that's not true for everyone.

Some people view food as nothing more or less than fuel for the body. That point of view is certainly true for some of the advocates of an ultra-low-fat, virtually vegetarian diet. During a radio interview in which I participated, Dr. Michael Jacobson of the CSPI was asked what he'd had for dinner the past evening. His meal consisted of a baked potato, a piece of squash, and a slice of bread. The host was not impressed with that kind of deprivation. Dr. Jacobson said he believed that food isn't all that important to him. Most of us, however, consider eating to be a pleasure.

Happily, many wonderful, delicious foods are naturally low in fat. Food manufacturers keep coming up with more and more low-fat and nonfat versions of dozens of favorites. There's even a company that produces beef products that are lower in fat than chicken breast without the skin. Part 4 of this book provides the details on easy and delicious ways to enjoy a low-fat diet without deprivation.

Certainly the first goal is to choose low-fat foods. But some foods just can't be duplicated or easily replaced. Sure, the McLean Deluxe hamburger at McDonalds is tasty, and at only eleven fat grams it's a great choice. But what happens when you have that Big Mac Attack? Wouldn't it be great if we could eliminate the fat from such foods, especially after enjoying them? And what about cholesterol? Sure, those egg substitutes are pretty good, but wouldn't you like a nice sunnyside-up egg breakfast at least once in a while?

Well, it turns out that there's a way to literally block the absorption of both fat and cholesterol in the foods you really want to eat. Talk about a revolutionary breakthrough!

BLOCKING FATS IN THE FOODS YOU EAT

It all started with a letter from one of my *Diet-Heart Newsletter* readers, wanting to know my opinion of a new weight loss product called SeQuester. A phone call to the company led to an interview with the company's president, "Buzz" Holcomb, who started that company, KCD Incorporated, because of his own marvelous results with the product, which had been invented by a physician.

Buzz told me how he personally lost fifty pounds by taking SeQuester and changing none of his eating habits. His wife went from 142 to 118 pounds. It was a gradual process, which did not give results overnight, but there was no question in his mind that SeQuester worked. Moreover, he pointed to results of clinical studies kept in the company files.

I remember telling the man that, as a medical journalist, I was a double skeptic, because of both my science and journalism training. Confident in his product, Holcomb challenged me to test it myself. And I did just that, along with reading everything I could dealing with the product and its ingredients.

SeQuester is a tablet composed of bovine (cow) bile in a special formulation with soluble and insoluble fibers. Bile, of course, is essential to the digestion of fats and is produced by the liver from cholesterol. On the package you'll see it listed as sodium choleate.

As the SeQuester tablet breaks up in the digestive tract, fat is attracted to the bile but gets caught in the mesh of those soluble and insoluble fibers. Fat builds up in the microscopic particle mesh, forming a larger particle that cannot pass through the walls of the intestine into the bloodstream. The fat is then eliminated in the bowel movement.

Right off the bat you should know that the Food and Drug Administration has reviewed the product and has issued a letter of approval for sale without a prescription. All ingredients in SeQuester are deemed to be "nondrug" and are on the generally-regarded-as-safe (GRAS) list issued by the FDA.

As determined by animal research studies, each SeQuester tablet is capable of immobilizing or sequestering about 6.0 grams of fat, 5.8 grams to be exact. This fat reduction has the potential for significant weight control or cholesterol management.

Weight loss in those using SeQuester exceeds that predicted by the sequestering of fat alone. Multiplying those six grams of fat by nine calories each, every tablet should remove fifty-four calories. Calorie removal itself is significant, but the soluble and insoluble fiber complex encapsulating the bile appears to further influence weight reduction. Interestingly, SeQuester suppresses appetite in those who need to lose weight, although I did not find that to be the case in my own situation or that of others who had no weight to lose in the first place. I learned that the Oakland Raiders football team uses SeQuester as part of its total nutrition and training program. The Raiders trainers find it helps build muscle tissue rather than fat in those athletes eating huge amounts of food.

But my immediate interest in SeQuester was not weight loss. What would be the effect of SeQuester consumption on cholesterol, I wondered? In some of KCD's clinical studies on weight loss, lipids were measured and, sure enough, cholesterol levels fell along with the pounds and inches. However, owing to FDA regulations, the company cannot make any cholesterol-lowering claims. SeQuester is sold exclusively as a weight-loss aid, available in most major drug stores and supermarkets. If you cannot find the product, you can call KCD directly at (805) 494-6687 to find a location near you.

I reported my findings in the October 1994 issue of my newsletter and began experimenting with SeQuester myself. My own cholesterol levels have been quite stable for the past several years, averaging between 165 and 175. My personal interest, then, was not so much to seek additional lowering but, rather, to see if I couldn't relax my fat restriction a bit.

Just about that time, Entenmann's introduced its reduced-fat doughnuts, with six grams of fat in each. Normally I would have opted for a piece of fat-free coffee cake, but I figured that the doughnuts would be a good part of the experiment. One SeQuester tablet to balance out one doughnut.

For three months I similarly calculated a bit of extra fat from extra oil used in my cooking or a piece of cheese in a restaurant and so forth. On a trip to New York, I gave in to the temptation of a corned beef sandwich and a bowl of chicken soup at the famous Stage Delicatessen. I preceded each of those little splurges with SeQuester. Even my friends and relatives noted how I was "cheating" on my usual low-fat diet.

Remember that all I wanted was to maintain my cholesterol level. Imagine my pleasant surprise to learn from Dr. Keenan that my test revealed a wonderfully low 151 TC, with similarly good measurements of the rest of my lipids. SeQuester has been part of my personal program ever since.

Then I started getting letters from my newsletter readers, thanking me for introducing them to this product. L.S. reported from Zephyr Cove, Nevada, that "In the past three months my cholesterol has dropped from 221 to 178, with similar improvement in HDL, LDL, and triglycerides."

J.W. of Long Island told me about attending a wedding out of town. "I took my SeQuester with me to try it. I really put it to the test. That night I ate 2 large pieces of pizza. For breakfast the next morning I ate about 2 scrambled eggs, 5 pancakes, and 6 small sweet rolls. After the wedding I ate a large piece of wedding cake with icing on it and a lunchmeat sandwich. Five days later I had my cholesterol checked. I was afraid to hear my results. I just knew it would go up. To my surprise it was 176 down from 204. Unbelievable! I went to the store to get more SeQuester."

D.S. of Odessa, Florida, said her results were amazing. "I have never been an overweight person (118 pounds) but for 20 years I have had high cholesterol. With a very stringent diet and 40 milligrams of Mevacor a day I have managed to reduce it from 300 to 230. I have been on SeQuester approximately 4 months now and my last cholesterol test was 195. I have even permitted myself to relax my diet a bit."

R.P. of Somerville, New Jersey, keeps detailed records of his cholesterol tests and sent me a copy along with a letter. "From the enclosed data you will see that the baseline cholesterol was 243. After 30 days on 5 milligrams of Mevacor daily the number dropped to 202. During the second 30 days I continued using the Mevacor, but added SeQuester. Cholesterol dropped to 174."

S.H. is a registered nurse in Hawaii. She wrote twice, once to tell me that, as director of education at a health clinic, she was going to do a personal experiment before recommending SeQuester to her patients. A few months later I got a second note: "I personally took SeQuester for one month and lost 4 pounds easily, and lowered my total cholesterol from a 'normal' (for me) of 220 to *206!* I didn't even diet as such."

When it came time to do my research with Dr. Keenan in Santa Monica, SeQuester was part of the program. You can check out the results of that study in chapter 13.

Additional studies are being conducted at the University of California at Los Angeles with Dr. David Heber and at the Wistar Institute in Philadelphia with Dr. David Kritchevsky. Both of those men, recognized as international experts in weight loss, cholesterol, and nutrition, are examining the long-term prospects for SeQuester.

How to Take SeQuester

You'll find SeQuester in the weight loss section of your drugstore or supermarket. Each box contains ninety tablets in three blister-pack cards. Make a point to keep a card of tablets in your kitchen, office, car, purse, and attaché case.

Doubtless other companies will try to infringe on the SeQuester patents and produce "copycat" products. While ingredients may sound the same, one cannot be sure of manufacturing processes and one cannot tell whether the copycats would work as well.

For the first two or three weeks, take one tablet with all three daily meals. The package directions suggest taking it thirty minutes before a meal. While that amount of time allows the tablet to disintegrate before you eat, you may not always remember. Just be sure to take the tablet either before you take the first bite or during the meal. Each tablet is a "fat sponge" for about six grams of fat, and food remains in the stomach for a few hours, so you'll benefit even if you take the SeQuester at the end of the meal.

Why take it with all meals, even if those meals are extremely low in fat? This regimen gives the body an opportunity to acclimate to the SeQuester and to build up a tolerance. Taking too many tablets right off the bat leads to gastric upset.

After the first few weeks, increase to two tablets before each meal for another few weeks. Please don't "jump the gun" and take more. Again, you might develop gastric upsets or even diarrhea. Give your body a chance to get accustomed to the bile/fiber formulation.

After the acclimation period of about six weeks, you can increase the dosage to three tablets before a fatty meal and perhaps drop down to one or two tablets prior to a meal with less fat. As time goes on, you may work your way up to even five or six tablets preceding a particularly rich indulgence. Conversely, be sure to take the tablets regularly, without skipping a day or two even if your meals are especially low in fat, so that your body remains accustomed to the SeQuester. If you do lay off the tablets for a while, for whatever reason, don't return to multiple-tablet doses; instead, build your way back up to avoid stomach upset.

For most people, six tablets as a daily average will provide excellent results. You will have sequestered about thirty-five grams of fat, vastly improving your diet. And, now and then, you may want to succumb to the siren call of the dessert cart after a festive meal or give in to that "Big Mac Attack."

Test SeQuester as part of this complete program for about ninety days, then have your cholesterol level checked. I think you'll be in for a wonderful surprise!

How Safe Is SeQuester?

SeQuester is a remarkably safe product with little if any downside. The ingredients are completely natural, and you should expect few if any adverse reactions if taken properly. As your body becomes accustomed to it, you might experience some slight gassy or queasy feeling. Just be sure not to take too many tablets at the beginning, lest you develop a bilious sensation and bloating in the evening or late at night. For most people, no problems. For a very few, gassiness persists; you then might want to take some activated charcoal tablets to counteract that effect. Again, taken properly SeQuester poses no difficulty.

SeQuester binds fats in the foods you eat and passes that fat out in the bowel movement. Stools will, therefore, have a higher than normal amount of fat. Not enough, though, to turn the stools greasy. Stools may turn a yellowish color and may float. That's completely normal and nothing to worry about. In fact, these changes show that the tablets are working. On the other hand, some people see no difference in the stools, and yet the tablets are doing their job.

If you develop any significant gastric upset or diarrhea, simply cut back on your dosage. Symptoms will disappear. There is no potential for any permanent injury or serious damage.

Studies have shown no problems in terms of SeQuester interfering with the absorption of either vitamin/mineral supplements or medications. Actually, as part of this complete program, you'll be taking vitamin supplements as detailed in coming chapters, and there's no chance that you'll not get enough. Remember, too, that SeQuester will bind about six grams of fat per tablet, only a part of the total fat content of any given meal. I mention this because some of the antioxidants you'll be interested in are fat-soluble vitamins with which a fat sequestrant like SeQuester might interfere; but that effect would be so small as to be negligible.

Currently there is no indication that SeQuester interferes with any medications or cholesterol-lowering agents, including niacin. If you are concerned about SeQuester interfering with your medications, simply take SeQuester and your medications at different times.

There are no contraindications for using SeQuester as part of a healthy lifestyle even for those with existing illnesses or conditions including liver, kidney, or digestive problems. Nor is age a barrier. Both elderly individuals and teens can benefit from taking SeQuester. The company president's mother, in her late seventies, uses SeQuester and it has greatly improved her cholesterol count, much to her physician's delight. And I've given it to my teenage children without concern. Ross's cholesterol tends to be elevated, and Jenny's weight can be a concern at times. Both Buzz Holcomb and I are devoted family men, and neither of us would in any way jeopardize our loved ones.

SeQuester as Part of Your Program

Let's say you're a 150-pound, moderately active individual who wants to follow a 20 percent–fat diet. Achieving that level would allow a total of fifty grams of fat daily, but perhaps that sounds a bit difficult to you. Maybe a 30 percent–fat diet, allowing up to seventy five grams of fat daily, would be easier. SeQuester allows you to, as it were, have your cake and eat it too.

Remember that SeQuester immobilizes about six grams of fat per tablet. Take four tablets daily, while adhering to an otherwise 30 percent–fat diet, and you're down to the fat from a 20 percent–fat diet. Although you're eating seventy five grams of fat, about twenty-five grams are sequestered, leaving only fifty grams to be absorbed.

You can look at SeQuester in two ways. First you might want it to help you lower your cholesterol further than you've been able to do until now. In that case, stay with your current diet plan and just take some SeQuester tablets to "squeeze" the fat down further. Second, you might want to liberalize your diet a bit, allowing yourself to have that occasional indulgence or a bit more fat daily. Either way, SeQuester can be a revolutionary cholesterol breakthrough!

ANOTHER FAT BLOCKER TO CONSIDER

Might I interest you in an appetizer of shellfish *shells?* It turns out that crushed exoskeletons, the shells, of crustaceans such as lobsters and shrimp taken in capsules can actually block the absorption of fat in the foods you eat. The product, called chitosan, is a type of animal fiber, amino polysaccharide, related chemically to plant cellulose. The chitosan has been chemically manipulated to give it a positive charge, allowing it to attract negatively charged fats and bile acids. Thus trapped, the fats are not absorbed and wind up in the toilet.

Chitosan is marketed by a number of companies worldwide. In the United States it is sold by the multilevel marketing company Interior Design Nutritionals, a division of NuSkin, and thus is available only through distributors, not in drug stores or other retail outlets. The brand name is FibreNet.

Articles published in the journals *Lipids* and *Bioscience, Biotechnology, and Biochemistry* in 1993 and 1995, respectively, have reported research indicating that chitosan blocks the absorption of four to six times its weight in fat. IDN recommends taking four capsules with lunch and another four with dinner. Those eight capsules contain a total of two grams of chitosan, which would block eight to twelve grams of fat. Obviously, that would make it a much less efficient fat blocker than SeQuester, which has the fat-blocking potential of nearly six grams of fat per tablet. Moreover, the cost of FibreNet is quite high, as much as three dollars per day. And FibreNet is contraindicated for anyone with seafood allergies.

FibreNet does have certain advantages, however. Clinical studies find virtually no gastric upset. And the chitosan takes care of any problems with regularity.

Again, the only way you can obtain FibreNet is through an IDN distributor. If you're interested in this product, you can call the company at (800) 487-2121 to be given the name and number of a distributor in your area.

BLOCKING THE CHOLESTEROL IN THE FOODS YOU EAT

For eleven years, since the time of my second bypass surgery in 1984, I had not eaten one egg yolk. It seemed a small price to pay to keep those arteries from clogging, and the egg-yolk substitutes were a lot better than when they first came out. But I have to admit that I missed those poached, sunnyside-up, boiled, basted, and other eggs. There's just no substitute for those yolks!

I haven't been alone in my avoidance of eggs and their cholesterol. Egg sales and consumption have plummeted to a fraction of their 1960s level. Even the egg industry has tossed in the towel and now recommends the AHA's limit of four eggs a week. Sensitive persons should eat none at all.

While other foods are rich sources of cholesterol, the egg has come to symbolize that deadly dietary component. A very nutritious, inexpensive food that nutritionists use as the gold standard of protein quality has come to be politically incorrect for those wishing to avoid heart disease.

But enough of that! The terrific news is that you can go back to enjoying those eggs as you like them. There's a way to block the body's absorption of the cholesterol we all want to stay away from so that the cholesterol levels in our blood rise not a bit. It's a wonderful story, so let me start at the very beginning.

Cholesterol, of course, is a member of the chemical family called sterols, which are present in every animal tissue. It is an animal sterol. Plants also contain sterols, which are termed phytosterols. Sort of the yin and yang of nature.

You'll remember that many years ago dietitians condemned shellfish for having very high levels of cholesterol. Those early measurements were totally inaccurate because they were counting not only cholesterol but also the phytosterols from the plants those animals ate. Shellfish are the vegetarians of the sea. In truth, certain shellfish have the lowest cholesterol content of any animal food; scallops contain a third of that found in chicken breast, for example. But those early measurement devices just couldn't tell the difference between cholesterol and phytosterol.

Well, neither can your body! Cholesterol is absorbed in the first one-third of your intestine by cell receptors that then pass it along into the bloodstream. Those receptor sites can't discern between cholesterol and phytosterols, and they'll fill up on whichever happens to be available. The phytosterols, however, are not absorbed into the bloodstream. The wonderful part of this fluke of physiology is that if those cellular docking sites are filled with phytosterols, there's no room for absorption of cholesterol, which simply passes along down the intestine and ultimately out with the bowel movement. Bingo!

Phytosterols are found in all plants, from fruits to vegetables to seeds to oils. Because they are soluble in fat, as is cholesterol, the principal concentration of plant sterols is in vegetable oils of all kinds. But plant sterols cause these oils to be cloudy, and food manufacturers remove them to provide the clear product that consumers prefer. Thus, there is no readily available source of concentrated phytosterols in our diet.

Interestingly, the Japanese make oil from rice bran, which they remove to produce the white rice they, too, prefer. But they leave the clouding phytosterols in that rice oil. Maybe that's one reason the Japanese have a low rate of heart disease.

The term phytosterols is generic, including all plant sterols. The principal phytosterols in nature are campesterol, stigmasterol, and beta-sitosterol. Often the latter is simply called sitosterol. Sitosterol is the most potent phytosterol for blocking the absorption of cholesterol. That discovery was made in the late 1940s at the laboratories of the Upjohn pharmaceutical company in Kalamazoo, Michigan.

During that time, steroid hormones were coming into vogue in the medical community. Cortisone was the miracle drug of its day. Upjohn discovered that those steroid hormones could be made from the soybean sterol stigmasterol. As part of his laboratory investigations at the time, Dr. Dury Petersen fed the soybean sterols to chickens. To his surprise he found that the chickens' cholesterol levels did not rise, even when fed a cholesterol-rich diet. But Upjohn was not particularly interested in that discovery; they wanted to sell cortisone.

So Upjohn bought crude soybean sterols from food companies such as General Mills, extracted the stigmasterol, and sold the rest, consisting of campesterol and sitosterol, to the Eli Lilly Company in Indiana. Lilly then concocted a cholesterol-lowering drug called Cytellin.

Cytellin was ahead of its time. Though it did lower cholesterol levels, most people and their doctors were not particularly aware of cholesterol as a risk factor in heart disease. Cytellin had no influence on the effect of fat on blood cholesterol levels; it only blocked the absorption of cholesterol. Moreover, according to reports I've read, the stuff was a foul-tasting fluid.

Research with phytosterols continued through the 1970s and into the 1980s. Probably the most definitive study came from the laboratories of Drs. Fred Mattson and Scott Grundy, then at the University of California at San Diego. They fed hospitalized patients scrambled eggs and sitosterol and found that the phytosterol blocked absorption of cholesterol, resulting in reduced cholesterol levels in the blood.

Often researchers used phytosterols as a general cholesterol-lowering agent rather than to specifically block the absorption of cholesterol in a particular meal. This meant that at one meal there would be more phytosterol than needed, when not much cholesterol was present in the foods, while at other times there wouldn't be enough to block the absorption of all the cholesterol available. Even so, studies showed total cholesterol reductions of 12 percent on average.

Dr. Mattson is now professor emeritus at U.C. San Diego. Dr. Grundy is now a world authority in diet, cholesterol, and heart disease at the University of Texas in Dallas. While attending a meeting of the American Heart Association, I asked him why the interest in phytosterols had dropped off. He felt that other agents available as cholesterol-lowering prescription drugs were more potent. Dr. Grundy, by the way, has done much of the research with the prescription cholesterol-lowering drug Mevacor.

No doubt a major factor in the decline of research comes from the fact that no major company produces phytosterols. As a plant substance, no one can hold an exclusive patent, and the money is in patented products.

The only study that showed no benefits in cholesterol lowering came from another Texas laboratory. Dr. Margo Denke studied thirty-three men who were already following a low-fat, low-cholesterol diet as well as taking prescription cholesterol-lowering drugs. The addition of phytosterols did not produce statistically significant additional cholesterol lowering for the average participant.

None of Dr. Denke's patients ate any eggs. Whatever small effect they achieved came from blocking the cholesterol in meats consumed. Even so, some of the men saw significant improvements, though not enough to influence the statistics of the entire group.

Finnish researchers shared their plant sterols results at the 1995 AHA meeting and published them in the November 1995 *New England Journal of Medicine*. For a one-year period, 153 subjects continued with their usual diet and lifestyle and used either regular margarine or a specially prepared margarine laced with phytosterols. Those subjects taking the sterols wound up with TC and LDL levels lowered by 11 and 15 percent, respectively, when compared with those consuming the regular margarine.

Reading through all the old and new research reports, I was fascinated by the idea of using phytosterols to liberalize my own diet. But I found that the plant sterols, once marketed widely in health food stores, were not available. There was never a clear focus as to how to best use them, and results weren't spectacular when the plant sterols were taken as a general cholesterol-lowering agent. Moreover, the dosages of phytosterols sold in the past were way too low to be effective. And, as I learned through the industry grapevine, often the purity was poor, with some products containing little if any active phytosterols.

To be effective, one has to counteract cholesterol with phytosterols on at least a one-to-one basis. And that's assuming a really high-quality phytosterol preparation. Since one egg contains about 220 milligrams of cholesterol, it takes at least that much phytosterol to block its absorption.

I turned to the company in the supplement industry I knew I could trust. The Endurance Products Co. in Oregon makes the niacin formulation Endur-acin and the antioxidants I've been taking and recommending for years. I knew that the owner of the company is a stickler for quality. Indeed, he was frustrated in his efforts to find a really good supply of phytosterols with which we could experiment. But finally he did locate a source of absolutely pure, potent material.

Phytosterols in the pure state are a white, slightly waxy substance. They are not soluble in water, so one could not mix them with orange juice or other beverages. In addition, they must be carefully tableted, since if phytosterols are too tightly packed, they may not break up in the digestive tract where they're to do their job. At first I made my own capsules.

My first experiments were done with my own family, and the timing couldn't have been better. We were scheduled to go on vacation to an island known for its French foods! We had our cholesterol levels measured and then headed off for two weeks of indulgence, including all that French cuisine and egg breakfasts three times a week. My son Ross's cholesterol level was rather high after a summer of picnics, parties, and hanging out with his high school friends. My daughter Jenny's cholesterol was perfectly normal, but she'd gained a few pounds during the leisurely summer months. My wife Dawn's level was a bit higher than usual, and mine remained at the healthy 165 to 170 level.

Before each fat- and cholesterol-rich meal, we all took tablets of SeQuester and capsules of phytosterols. I must admit the food was delicious. And those eggs were wonderful! Then came the marvelous results when we returned and retested those cholesterol measurements.

Ross's cholesterol fell all the way down to normal. Jenny's remained at a normal, healthy count—and she actually lost three pounds along the way. Dawn's cholesterol came down, while her weight remained the same even after those rich meals. And my own numbers stayed the same. The eggs had no negative effect.

Please let me hasten to say that I don't endorse eating that way all the time. Back home we quickly returned to our usual healthy eating habits, centered around low-fat foods, as I detail in part 3 of this book. In fact, I invite you to enjoy "Dinner with the Kowalskis" by way of the month of family recipes in the book. However, we all now regularly eat real, delicious eggs every week, usually on weekends. But let me go on with the phytosterol story.

My most dramatic proof of effectiveness came courtesy of my friend and financial adviser Gerry Gersten. This is a man who has had seven angioplasties before "getting religion" regarding his health. I worked with him closely, and he and his wife Claudia read my books and followed the program to the letter. In addition, Gerry took a combination of cholesterol-lowering drugs under his cardiologist's supervision. His was a particularly difficult case. But finally his cholesterol level normalized at about 165 to 170 on a regular basis, with an LDL around 100. He stayed that way for about two years, and then I suggested that he start eating eggs!

To say that Gerry was shocked would be an understatement, and his wife was absolutely appalled that I would have him take such a chance. Even after his cardiologist, who knows my work, gave his permission, Gerry was skeptical. Gerry assumed that the experiment would fail, since his was such a resistant cholesterol problem to begin with, and he wanted to know how long it would take to get the count back to normal—assuming that the numbers would go up after a month of eating eggs.

For one month, Gerry ate eggs three times a week. Sometimes it was Egg McMuffin, though he told them to hold the cheese. Sometimes he'd have pancakes and eggs, or Canadian bacon and eggs, and a few times he cheated with a little regular bacon, done crisp the way he likes it. Before each meal, Gerry took a couple of SeQuester tablets and phytosterol capsules. Then came the moment of truth, and I must tell you that Gerry was more than a little concerned.

Well, he need not have worried. Total cholesterol was lower than ever before at 156, LDL cholesterol was down to 90, and Gerry's triglycerides, which had never been lower than 225, were at 175. He's enjoyed those eggs ever since, typically once or twice a week, mostly on weekends.

By now you must be asking, but is it safe? Can I use phytosterols often or just once in a while? This sounds too good to be true; what's the downside? The good news is that there simply isn't any downside at all. Phytosterols are one of the safest substances you could possibly ingest. To quote Dr. Grundy, "Phystosterols have the added advantage of causing little or no side effects, a necessary property where lifetime therapy is often necessary." And Dr. Denke concurs, saying that, "Except in patients with sitosterolemia, plant sterols are poorly absorbed and have been associated with no known toxicity."

That one exception, sitosterolemia, is a very rare metabolic disorder in which afflicted persons absorb phytosterols and are not able to excrete it. In those cases, sitosterol builds up in tissues and could lead to health problems in much the same way as cholesterol does. But people with this disorder develop problems eating a normal diet containing fruits and vegetables, sources of phytosterols in small amounts. The bottom line, then, is don't worry about it. If you have sitosterolemia, you'd have known long ago.

For all the rest of the millions of us, phytosterols pose no problems even if eaten in huge quantities, much less the small amounts needed to block the absorption of cholesterol. To quote Dr. Grundy again: "By the judicious choice of foods and phytosterols, a proper balance of cholesterol and plant sterol intakes could be achieved. This would mitigate one reason for restricting the consumption of eggs, dairy products, and meat." Put simply, balance out the absorption of cholesterol with phytosterols and enjoy the foods you really like. You can use SeQuester to block out the fat that those foods also contain. Eggs, for example, have five grams of fat per yolk in addition to the cholesterol. Use SeQuester to block it.

Take a look at the chart on page 98 to see just how much fat and cholesterol lurk in the foods you've probably been avoiding or limiting. You'll want to block that cholesterol with at least a one-to-one dose of phytosterols. The phytosterols I recommend you use come in 400-milligram tablets, so calculate accordingly. For meals containing any kind of meat, one capsule will effectively block the cholesterol. Eggs raise cholesterol levels more than other foods such as shrimp, even if the total amount of the cholesterol found in those foods are equal. For eggs, then, to be on the safe side, I advocate one tablet per egg yolk. Perhaps less would be okay, but this amount is absolutely certain to zap all the cholesterol out of those delicious yolks. Take the tablets thirty minutes before meals.

I noted earlier that phytosterols were previously available in health food stores, but that the dosages and purity were a problem. No doubt a number of companies will bring back the phytosterols when the word gets out by way of this book, but I have no idea how effective they'll be. I'd hate to see you take an ineffective product to deal with something as important as your cholesterol level. To be on the safe side, I suggest you stick with the same phytosterols that I've used in my own research and that I personally take and give to my family. You can order directly from the company, and they'll ship the phytosterols directly to your home. Because there's no advertising or retail store markups, the phytosterols are actually less expensive that way. Write or call:

Phytosterols
Endurance Products Company
Post Office Box 230489
Tigard, OR 97281-0489
(800) 483-2532

CHOLESTEROL AND FAT CONTENT OF COMMON FOODS

FOOD	CHOLESTEROL (MILLIGRAMS)	FAT (GRAMS)
CHEESE (ONE OUNCE)		
American	27	9
Brie	29	8
Cheddar	30	9
EGGS		
One large chicken egg	220	5
Caviar (1 tbsp/40g)	94	2.9
Egg McMuffin (with cheese)	260	16
FAST FOODS		
Big Mac	83	35
Wendy's Double Hamburger	150	30
MEATS (3.5 OZ, COOKED)		
Beef brisket, fat & lean	92	35
Round steak	96	15
Tenderloin, fat & lean	86	17
Tenderloin, lean only	84	9
POULTRY		
Chicken, dark w/skin	92	16
Chicken, dark wo/skin	93	10
Chicken, light w/skin	84	11
Chicken, light wo/skin	85	4.5
Turkey, dark w/skin	89	11.5
Turkey, dark wo/skin	85	7.2
Turkey, light w/skin	76	8.3
Turkey, light wo/skin	69	3.2
Chicken liver	631	5.5
SHELLFISH (3.5 OZ RAW)		
Clams	29	0.7
Crab	35	0.5
Crayfish	118	0.9
Lobster	81	0.8
Scallops	28	0.6
Shrimp	130	0.6

CHOLESTEROL AND FAT CONTENT OF COMMON FOODS

FOOD	CHOLESTEROL (MILLIGRAMS)	FAT (GRAMS)
VARIETY MEATS (3.5 OZ, COOKED)		
Brains	2,000–2,500	10–16
Heart	193	5.6
Kidneys	387	3.4
Liver	389	4.9
Pâté (1 oz)	43	5–12
Tripe	95	4.0

You can also obtain the same high-quality phytosterol tablets marketed as SeQuester 4: Phytosterols in drug stores, some large supermarkets, and other retail outlets. The KCD company that makes SeQuester arranged with Endurance Products to market phytosterols through retail outlets. I can't vouch for the quality or performance of other products that may appear.

I've said this before, but it bears repeating. The use of SeQuester and phytosterols allows us all to be far more flexible with our diets than ever before. Truly this represents a twenty-first-century revolution in nutrition and health. But these products should not be used to replace good eating habits. The low-fat diet should still be the goal and the centerpiece of a truly healthy lifestyle. For example, we still need lots of fresh fruits and vegetables as well as high-fiber breads and cereals.

For years, I walked the straight and narrow path of low-fat eating. I chose the foods that were naturally low in fat and cholesterol—difficult, but not all that bad when I considered the alternative. Then the food industry came up with all sorts of low-fat and nonfat versions of foods I'd avoided until then. That was a marvelous evolution. And now we have SeQuester and phytosterols to block the absorption of fats and cholesterol in the foods we want to enjoy at least once in a while. That's a revolutionary breakthrough. And for you it can be a revolutionary reality!

· 8 ·

ACES OF HEARTS

It's no surprise that many health professionals have a negative knee-jerk reaction to the concept of vitamin and mineral supplementation. For years, since the initial discovery of vitamins and their functions and deficiencies starting in the 1920s, charlatans have made wild, unsubstantiated snake-oil claims for megadoses of this, that, and the other thing. Even today, a trip to the health food store is a lesson in unscientific thinking.

The traditional thinking has been that one can get all the nutrients necessary for good health by eating a wide variety of foods in a balanced diet. Intake levels have been set for vitamins and minerals based on amounts determined to prevent deficiency states in most people. Take any more, the established consensus stated, and you'd simply have expensive urine.

So when some researchers who were not in the mainstream of certain universities and research centers, who did not publish in the "correct" scientific journals, and who did not attend the "recognized" conferences and meetings came up with the first suggestions of harmful substances known as "free radicals," they were dismissed as "the lunatic fringe." Those free radicals, they said, were unstable chemicals that could damage cells throughout the body. The process was likened to oxygen rusting iron. The results were degenerative diseases and aging, and the solution was to take antioxidant vitamins and chemicals.

Fast-forward to the present: The mainstream researchers are publishing data in the correct journals and presenting them at "recognized" scientific meetings around the world that validate the concepts of oxidative damage to the body. But unlike their maverick predecessors, most of these established researchers are not willing to recommend supplementation for the general public.

You need to understand the research that has been done so that you can make decisions based on your own needs. The data are compelling. In the coming pages I'll share benefits in terms of prevention of heart attack, stroke, angina pains, and the clogging of the arteries in the legs that leads to the pain known as intermittent claudication. The underlying mechanism by which antioxidants appear to work involves the prevention of oxidation of LDL and Lp(a) in the bloodstream which, in turn, prevents arterial clogging.

To really get a handle on that mechanism of antioxidants' action, let's take a brief look at how and why arteries clog in the first place. It all starts with the body's natural attempt to stay healthy. When a foreign intruder enters the bloodstream, bacteria for example, white blood cells come to the rescue and attack like Pac-Man. Usually the body views cholesterol, both LDL and HDL, as normal in the bloodstream. But when the LDL becomes oxidized, a type of white blood cell known as the macrophage views it as foreign. Macrophages gobble up the oxidized LDL and Lp(a) voraciously and turn into what are termed foam cells. Those foam cells, bloated with fats and cholesterol, enter the walls of the arteries, usually at sites of microscopic injuries and where the artery is stressed, such as at twists and turns. Eventually these foam cells combine with the blood's clotting material called fibrinogen to form a soft plaque that is subsequently hardened by calcium. You can read about this in greater detail in chapter 1.

The important point here is that if LDL and Lp(a) are not oxidized, they are not sucked into the plaque-forming process. Of course it's better to have as few molecules of LDL and Lp(a) as possible to keep the clogging from happening. But everyone has at least small amounts of these particles in the bloodstream. So the next best thing is to keep them from oxidizing. That's where the antioxidants come into the picture. Do we have evidence? Tons of it!

One of the leading research centers for antioxidant investigation is the Texas Southwestern Medical Center in Dallas. There Dr. Ishwarlal Jialal laid the foundation for vitamin E's ability to prevent LDL oxidation. In a study he presented at the AHA's annual scientific session, Dr. Jialal explained that 800 IUs of vitamin E reduced oxidation by 62 percent. At the same meeting, he reported on work showing benefits of beta-carotene as well in preventing macrophage gobbling of LDL and thus in stopping the clogging process.

Publishing in the AHA's official publication *Circulation* in 1994, Dr. Jialal wrote of thirty-six healthy male volunteers who were given a "cocktail" consisting of 800 IUs of vitamin E, 1,000 mg of vitamin C, and 30 mg of beta-carotene. Again, the oxidation of LDL was effectively prevented.

Very importantly, Dr. Jialal has noted no side effects with antioxidant dosages of vitamin E. I'll cover the safety issue in more detail on page 107.

As any reputable scientist will tell you, one study or even two does not necessarily prove a concept to be true. The acid test for truth is termed "reproducibility." Simply enough, do other researchers get the same results when they test the concept at their laboratories. The antioxidant theory passes that test with flying colors.

At the University of Minnesota's School of Public Health, laboratory studies of blood samples from ten volunteers who took 800 IUs of vitamin E daily for just two weeks showed up to a threefold increase in their LDL cholesterol's resistance to oxidation. As Dr. John Belcher reported in the journal *Arteriosclerosis and Thrombosis,* elevated levels of vitamin E in the blood appeared to prevent or reduce the toxicity of oxidized LDL, that is, its ability to injure the endothelial cells that line blood vessel walls.

Benefits of antioxidants have been demonstrated for both men and women.

The Nurses' Health Study is a long-term project involving more than 87,000 women aged thirty-four to fifty-nine years from across the United States. Over the course of eight years, 17 percent of the nurses took vitamin E supplements at least some of the time. During that time, 552 cases of heart attack were diagnosed in the test group. But after adjusting for age, smoking, obesity, exercise, and other risk factors, the nurses who took vitamin E had only two-thirds the risk of cardiovascular disease compared with those not taking the supplements. Women who took vitamin E for more than two years had about half the risk.

Meir Stampfer, M.D., associate professor at Harvard's School of Public Health, was one of the principal investigators of the Nurses' Health Study. The results surprised even him. It's worth directly quoting him from an interview when the study was presented at the AHA meeting in 1993:

> *I'm skeptical by nature but I was even more skeptical going into this study. It just didn't seem plausible that a simple maneuver like taking vitamin E would have such a profound effect. So even though there was a lot of sound scientific basis for the hypothesis that antioxidant vitamins can reduce heart disease, I expected to show that this was not in fact a true association.*

A parallel study was performed with participants in the ongoing Health Professionals Follow-Up Study involving nearly 46,000 men ages forty to seventy-five years. Again, after adjusting for major cardiovascular disease risk factors, men who had taken vitamin E for more than two years had a 26 percent lower risk of heart disease than those not taking the vitamin. Men taking the most vitamin E also had a significant reduction in overall mortality. Benefits of taking beta-carotene were also seen.

The research continues to pour in from all over the world. Researchers from Scotland reported in the *American Journal of Clinical Nutrition* that both smokers and nonsmokers who took vitamin E had less LDL cholesterol oxidation than those who didn't. Swedish workers linked the severity of coronary atherosclerosis in thirty-five men surviving heart attacks with the susceptibility of their LDL to oxidation in the British journal *Lancet*. Finnish investigators also reporting in *Lancet* found that LDL oxidation in sixty men correlated with the amount of plaque clogging the carotid arteries in the neck. And at the 2nd International Conference on Heart Health in 1995, Indian researchers told of linking levels of antioxidant vitamins in the blood with coronary artery disease.

Not only has there been international validation of the benefits of antioxidants but also investigators have demonstrated these benefits in a number of different cardiovascular conditions.

Blood clots frequently precipitate a heart attack by stopping the blood flow in a clogged artery. Preventing the formation of these clots could, in turn, prevent heart attacks. It turns out that antioxidants do just that. Writing in the journal *Blood,* doctors found that clotting was reduced 75 percent after two weeks of taking 200 IUs of vitamin E daily. A dose of 400 IUs cut clotting by 82 percent. They reported that "it was especially gratifying that 'reasonable' doses of vitamin E that had no untoward side effects were able to accomplish such reduction."

Did others find similar benefits of antioxidants in terms of blood clotting? Researchers at Boston University School of Medicine came up with virtually identical results and reported them in *Circulation* in 1994. Scottish investigators wrote in the *American Journal of Clinical Nutrition* that same year that antioxidant intake was responsible for decreasing the number of platelets responsible for clotting in the blood.

Angina pains following exercise are the result of arterial blockage. If antioxidants would prevent such blockage, it could be theorized that people with more antioxidants in their bloodstreams would experience less angina. The test of that theory was published in *Lancet*. Authors of that article measured vitamins A, C, and E and beta-carotene in 110 men with angina and compared them with levels in 394 control subjects without angina. Sure enough, the more antioxidants in the blood, the greater the protection against angina.

Stroke occurs owing to blockage of the carotid arteries in the neck that supply blood to the brain. Three separate teams of researchers reporting at the 1993 epidemilogy conference sponsored by the AHA correlated consumption of beta-carotene and vitamin E with a reduced risk of stroke. A Harvard study demonstrated that women regularly eating foods containing antioxidant vitamins had less than half the risk of stroke compared with women who ate such foods infrequently. Beta-carotene was associated with the greatest risk reduction.

A Texas study, on the other hand, found the greatest risk reduction in those consuming the most vitamin E rather than beta-carotene. Researchers measured the impact of antioxidant consumption on the wall thickness of carotid arteries. Thickening of the arterial walls signifies increased stroke risk. More than ten thousand men and women were included in the study.

The third study came from Finland where scientists found low levels of antioxidants in the blood associated with increased arterial wall thickness. Both vitamin E and beta-carotene were linked to the stroke risk.

Peripheral artery disease refers to clogging of vessels in the legs, resulting in pain when exercising. In the Edinburgh Artery Study, both vitamin E and vitamin C showed a protective effect in about sixteen hundred men and women aged fifty-five to seventy-four years. Those with higher vitamin intakes suffered less peripheral artery disease. The benefits of vitamin C were principally shown in smokers, which comes as no surprise, since smoking depletes the levels of antioxidants in the blood.

Bypass surgery can be a lifesaver for heart patients but also places a tremendous burden on the heart. That's because free radicals form in the heart or any other organ temporarily deprived of oxygen, as happens during surgery. Those free radicals play havoc on the heart's tissues. Vitamin E, given for two weeks before bypass surgery provided protection against those free radicals, as shown in a study at the University of Toronto. Researcher Terrence Yau, M.D., pointed out that vitamin E is the major, and perhaps only, fat-soluble antioxidant in human tissue. He explained that vitamin E is the only antioxidant that penetrates the fat membrane around the heart muscle cell to reach the sites where free radicals do their damage.

Strenuous exercise, good for the heart, can induce formation of free radicals. Stop doing the exercise? Absolutely not. Instead, prevent those free radicals from doing their damage in oxidizing LDL. Supplementation with 300 IUs of vitamin E effectively prevented exercise-induced oxidation, as reported by researchers in the *International Journal of Biochemistry*.

While prevention of heart disease is preferred, we can all benefit from regression. Years ago doctors believed that heart disease was permanent; once the arteries were blocked, that was that. Today we know we can make the disease go away. And antioxidants can help.

As usual, the first indications of antioxidant benefit in heart disease regression came from animal research. In a study at the University of Mississippi monkeys ate regular chow, a high-fat diet, or a high-fat diet supplemented with vitamin E. Chow-chomping monkeys developed no blockages in their carotid arteries. Those eating a high-fat diet showed an average of 87 percent blockage, and those given vitamin E along with the high-fat diet had a lesser (61 percent) blockage.

After completion of that phase of the Mississippi research, the monkeys continued to consume supplemental vitamin E. Two years later, the blockages had diminished to 35 percent.

That study was published in 1992, with the authors concluding that human research was needed to confirm their results. That confirmation came in 1995, reported in the *Journal of the American Medical Association.* Data were collected from 156 men aged forty to fifty-nine who had previously had bypass surgery performed and who were engaged in a test of cholesterol reduction with the vitamin niacin in combination with the prescription drug cholestipol. Indeed, those with lowered cholesterol levels were demonstrated by angiogram to have experienced either no further progression of the disease or even regression.

Investigators at the University of Southern California went back to the data to learn which of the men might have been taking antioxidants during the course of the study. Indeed, those taking vitamin E supplements of at least 100 IUs daily had a much better outcome than those not taking the vitamin. Antioxidant vitamin intake reduced progression of coronary artery disease and was signficantly associated with regression of the disease.

WILL THE BEST ANTIOXIDANT PLEASE STAND UP?

Many antioxidant researchers refer to combinations of vitamin E, vitamin C, beta-carotene, and the trace mineral selenium as a "cocktail." That reminds me of a bartender asking, "What'll you have?" Is one better than the others, or should we take some of everything? The answer, paradoxically, to both questions is yes.

Beta-carotene is the best known of a group collectively known as carotenoids, nutrients found in orange vegetables, and is the precursor of vitamin A. While vitamin A is a potent antioxidant itself, consuming large doses, especially through supplementation, can have significant adverse effects. Beta-carotene is converted to vitamin A in the body, and large doses have no apparent ill effects. But can it protect against heart disease?

Preliminary data indicating beta-carotene's worth were brought to the public in 1990 by researchers at Brigham and Women's Hospital in Boston. In that study, 333 patients with documented coronary disease were given either fifty-milligram tablets of beta-carotene or a placebo every other day. Those receiving the beta-carotene suffered about half as many cardiac events such as heart attacks or the need for surgery as those getting the fake pills. Again, there were no significant side effects.

Two years later Dr. Ishwarlal Jialal at Southwestern Medical Center in Dallas found that beta-carotene inhibited LDL oxidation. The nutrient also prevented macrophages from gobbling up the LDL in the atherogenic process.

At the scientific sessions of the AHA in 1994, three papers were presented showing the benefits of beta-carotene in preventing LDL oxidation. Two of those papers also showed a correlation between the amount of beta-carotene in the blood and the risk of heart attacks.

Late in 1994 the *Journal of the American Medical Association* published an article from the University of North Carolina titled simply "Serum carotenoids and coronary heart disease." Considering normal risk to be 1.0 on the study's scale, those with the highest level of carotenoids in the blood had a relative risk of heart disease of 0.64. For men who had never smoked, the risk dropped to 0.28. The obvious conclusion to be drawn was to quit smoking and start eating vegetables and consuming supplements rich in the carotenoids in general and beta-carotene in particular.

Vitamin C, also known as ascorbic acid, is the most popular vitamin supplement in America. Linus Pauling believed that it would protect against the common cold, but does it provide protection from heart disease? Research done at the University of California at Los Angeles and published in 1992 revealed a much lower death rate among those who took vitamin C supplements when compared with those who, although consuming plenty of the nutrient in various foods, did not supplement their diets. Dr. James Enstrom studied more than eleven thousand men and women. The more vitamin C they consumed, the fewer deaths they suffered, particularly from heart disease.

Frankly, vitamin C doesn't appear to be as potent an LDL antioxidant as vitamin E, but the protection it conveys against heart disease is very real. How does it do that? Research sponsored by the National Institutes of Health at the Human Nutrition Research Center in Beltsville, Maryland, points to vitamin C's influence on the good cholesterol, HDL. After adjusting for other risk factors, investigators found less heart disease in those consuming well above the recommended amounts of vitamin C. In both men and women the mechanism of action involved appeared to be an elevation of the protective HDL, which pulls cholesterol out of artery walls rather than depositing it there.

Selenium is a trace mineral found to be inadequately represented in the majority of men and women, despite an otherwise balanced diet. Like the vitamins we've been studying, selenium acts as an antioxidant. It is a vital component of the enzyme glutathione peroxidase, which neutralizes harmful free radicals. Those consuming inadequate amounts of selenium have been found to have reduced glutathione peroxidase activity and thus may be more susceptible to the effects of free radicals. Also, selenium appears to act in concert with vitamin E in its antioxidant activity protecting LDL.

Two separate studies in 1989, one published in the *British Journal of Nutrition* and the other in *Free Radical Biology and Medicine,* demonstrated the benefits of selenium in protecting against LDL oxidation.

The action of selenium is a bit different from that of other antioxidants. It defends the endothelial cell lining of arteries against the assault of oxidized LDL and also increases production of prostacyclin, a hormonelike substance that protects the heart while inhibiting production of thromboxane, which has been strongly implicated in the development of atherosclerotic plaques.

Therefore, while most people don't hear much about it, selenium ought to be part of the antioxidant protection package. There we have it: ACES of hearts.

SAFETY OF ANTIOXIDANT THERAPY

The term "megadose" takes on negative connotations, especially when used by those who still doggedly stick with the ancient advice to "get all the nutrients you need from a balanced diet." The Recommended Dietary Allowance (RDA) for vitamin E is 15 IUs, which is considered to be adequate to prevent deficiency symptoms in healthy adults. Taking 100, 400, 800 IUs or more certainly falls into the megadose category. The same is true for vitamin C with its RDA of sixty milligrams. That much may prevent scurvy, but it takes many times more than sixty milligrams per day to provide antioxidant protection. Are such doses safe?

In double-blind studies of vitamin E with adult subjects, relatively few side effects have been seen, even at doses up to 3,200 IUs daily. Are side effects possible? Practically every substance known to man can produce an adverse reaction in certain individuals. The studies cited previously in this chapter indicated no side effects. Most researchers report none at all. Yet observed side effects over the years have included gastrointestinal disturbances, fatigue, and elevations in serum triglycerides.

There is also the rare occurrence of slight gastrointestinal bleeding. Some naysayers have pointed to this side effect to justify their reluctance to recommend antioxidants for everyone. They note that aspirin can also cause bleeding, and if aspirin and vitamin E were combined, they could even precipitate a particularly rare type of stroke termed a hemorrhagic stroke caused by bleeding in the brain. The odds against this would be akin to being struck by lightning while being devoured by a shark, but I mention it only to be perfectly candid in presenting both sides.

Are there risks for ingesting large amounts of beta-carotene? Well, if you take huge dosages you just might turn orange, literally. That might be a signal to back off a bit. While vitamin A can be toxic to the liver in megadose quantities, no such problems present with beta-carotene. Think about it this way: Have you ever heard of a dietitian telling you not to eat too many vegetables? Yet one cup of carrot juice at lunch and a sweet potato for dinner will yield a whopping thirty-four milligrams of beta-carotene, more than has been used in most research studies employing supplements.

In two studies, in 1995 and 1996, smokers taking beta-carotene developed lung cancer at a higher rate than smokers receiving a placebo. Researchers were hoping for the opposite. Why did that happen? No one really knows. But we do know that lung cancer takes a long time to develop, that the study participants had been smoking for many years, and that the odds against any vitamin protecting them against a condition unequivocally linked with cigarette smoking were pretty high. Rather than taking vitamin pills, smokers should quit.

Other than in those two studies, no ill effects have been ascribed to beta-carotene regardless of dosage.

Linus Pauling advocated taking ten grams of vitamin C or even more. Even at those astronomical dosages, the worst thing that can happen is slight diarrhea, which subsides when one cuts back on the vitamin intake. At dosages studied for antioxidant purposes, about one thousand milligrams or one gram, there appears to be no downside at all.

Finally we come to selenium, the trace mineral that is considered "safe and adequate" at fifty to one hundred micrograms daily consumption. There is no established RDA. But we do know that most people don't get that much in their normal diets. So a supplement of one hundred micrograms can be expected to do nothing but good.

PILLS OR PRODUCE?

Many of the research studies linking antioxidant intake with protection against heart disease have looked at consumption of fruits and vegetables. Some of those researchers have concluded that the public should concentrate on increasing daily servings of those foods in the diet rather than taking supplements.

There are a lot of good reasons to make a conscious effort to eat more fruits and veggies. Take beta-carotene, for example. That's just one of about four hundred known carotenoids found in orange vegetables. It's very possible, if not probable, that those other carotenoids also provide health benefits. It may very well be that the reason vegetarians are typically found to be healthier than meat eaters is because of their increased intake of fruits and vegetables rather than their avoidance of animal foods. And, on a practical note, if one puts more plant foods on the plate, there's less room left for the animal foods that are high in saturated fats.

Authorities call for us to consume at least five servings of fruits and vegetables daily, with the emphasis on "at least." At first that amount of consumption seems formidable. But bear in mind that a "serving" is quite small. That's just one carrot, for example, or a half of a mango, or one slice of watermelon. For most people, one serving is really two. Check the charts in this chapter to see how you can get quite a lot of antioxidants from commonly enjoyed fruits and vegetables. That's definitely the place to start.

I concur with many authorities, those who have been doing the research with antioxidants, that even a diet rich in fruits and vegetables can profit from supplementation with vitamin C and beta-carotene.

When it comes to vitamin E, it's practically impossible to consume in foods the amounts that have been shown to be advantageous as antioxidants. Vitamin E is found in various oils, nuts, and whole grains. If nothing else, most of us are trying to limit the amount of fat in our diets, and that means keeping oils and nuts down to a minimum. One tablespoon of soybean oil has 1.5 mg of vitamin E; that's the equivalent of 2.5 IUs. The richest source of vitamin E is wheat germ oil, in which few of us partake regularly; it has 20.3 mg per tablespoon, 30 IUs. You'd have a long way to go to get to 400 IUs daily.

The richest sources of selenium in the diet are liver and kidneys, with a lesser amount in seafood and still less in plant foods. The selenium content of foods varies considerably, based on the amount of the mineral in local soils. While it's likely that many adults will consume only small amounts, supplementation with from 50 to 100 micrograms can't do any harm and very well may provide the edge in antioxidant protection. Don't worry about toxicity, as it would take at least 5 milligrams to do harm. That's the equivalent of 5,000 micrograms. (One milligram is 1/1000 of a gram; one microgram is 1/1,000,000 of a gram.)

CONVERTING MEASUREMENTS OF VITAMIN E AND BETA-CAROTENE

Beta-carotene is measured in terms of vitamin A activity, since it is the precursor of vitamin A, which is always listed in IUs. One milligram of beta-carotene equals 1,667 IUs. Thus a 25,000 IU tablet or capsule would contain 15 milligrams. The actual conversion to milligrams from IUs varies a bit, depending on the beta-carotene's actual vitamin A activity. Roughly, however, you can calculate that 6 milligrams of beta-carotene equals 10,000 IUs.

Vitamin E is typically measured in IUs but now and then you'll see it in milligrams. Conversion depends on the form of vitamin E involved. Natural *d*-alpha tocopherol converts as 1.49 IUs per milligram. The natural vitamin E in its acetate form converts as 1.36 IUs per milligram. For synthetic acetate the equation is 1.0 IU to 1.0 milligram. And the seldom seen synthetic alcohol vitamin E converts as 1.1 IUs per milligram. Synthetic vitamin E will be listed as *dl*-alpha-tocopherol.

You might also see "mixed tocopherols" on a label; in that case, figure 1.25 IUs per milligram. Alpha is more potent.

NATURAL VERSUS SYNTHETIC VITAMINS

No one in a health food store or selling supplements as a distributor of some multilevel-marketing company will agree with what I'm about to tell you, but it happens to be the truth. For the most part, it makes no difference whether a vitamin comes from some natural source or has been manufactured synthetically. The body recognizes and utilizes vitamin C, vitamin E, and beta-carotene just the same, whether natural or synthetic.

One milligram of natural vitamin C or beta-carotene has the same potency as one milligram of the synthetic form. However, the natural form of vitamin E (designated by the letter *d* as in *d*-alpha-tocopherol) is more potent than the synthetic form (designated by the letters *dl.*)

The claims made by certain companies for their products are more a matter of marketing than science. Think about this: Scientists all over the world have gotten similar results with antioxidants in their research, yet the tablets and capsules they use have come from dozens of different companies.

Don't believe that a bottle of vitamins is better just because it's more expensive. On the other hand, a bargain brand may not be a good buy if it doesn't deliver the dosage of nutrient listed on the label or if that nutrient isn't released properly as the tablet dissolves—or doesn't dissolve—in the gastrointestinal tract. Stick with middle-of-the-road-priced products by recognized companies or distributed by major health food stores or drug stores.

I personally get my antioxidants by mail from Endurance Products, a company I know to produce the best quality at very reasonable cost. Call them at (800) 483-2532 or write to P.O. Box 230489, Tigard, OR, 97281-0489 to obtain order forms.

THE FINAL DECISION IS YOURS

No official medical organization such as the AHA or AMA has come out with a recommendation to take antioxidants. They say that definitive evidence is not yet available. Frankly, the kind of study that would be definitive would require millions of dollars and would span decades. It would mean tracking thousands of men and women over the entire length of time heart disease takes to develop. One group would be given antioxidants, another placebos. Then all the variables would have to be considered. The group would have to be large enough to ensure representation of all sorts of healthy and unhealthy men and women. And the dosages of this, that, or the other antioxidant would have to be decided. Then one would need the consensus of committees of researchers and organizations. Good luck. We'll all be long gone by the time they'd get it together, if they ever do.

Asked whether they personally take supplements themselves, the antioxidant researchers typically say yes. Asked whether they would recommend antioxidants for friends or family members, especially for those at risk of heart disease, the response is almost always yes.

One group has taken a stand on the issue. The Alliance for Aging Research, a nonprofit group comprised of researchers, nutritionists, and consumer advocacy organizations, has made specific recommendations in regard to vitamins E and C and beta-carotene to prevent age-related disease. It's guidelines are based on more than two hundred clinical and epidemiological studies done over the past two decades, all of which have shown a correlation between antioxidants and disease prevention. The Alliance recommends these daily amounts:

Vitamin C: 250 to 1,000 mg
Vitamin E: 400 to 800 IUs
Beta-carotene: 10,000 to 25,000 IUs

These guidelines came out prior to a study by Dr. Jialal at the Southwestern Medical Center in Dallas, which found benefits of going up to 1,200 IUs of vitamin E daily. The Texas research showed that doses of 200 IUs to 1,200 IUs of vitamin E provided increasing protection against oxidation of LDL and potential for development of heart disease. But there was a diminishing return, with no additional benefits seen for doses over 1,200 IUs. Dr. Jialal believes that the optimal dosage is probably 800 IUs, and there's plenty of research data to back him up from other investigators. In fact, if one were to decide to take only one antioxidant, it probably should be vitamin E, at 400 IU twice daily with meals containing at least a bit of fat, since vitamin E is a fat-soluble vitamin as compared with vitamin C, which is water soluble.

While most discussions of antioxidants focus on vitamins C and E and beta-carotene, I believe there is good reason to include selenium in the daily regimen. A fifty- or one-hundred-microgram tablet is sufficient.

As we have seen in reviewing the antioxidant literature, both men and women have been included in studies, and both show benefits of antioxidant consumption, definitely as part of the diet and probably through supplementation. Since heart disease begins in childhood, it's never too early to teach youngsters good dietary habits, which means eating plenty of fruits and vegetables each and every day. With the exception of a one-a-day type vitamin/mineral pill, supplementation in childhood doesn't seem warranted or advisable.

Your doctor should be aware of all your health habits, both good and bad. By all means let him or her know if you are taking antioxidants so that information can be included in your chart and considered in decisions regarding your health care.

I have personally been taking antioxidants since my second bypass in 1984, the time when I began my active efforts to save my own life. I consider them to be an integral part of my personal program. Even though my LDL cholesterol count remains at a safe, low level, I don't want that LDL oxidizing in my arteries and doing damage. How much protection those antioxidants have given me over the years I don't know for certain. I do know that my heart health is excellent, far better that of most others with my health history, and I want to keep it that way.

But what about that study indicating that beta-carotene provided no benefit, you might ask? In January 1996, results of the Physicians' Health Study showed that doctors taking the antioxidant for a number of years were not any better off than those not taking it, in terms of heart disease. It did no harm, but it apparently did no good. Well, that was just one study. Many others have shown benefit. In fact, that was the only one which did *not* show benefit. So I continue to take beta-carotene, both as supplements and by way of the fruits and vegetables that are rich sources.

"So how much do *you* take, Bob?" That's a question I hear every time I speak to groups around the country. While I don't say that my regimen should be the standard for everyone, here's my daily intake, spread over the course of the day: 1,000 mg of vitamin C; 800 IUs of vitamin E; 25,000 IUs of beta-carotene; and 100 mcg (micrograms) of selenium. That's over and above my dietary intake, which provides significantly more, since I do make a point of enjoying lots of fruits and veggies every day. Those antioxidants are my ACES of hearts.

GOOD SOURCES OF VITAMIN C

The following foods all have at least 20 milligrams of vitamin C per serving, a third of the U.S. RDA. All nutrient levels are approximate, and will vary.

FOOD	SERVING SIZE	VITAMIN C (MG)
FRUITS		
Papaya	1/2	94
Orange, California navel	1	80
Cantaloupe	1/3	75
Kiwi	1	75
Orange, Florida	1	68
Currants, black	1/4 cup	51
Grapefruit, pink or red	1/2	47
Watermelon	1 slice	46
Strawberries	1/2 cup	41
Grapefruit, white	1/2	39
Mango	1/2	29
Starfruit (carambola)	1	27
VEGETABLES*		
Bell peppers, sweet red, raw	1/2 cup	95
Chili peppers, hot red or green, raw	1/4 cup	91
Broccoli	1/2 cup	58
Brussels sprouts	1/2 cup	48
Bell peppers, sweet green, raw	1/2 cup	45
Kohlrabi	1/2 cup	45
Snow peas (edible pod)	1/2 cup	38
Sweet potato, baked	1 medium	28
Cauliflower	1/2 cup	28
Kale	1/2 cup	27
Potato, baked with skin	1 large	26
Cabbage, red	1/2 cup	26
Tomato, raw	1 medium	24
Cabbage, bok choy	1/2 cup	22
Turnip greens	1/2 cup	20
JUICES		
Orange juice	6 fl. oz.	93
Grapefruit juice	6 fl. oz.	70
Cranberry juice cocktail	6 fl. oz.	67
Tomato juice	6 fl. oz.	34

*Cooked, unless otherwise specified.

Source: ESHA Research, Salem, Oreg.

GOOD SOURCES OF BETA-CAROTENE

The following foods all have at least one milligram of beta-carotene per serving, a significant amount. While there is no official U.S. RDA for beta-carotene, three milligrams is equivalent to 5,000 IU, the U.S. RDA for vitamin A. All nutrient levels are approximate, and will vary.

FOOD	SERVING SIZE	BETA-CAROTENE (MG)
FRUITS		
Apricots, dried	10 halves	6.2
Cantaloupe	1/2	4.8
Apricots, fresh	2	2.5
Grapefuit, pink or red	1/2	1.6
Mango	1/2	1.4
Watermelon	1 slice	1.1
VEGETABLES*		
Sweet potato	1 medium	10.0
Chicory, raw	1 cup	6.2
Carrot, raw	1 medium	5.7
Spinach	1/2 cup	4.9
Turnip greens	1/2 cup	3.9
Pumpkin	1/2 cup	3.7
Collard greens	1/2 cup	3.4
Swiss chard	1/2 cup	3.2
Kale	1/2 cup	3.0
Winter squash	1/2 cup	2.9
Spinach, raw	1 cup	2.3
Spaghetti squash	1/2 cup	1.9
Mustard greens	1/2 cup	1.9
Beet greens	1/2 cup	1.8
Dandelion greens	1/2 cup	1.4
Bell peppers, sweet red, raw	1/2 cup	1.1
Romaine lettuce, raw	1 cup	1.1
Broccoli	1/2 cup	1.0
JUICES AND SOUPS		
Carrot juice	1 cup	24.2
Gazpacho	1 cup	11.7
Tomato juice	1 cup	2.2
Vegetable soup	1 cup	1.9
Manhattan clam chowder	1 cup	1.9
Vegetable and beef stew	1 cup	1.7
Split-pea soup	1 cup	1.4

*Cooked, unless otherwise specified.

Source: United States Department of Agriculture/National Cancer Institute

· 9 ·

Niacin and Your Heart: *A Lifesaver Revisited*

Eighty percent of the cholesterol in your bloodstream got there through the body's own production in the liver. Diet is responsible for only 20 percent. So, while it's a good idea to control those dietary factors, many if not most of us with cholesterol elevations will need help with that 80 percent. For me and for thousands of others that help has come from the vitamin supplement niacin.

I first learned about niacin in 1984 when I desperately needed something to get my own numbers under control to save my own life. Facing my second bypass surgery, I knew that cholesterol was the culprit. Something had to be done.

As a medical journalist, I gave myself the assignment of reviewing the scientific literature. That's when I started to read about niacin, and I haven't stopped yet. Following the program I put together, which included daily supplementation with large doses of that vitamin, my cholesterol level plummeted from a dangerously high 284 to 169 in only eight weeks. The regimen worked as well with others, I wrote *The 8-Week Cholesterol Cure,* and soon niacin got international attention.

"The Amazing Story of Niacin," as I titled the chapter in that book, began in 1955 with the discovery by two Canadian physicians, Drs. Hoffer and Altschul, that the vitamin effectively lowered cholesterol readings. That was before many people paid much attention to cholesterol and its link with heart disease. For the next twenty years or so, not much niacin research was conducted. Then the data started trickling in, and the trickle became a flood that continues to pour through the medical journals month after month.

Today niacin is recommended as the agent of first choice by the National Cholesterol Education Program for those for whom diet alone isn't enough. Even after the introduction of potent prescription-only drugs, niacin alone deals with all aspects of the lipid profile. According to one of niacin's pioneering researchers, Dr. William Parsons of Scottsdale, Arizona, "If every doctor in the country were good at niacin and would use it in preference to other medications, probably 90% or more of patients needing cholesterol control could take the drug successfully. This would literally save billions every year."

What makes niacin so superior over every prescription drug on the market? Why doesn't every doctor recommend it for his or her patients? Will niacin be the lifesaver for you as it has been for me? Let's start at the beginning.

Niacin, also known as nicotinic acid, is sometimes called vitamin B_3. As a vitamin found in a wide variety of foods, niacin has an RDA of only twenty milligrams to prevent the deficiency state pellagra. These small amounts of niacin found in the diet have no effect on cholesterol, but when used in what are termed "pharmacologic doses," niacin battles cholesterol as well as or better than any prescription drug. In fact, doctors writing in the literature refer to niacin as a drug because of its dramatic effects on the body.

When niacin enters the bloodstream, the liver proceeds to break it down first to a derivitive called niacinamide and finally to nicotinuric acid, which is excreted in the urine. It is during this metabolic process that niacin appears to work its magic. There in the liver niacin interferes in some way that is not yet fully understood with the formation of very-low-density lipoprotein (VLDL) cholesterol and subsequently with the manufacture of low-density-lipoprotein (LDL) cholesterol. At the same time, niacin decreases the amount of lipoprotein(a) and triglycerides. It transforms small, dense LDL subparticles into less dangerous larger, looser molecules, and for good measure, results in often dramatic increases in the protective HDL molecules that shuttle cholesterol back to the liver for proper disposal. While at first all this might sound like snake oil, scientific research documents every capability of niacin.

- Total and LDL cholesterol levels fall by an average of 20 to 40 percent. This fall has been documented again and again at the University of California, the University of Southern California, the University of Minnesota, the Health Sciences Center at the University of Texas, the Oregon Health Sciences University, and research institutions around the world. Used in combination with the prescription drug colestipol, niacin produced lipid improvements that were associated with reversal of heart disease at USC in Los Angeles. Dozens of studies have confirmed niacin's effectiveness.
- Lipoprotein(a) counts were down 35 percent with administration of niacin in research done at Oregon Health Sciences University. At the internationally renowned Karolinska Institute in Sweden, Lp(a) came down an average of 33 percent in all patients treated with niacin. The Clinical Center of the National Institutes of Health reported in the *Journal of the American Medical Association* that "strong consideration should be given to including nicotinic acid as part of the pharmacologic regimen" for treating Lp(a) elevations. A case his-

tory presented in the NIH report demonstrated a patient's Lp(a) cut in half in three months of niacin treatment.

- Triglyceride measurements fall precipitously with niacin. Only one prescription drug, Lopid (gemfibrozil), can lower triglycerides effectively. The higher the initial triglyceride levels, the greater the response. The ability to bring triglycerides down is directly proportional to the dosage used in most cases. Patients participating in the Coronary Drug Project, a long-term, nationwide, double-blind study, experienced anywhere from 15 to 30 percent triglyceride reductions. In an NIH-sponsored study, triglycerides fell an average of 52 percent. Regardless of percentage of improvement, niacin can bring triglycerides to normal even if one begins at very high levels of triglyceride elevation.
- Small, dense LDL particles are improved significantly by taking niacin, resulting in larger, less dense molecules. Research at the University of California at Berkeley found that those with the smallest particles are at three times the risk as those with the largest LDL particles. And in another study at the same center, niacin was found to significantly increase LDL diameter.
- Protective levels of the good cholesterol, HDL, rise in those taking niacin. Improvements in HDL occur in both patients with elevated and patients with normal triglycerides, whereas the drug Lopid works primarily when triglycerides are up. Often HDL improvements can be achieved even with low niacin dosages, as documented by physicians at Hadassah University Hospital in Israel. They used less than five hundred milligrams of niacin to produce significant HDL gains. At the Mayo Clinic in Rochester, Minnesota, 63 participants in a cardiac rehabilitation program who had low HDL levels experienced an average of 18 percent increase with niacin. An increasing number of physicians and researchers are concluding that raising HDL levels can decrease the risk of heart disease, and niacin does it most effectively. Doctors at the Ochsner Clinic in New Orleans achieved a 32 percent improvement in HDL levels.
- Platelet aggregation and resulting blood clotting are inhibited by niacin via production of the prostaglandin called prostacyclin (PGI_2). Prostaglandins are hormonelike substances present throughout the body in tiny quantities. They have both positive and negative effects, and hence their balance is crucial. Prostacyclin counteracts the negative prostaglandin thromboxane, which adversely influences blood clotting and arterial clogging. We want more of the prostaglandin prostacyclin to offset thromboxane's potential harm. Niacin does just that.
- The risk of dying of heart attack dropped significantly in patients taking niacin. Those taking niacin as part of the Coronary Drug Project, the

longest running such study, were far less likely to suffer a myocardial infarction. Which of the many beneficial effects niacin offers was responsible? No one knows, but researchers do not dispute niacin's stellar performance.

• No prescription drug can match niacin's total performance. The newest class of drugs, collectively termed the "statins," can bring total and LDL cholesterol levels down but do not compare with niacin's effectiveness in raising HDLs and lowering triglycerides and Lp(a). These drugs include Mevacor (lovastatin), Zocor (simvastatin), Lescol (fluvastatin), and Pravachol (pravastatin). Lopid (gemfibrozil) has an effect on triglycerides and HDLs but does not do nearly as well in controlling total and LDL cholesterol. The resin drugs, including Colestid (colestipol) and Questran (cholestyramine), have only small effects on cholesterol when taken alone, and they actually raise triglyceride levels.

• Doctors can prescribe niacin in combination with one of the drugs for patients with particularly difficult lipid problems. As reported in the *American Journal of Cardiology* in 1994, for example, niacin and fluvastatin produced a 40 percent LDL reduction; niacin alone yielded a 25 percent drop. *Preventive Cardiology* that same year reported a 49 percent drop in LDL with the combination of niacin and pravastatin. And niacin has been used for years in combination with the resin drugs, resulting in lipid improvements associated with reversal of heart disease. Arteries photographed by angiography were less clogged after treatment at both the University of Southern California and the University of Washington.

• Niacin vastly improved lipids when combined with the drug pravastatin in a University of Kansas study presented in 1995 at the AHA meeting. Pravastatin alone, in a 20 mg dose, achieved a 14 percent reduction in LDL and no change in HDL, along with a 15 percent drop in triglycerides. The ratio of total cholesterol to HDL fell 15 percent. When three grams of niacin were added to the program, HDL rose by 29 percent, triglycerides came down 42 percent, LDL fell 25 percent, and the cholesterol/HDL ratio plummeted by 41 percent.

• Combining niacin and the statin drugs has been shown to be both safe and effective. It's the "extra whammy" doctors sometimes need for especially difficult cases. In another presentation at the 1995 AHA meeting, Dr. John Guyton of the University of North Carolina called niacin his "secret weapon" against elevated cholesterol and heart disease.

• So why don't doctors recommend niacin more often? Since niacin is a relatively inexpensive vitamin supplement, available at any pharmacy or health food store, manufacturers do not send salesmen into doctors' offices.

Conversely, pharmaceutical companies enjoy huge profits from drug sales and deluge physicians with information about their products.

In all honesty, far more practicing physicians have begun to prescribe niacin in recent years. That's the combined result of my books along with the information directed at doctors by the National Cholesterol Education Program in Washington. NCEP strongly recommends considering niacin to treat patients with elevated cholesterol levels.

But doctors still do not understand niacin as well as they do the prescription drugs. That's because niacin requires more doctor-patient interaction and communication, owing to some of the potential side effects of the vitamin.

- Is niacin a vitamin or is it a drug? In the scientific literature, researchers refer to niacin in large doses as a drug. They use that term because in those large, pharmacologic doses niacin has effects on the body beyond its benefit as a vitamin in preventing pellagra. In that respect, researchers also call large doses of vitamin C—or any other supplement—a drug.
- Certainly niacin should be used with respect and caution. As I will detail shortly, large doses of niacin have the potential for certain adverse reactions or side effects. Since it works in the liver to correct cholesterol problems, and it is metabolized there, niacin does place a certain extra load on that organ. As a result, those taking it should see their doctors regularly to have their liver functions checked. And because niacin has a number of contraindications, not everyone should take it, and everyone should discuss niacin with his or her physician before starting treatment.

NIACIN'S SIDE EFFECTS AND ADVERSE REACTIONS

Virtually everyone taking standard, unmodified, crystalline niacin experiences the "niacin flush." Some people react more strongly than others. While the reaction is totally harmless, it is uncomfortable. Flushing can be described as a reddening of the skin along with a prickly, burning sensation that occurs twenty to thirty minutes after taking a dose of niacin and lasts ten to twenty minutes on average. Flushing typically diminishes as one continues to take niacin and the body becomes accustomed to it.

One can lessen the niacin flush in a number of ways. First, it's best to take niacin with food at meals with plenty of fluids. Second, taking an aspirin tablet prior to the niacin eliminates or at least weakens the flush. Third, one can take modified niacin in slow-release or sustained-release formulations. One such preparation that I'll discuss more fully later practically wipes out the niacin flush.

Some individuals may experience a variety of gastrointestinal disturbances with niacin. I've found that to be the case mostly in those who take certain slow-release preparations, which include other ingredients in the formulation to slow down the niacin's release. It appears to be those other agents, termed "excipients," which present the problems. However, any niacin tablet or capsule can produce GI upset occasionally. Not often, but it does happen.

Many niacin users report itching to one degree or another. Dry skin occasionally accompanies its use. In rare instances one may develop a rash, typically on the chest and shoulders. Such a rash indicates an inability to tolerate niacin, and its use should be discontinued.

Niacin lowers glucose tolerance, the body's ability to maintain fairly constant blood sugar levels, to a certain extent. This is not a problem for normal, healthy individuals but may limit the use of niacin in those with diabetes. On the other hand, some physicians may simply wish to monitor patients with diabetes more carefully rather than depriving them of the benefits of niacin. That's certainly the case for Dr. Charles Keenan of Santa Monica, California. He has successfully used niacin with his diabetes patients for years.

Although loss of appetite is listed as a possible side effect in the medical literature, I've never heard of this happening either from my readers who have corresponded with me over the years or from physicians who routinely prescribe niacin.

Development of a vision problem termed maculopathy has been reported to occur in approximately 0.67 percent of patients taking niacin. The condition is completely reversible when one stops treatment. The authors of a report on niacin-induced maculopathy stated that "only those who experience visual symptoms need to be ophthalmologically evaluated." This is truly rare and has been associated with doses higher than most authorities feel are needed for cholesterol control. Check with your doctor if you do happen to develop blurred vision; if niacin is responsible, your doctor will either modify your dosage or suggest you discontinue usage.

Niacin may slightly increase the production of uric acid in the blood. For the vast majority of people, this poses no problem, since uric acid levels remain comfortably within normal limits. However, even slight elevations of uric acid can result in episodes of gout in individuals who have that disorder to begin with.

Doctors should routinely monitor liver function by testing for liver enzymes in the blood of those taking niacin. Slight elevations in those enzymes are not cause for alarm and are rather common in niacin takers.

Dr. Robert Kreisberg of the University of Alabama School of Medicine put the matter of niacin and liver function into a clear perspective in an editorial appearing in the October 1994 issue of the *American Journal of Medicine.*

> *Increased liver enzymes become an indication for stopping niacin therapy only when they are more than three times the upper-normal-limit. In my experience, I have found that physicians are too quick to discontinue niacin, and for that matter, other hypolipidemic drugs, because of mild or trivial changes in liver enzymes and explain to patients that the drug was "hurting their liver"; perhaps this is understandable in our litigious society.*

In practical terms, how many people will be able to take niacin? The issue of flushing is really a matter of nuisance. Unpleasant, sure, but such flushing tends to dissipate quickly after one's body gets used to the niacin. Moreover, as discussed, there are ways to effectively deal with flushing. Increases in uric acid and decreases in glucose tolerance are problems only for those with either gout or diabetes. Gastrointestinal disturbances can be eliminated by switching brands. Blurred vision occurs only rarely, as does loss of appetite. In the Mayo Clinic study I referred to earlier, all sixty-three participants were able to take niacin without intolerable side effects, according to the authors. Some researchers report a small drop-out rate during studies designed to investigate niacin's benefits, owing to side effects. But as niacin expert Dr. Parsons of Arizona put it, probably 90 percent of patients can take niacin when properly educated as to its use.

How often should one check liver enzymes? After your doctor approves niacin for you, he or she will want to test your liver enzymes in about two to three months. If all's well, as it most likely will be, the next test should be six months later. Most physicians will want to run liver enzyme tests twice a year thereafter. The test is easily performed with the same blood sample that will be drawn to check your cholesterol levels, which you'd want to do anyway.

But some people should not take niacin at all. There are definite contraindications to niacin usage. They include

- Pregnancy
- Severe cardiac arrhythmias
- Active peptic ulcer

- Gout
- Prior liver disorders, including hepatitis and cirrhosis
- Previous inability to tolerate niacin as evidenced by severe skin rash or greatly elevated liver enzymes if those conditions did not respond to dosage modifications
- Heavy alcohol use/abuse and possible subclinical liver damage, which would not normally be detected until the liver is further challenged by niacin

Why bother to take niacin when there are so many possible side effects and adverse reactions? Well, first of all I don't think everyone should take it. Of all the men and women whose lipids need modification, many if not most will be able to slash their risks by employing the other aspects of the program in this book. Dietary improvements, soluble fibers, and fat/cholesterol blockers can and will dramatically help most cholesterol problems and will greatly reduce the risk of heart disease, especially when combined with regular exercise, stress reduction and relaxation techniques, antioxidants, and other dietary supplements such as the B vitamins to prevent accumulation of homocysteine. Such individuals wouldn't need to take niacin even if it was as free of potential problems as water.

But as one who has literally come to the precipice of death, I view heart disease as a personal enemy. There is no way for me to express my strong emotions when I think of the millions of people who will needlessly suffer heart attacks and die because of coronary heart disease. I am firmly convinced that niacin has helped to save my life and that it can save the lives of others.

Bringing cholesterol levels down to 215, let's say, from a previous level of 240 is a step in the right direction, but it's just not enough. Yes, risk has been reduced, but risk still exists. Quite often it will take niacin—or some other agent—to bring lipids into the completely safe zones I've detailed throughout this book. That's particularly true if you have other risk factors, such as hypertension, diabetes, family history, or certainly a previous diagnosis of heart disease. Don't just cut that risk, eradicate it! A little flushing is a small price to pay.

While I further believe that niacin should be one's first choice and that it has enormous advantages over the prescription-only cholesterol-lowering drugs, not everyone can take it, owing to one of the contraindications discussed earlier. Other niacin users will develop abnormal liver enzymes to the extent that their doctors suggest that niacin isn't for them.

In those cases, one must be practical and Machievellian and accept the need for the prescription drugs when other lifestyle modifications don't achieve adequate cholesterol control. The safety of the statin drugs has been well established in the millions of patients who have used them since the first such agent, Mevacor, was approved in 1987. The importance of controlling the full lipid profile is so vital that I think one should do whatever is necessary to eliminate those risks. And, of course, if you and your doctor do decide on a prescription drug, simply use it to replace the niacin in this complete program to eliminate heart disease risk. By doing so you will ensure maximum impact on all lipid-involved risks, and you will also limit the amount of drugs you'll have to take.

Neither niacin nor prescription drugs should ever be viewed as an alternative to lifestyle improvements, both dietary changes and exercise routine, as well as other risk-reducing suggestions I've made in this book.

HOW TO TAKE NIACIN

Before taking niacin, be certain to discuss it with your physician. He or she may have suggestions regarding appropriate dosages. I provide the following information as reference for both you and your doctor. In fact, you may wish to photocopy this entire chapter for him or her.

To achieve cholesterol reductions, doses of niacin have ranged up to 8 grams a day and more. In the Cholesterol Lowering Atherosclerosis Study (CLAS) at the University of Southern California, which documented reversal of heart disease, researchers gave patients an average of 4.3 grams of niacin daily. However, much lower doses have been shown to be effective, especially in combination with other approaches.

The maximum niacin dosage daily should not exceed 3,000 mg (3 grams) of standard, immediate-release (IR) niacin or 1,500 mg (1.5 grams) of slow-release (SR) niacin. SR niacin formulations have been noted to have both twice the effectiveness and twice the toxicity of IR preparations. SR niacin is, therefore, a double-edged sword. These dosages have been shown to provide maximum benefits while resulting in minimal side effects. Larger dosages are more likely to result in adverse reactions, including abnormal liver enzymes.

When used exclusively for the purpose of raising abnormally low levels of the protective HDL cholesterol, lower dosages are often effective. Research in Israel has indicated that a daily dose of five hundred milligrams of IR niacin can significantly raise HDLs.

To be most effective, niacin doses should be divided and taken three times daily, preferably with meals. While twice-a-day dosing may be more convenient, it is not as effective.

To be sure that I don't forget to take my niacin, I keep a supply in my bathroom, kitchen, car, office, attaché case, and travel toiletry case. I use divided containers found in all pharmacies to store both the niacin and antioxidant and vitamin supplement dosages for the week.

Traditionally, niacin therapy is begun at low doses and gradually increased to minimize the flush and to allow the body to become accustomed to it. While your physician may have other recommendations, which you should follow, the following dosage schedule has been suggested frequently in the medical literature to achieve a final dosage of 3,000 mg (3 grams) of IR niacin.

DOSAGE SCHEDULE FOR INITIATING NIACIN THERAPY (IR)

First three days:	one 100 mg tablet three times daily = 300 mg
Next three days:	two 100 mg tablets three times daily = 600 mg
Next three days:	three 100 mg tablets three times daily = 900 mg
Next three days:	four 100 mg tablets three times daily = 1,200 mg
Next three days:	one 500 mg tablet three times daily = 1,500 mg
Next three days:	one 500 mg tablet plus one 100 mg tablet three times daily = 1,800 mg
Next three days:	one 500 mg tablet plus two 100 mg tablets three times daily = 2,100 mg
Next three days:	one 500 mg tablet plus three 100 mg tablets three times daily = 2,400 mg
Next three days:	one 500 mg tablet plus four 100 mg tablets three times daily = 2,700 mg
From then on:	two 500 mg tablets three times daily = 3,000 mg

Slow-release and sustained-release niacin formulations are an effective way to reduce or even eliminate the niacin flush. Again, the maximum dosage should be 1,500 mg. Although flushing may not be a problem, it is still better to gradually increase the dosage of SR niacin. The following dosage schedule allows the body to acclimate to the niacin. Dr. William Parsons suggests that an accelerated schedule, with 500 mg the first week, 1,000 mg the second, and 1,500 mg the third, might reduce the potential for flushing even further. Compare his approach with the following.

DOSAGE SCHEDULE FOR INITIATING NIACIN THERAPY (SR)

First week: one 250 mg tablet morning and evening = 500 mg
Next week: one 250 mg tablet morning, noon, and evening = 750 mg
Next week: two 250 mg tablets morning, noon, and evening = 1,500 mg
Thereafter: one 500 mg tablet morning, noon, and evening = 1,500 mg

Is Slow-Release Niacin Safe?

Beginning in 1990 a number of reports warned about the potential hazards of SR niacin preparations. The concerns were based upon a case history involving a man who, at his physician's prescription, had been taking a daily dose of 6,000 mg (6 grams) of IR niacin. He then switched to an SR niacin formulation he purchased at a health food store. By doing so, the man effectively doubled his dosage to 12,000 mg (12 grams) of niacin daily. The result was tragic: liver failure and the need for liver transplant.

That was an extreme case. Normally niacin-induced liver problems are shown by elevated liver enzymes and symptoms including nausea and vomiting, typically reversible after ceasing to take the niacin. There was only one case in which a person actually experienced liver failure.

But was the SR niacin responsible for the liver failure? Many stores overreacted and discontinued sales of SR niacin; reports urged banning the formulation and allowing only IR niacin to be sold. In truth, the man in question took a massive dose of niacin. No responsible person would recommend such dosages. He took four times the amount needed for cholesterol control.

Practically any substance can do severe damage and even cause death when taken in excess. Overdoses of aspirin can be fatal, yet the benefits of aspirin are recognized and reasonable care is taken when using it.

Slow-release niacin is completely safe when taken properly and when monitored by a physician. I began taking niacin in 1984 to control my own cholesterol levels. At that time, and for the next four years, I took three grams of IR niacin daily. My liver enzymes were always monitored and remained in the normal zone. The flush didn't bother me.

Then in 1988 I learned about a newly developed SR niacin called Enduracin. The maximum dosage was to be 1,500 mg, and the product was said to be free of nuisance side effects including flushing and GI upset sometimes seen with other SR preparations. Endur-acin was thought to be more effective than IR niacin. So I tried it. Sure enough, the slight flushing that had persisted for years with IR niacin was gone, and my cholesterol levels were actually lower than they had been before. I told my friend and physician, Dr. Charles Keenan of Santa Monica, about it, and he subsequently prescribed Endur-acin for his patients with fabulous results. He's been using it in his own practice ever since and takes it to help control his own cholesterol.

Dr. Keenan is a member of a medical family. Three of his brothers are also physicians. One of them, Dr. Joseph Keenan, is a professor of medicine and researcher at the University of Minnesota. The two brothers spoke together about Endur-acin and the terrific results seen, and Joe became intrigued. That led to a series of research studies at the University of Minnesota exploring the potential of Endur-acin as a cholesterol-reducing agent.

Dr. Joseph Keenan's first research with Endur-acin was published in the *Archives of Internal Medicine* in July 1991. Working with 201 men and women ages twenty to seventy years with elevated cholesterol levels, he found that 1,500 mg of Endur-acin lowered total cholesterol by 13.3 percent, LDL cholesterol by 19.3 percent, and the important TC/HDL ratio by 19.4 percent. HDLs rose, and triglycerides also fell. The drop-out rate due to side effects was only 3.4 percent, and participants had no problem in complying with the niacin dosage.

Dr. Keenan also reported that higher doses of 2,000 mg/day resulted in elevated liver enzymes. Moreover, HDL levels began to fall rather than rise. It was a matter of diminishing returns. Although the LDL levels fell, so did the HDLs, and the ratio did not appreciably change. He concluded, therefore, that 1,500 mg/day of Endur-acin was both safe and effective.

As interest in my book *The 8-Week Cholesterol Cure* began to spread around the world, medical authorities in the Russian government approached Dr. Keenan to collaborate with research in the then Soviet Union. He and Dr. D. Aronov of the National Research Centre for Preventive Medicine in Moscow subsequently published a series of papers reporting the effectiveness of the cholesterol-control program utilizing 1,500 mg of Endur-acin. That research has continued, and most recently was presented at the 2nd International Heart Health Conference in Barcelona in 1995.

Thus the credentials for Endur-acin are quite impressive. But why is this SR niacin preparation better than any other? Endur-acin is a formulation of pure niacin impregnated in a wax matrix tablet. Rather than dissolving, Endur-acin gradually releases niacin as it is leached from the tablet. The emptied wax tablet typically crumbles but sometimes passes through the digestive tract intact. Sometimes people have been concerned, especially when they've seen the tablet in their bowel movement stool. But by the time it passes, no niacin remains.

Owing to the very precise delivery system afforded by the wax matrix, Endur-acin delivers a predictable niacin dosage day after day. Because so little leaches out at a time, the niacin flush is virtually eliminated. Very few people experience even the slightest flush. In addition, because the niacin is continuously available to the liver, it controls cholesterol levels very effectively.

Do not forget, however, that Endur-acin is an SR niacin and as such its toxicity potential, as well as its effectiveness, is doubled. While clinically proven safe at recommended dosages, higher dosages may lead to problems. Don't experiment!

NOTE: WHILE THE MAXIMUM DOSAGE OF ENDUR-ACIN IS 1,500 GM/DAY AND 3,000 MG/DAY FOR IR NIACIN PREPARATIONS, NOT ALL INDIVIDUALS WILL REQUIRE THAT AMOUNT. YOU MAY FIND THAT LOWER DOSAGES ARE SUFFICIENT. WORK WITH YOUR DOCTOR TO DETERMINE EXACTLY THE RIGHT DOSAGE FOR YOUR AS PART OF THIS COMPLETE CHOLESTEROL CONTROL PROGRAM.

It is important to note that I have no financial or other vested interest in Endur-acin. I simply believe that, in my experience and that of others, it is the best SR niacin available. Endur-acin is produced by the Endurance Products Company in Oregon and sold to Walgreen Drugs, which sells it in both 250 mg and 500 mg strengths. Osco Drugs and Savon Drugs also sell Endur-acin labeled as such. In Vancouver, Canada, Endur-acin is available under the Stanley Drug label. You can also obtain Endur-acin directly from the company; it's less expensive that way. Endurance also produces an excellent IR niacin as well as antioxidants. Write or call for order forms:

Endurance Products Co.
P. O. Box 230489
Tigard, OR 97281
(800) 483-2532

Combination IR and SR Niacin Regimen

Through the years I've continued to monitor the medical literature regarding niacin and its benefits for cholesterol control and prevention of heart disease. Reading a report in the *Journal of the American Medical Association* in early 1994, I learned that researchers had found that SR niacin lowered LDL cholesterol significantly more than IR niacin did. Conversely, IR niacin did a better job of increasing HDLs and lowering triglycerides.

I spoke with Dr. Joseph Keenan about this report, and he indicated that his experience was similar. We discussed possible combination regimens and came up with an approach that I experimented with myself, using both SR and IR niacin. In the past, although the total and LDL cholesterol levels had been quite good, my HDL counts were less than wonderful. Typical measurements were in the very low 30s, and my triglycerides remained in the 180 to 230 range; not that bad, but not great. And I was very aware of the research showing that low HDL in the presence of even slightly elevated triglycerides posed an independent risk.

After three months on the combination IR/SR schedule, my test showed an improvement in HDL to 38 and triglycerides at an even 100. Terrific! Subsequent tests demonstrated continued improvement with HDL measurements as high as 42, which, for me, was tremendous. Triglycerides remained comfortably low.

I reported my findings to the readers of my *Diet-Heart Newsletter* (see page 184) and asked for feedback from readers who tried the combination themselves. A number responded, and their findings were similarly positive. Inspired by my success, Dr. Joseph Keenan plans to research the IR/SR combination.

Talk with your doctor about this combination. If he or she agrees that it's worth trying, you might want to consider the regimen that I've found successful.

DOSAGE SCHEDULE FOR IR/SR NIACIN COMBINATION

Morning:	One 500 mg SR niacin (Endur-acin) plus one 500 mg IR niacin
Afternoon:	One 500 mg IR niacin
Evening:	One 500 mg SR niacin (Endur-acin)

Note that I've substituted my previous afternoon dosage of one 500 mg SR niacin (Endur-acin) with two 500 mg IR niacin tablets, which I take in the morning and afternoon. Remember that 500 mg of SR equals 1,000 mg of IR. Therefore, the effective dosage remains the same.

But These Niacin Substitutes Don't Work

Virtually every medical report on the subject begins with words to the effect that "Niacin is an effective treatment for lowering cholesterol levels." Fortunately, as an over-the-counter supplement sold in pharmacies, health food stores, and by mail order, niacin remains very inexpensive, especially compared with the prescription drugs, but be cautious about choosing from the niacin preparations you see for sale. Not all of them work.

Niacinamide is the metabolic breakdown product of niacin. Used in supplements, it satisfies one's vitamin requirement for niacin. However, niacinamide has no effect on lowering cholesterol.

Inositol nicotinate sometimes is labeled as "no-flush niacin," but like niacinamide, it does not lower cholesterol. Do not believe any salesperson in a health food store who argues to the contrary. There is no clinical evidence that inositol nicotinate has any effect on cholesterol.

Combination niacin products are frequently found in health food stores. These products may also include dietary fibers, antioxidants, and other supplements. The amounts of niacin and the other ingredients are typically too low to have an effect on cholesterol. If a combination includes, say, 50 mg of niacin, you'd have to take a lot of those capsules or tablets to reach an effective dosage. The same applies to a soluble fiber that might be included. Not only are such preparations ineffective as such, but they also are horribly expensive when compared with similar doses of the individual components. Buy and take them separately.

Should Niacin Be a Prescription Drug?

Niacin is available without prescription in the United States as a "nutritional supplement." Noting the potential toxicity of niacin, especially if used without any medical supervision, some doctors have urged FDA to restrict sales to prescription only. I can understand such caution, but I personally believe niacin should remain available without prescription. My main reason is cost, which would double, triple, or more if niacin had to be regulated by and relegated to the bureaucracy required for prescription drugs. As it is now, niacin is available to everyone, regardless of economic status, and heart disease is an equal-opportunity killer. Niacin should not be restricted to only those who can afford the higher prices of prescription drugs. Additionally, the over-the-counter status niacin now has provides a certain degree of freedom for the individual. You feel more in control than when having to take a prescription into the pharmacy every time you need a niacin supply.

That said, I must reiterate my feeling that niacin should be used under medical supervision. You need to have those liver enzymes checked now and then, and only a doctor can perform the tests for you. Actually, that's not at all inconvenient, since you'll want to know how your lipid profile is coming along from time to time, and you can check all the measurements at one time. Niacin can be an enormous help, in fact a lifesaver, in our fight against heart disease. Don't let it hurt you in the process.

In the decade since I wrote *The 8-Week Cholesterol Cure,* niacin therapy has become more medically utilized. During that time thousands of my readers have written to express their thanks and to share the wonderful news of their results with me. Those results have been dramatic and have signaled unprecedented heart disease protection for those men and women. Today we know that niacin has benefits well beyond those recognized in 1984 when I began my personal experience with it. Niacin will be an integral part of our battle with heart disease well into the twenty-first century. I'm glad you know about it.

· 10 ·

Exercise Your Heart, Exorcise Your Cholesterol

Even if you're absolutely set against exercise and define yourself as the ultimate sofa spud, please bear with me through this short chapter. To begin with, I can really relate to you. As a kid in elementary school in the '50s I flunked the president's physical fitness test while almost everyone else passed. I was always the last one picked for any team sport. No, I am not now nor have I ever been an athlete with a natural attraction to fitness and exercise.

To make matters worse, I went to college in the 1960s, a truly self-destructive era. No one exercised. If anyone was running on campus, you could assume that a cop was after him! And after college I became a typical American, sedentary office worker.

Looking back on those days I realize that I was always tired and never felt really good. Yawning every afternoon. Nodding off in meetings, even interesting ones. Not sleeping well at night and having a tough time getting up in the mornings. Lousy at sports—I tried skiing but just couldn't get my body to do the turns.

When I had my heart attack and first bypass surgery in 1978 at the tender age of thirty-five, there was no such thing as cardiac rehabilitation, and I got no advice about exercise. So if I did anything strenuous, I was scared that I'd have another attack.

Then in 1984 my life changed. On July 3 I had my second bypass operation, and three weeks later my cardiologist had me—much against my will—in a rehab program. Little by little I came to life: walking slowly on the treadmill, riding slowly on the bicycle. Everything I did at the beginning I did slowly. But by the end of just six weeks, I was feeling better than at any time I could recall. By the end of the twelve-week program, I was well on my way to enjoying a life of fitness that I'd never experienced before.

So, there you are. You're not reading the advice of some Olympic athlete or a wild-eyed fanatic. Simply enough, if I could make the transformation, anyone can!

Looking back at things, it's too bad it took such a near-catastrophic illness to turn me around. I think of all those years I could have enjoyed more. Sooner would have been better than later, but later was way better than never. And now I swear I'll never go back to the old ways. Life is a lot more fun when you have the energy to enjoy it.

ACTIVATE YOUR HEART

Certainly this isn't a book for sick people. It's for those who want to prevent problems and for those who want to enjoy their health and their life. But the one thing that I learned in cardiac rehabilitation that applies to an exercise program for everyone is the word "slowly." It took years to get to your level of sedentary lifestyle, and it'll take some time to get going. How long? Ninety days. Give yourself just ninety days. Make a promise, a commitment, to follow the advice in this chapter, and I promise, in turn, that by the end of that time you'll be converted for life. You won't want to give up the way you feel!

Dr. Sidney Smith, president of the AHA in 1995, dedicated his year in office to encouraging other doctors to urge their patients to adopt a lifestyle of heart disease prevention. He strongly criticized the fact that only one out of every three patients gets the guidance he or she needs to prevent a second heart attack or bypass.

Whether you're trying to prevent a first heart attack or a second one, exercise just has to be an integral part of the program. Yet the word "exercise" itself is enough to turn off most people. If you're one of those, you'll be pleased to know that you don't need to exercise in the Jane Fonda or Susan Powter sense of the term. You just need to get active, to just move your body.

Researchers at the Aerobics Institute in Dallas wanted to know just how fit people had to be to prevent degenerative illnesses such as heart disease. Dr. Steven Blair and his associates studied thousands of men and women, putting them into one of five categories of fitness and regular activity. He expected to see a linear increase in health, a bigger payoff, with every increment of exercise. The results were amazing.

To no one's surprise, those in the top category of fitness were the healthiest. But those in the second-from-the-bottom level, just above the truly sedentary couch potatoes who did absolutely nothing, got almost as much benefit from a minimum of activity as those in the top tier. The lesson learned: It doesn't take much effort to protect your health adequately.

But how can one measure the activity needed to achieve health and vitality and to prevent heart and other diseases?

In the past, people were forever talking about heart rates and measuring their pulses. That's really not practical. Who wants to become obsessed with measuring heartbeats while exercising? And, it turns out, that's not at all necessary. The trick to effective exercise comes down to a concept known for many years by exercise physiologists, but seldom shared with the rest of the world. It's a way of thinking about activity known as METs, and it's really simple.

When you're completely relaxed, just sitting in a chair quietly or lying in bed or on a couch watching television, you're burning enough energy to keep your internal organs operating and your body alive. And that amount of energy, regardless of your age, sex, height, or weight, is one metabolic unit of activity: one MET. It's the lowest metabolic level of activity. Get up from that chair to open the window or find a snack, and you've stoked up your body's furnace to two METs.

The thinking behind the MET is very logical and easy to understand. When we engage in any physical activity, the heart beats to match demand, to pump out the amount of oxygen-carrying blood needed. Some activities require 50 percent of an individual's maximal capacity. Others call for 60 percent. Still others may need even more.

At the same time, our lungs are pumping oxygen-rich air in and carbon dioxide–laden air out. Again, we have maximal capacities for vigorous breathing. The scientific term for this is VO_2 max, referring to the maximum volume of oxygen we can accomodate. That's all you need to know.

Put the two, heart rate and breathing rate, together, and you have a measure of physical performance or level of activity. This measure is termed the "metabolic equivalent," or MET. Virtually every human activity can be broken down to the effort required, measured in METs. Take a look at the table at the end of this chapter for a listing of daily activities and their MET ratings.

Remember that I said that *activity, not exercise, is the key to health and fitness.* Anyone would have to agree that walking briskly for thirty to forty minutes a day, at about 4 to 4.5 miles per hour, is sufficient daily exercise. That walk will burn from four to six METs. You can get the same benefit by performing activities requiring half the METs for twice the time.

Maybe it's a very busy day, and you just don't have the time to take that thirty- to forty-minute walk. Instead, concentrate on activities that require the same METs: climbing the stairs instead of using the elevator; picking up the pace of your housework; stepping lively when you need to get from one place to another, whether from your car to an office through the parking lot or down the hallway from one office to another or doing your grocery shopping and getting the dry cleaning.

Yes, I said that measuring your heart rate isn't necessary. But just to prove a point, put your finger to the side of your neck while you are doing some of those relatively low-MET activities. You'll find that your heart is beating faster and you're breathing more deeply than when you are at rest.

Of course, the flip side of that coin is also true. You can get the benefit of a low-MET activity by doing activities requiring twice the METs for half the time. Instead of walking at four miles per hour for forty minutes, you can jog at five to six miles per hour for twenty minutes. It's your choice. Hate to jog but love to dance? Get into the habit of square dancing or folk dancing on a regular basis. Ronald Reagan actually enjoyed chores on his California ranch and spent a lot of his free time clearing brush. That was just as beneficial as Bill Clinton's jogging, and since Reagan really enjoyed himself, probably a lot healthier.

Most people think that medicine has to taste bad to be effective. They apply that same thinking to activities, concentrating on what might be distasteful efforts to them, what they would call "exercise." Instead, concentrate on the things that are fun for you, whether that might be riding a horse, pedaling a bicycle, or clearing brush. You can kill two birds with one stone by picking up the pace of active work, thus increasing the METs you use, as shown in the table.

WHY BOTHER TO MAKE THE EFFORT?

I could cite chapter and verse from the scientific literature to try to make a convincing argument for the health benefits of exercise. Just lifting the many volumes of books and journals is a lot of exercise in itself. I'll spare you the details, but here are the healthful effects of regular physical activity.

- You'll feel better. Whatever activity you choose, when the heart and breathing rate increase to a point that you're breathing deeply and have at least a little perspiration, your body produces a soothing chemical called beta-endorphin. The calming effect of the substance, chemically related to morphine, can last the entire day.

Most psychologists recognize exercise as one of the best ways to reduce stress. Especially when done on a regular basis, exercise can and will enable you to cope with stress more effectively.

- You'll sleep better. Exercise promotes the release of another chemical, this one in the family of neurotransmitters, known as serotonin. In fact, pharmaceutical companies keep trying to develop drugs that increase serotonin levels to sell as tranquilizers. Exercise is a natural way to produce serotonin to ensure better sleep at night.
- You'll be more productive at work. Most people feel sleepy by midafternoon. Those who regularly exercise find that midday letdowns are a thing of the past. Their stamina increases along with their ability to concentrate. In a survey of highly successful men and women in a number of professions, Dr. Kenneth Pelletier of Stanford University found that virtually all had a regular schedule of physical activity and that they credited their productivity to their exercise habits.
- You'll enjoy sports and leisure recreation more. Whether you play golf or tennis or any other sport, you'll find that you do it better and enjoy it a lot more when you get regular exercise rather than being a "weekend warrior." That'll probably result in your playing those sports more often and getting even more exercise.
- You'll live longer. Here's a little detail that most people find at least moderately interesting. Two large studies published in the *New England Journal of Medicine* in 1993 provided the scientific proof that physical fitness prolongs life. And another one reported in the *Journal of the American Medical Association* in 1995 showed that the more strenuous one's physical activity—call it exercise or sport or play—the longer one is likely to live. The same study showed that even nonvigorous activity prevented heart disease.
- You'll control your weight more easily and be able to eat more. Not only do you burn calories during physical activity, but also the body's metabolism remains revved up for hours afterward. In addition, as fitness levels increase, you'll build more lean muscle tissue. Since only muscle tissue can burn calories, acting as the body's furnace, you'll be able to consume more food without gaining weight. More about all this in chapter 12's discussion of weight control.
- You'll stabilize blood sugar levels and control diabetes. Along with weight loss, regular physical activity can virtually eliminate the symptoms and health hazards of type II, non-insulin-dependent diabetes. Exercise has an insulinlike effect.
- Your blood pressure will fall. While scientists were initially skeptical,

data now demonstrate the incredible effectiveness of lifestyle modifications, including exercise, to control mild to moderate hypertension without the need for drugs. Even patients with severe blood pressure elevations are likely to lessen their drug requirement when they regularly exercise.

- Your cholesterol levels will improve across the board. The bad LDL cholesterol comes down with regular exercise, while HDL levels rise. In fact, the more one exercises and the more strenuous that exercise, the greater the HDL gain. Triglycerides fall as well. LDL and total cholesterol come down with the weight loss that typically results from exercise.

- You'll be less likely to form blood clots that can precipitate heart attacks. In sedentary individuals, sudden bursts of activity can cause blood clotting. That may explain why some people have heart attacks when doing unusual activities such as snow shoveling. But those who do exercise on a regular basis are protected against this tendency of the blood platelets to form clots. Again, the more one exercises, the greater the protection.

- You may develop collateral circulation. Doctors have found tiny collateral arteries that provide a kind of "natural bypass" around clogged arteries. Many believe that vigorous exercise can contribute to the formation of those new arterial pathways.

- You'll prevent heart attacks. Do at least two hours of vigorous activity a week, and you can reduce your risk of having a heart attack by as much as 70 percent. Both strenuous and nonstrenuous activity provide protection, and the amount of time spent doesn't have to be as much as previously thought, as shown in research published in the *New England Journal of Medicine* in 1994. The benefits of exercise in that study were over and above any other factors such as cholesterol level or blood pressure. In other words, even if a person smoked, he would benefit from exercise. And, again, while low levels of activity were protective, the most active and physically fit men enjoyed the greatest protection.

- You'll recover from a heart attack faster and prevent a subsequent event. Data have come in from all over the world. If a person begins an exercise program after suffering a heart attack, his or her recovery will be far more successful than if he or she remains sedentary. That success can be and has been measured in a number of ways. Less anxiety and depression. Reduced risk of a second attack. Faster return to work and regular activities. Improved outlook. Better sex lives. Exercise is the best prescription a doctor can write for the recovering heart patient. Those who do the minimum amount of recommended physical activity do very well; those who do more do better.

HOW MUCH IS ENOUGH? TWO THEORIES

Looking at the list of benefits of exercise and physical activity I've just provided, one might wonder if it isn't too good to be true. The documented fact remains that if exercise could be "bottled," it would be the greatest miracle drug of all time. But what should be the dosage of that "drug"? If a little is good, is more better?

No, I'm not reneging on what I said earlier. Just being more active than the typical couch potato will convey tremendous protection against heart disease and will provide the benefits I listed.

The American College of Sports Medicine prescribes moderate exercise for shorter periods that add up to thirty minutes or more, at least five days per week. Unfortunately, only 22 percent of all American men and women now get even that moderate level of activity, according to data from the Centers for Disease Control and Prevention (CDC).

In the past, experts' guidelines called for vigorous, continuous exercise for at least twenty minutes or more, three to five times per week. The new recommendations come mostly from epidemiological studies showing that even moderate exercise or physical activity is associated with reduced risks of chronic disease, especially heart disease.

Steven Blair, of the Institute for Aerobics Research in Dallas says that he and others made a mistake in their earlier recommendations. The emphasis used to be on sustained activity. Then research done at Stanford and elsewhere demonstrated that activity added up: Ten minutes here, fifteen minutes there, five minutes another time, it all adds up.

So how many people actually are engaged in physical activity at those recommended levels? Very darned few. Nearly 60 percent of the U.S. population fall into the category of true couch potato, living a sedentary lifestyle, according to a CDC survey. Sedentary lifestyle alone is said to be responsible for 250,000 deaths a year.

Call it "exercise lite" or anything you wish, but the new guidelines are really easy to achieve. Ultimately the physical activity should add up to the equivalent of walking briskly two miles a day. Again, whether that activity comes during one stint or two or three makes no difference at all, and it can take the form of any physical activity you like to do, choose to do, or have to do. Things you like may include gardening, dancing, tennis, or other sports. Activities you choose to do might be riding an Exercycle or walking on a treadmill in order to get "the job done" efficiently and regularly, whether in a gym or at home. And things you have to do might be housework, chores around the house, waxing the car, or whatever. Of course all three categories of activities all add up together.

Maybe it's our Puritan background, but Americans tend to think of exercise in the strictest terms. Most would not think of golf as exercise. But when Purdue University exercise physiologist Darlene Sedlock studied the work output of a 150-pound golfer walking and carrying his or her clubs rather than riding in a cart, she found that the eighteen-hole game was the equivalent of running six miles. That golfer will burn 660 calories more than if he or she were just sitting around. Digging in the garden, Sedlock learned, took 540 calories per hour. Pushing a lawnmower required 470 calories per hour. In fact, Dr. William Castelli of the famous Framingham Heart Study mows his own lawn as one of the ways he stays fit.

Getting back to those things you have to do; they can really use up calories fast. Carrying groceries up the stairs means you're working at 8 METs, the same as running at 5 mph. Shoveling snow is a 5 MET activity, equal to hiking. The same holds for moving furniture and pushing that lawn mower. Scrubbing floors takes 5.5 METs. Whether you're carrying and stacking firewood, digging in a garden, or actively playing with children, you're operating at 5 METs. And here you thought you had to go to the gym!

No doubt about it, get thirty minutes of activity every day and you'll significantly reduce your risk of heart disease. But, again, is more better? And, if so, is there a limit, a point of diminishing returns?

Dr. Kenneth Cooper, who coined the term "aerobics" and founded the Institute for Aerobics Research in Dallas says that if you're doing more than fifteen miles a week—walking, running, or whatever equivalent—you're not getting any additional protection from heart disease. There may be other reasons to do more, but fighting heart disease isn't one of them. Still, most people don't do fifteen miles a week. Far from it.

In a very real way, the science hasn't changed much in the past years, just the ways of interpreting the data from an increasing number of studies. Dr. Cooper advocates fifteen miles a week. He is a runner, so his fifteen miles might be three days of running five miles a day. That's what he's been recommending for years. The College of Sports Medicine now sets guidelines at the equivalent of two miles a day. Well, that's fourteen miles a week. Just about the same.

In a 1991 article in *Circulation*, researchers reported that "vigorous" exercise was needed to avoid heart attack and stroke. The researchers determined that exercise training at a high level of intensity significantly increases the ability of men's blood to dissolve blood clots and to prevent clot formation. The intense exercise done was strenuous walking, jogging, and bicycling for forty-five minutes four or five times per week. If you multiply that out, the task doesn't seem so daunting. Those men were doing a total of three to four hours of activity a week. Figuring they were averaging 4.5 miles per hour walking or jogging, that comes out to—once again—about fifteen miles a week.

It doesn't make one bit of difference whether you run those fifteen miles in three outings or walk them one mile at a time twice a day throughout the week. For that matter, you can replace the running or walking with any activity that gets your body's organs functioning beyond the METs required to maintain a prone position on the couch.

That does it for aerobic exercise/activity. But don't stop there. Fill out your exercise regimen with sessions of both strength training and stretching to achieve maximum fitness.

GRANDMA THE WEIGHT LIFTER

Don't roll your eyes at the suggestion of strength training. It doesn't mean that you have to pump iron like Arnold. The inevitable truth is that as we get older—and that happens to all of us one day at a time—we lose body strength. That loss is imperceptible over the years, and then one day, all of a sudden, you realize that you can't get up from a chair without assistance or do any number of things you used to take for granted. But such deterioration doesn't have to happen.

Researchers from Tufts University Center for Aging have done some work that puts the movie *Cocoon* to shame. They took people in their eighties and nineties, unable in many cases to walk without a walker, and for a mere six weeks put them into training on Nautilus machines. The result was virtually miraculous. It was like Lourdes.

As part of the study, the participants returned to a sedentary lifestyle, without the exercise. Benefits quickly disappeared. There was an uproar: "Give us back our exercise!" As I've said before, give exercise a chance, and you won't want to give it up when you see how it can change your life. If it can work for folks in their eighties and nineties, it can work for you.

What does it take? Figure about twenty minutes three times a week. That's all you need. No doubt the best way to do strength training would be to work out in a gym with Nautilus or other equipment. The first sessions should be with someone who can instruct you in the best, most efficient, and safest techniques. You don't need a fancy health club; the local YMCA is just fine.

Resistance training, as researchers refer to strength exercising, has a number of benefits beyond toning one's body. Blood pressure falls significantly. Weight control is more efficient. Levels of the protective HDL cholesterol rise while the harmful LDL falls. And both blood sugar and insulin levels improve.

No question about it, the toughest part is to get going. After getting into a routine, fitness programs become a part of your life. You won't want to give it up.

Start by taking a walk—perhaps just one block or two. Dust off the bicycle in the garage or do that gardening you've been putting off. Promise to do something active for at least twenty to thirty minutes daily, to the point that you can feel your heart beating firmly and you perspire slightly. Keep a journal listing the day's activity. You'll be amazed at how quickly you'll develop your stamina and start feeling better.

Think about that heart beating inside your chest. Think of it as your friend, your "pet" perhaps. That heart works all day long; it never rests. It works for you. Now do something for your heart. Exercise can take you from athero-genesis to athero-exodus!

ENERGY REQUIREMENTS OF COMMON ACTIVITIES IN METS

1 MET (Metabolic Equivalent) equals the amount of energy needed when the body is at rest.

Sleeping	Sitting quietly in a chair
Lying in bed	

2 METs equal twice the amount of energy used when at rest.

Standing	Playing cards
Talking	Light housekeeping (dusting)
Walking (1 mph)	Typing/word processing
Reading	Shaving
Writing	Dressing/brushing hair

2–3 METs

Walking (2 mph)	Moderate housekeeping (light laundry)
Playing piano	Meal preparation
Playing golf (electric cart)	Bicycling (5 mph)
Bathing/showering	Bowling
Washing hair	

3–4 METs

Walking (3 mph)	Heavier housework (scrubbing dishes)
Bicycling (6–7 mph)	Ballroom dancing (foxtrot)
Driving a car in light traffic	Factory labor
Climbing stairs slowly	

4–5 METs

Walking (4 mph)	Playing badminton/light tennis
Bicycling (8 mph)	Heavy housekeeping (mopping, vacuuming)
Gardening/raking	House painting
Light carpentry	Driving a car in heavy traffic
Mowing lawn (power)	Washing windows

5–6 METs

Walking (4.5 mph)	Golfing (carrying/pulling clubs)
Bicycling (10 mph)	Very heavy housework (scrubbing floors)
Roller-skating	Carrying wood or groceries
Light shoveling, digging	Social dancing (tango)

6–7 METs

Walking (5 mph)	Mowing lawn (push mower)
Bicycling (11 mph)	Square dancing
Playing tennis (singles)	Splitting wood
Waterskiing	Snow shoveling
Swimming leisurely	Moving furniture

ENERGY REQUIREMENTS OF COMMON ACTIVITIES IN METS

7–8 METs

- Jogging (5 mph)
- Bicycling (12 mph)
- Downhill skiing
- Canoeing
- Swimming laps (slow)
- Playing football
- Horseback riding at gallop
- Climbing hills (moderate)
- Climbing stairs (continuous)
- Playing tennis (competitive singles)

8–9 METs

- Jogging (5.5 mph)
- Bicycling (13 mph)
- Swimming laps (fast)
- Cross-country skiing
- Playing basketball
- Carrying groceries upstairs

10+ METs

- Handball, racquetball, squash
- Climbing hills with a load
- Jogging (6 mph and faster)

· 11 ·

Happy Heart, Healthy Heart

Even in the face of adversity and numerous hardships, my father was a very happy man for most of his life. He loved my mother enormously, adored his children, and truly enjoyed his work as a pharmacist who was greatly respected and valued in his community. He was remarkably healthy and relished every day of his life. Then a tragedy struck, an occurrence that produced such stress that his life came apart. Simply enough, Dad was unable to cope with that stress or to just walk away from it. Within a year he died of a massive heart attack at the age of fifty-seven.

My brother was one of the most happy-go-lucky guys I ever knew. A series of bad investments and business decisions financially ruined him, and he was so overwhelmed by stress that for years he awoke every night in a cold sweat. His heart attack hit at age forty-nine.

As I've traveled the country speaking with heart patients I've heard it over and over: "Stress caused my attack." More pursuasive than such anecdotal stories are the data piling up in the medical literature and being presented at virtually every scientific conference linking the emotions with heart disease.

There's no doubt in my mind that stress will eventually be listed as a major risk factor, right up there with high blood pressure, cigarette smoking, elevated cholesterol counts, and sedentary behavior. The only reason that stress isn't already included as a risk factor is the difficulty in quantifying and measuring what we call stress. What may be horribly stressful to me might be easily shrugged off by another person.

It's difficult even to give stress an absolute definition. Determinations of stress are far more subjective than objective. Are you more angry today than you were yesterday? Did your reaction to your boss or your spouse or your kids rate a four or a seven or a nine on a scale of one to ten?

What we do know for certain is that depression appears to be an independent predictor of heart disease. Researchers from Johns Hopkins in Baltimore and McGill University in Montreal collaborated in collecting data that they shared with the scientific community in 1994. In nearly twelve hundred medical students from the classes of 1948 to 1964 who were studied for thirty-five years, depression was directly associated with heart attacks even after adjusting for other risk factors. In other words, take two men having similar levels of cholesterol, blood pressure, and so forth, and the depressed individual has a far greater risk of suffering a heart attack, according to the Hopkins investigators.

In Montreal, Dr. Nancy Frasure-Smith found that depression that develops following a heart attack continues to increase the risk of dying over an eighteen-month period. Conversely, those patients without depression were likely to make a complete recovery.

You can add anger to the emotions that place our hearts in jeopardy. A team of scientists from Harvard Medical School asked more than sixteen hundred men and women in fifty-three hospitals to evaluate their anger one week after their heart attacks. Again, influences of other risk factors were canceled out. Bingo. The average risk of heart attack was increased by 2.3 times in the two hours following the onset of moderate or greater anger. Those were not happy people.

The study of the heart's emotions remains in its infancy when compared with, say, our knowledge of hypertension. It's a lot more difficult to really get a handle on this risk factor. Moreover, our assessment of the impact of our emotions has changed significantly over the past several years.

In the 1970s, the emphasis was on the "Type A" personality: the time-driven, ambitious, impatient person was thought to be at risk. Taken to its logical conclusion, that description means that every successful doctor, lawyer, and businessperson is a cardiac time bomb. Think about those arrogant, impatient, obnoxious orchestra conductors. They wave their arms a lot, burning many calories. And they don't bottle up their frustrations. They live well into their eighties.

Then the focus narrowed. Maybe it was certain traits within that personality spectrum that placed certain men and women at risk. In the 1980s Dr. Redford Williams of Duke University zeroed in on anger and hostility. Those were emotions that could actually be measured by way of a personality inventory. Sure enough, in both doctors and lawyers studied, those with higher measured assessments of anger and hostility as students later suffered early heart attacks. Calmer individuals were spared.

Currently psychologists emphasize the importance of depression, anxiety, and a general feeling of hopelessness, in addition to anger and hostility. In a more general sense, happy hearts are healthy hearts. Unhappy hearts are at risk.

Physicians tend to be a very pragmatic lot. Why should an intangible emotion have a physical effect? As one world-renowned cardiologist told me a number of years ago, no psychological stress could make the heart beat as fast, or at least any faster, than demonstrated during physical exercise on a treadmill test. Therefore, he reasoned, psychological stress could be no riskier than physical stress. In fact, he posited, since physical stress in the form of exercise was known to strengthen the heart, so, too, might psychological stress. He was wrong, and doctors now are paying more attention to stress as a risk factor in heart disease.

Today, however, we are aware of just what psychological stress does to the body. We can measure the chemical changes just as certainly as we can measure cholesterol levels or blood pressure. Simply enough, we are physiologically different when we are happy as compared with when we are unhappy.

What, you might be asking by this point, is this chapter doing in a book on diet and cholesterol? Well, it turns out that the emotions are strongly linked with both our cholesterol levels and with the degree of clogging of our arteries.

Meet George Kaplan, Ph.D., chief of the Human Population Laboratory in the California Department of Health Services in Berkeley. He and his coworkers examined the medical records of eleven hundred men in a Finnish heart study that investigated the medical and lifestyle influences on the development of atherosclerosis. They learned that depression intensifies the buildup of fatty deposits in both coronary and carotid arteries by amplifying the effects of other risk factors and thus increasing the chances of suffering a heart attack.

Kaplan found that smoking almost tripled the amount of atherosclerosis in the arteries of depressed men. The impact of LDL on clogging was nearly double in depressed men when they were compared with more emotionally happy individuals. Men who were depressed and had high circulating levels of the protein fibrinogen, an essential part of blood clot formation that encourages plaque development in the arteries, were almost four times as likely as men who were not depressed to develop these deposits in their blood vessels.

One of the arguments used against the belief that cholesterol elevations are responsible for heart disease has long been the observation that while one person with a high count has a heart attack, another person with an equally elevated level doesn't have heart disease. As Dr. Kaplan points out, the psyche very well may be the critical factor.

What if the cholesterol level isn't so high that it narrows the arteries? Would negative emotions still have an impact? Definitely. Anger results in the release of the biologically toxic chemical cortisol from the adrenal glands. That cortisol causes a spasm in the arteries of the heart, stopping the flow of blood to the heart's muscle. The result is either angina pain or even heart attack. Combine such a spasm with already narrowed arteries, and the situation could be and often is fatal.

We know that the good cholesterol HDL can block the deleterious effects of the bad LDL. But those who easily become angry and who register other negative emotions have lower levels of HDL. A coincidence? Dr. JoAnn Manson at Brigham and Women's Hospital in Boston explains that every time one experiences a strong emotional response, the body produces more cortisol and adrenaline, both of which lower HDL.

But what about more chronic, lingering, negative emotions, such as what might be termed hopelessness? Such individuals are sad, lack optimism, and are, again, unhappy. They aren't overtly angry or hostile. They wouldn't be diagnosed as clinically depressed. They're mildly depressed. If nothing is done about that chronic unhappiness, these people progressively damage their cardiovascular systems.

One researcher looking at this problem is Dr. Robert Anda of the Centers for Disease Control and Prevention in Atlanta. He and his team tracked nearly three thousand adults for twelve years, all of whom were free of heart disease and other chronic illnesses at the start of the study. About 11 percent of the volunteer subjects had symptoms of mild depression; another 11 percent cited moderate hopelessness, and 3 percent reported severe hopelessness. All three groups had a significantly higher heart disease death rate over the years than more emotionally healthy individuals.

Death was four times greater in those with severe hopelessness than in those without such negative emotions. Nonfatal heart attacks were also more prevalent in the unhappy individuals. Dr. Anda speculates that prolonged depression and hopelessness may contribute to heart disease by promoting the formation of blood clots and the thickening of arterial walls.

Then there's blood pressure, another major risk factor for heart disease as well as for stroke. Looking at participants in the Framingham Heart Study in Massachusetts, investigators found that heightened anxiety, intensified anger, and suppressed expression of anger increase the risk of hypertension.

Blood pressure rises with anger, and when that anger subsides, the pressure goes back to normal in healthy persons. That's referred to as labile hypertension. But when emotional flurries get strung together on a regular basis, the pressure rises and falls for a while but eventually stays up. Liken the phenomenon to a rubber band losing its ability to spring back after being stretched too often and too far.

Many people living in our fast-paced, uncertain society have feelings of anxiety. Most manage to cope. But for some that anxiety becomes severe. Doctors at Harvard's Department of Health and Social Behavior tracked nearly fifteen hundred men for up to thirty-two years, noting symptoms of severe anxiety and observing their heart health. Compared with men showing no symptoms of anxiety, those with two or more symptoms had more than three times the risk of a fatal heart attack and more than five times the odds of sudden death.

This is all quite frightening stuff, and I hope reading it hasn't caused too much anxiety for you! The good news is that, as for other risk factors, one can modify behaviors to lessen the danger of negative emotional states. No, this does not mean converting to a life of passivity and purposelessness, and I'm not going to waste paper on publishing more bromides of count your blessings and smell the roses. However, coming to grips with one's emotions is an integral part of a heart-healthy lifestyle. The solutions are real and they work.

For openers, stress in itself is not a bad thing. We all experience stress in various forms, and life wouldn't be very interesting without the challenges we face. But how we deal with that stress makes all the difference in the world. In one way, that cardiologist I spoke of earlier was somewhat correct in comparing physical and psychological stresses. By purposefully adapting to them, we can become more capable of enduring both.

One does not begin a physical fitness program by going out and running a marathon or entering a weight-lifting contest. It starts with a walk around the block and perhaps a few sit-ups. Similarly, we learn to strengthen our resistance to stress a little at a time, and we just might need a personal trainer to get us started.

You need a blood test to determine your cholesterol count, and your doctor can measure your blood pressure. But only you can determine whether you're at risk because of your emotional state. This may seem simplistic to many researchers, but over the years I've come to the conclusion that answering just one question makes the diagnosis: Are you happy or unhappy?

You could take personality assessments and subject yourself to psychological profile analyses to determine your anger, hostility, depression, anxiety, hopelessness, or any other emotion. But you can easily cut out the middleman and just ask yourself, Am I happy or unhappy?

Of course, that's not like asking whether you're pregnant or not pregnant. There's a lot of gray between the black and white. Those shades of gray are going to describe mainly a relatively happy state of affairs. If you're unhappy, that's pretty certain, and that unhappiness, my friend, puts you at cardiac risk every day it continues.

Lowering your cholesterol level and blood pressure can certainly provide a sense of satisfaction and gratitude that your risk has been reduced. I doubt, however, that such accomplishments will leave you feeling exuberant for days and years to come. On the other hand, overcoming your current state of unhappiness can make you feel, well, happy! Even if you're happy now, you can get happier! Again, I risk seeming simplistic in this analysis, but sometimes the most significant truths are, indeed, quite simple.

How does one begin to seek happiness? Seeking a guru at the top of a Tibetan peak isn't very practical and probably wouldn't be too productive anyway. However, it is possible to change, to make emotional adjustments. Don't curse the dark; light a candle. As we'll see, there are a number of ways to light the dark. Besides candles there are flashlights, bonfires, and lamps. Each must find his or her own way, but knowing the options is a start.

IDENTIFYING YOUR UNHAPPINESS

Why aren't you happy? Do you know? Can you say with honesty to yourself that if you were to make a certain change or attain a given goal that you would be happy? Then, by all means, go for it. The cause of unhappiness may be your job, your spouse, or some factor only you know. Is it worth dying for? Few things in life are. Cutting loose from the cause of your unhappiness might be difficult in the short term, but the change is essential for long-term health.

It may well be that you're unable to identify the cause of your distress. You may answer yes to a number of the following:

- Difficulty in sleeping at night
- Little motivation to get out of bed in the morning
- Little enjoyment in life's pleasures
- Thoughts about death being an alternative
- Lack of satisfaction in vocation or avocation
- Frequent sadness, hopelessness, crying

If more than one of these phrases apply to you, I strongly urge you to seek professional counseling. Such depression classifies as a life-threatening illness and calls for more than a quick fix.

If you were to cut yourself in the kitchen and bright-red, arterial blood was spurting from the wound, you wouldn't apply a Band-Aid. It's time for stitches only a health professional can provide. If you broke your leg falling from a ladder and the bone protruded through the skin, you wouldn't ignore it. You get the point. Depression is very real and nothing to be ashamed of when revealing it to a professional healer.

Start with your own physician. You'll probably be surprised that he or she registers no shock. That's because depression is so common today and so frequently treated. The only way depression can get better is to treat it. Your doctor has a number of options at his or her disposal. One option is a referral to a psychologist for what will most likely be a remarkably short period of counseling. Happily, most insurance plans cover psychological care. Your physician may opt to prescribe one of the antidepressant drugs such as Prozac. Taken on a short-term basis, such agents have proven remarkably effective. They can lift you out of depression enough for you to recognize the potential for happiness you actually have but were blinded to by your emotional state.

Much has been written about Prozac, and there is little point in duplicating that effort. Suffice it to say that if antidepressants are used properly and with adequate guidance, those drugs can be the equivalent of a life preserver tossed to a drowning man.

Getting out of a deep rut is important. It is then necessary to take an active role in maintaining one's psychological equilibrium, which takes a certain amount of effort. View your work as your program of psychological fitness, which, just like physical fitness, you have to do by and for yourself.

WILLINGNESS TO CHANGE

Dr. Suzanna Kobasa of the University of Chicago found that the happiest, least stressed individuals are those who have the "three *C*s" in their lives: commitment, challenge, and control. Commitment might be the result of one's belief in one's work or career or devotion to one's family. Challenge provides a sense of satisfaction in seeing a job done well, whether in one's work, play, church efforts, family, or other endeavors. Finally, and possibly most importantly, control means having a reasonable degree of freedom to "do it my way."

While top executives may be perceived as having the most stress, in truth middle managers are under the greatest duress. Top executives make the decisions and see them through. Those in the middle are expected to perform tasks and to achieve levels of performance whether they agree or not with a given approach or management philosophy. They're the ones who have the heart attacks. I spoke of orchestra conductors a while back; they, too, have a remarkable degree of control, commitment, and challenge, and, not surprisingly, live long lives free of heart disease.

An underlying sense of pessimism pervades the unhappy spirit, and as one might expect, those classified as pessimistic are prone to heart disease. In fact, patients with pessimistic views regarding their recovery following heart attacks are far more likely to have a self-fulfilling prophecy. Whether one is optimistic or pessimistic plays an enormous role in all aspects of life and ultimately determines happiness or unhappiness. The salesman who continues to believe that this is the day he'll make that big sale is the one who eventually will do so. The only way to get that girl to say yes to a date is to ask her. To some optimism comes easily; for others, it has to be learned. To that end I would enthusiastically recommend another book for your reading: *Learned Optimism* by Martin Seligman, Ph.D., professor of psychology at the University of Pennsylvania. Be an optimist and believe that reading it will help change some of your attitudes!

STRESS BUSTERS (WHO YA GONNA CALL?)

Not too long ago, the connections between doing one thing and achieving another were not well understood. How could sitting quietly and attempting to think about nothing cause one to be more relaxed, at ease, and healthier? That millions of men and women from cultures all over the world had been doing meditation for centuries didn't really prove its validity.

Then scientists began to measure the changes in the body's chemistry and physiology achieved by those practiced in the skills of meditation and found reduced blood pressure and heart rate. They recorded significant changes in brain waves on sophisticated EEG (electroencephalogram) machines. They measured increased levels of calming neurotransmitter hormones in the blood, and they concluded that all these things could and would make one's risk of heart disease plummet.

For some, meditation has been a part of life as far back as they can remember. They call it prayer. Dr. Herbert Benson of Boston Deaconess Hospital wrote about meditation in his first book *The Relaxation Response* and followed that up with another titled *Beyond The Relaxation Response* when he saw the enormous power of prayer as a calming practice.

While prayer calls for one to pay active attention to the words mentally recited, meditation seeks to free the mind of all conscious thought. Some individuals are able to learn the process themselves, perhaps aided by one of the many books on the subject. Others benefit from training available in every city at YMCAs and elsewhere; yoga centers will typically have information as to where one can take lessons on meditation.

For those who prefer a high-tech approach to relaxation, biofeedback might be just the thing. Here, too, some training can facilitate the technique. Biofeedback is predicated on the individual's ability to consciously alter physiological states of the body. We all can do a bit of this without any instruction. By actively controlling one's breathing, for example, one can reduce one's pulse rate. Devices enable one to physically measure physiological changes brought about by conscious effort in much the same way that lie detectors measure galvanic skin responses.

One of the most remarkable demonstrations of how the mind and body work together involves the simple act of smiling. When you move your facial muscles into that posture known as a smile, your body releases a number of calming substances, including serotonin, and your immune system is activated to enhance good health. Conversely, when you scowl in anger, your body secretes deleterious hormones that constrict the blood vessels, raise LDL counts, increase blood pressure, and make you feel on edge and uncomfortable.

Well, that's very nice, you might say, but you don't often feel like smiling, especially when things happen that make you angry and hostile. Okay, here's the really remarkable part. Your body responds favorably when you smile even when you don't feel like it. If you're feeling angry, force yourself to smile through whatever unpleasantness you're experiencing—a traffic ticket for example—and it will be almost as though you've swallowed a Valium. Give it a try; what do you have to lose except your anger?

Want another sure-fire way to change your mood for the better? Try breathing. Sure, you breathe all the time, but this kind of breathing is deep and deliberate. It forms the basis for all relaxation techniques and may be enough in and of itself to provide the regular calming that you need.

The difference between the regular breathing we do unconsciously and deep therapeutic breathing is like the difference between getting up from the sofa to get a snack during a TV commercial and jogging. Breathing for relaxation and to calm you during tough times has marvelous restorative powers and, like smiling, results in the flow of beneficial hormones and neurotransmitters that favor heart health, including the reduction of LDL cholesterol.

Breathing for relaxation takes no special equipment, clothing, or facilities. You can and should try to do it every day, especially during tough, difficult moments. But recognize that this is a skill and, as such, requires practice to make perfect.

One man I counseled at a cardiologist's support group session in Chicago complained that he found himself under a lot of stress when driving his car. Other drivers just drove him nuts when they'd cut him off, change lanes erratically, or steal his parking space. It seemed that every time he got into his car, his level of stress skyrocketed. Deep breathing, he said, did no good.

I asked whether he ever practiced that deep breathing at times when he wasn't under stress. The answer was no. I then suggested that he do so, developing the skills that he could later use in those stressful driving times. Unlike most people, George was willing to give it a try, and a few months later he reported that deep breathing really did work.

It's really too bad, but most people really won't give relaxation techniques a legitimate trial. I'm certainly not the first person to write about the value of deep breathing, and very likely you've read about it before. But you probably have not attempted to make it part of your life. You'll convert to skim milk, avoid eggs, take antioxidants, and do all sorts of other things to control your cholesterol level and improve your heart's health, but you won't do something as simple as breathing. Kind of silly, don't you think?

Well, here's the way to do it. At least once a day, every day, set aside a few minutes to relax and do some deep breathing. Pick a spot where you can be alone, without interruption, where it's quiet and dimly lit. You can sit in a comfortable straight-backed chair or on the floor with your back against the wall and your legs crossed. Close your eyes, put your hands on your thighs, and keep your elbows close to your hips. Let your head fall slightly forward and begin to take a deep, deep breath in through your nose, such that your head rises up from your chest and you feel the air filling your lungs to their fullest capacity. Pay attention to that breath. Feel the air. Sense your rib cage expanding to accomodate all that air. Now hold your breath for a few seconds. Then slowly, slowly release it all, feeling your body literally deflating like a balloon with a slow leak. Then begin the process over. Start with two minutes and build to ten. Afterward you'll feel relaxed, even the first time, and it just keeps getting better.

While doing your deep breathing, don't think about your work, your kids, your finances, or anything else in your life. Picture an idyllic setting of your choice: a mountain glade with a stream running through it, a pristine beach with the waves gently rolling in, the woods on a crisp autumn day as the leaves turn beautiful colors of gold, red, and orange. Take yourself to that special place in your mind, all the while deeply breathing in and out.

I do not want to be redundant about this, but remember that deep breathing as a relaxation technique is a skill. Try it without any previous practice when stressed, and as George found, it won't work. But when you learn to "turn on" this special tool, it will be at your disposal not only during times of relaxation but also when stresses threaten your well-being.

MINDFULNESS

The swamis called it "walking meditation." Rather than sitting quietly and passively, as is the case for standard meditation, this is the practice of being acutely conscious while being active. An example of mindfulness is paying concentrated attention to one's breathing while briskly walking, jogging, or swimming. No longer is that activity boring. Rather, it is filled with awareness of the body's natural functions. One feels also the heart beating, far faster than when at rest, pumping blood throughout the body. Sweat begins to form on the forehead and to wet the T-shirt, and it feels good because one is aware of how the body is purifying and cooling itself. Concentrate on the miracle of walking, balancing on one foot while swinging the other leg. Appreciate your body.

I'll admit that I'm not an accomplished meditator in the classic sense. Sit for a while and do some deep breathing, sure. But to meditate is, for me, uncomfortable. For others I've spoken with, meditation is daily renewal, a part of life that is wonderful and something to look forward to. But not for me. By all means try it. It might be right for you.

For me, mindfulness or walking meditation is perfect. I become acutely aware of my body and the things around me. Out early in the morning, I pay close attention to the dew on the ground and hanging on the needles of pine trees. In the afternoon I revel in the sensation of the sun on my skin. Later in the evening, I glory in watching the sunset. Now, I don't mean just noticing those things. I mean spending a great deal of time concentrating on them—catching the glistening of that dew, studying the colors of that sunset. Whatever the time of the day, I immerse myself in the marvels of my body's functioning.

I know that, but for the grace of God and my determination to fight for my health, my heart disease might well have killed me. Just as I hated the disease as I would a most loathed enemy and destroyer, so now I love my health and well-being. I don't take that health for granted. I worked hard to attain it, and I continue to work hard to maintain it. As I walk on the beach or climb the stairs in a building instead of using the elevator or work out in the gym every morning when not traveling, I feel my health. I sense it flow through me.

Most people just don't get it. They don't realize how wonderful life and health are. They don't give their bodies a second thought. One such person was a patient of Dr. Martin Rossman in Mill Valley, California. Marty worked with her as she recovered from a heart attack at the fairly early age of fifty-six; he guided her through a process known as imagery. As time went on, Sally made a new friend: her heart.

She had really paid no attention to that magnificent organ in the past. Like millions of Americans, Sally abused her heart with a high-fat diet, cigarette smoke, and sedentary behavior. After her MI she changed those lifestyle behaviors but needed more. Dr. Rossman taught her how to have a conversation with her heart, to get to know it as a friend, to be aware of its untiring activity in her chest, providing blood as needed. Today she pictures her own heart in a very real way and thinks about it and "communicates" with it regularly when walking, working, or relaxing. I'm sure that Sally and her heart will get along beautifully for many years to come. She and her heart are healthy and happy.

WHAT'S MOST IMPORTANT?

What's the most important thing you can do to protect your heart against disease? Lowering cholesterol levels? Losing weight? Controlling blood pressure? Quitting smoking? Exercising regularly? Certainly those are all major components in this or any program of heart health. But, in a very real way, this chapter may be the most important chapter in this entire book. I truly believe that to have a healthy heart you must have a happy heart.

How can anyone be expected to follow a low-fat diet or quit smoking or choose exercise over an extra thirty minutes in bed when that person is unhappy? Why bother to save a life that isn't worth living? When one is depressed or angry, that bacon, double-cheese, monster burger washed down by an extra-rich chocolate milk shake and accompanied by a mountain of fries can be one of life's small consolation prizes. Give such food up? Hell no, make that with double the special sauce! Only when one reaches some state of happiness can one expect to go on to that next plateau of seeking improved health.

Think about it. Stress, anger, unhappiness, whatever you want to call it, not only sets the stage for heart disease by raising blood pressure and cholesterol, bringing on spasms of the arteries, and all those terrible things, but also may be the precipitating factor for a heart attack. I know that was the case for my father, my brother, countless people I have spoken with, and myself. Emotional distress is a major risk factor. But, unlike those other risk factors, there is no pleasure in stress, anger, or hostility. You may enjoy that cheeseburger or cigarette, but there's no joy in being unhappy.

Like all risk factors, however, this one can be modified. Maybe the solution for you will be as simple as doing some deep breathing. Maybe you need something more, such as biofeedback. Or perhaps you'll require professional assistance in counseling or medication. Truly that's no different than how one person can lower his cholesterol with just a few dietary changes while another might need a dose of niacin or even prescription medications to control hers. The important thing is to get the job done.

You and your heart will be happy that you did!

· 12 ·

The Ultimate Solutions for Weight Control

Read the title of this chapter carefully. It says solutions, not solution. Weight loss and weight control are highly complex physiological and psychological matters, which are not served by a one-size-fits-all approach. While everyone who has weight to lose has much in common with others, differences must be considered. We'll look at those commonalities and special needs in this chapter.

Overweight poses problems of epidemic proportions in the United States. A study published in the *Journal of the American Medical Association* in 1994 revealed that one-third of all U.S. adults are considered overweight, weighing between twenty and twenty-four pounds or more than they should. That's not just a cosmetic concern.

Obesity, weighing 20 percent or more over what you should, is a health hazard. Losing weight lowers blood pressure, often to a degree that makes taking hypertension drugs no longer necessary. Attaining a healthy weight can virtually eliminate the symptoms of non-insulin-dependent Type II diabetes. When weight comes down, so do cholesterol counts. Conversely, keeping those pounds on threatens one's life by way of high blood pressure, diabetes, and cholesterol elevations.

And women, especially, may suffer even more. Looking at the data from the Nurses' Health Study in Boston, Dr. JoAnn Manson found that those who gain even a modest amount of weight over the years have an increased risk of heart disease as compared with those who keep their weight steady. The Harvard study, published in 1995, tracked the health of 115,818 RNs since 1976. At that time, the women were asked how much weight they had gained since they were eighteen.

In the years between 1976 and 1995, those gaining 11 to 17 pounds had a 25 percent higher risk of heart disease. Women who put on 17 to 24 pounds increased their risk by 64 percent, and the nurses who had gained more than 44 pounds tripled their risk.

IDEAL WEIGHT VERSUS HEALTHY WEIGHT

Which weight tables are most appropriate? You know the ones: a range of so many pounds for varying height for men and women, sometimes also considering body-stature type. In my opinion—and that of many weight experts—those tables are worthless.

The ranges stated are so wide that they have no meaning. The proportion of lean muscle tissue and fat is not considered and special medical conditions are not taken into consideration. Let's shoot, instead, for a healthy weight.

For example, as little as a 5 percent reduction in weight can reduce blood pressure significantly. But diabetic patients in that condition might have to achieve a 15 percent weight reduction to see an improvement.

It's rather unrealistic to shoot for an "ideal" weight that one never attained even twenty or thirty years ago. A healthier approach would be to aim for what you weighed at, say, age eighteen or before you started to gain. If you think back, that was probably when you felt best as well. Did you weigh 130 pounds then? If not, don't try to achieve an "ideal" weight of 130 pounds now.

Don't give in to popular old-wives' tales. There is no physiological reason to weigh more after you've had children. If you were a football player in college, don't believe that muscle turns to fat.

But weight alone tells only part of the story. Yes, as we age, there is a tendency to gain weight, but aging is no excuse. What really happens is that, for most of us, the proportion of muscle and fat tissue changes owing to an increasingly sedentary lifestyle. In fact, even those who weigh exactly what they did in college are likely to be "overfat" if not overweight.

Science has an explanation. Only muscle tissue is capable of burning calories for energy. The larger the proportion of lean muscle tissue, the more calories one can consume without gaining weight. That's one reason most men can eat more than most women of the same age and circumstances. As physical activity lessens, muscle tissue diminishes. It's the old "use it or lose it" adage. With less muscle to burn calories, even the same diet will eventually lead to weight gain.

The process is insidious, going entirely unnoticed perhaps for years. Gradually the lost muscle is replaced by fat. At first there is no weight gain, as the exchange is pound-for-pound. Slowly the body, with far less muscle tissue acting as the calorie-burning engine, is no longer able to use incoming food as energy and deposits it as fat. One can honestly say that "I eat no more today than I did before, but I keep putting on weight."

Does everyone go through this unpleasant process? No. Some avoid it partially or entirely by maintaining a lifestyle that includes regular physical activity to maintain and perhaps even increase their body's muscle tissue. More about that later.

The first thing to do is to set a reasonable goal for your healthy weight. Fitting into a dress size you were never able to wear before is not reasonable. Getting back down to your early adult weight when you were feeling healthy, energetic, and terrific is.

Expect success. Don't let those scary headlines about 90 percent failure rates concern you. First, those numbers come from the totality of commercial weight-loss industries that are often more geared to profit than health. Second, science and medicine have more answers today that can help ensure your success. Third, even a 90 percent failure rate means a 10 percent success rate. There's no reason why you shouldn't be the one to succeed.

DEAR DIARY

What did you eat yesterday? How about last week? Most people can't come even close to remembering accurately. A 1994 study demonstrated that dieters unable to lose weight on a 1,500-calorie diet underestimated their caloric intake by 500 calories per day as well as their exercise output by about 1,000 calories per day.

They weren't deliberately lying. It's just difficult to remember accurately things we don't pay much attention to.

Many overweight men and women truly believe they eat "like a bird." Well, that's probably accurate, since birds may not eat all that much at one sitting, but they tend to eat almost continuously. So how much do you really eat? And even more importantly, what do you really eat? Probably you don't know the answers to those questions with any accuracy or precision.

As a very useful first step, then, start keeping a food diary. Record everything you put into your mouth—everything you eat or drink—including water. Do that for a couple of weeks, and you'll probably amaze yourself. You needn't share your journal with anyone else. It's not meant to embarrass you but, rather, to start an education process.

It doesn't matter whether your target healthy weight calls for losing ten pounds or one hundred. You need to know your starting point accurately. Scientists call that the "baseline." Then looking at your own records you'll be able to make some judgments about the necessary changes.

Virtually every weight-loss expert I've talked with over the years agrees with this approach, yet most shake their heads when thinking about how few people follow it. Maybe people think it's too much trouble. Perhaps they don't want to admit their own behaviors, even to themselves. But if you can overcome your reasons for resistance, the food diary can mean the difference between success and failure.

It doesn't have to be anything fancy. My preference is a small, spiral-bound notebook you can keep in your purse or pocket along with a pencil or pen. Be as detailed as you possibly can be. Remember that this is science, and you don't want sloppy data. If you've marked down "a handful of mixed nuts," take another handful and count those nuts. But don't eat that second handful. Don't let alcohol blur your perceptions: was it really two drinks, or more like three or four? Remember, no one will see this diary but you. Don't cheat yourself.

SNACKING: THE AMERICAN OBSESSION

No one in the world snacks like we do in America. One of the reasons for the early economic woes of EuroDisney was the poor sales of snacks as compared with those at the Florida or California parks. I won't point any fingers, but think about your own habits and look at your food diary.

Probably the worst part of the American snacking obsession isn't so much the habit itself as much as what we snack on. Most people don't reach for an apple or a bunch of grapes or a breadstick or a carrot. Chips, cookies, candies, cakes, and pies are the snacks of choice. Calories pile up fast.

Frequently an overweight individual skips breakfast, has a tiny lunch, then a horrible, enormous dinner. Worse, eating continues through the entire evening, often a response to stress. Compare that eating style with what most authorities, including UCLA's Dr. Heber, consider to be the most healthful approach: several small meals throughout the day. While four to six or seven meals daily may make sense theoretically, most Americans wouldn't find that practical.

But it is possible, and even practical, to hit a healthy compromise. Start with a good breakfast of your choice. Have a lunch that you've planned in advance. See chapters 23 and 24 for some suggestions. Then don't allow a long time to pass before your next food intake.

If you're ravenous when you sit down to dinner, you'll eat beyond your needs, before the body's blood glucose "fuel gauge" has a chance to kick in. Here's when snacking can be healthful and actually part of a weight-loss plan.

Have something to eat at least an hour before dinner. A classic study at Michigan State University by Dr. Olaf Mickleson showed that people lost weight by regularly eating two slices of bread before meals. They effectively killed their appetites, as the bread resulted in a rise of blood sugar signaling satiety to the brain. When the bread eaters sat down to the evening meal, they just weren't as hungry and they ate less. Other experts update that approach by suggesting a piece of fruit in addition to the bread, since most of us do not get the daily five servings of fruits and vegetables.

But what about the evening snacking? Probably if you eat less for dinner, and do so less ravenously, you'll lessen your compulsive snacking afterward. First, you won't set up a release of huge amounts of insulin, which require carbohydrates to balance off. Second, you won't have set up the "feeding frenzy" that lasts from dinner to bedtime.

With today's frenetic schedules, seven hours might pass between lunch and dinner. If that's the case for you, consider two snacks during that time. In a very real sense you're now up to five meals daily. Next, put off having that dessert at the dinner table. Instead, save it for later as a snack. You just hit meal number six.

But what about classic American snacking? Many dietitians recommend replacing the chips with sliced fruits and the mixed nuts with carrot sticks. Some people can actually pull that off. Not many, but some. If you're one of them, terrific.

If not, you might consider swearing off snacking entirely. View snacks, even the nonfat versions, in the same way that smokers trying to quit view cigarettes. It's almost impossible to "cut back" rather than going "cold turkey." Find something else to occupy yourself at the times you normally snack. Take a walk. Read a book. Go to a lecture—do anything, go any place, where you're not likely to tear open a bag of corn puffs or a Butterfinger.

Snacking is a habit. You can break that habit.

BEHAVIORAL MODIFICATIONS

Weight-loss techniques have, like most things, changed over the years. Some things are fads and deserve to be forgotten. Others are relegated to lesser importance. That's the case with the approach called "behavioral modification" that was so popular in the 1970s.

The prevailing theory back then was that our eating habits were largely responsible for weight gain. Eating too fast resulted in eating too much, so put your fork down between bites. Chew your foods so many times before swallowing. Never eat in front of the television. Use smaller plates. Make food more attractive and savor every bite. The advice went on and on. Valid? Such techniques might be helpful to some people, but they don't really get at the underlying problems, both physiological and psychological.

On the other hand, those little tricks can be a useful adjunct to a complete program of limiting calories and increasing exercise as we'll discuss in detail in the balance of this chapter. There's no doubt that if you snack when watching TV, breaking that habit will help.

SUPPORT GROUPS AND COMMERCIAL CENTERS

Are you the kind of very open person who might actually enjoy talking about yourself in front of a group of people? Then "confessing" on a regular basis at Overeaters Anonymous might be useful. If you're a private person, and sort of shy, this is not the way to go.

Support groups can be the secret ingredient in success, or they can actually undermine your efforts and lead to failure. Before making a commitment of any kind, take the time to check out the group thoroughly. Only you can make the final decision. Realize that groups differ significantly, and while one may turn you off, another might offer the assistance you need.

As a general rule, women do better with support groups than do men. That's also true for cigarette-cessation programs. But that doesn't mean that all women will benefit or that no men will.

Weight loss has become a multibillion-dollar industry. While commercial weight loss centers aren't as popular as they were in the 1980s, they remain an option to consider.

Quality of service varies considerably from one company to another. Investigate thoroughly just what you're getting for your money. Get it all in writing. If the company relies on prepackaged foods, calculate the realistic cost over the expected weight-loss period. Learn about the counselors. Some companies offer the services of registered nurses and nutritionists, while others hire previous customers. Talk with someone who has gone to the center you're considering.

Do such centers work? Typically one can expect to lose weight as promised, by following the program faithfully. The problem lies in maintenance of that weight loss. Long-term results are less than wonderful. Still, for some individuals the commercial weight-loss centers can provide a jump start to a successful effort.

How would you like to find a weight-loss center that provides a physician specially trained in obesity management, nutritionists and dietitians who can tailor a diet to your personal needs, psychologists and counselors to help you with emotional hurdles, exercise physiologists to function as personal trainers, and even researchers who can potentially apply cutting-edge technology that won't be available to the public for years? Sound too good to be true? You can find such centers in virtually every major metropolitan region of the United States. They're found in major academic centers such as Harvard in Boston; Columbia/St. Lukes in New York City; UCLA in Los Angeles; Mayo Clinic in Rochester, Minnesota, and satellite centers elsewhere in the country; Baylor University in Texas; the University of Chicago as well as Northwestern University and others in that city; and virtually everywhere there is a medical school. Most people don't realize these are open and available to the public. And you'll get the very best care possible. Just call the nearest center and ask for information about weight-loss programs.

THE ESSENTIAL COMPONENT FOR SUCCESS

Suppose I told you that a "secret, magic component" of a weight-loss program could (1) help your body burn more calories and do so more efficiently; (2) help end the vicious cycle of insulin resistance; (3) release stored fat to be burned; (4) help you sleep better, perform better at work, and put you in a better mood; (5) build self-esteem; (6) improve your figure as well as decrease your clothing size; (7) lose weight consistently, helping to avoid plateaus; and (8) provide the best known insurance against gaining weight back. Oh, and as fringe benefits that magic component will help protect you from a number of degenerative diseases and contribute to a longer, healthier, happier life. Sound like snake oil?

There's nothing magic about that component. It belongs in everyone's life, whether trying to lose weight or not. It's physical activity, otherwise known as exercise. Now, before you turn the page and refuse to read any more about this magic ingredient, give me a chance, please. Just read the facts and make your own decision.

FACT: The only tissue in your body capable of burning calories is lean muscle. The more you have, the more calories you can burn. One of my wife Dawn's good friends is younger and taller than she is. Yet Dawn can eat more food and has an easier time controlling her weight. Her friend gets frustrated because every bite puts on another pound. Simply enough, Dawn is in better physical condition, has a better percentage of lean to fat tissue, and exercises regularly.

As one starts an exercise program, the percentage of fat drops while that of lean tissue increases. There may not be any weight loss at first, but clothing sizes drop and the body looks better. As the amount of muscle increases, the number of calories regularly burned grows, since the new muscle tissue needs additional energy.

Ironically, even when one loses weight by simply cutting calories, the body is incapable of burning calories any better than it did previously. With extreme regimens such as the OptiFast program used by Oprah Winfrey, significant amounts of lean muscle tissue are lost along with the fat. Thus the person is actually less capable of burning calories than before starting to diet. That was Oprah's problem. Sure, she was wearing those Calvins and smiling, but she had the deck stacked against her. Even small amounts of food inevitably would bring the weight back. And it did, in front of millions of her fans.

Today Oprah maintains the weight loss she achieved by using the identical combination of components I'm proposing to you: cutting back on fats and sugars and increasing exercise.

FACT: Any and all exercise counts. The "no pain, no gain" philosophy of the 1980s is totally out of date. Today we know that it's a matter of staying active on a daily basis. For more on this, see chapter 10.

FACT: Sign up a friend to make the commitment to exercise with you, and you're more likely to succeed. You encourage her; she'll encourage you. It's tough to decide not to take that walk or jog when someone's waiting for you to join her, and you've made that commitment to her.

FACT: Do something you enjoy, and you'll stick with it. If you hate sitting on the stationary bike peddling to nowhere, don't even bother. I like to use a treadmill, stair climber, or other equipment while listening to the morning news at a gym. Dawn hates exercising in the morning, and she hates those machines. So she takes all sorts of classes in the afternoon after work.

FACT: It's best to do a variety of activities. Swim one day, walk another, go bicycling the third, and so on. You will work more different muscles, and you'll be less likely to get bored. Skip rope. Play with a hula hoop. Go dancing.

FACT: We all get less and less flexible as we age, and that leads to disabilities. Part of an exercise program should include stretching of all sorts. I strongly advocate yoga. Look for a tape in your video store to buy or rent or attend a class at a YMCA or local gym.

FACT: Muscle grows when it's used and atrophies when it's not. Since we want to build as much muscle as we can, seriously consider a program of strength training. As a side note, it's never too late to start. Remember that a group of retirement home residents in their nineties were started on Nautilus-type equipment. At the beginning of the program sponsored by Tufts University in cooperation with the National Institutes of Health, the men and women were truly frail, unable to get out of chairs without assistance. At the end of just six weeks, they were rejuvenated beyond their wildest dreams.

FACT: Keep a little log to record your progress. Note the day and date, what you did, how you felt, and so forth. You'll be amazed at how much you've improved when you look back at those early entries after a few weeks.

FACT: You'll do better if you set certain goals and promise yourself a reward. "If I stick with my program for two weeks in a row, I'll get a manicure." "At the end of the first month, I'll buy that book I've been wanting to read."

FACT: Within a few weeks, you'll start feeling better, sleeping better, working more productively, and noting improvement in just about every aspect of your life. After ninety days, only three months, your activity program will become so much a part of your lifestyle that you won't want to give it up. It's just as easy to form good habits as bad.

Think of yourself as a physical person. Walk the stairs instead of taking the elevator. Choose the parking place farthest from the store. Breathe deeply, thinking about your breaths as you exercise rather than taking them for granted. Walk with purpose.

Is Fast or Slow Exercise Best for Weight Loss?

Many magazines have featured articles claiming superiority of slow-paced exercise for weight control. The idea has been that such workouts, including walking rather than jogging, burn fat, while more strenuous activities expend carbohydrates. But it's not quite that simple.

Recent research has shown that slow-paced exercise has to be maintained for long periods of time to be effective. Yes, walking four or five or more miles burns fat somewhat better than does jogging that same distance, but the problem for most people is time. The faster one goes, the quicker the workout is over, and the energy expenditure is the same for covering that distance whether by walking, brisk walking, jogging, or running.

Second, research at Georgia State University demonstrated that the kind of calories you burn during a workout isn't as important as the fact that you've used up those calories and have created a caloric deficit. Your body makes up that deficit later, and according to physiologist Jeffrey Rupp, it does so by taking fat from your stomach and hips.

In the Georgia research study, a group of overweight women walked on a treadmill. Some burned three hundred calories by walking slowly, while others used up the same energy at a brisker pace. They "walked" four times a week for three months. Both groups lost 3 percent of their body fat. Dr. Rupp came to the same conclusion: If time is a consideration, get the exercise done as quickly as you can. When you have some leisure time, say on a weekend, take a nice lengthy, leisurely hike or bike ride.

Picture yourself as you want to be, as you know you can be. Close your eyes and call up that positive image frequently. Soon it will be a reality.

LIFESTYLE, NOT DIET

Weight control doesn't have to involve elaborate trendy fads or even major changes in the way you eat. I harken back to thoughts of realistic expectations of a healthy weight. Whatever you do has to be realistic enough to expect to do it for the rest of your life; otherwise, don't bother. If you diet by switching from beef to tofu—and you happen to hate tofu—it won't be long before you go back to your old habits. Going on a diet almost by definition means that you will go off that diet.

Most authorities agree that the two nutrition components to cut back on for weight control are fat and simple sugars. Those two represent concentrated sources of calories and can easily be replaced by complex carbohydrates and protein.

Simple sugars may not be a problem for most people, as I explain in detail on page 200. But they're on the taboo list for those wanting to lose weight for two reasons. First, simple sugars supply calories without nutrients. Second, they invoke a release of insulin into the bloodstream, which actually creates cravings for more sugar; leads to retention of salt and fluid; raises triglyceride levels in the blood; and has a negative impact on well-being, mood, and sleep. Especially during the early stages of weight loss and at least until one is well into a maintenance phase of control, it's best to avoid sugar as much as possible.

For someone with just a bit of weight to lose, cutting back on calories in general, and on fat and sugar in particular, will achieve weight loss. For those with a significant amount of weight to lose, sugar can be particularly insidious. It involves a condition known as insulin resistance, an area of expertise of Dr. Calvin Ezrin, an internationally renowned endocrinologist at UCLA.

For insulin-resistant individuals, typically weighing at least 20 percent more than their healthy weights, the hormone insulin no longer efficiently disposes of blood sugar (glucose) by either supplying immediate energy needs or storing it for later use. Therefore, instead of falling in response to insulin, blood sugar levels rise and the pancreas secrete more insulin in a further effort to metabolize the glucose. The resulting increased level of insulin in the blood has several negative consequences.

High levels of insulin interfere with sodium and water metabolism. Tissues retain sodium, which, in turn, retains water. Much of the excessive weight in such individuals is, indeed, caused by water buildup. Sugar levels start to rise in the blood, often signaling a sort of prediabetic condition. Many such persons go on to develop frank diabetes.

Many obese patients have compelling carbohydrate cravings that have been linked with a deficiency in serotonin. The resulting state of anxiety, mood swings, depression, and sleep disturbances make weight control even more difficult and prevent proper exercise.

Desperate for serotonin, the brain resorts to manufacturing more by a complex insulin-mediated disposal of amino acids out of the bloodstream that spares tryptophan, the building block of serotonin. The amino acid shift that promotes the easy entry of tryptophan into the brain is brought about by insulin. This temporary increase in serotonin accounts for much of the "comfort" that these patients feel after glutting on carbohydrates. However, the comfort is short-lived and the prolonged fat-building, salt-retaining, and appetite-stimulating adverse effects of insulin remain to compound the initial obesity.

If that sounds like a terrible, vicious cycle, it is. It helps to explain why greatly overweight persons have such a difficult time in losing weight. It also provides an understanding of why those men and women are often in a poor mental state. Tragically, they turn to the very things that caused the problems to begin with: fat and sugar.

And there's more. Triglyceride and cholesterol levels rise. Blood pressure increases significantly. The risk of heart disease multiplies geometrically.

Virtually eliminating the simple sugars and relying on protein and complex carbohydrates while increasing physical activity a little at a time can bring insulin resistance under control and lead to very satisfying weight loss. If this description fits you, a physician's care will help. To find the right doctor, call one of the organizations mentioned on page 176.

The paradox of the 1990s has been how so many people have switched to nonfat foods in the hopes of weight control as well as cholesterol lowering only to find that they actually gain weight. Most of those products replace fats with sugars, and the result is a calorie count as high as the original. All things considered, that's not bad, and certainly might help if cholesterol management were the only consideration. Moreover, the idea should be to replace one serving of a high-fat food with one serving of the nonfat counterpart. But, too often, that's not what happens. The nonfat label seems to give people the green flag to eat all they want, and their calorie intake goes beyond what it was before.

Cut fat, cut calories, lose weight. It really is that simple. One gram of carbohydrate contains four calories. The same for protein. But that gram of fat socks you with at least nine, and most nutrition researchers now believe eleven, calories. For the record, a gram of alcohol provides seven calories. In practical terms, a twelve-ounce can of beer has about 150 calories; a seven-ounce glass of wine 140 calories; and a 1.5-ounce shot of 80-proof spirits has about 100 calories. But while those seem like large amounts, they pale in comparison with fatty foods.

Cut back on fat without replacing those lost calories with sugars, and you'll lose weight. How can one do that painlessly? Certainly I've spelled out the details of how one can eat virtually everything one wants without paying the "fat-tax" throughout this book: snacks, breakfast, lunch, dinner, and even meals in restaurants. Let's look at some specific examples of just how this works to facilitate weight loss.

Start with some ground beef for whatever dish you'd like to prepare. USDA standard ground beef is 30 percent fat, yielding 270 calories just from the fat. Use my method of trimming off the fat from a piece of round steak prior to grinding, and you get just 5 percent fat with only 45 calories from the fat. That's a savings of 225 calories in only one 3½-ounce serving.

Prefer a steak? A 6-ounce cut of choice filet mignon has nineteen grams of fat, yielding 171 fat calories. The same size portion of filet mignon from Meucci Beef (see page 239) has only four grams of fat, yielding 36 calories. You save 135 calories.

You never outgrow your need for milk, but you don't need the fat. An eight-ounce glass of whole milk has eight grams of fat and 150 calories; cut back to 2 percent low-fat milk and you're down to five grams of fat and 121 calories. The next step is to 1 percent low-fat milk, and the fat-gram count is two with a calorie count of 100; graduate to skim (nonfat) milk, and you'll get less than a gram of fat and just 90 calories. Calculate your savings each step of the way.

Next we go to cheddar cheese. A one-ounce slice of the full-fat variety provides nine grams of fat and 60 to 70 calories. Opt for Borden's Lite slices with one gram of fat each, and you'll save 30 to 40 calories. Prefer the richness of Kraft Healthy Favorites cheddar? It has four grams of fat and 70 calories, with a savings of 30 calories per ounce.

Margarine for your toast? One tablespoon of I Can't Believe It's Not Butter yields ten grams of fat and 90 calories. Pick up the Lite version instead, and you're down to seven grams and 60 calories, a savings of 30 calories. And when it's time to sauté some onions, do it with butter flavor Pam and you'll get rid of practically all the fat and calories. Use the I Can't Believe It's Not Butter spray to "lubricate" an ear of corn and zap all but a fraction of a gram of fat and a smattering of calories.

Beliefs and philosophies regarding weight loss come and go, but certain facts are immutable. The most principal of these is that 3,500 calories equals one pound of fat. Cut that amount of calories and lose one pound of fat; add an additional 3,500 calories and gain a pound of fat.

To make a point, let me jump back to simple sugars for just a moment. Dawn's late father Ben decided that he needed to lose about ten pounds. At that time he was in his early seventies. The way he'd do it, he told the family, was to quit using sugar in his coffee. Everyone laughed. How could such a little thing make a difference? But Ben was resolute and stopped putting those two teaspoons of sugar into his five daily cups of coffee.

Now for a little mathematics. At 16 calories per teaspoonful, multiplied by ten teaspoons per day, that sugar came out to 160 calories daily. By eliminating it, Ben cut out 3,500 calories every twenty-two days. So every twenty-two days Ben lost a pound. In less than eight months, he'd lost his extra ten pounds just as he planned.

As we saw with the examples I used, cutting back on fat can produce even more dramatic caloric deficits. Just by choosing foods with little or no fat and getting some regular exercise, one can gradually attain the target healthy weight.

FEED THE BODY YOU WANT

On page 44 I go into some detail as to how to calculate the grams of fat to allot yourself in order to bring the calories from fat in your diet down to 20 percent. And I provide some examples of fat allotments for men and women with varying levels of activity and healthy weights.

Now let me introduce a concept that I've found very helpful for people when I've done presentations throughout the country. If you don't like the body you have, feed only the body you want and the rest will eventually go away. You'll starve those extra, unwanted pounds right out of existence.

Take a look at that table on page _____. Find the healthy weight you'd like to achieve. Note the fat-gram allotment for that person at that level of physical activity. That's the allotment to gradually attain the body with the healthy weight you want. Sounds simple, doesn't it? But it's true, and it works beautifully.

A woman in Topeka, Kansas, wrote to tell me her story. She had gradually seen her weight go from 125 pounds when she was married to 140 pounds after children. After hearing me speak, Mary decided to feed only the 125 pounds she felt healthy with ten years ago.

Moderately active, Mary determined that she needed fourteen calories to maintain each pound of healthy weight. That meant 1,750 calories daily. Wanting to follow my 20 percent of calories-as-fat approach, she calculated that 350 calories would come from about forty grams of fat. She avoided simple sugars of all kinds. Otherwise, Mary ate what she wanted. And every two to three weeks, she'd look at the scales and see that she'd lost a pound. Within months, Mary arrived at her target healthy weight, and she said, "I never felt like I was on a diet, and I never expect to gain those pounds back again."

Other readers have reported, more typically, that they followed the program in my original book to lower their unhealthful levels of cholesterol and found, much to their delight, that weight came off without even trying.

But today it's a lot easier to lose weight than it was back in 1987 when *The 8-Week Cholesterol Cure* was first published. First, there are so many more foods available to all of us that are reduced in fat and calories. Using those foods as ingredients in the recipes we enjoy as our personal favorites, we will automatically slice off calories and lose weight. Every dish you love can be a "diet" food!

Second, thanks to SeQuester, one can literally reduce the fat in the foods one eats. See chapter 7 for details. In terms of weight control, this product can make a lot of difference. Each tablet prevents the absorption of about six grams of fat. That's 45 to 66 calories, depending on whether one counts fat as 9 or 11 calories per gram. Round it off to 50 calories saved per tablet consumed with meals. It just keeps adding up.

Moreover, research with the product at UCLA indicates that there may be something more involved in weight loss than just prevention of fat absorption. SeQuester appears to somehow curb the appetite as well.

After I reported the product in my *Diet-Heart Newsletter* (see page 184), I started getting wonderful letters full of success stories. Readers told me how their cholesterol levels fell and how they lost weight as well. A health professional in Hawaii wrote that she took one tablet a day for one month and lost four pounds while reducing her cholesterol level from 220 to 206. She was adamant that she did not diet, did not change her eating patterns, but still lost that weight.

SeQuester is not a panacea. It should not replace good eating habits. It would be absurd and unhealthful to swallow handfuls of tablets in an effort to block the fat from high-fat foods at every meal. But as part of a total program, or to allow a special treat or a night out on the town now and then, SeQuester can be very helpful.

A FASTING WAY TO WEIGHT CONTROL

Controlling weight is a matter of controlling calories. No one meal causes a person to become overweight, and no one day's calorie counting will allow you to lose that weight. Weight control is a matter of balance, calories, and exercise over a period of time. Think of your weight as a sort of bottom line on your body's accounting ledger sheet at the end of a month. Everything you did during that month tallies up to the total registered on the bathroom scales.

Just as that special treat or that restaurant meal is merely part of the whole caloric intake, accounted for on one side of the ledger, picking a day a week to fast can make up for those indulgences on the other side of the accounting book.

No, there's nothing unhealthy about fasting now and then, as long as you remember to drink plenty of fluids. That means at least eight eight-ounce glasses of fluid during the day, mostly as water. Flavor that water with a twist of lemon or a squeeze of lime. Keep a jug handy.

Juices can replace part of the water, but remember that all juices have calories. Here's a breakdown for eight-ounce glasses of some fruit and vegetable juices:

Apple juice	120
Carrot juice	70
Cranberry cocktail	140
Grapefruit juice	100
Orange juice	110
Tomato juice	50
V-8 juice	50

As you can see, those calories could add up mighty fast during your fast. You might want to limit yourself to a glass of fruit juice in the morning and one of vegetable juice in the evening, and lots and lots of water in between. You can also enjoy artificially sweetened soft drinks or iced tea in moderation.

I've suggested this approach for many years. Some find a day of fast to be absolutely liberating, a day not to worry about meal planning. One woman told me she used the time saved in food preparation and eating to do extra-long walks on her fast day. A day of zero calorie intake really affects the week's total, but it's not for everyone. Some find themselves hungry and thinking about food all the time. Certainly that's not healthy. The last thing an overweight person needs is to obsess about food! Will it work for you? You won't know until you try it. You might even want to designate two days a week, say, Tuesdays and Thursdays, as your fast days.

If a complete fast is just too much to undertake, consider a day or two of extremely limited calorie intake. It's really true that Tommy Lasorda of the Los Angeles Dodgers lost weight with SlimFast shakes replacing meals. We talked about it in the dugout when I was working with the Dodgers in a program to improve school lunch programs in California. Any of the commercially available diet shakes will do.

Meal Replacement Can Be Effective in Weight Loss

No question but that the various meal replacements work. The most common approach is to replace breakfast and lunch with shakes and have a "sensible dinner." That's sort of backward if you think about it. Most people don't "pig out" at breakfast or lunch, and one can come up with any number of low-calorie options for those meals. It's at dinner that most of us pile it on and on and on. So why not eat sensible breakfasts and lunches and replace some of the week's dinners with those shakes? Again, you may find this liberating in terms of the time saved, especially if you don't have to prepare dinner for others. Instead of eating, go shopping, or to a movie or the museum.

The reason the meal replacement programs don't have a good long-term record comes down to the reality of eventually going back to one's old eating habits. However, the approach can work if you use it as a crutch to lose weight while learning to control calories by limiting fat as shown elsewhere in this book. Moreover, there is no reason why your long-term maintenance program shouldn't include a meal replacement here and a day of fasting there.

Weighing in your success on the bathroom scales should be triumphant. But don't expect overnight results. It took you years to gain that weight, and it'll take some time for you to lose it. In fact, surveys show that weight lost slowly is most likely to remain off. So stay away from those scales for at least a week, and don't weigh yourself more than twice a week thereafter. After the weight is gone, use the scales as your barometer for your maintenance program. If you see a pound or two of gain, that's the time to get rid of it, when it's still easy to do.

THOSE BEST-SELLING DIET BOOKS

Dozens of books have hit the best-seller lists by promising to be the ultimate word on permanent weight loss. Yet one needs only to look around to see that, as a nation, we've grown heavier and heavier since the 1960s. Today one out of three adults is overweight. So what's wrong with those books?

Eat More, Weigh Less sounds like a wonderful promise, and it is as long as what you want to eat is mounds of vegetables. It's true that nobody ever got obese from eating too much steamed broccoli. It's a rare individual who will be willing to change his or her entire life to accommodate the ultra-low-fat, mostly vegetarian diet advanced in this book. The editors at *Glamour* magazine challenged themselves to follow the program, and they confessed in print that, as healthy as the diet sounds on paper, they just couldn't do it for any length of time in real life.

Fit For Life continues to sell well in paperback, with millions of copies in print. The Diamonds, too, advocate a vegetarian diet; theirs allows no animal products at all. They give their program a twist by proposing that certain foods should not be eaten in combination with other foods, lest they not be digested properly. Nonsense and nonscience. That theory was first proposed in the 1920s and has been completely debunked.

Dr. Atkins' Diet Revolution lets you eat all the fatty foods you want, just as long as you eat no carbohydrates. This results in an unhealthful state of severe ketosis, which is measured by diabetes urine-testing strips. Ketosis results from the formation of ketones, improperly metabolized sugars, in the blood and urine. Ketosis is a symptom of diabetes and starvation. A mild state of ketosis, as occurs when following a diet that emphasizes protein and limits carbohydrates, isn't necessarily a bad thing, but severe ketosis is unhealthy. In addition, the high-fat diet advocated by Dr. Atkins significantly elevates cholesterol levels in the blood. His program has been severely criticized by virtually every nutrition authority. The worst part of the Atkins diet is that once you stop the diet, the weight comes back with a vengeance.

Are any good weight-loss books available? Dr. Katahn's *T-Factor Diet* and Covert Bailey's *Fit or Fat* books are both based on a sensible, scientifically sound approach of limiting fat and increasing exercise. Both are well written and well documented. I highly recommend them, especially for those with a moderate amount of weight loss to achieve.

If you have a significant overweight problem of fifty or more pounds, and especially if you suffer from Type II diabetes, the book to read is *The Type II Diabetes Diet Book: The Insulin Control Diet* by Dr. Calvin Ezrin and myself, published by Lowell House. There's even a chapter to share with your doctor, informing him or her about the concepts of this program, which is designed to deal with the problem of insulin resistance.

ONE PILL MAKES YOU LARGER, ONE PILL MAKES YOU SMALL

Jefferson Airplane's homage to Alice in Wonderland, "White Rabbit," captures the essence of the hope for a magic pill. While no such miracle exists, there are chemical crutches that can help.

Doctors no longer prescribe amphetamines the way they did in the 1960s and 1970s. Those drugs are far too addictive and, in the long run, weren't very effective. A chemical with a similar mechanism of action can be found in any drugstore. Phenylpropanolamine (PPA) is the active ingredient in dozens of weight-loss nostrums that one can buy without a prescription. It works like a mild form of the amphetamines of old, depressing appetite by revving up your metabolism. Unfortunately, PPA's effectiveness, like that of amphetamines, lasts only two to three weeks. After that time the body adapts, and appetite returns to normal. PPA also has the adverse reaction of jangled nerves akin to the effect of drinking too much strong coffee.

Newer weight-control drugs are far more effective than PPA. Fenformin and fenfluramine came off patent in 1995, and thus less expensive generic versions are now available. When used properly under medical supervision both can be useful adjuncts to other weight-loss efforts. The combination of both, termed "fen-fen therapy," has produced dramatic responses. Other drugs are in final stages of testing and will be available through a physician.

Every magazine and newspaper carried the news in 1995 that genetically obese mice given an engineered hormonal protein termed leptin lost weight dramatically. Within weeks of getting leptin, the obese rodents shed half their weight and soon resembled their slender counterparts. Even slender animals lost weight when given the protein. Clinical trials are scheduled for 1996, but it will be years before a drug will come to market.

For those who have tried every other approach and failed, the last resort for weight loss can be gastric surgery. Doctors reserve this drastic measure for when no other hope remains.

At one end of the spectrum, 5 percent of men and 10 percent of women have a genetic predisposition to obesity. For them, the effort to attain and maintain a healthy weight is an exceptionally difficult and life-long battle. Genetically obese individuals never feel satisfied from food and continue to crave food beyond all reasonable needs of the body. At the other end of the spectrum are those who merely would like to lose five or ten pounds for cosmetic reasons (although science has shown that even slight weight gain is unhealthful). In the middle of the spectrum are millions of individuals who are clinically overweight, that is, 20 percent or more over their healthy weights.

No matter where one fits into that spectrum, however, everyone must ultimately take in fewer calories and expend more energy in exercise. Granted, that's easier for some than for others, and for those who have tried and failed again and again, assistance is available.

FINDING A DOCTOR TO HELP

I've already mentioned the potential of university-based weight-control centers throughout the United States. In an ideal world, everyone who needs that help would have it available. But in reality those centers may not be accessible to you. That leaves patients to rely on their physicians. But doctors have been notoriously ineffective in dealing with weight problems.

Historically, physicians have been trained to treat every ailment or complaint with drugs or surgery. Diagnose the condition, determine the proper treatment, receive proper gratitude from the cured patient, and move on. Dealing with weight problems isn't that easy; it requires a lot of caring and counseling. Not every doctor can do that, but there are organizations that can help you locate one in your area.

The Weight Information Network is a function of the National Institutes of Health in Washington, D.C. Call them at (301) 951-1120 for a medical referral.

The American Society for Clinical Nutrition (ASCN) offers a list of experts in various geographic locations. Call ASCN at (301) 530-7110.

The *American Board of Nutrition* certifies specialists in nutrition in general and weight control in particular—similar to board certification in other medical specialties. For a list of certified physicians in your area, call (205) 975-7110.

Very frequently, depression accompanies overweight. That certainly is true in cases of insulin resistance, and is often a contributing factor for other overweight men and women. Food can be the only consoling element in a person's life. Depression in and of itself can make weight control difficult, if not impossible, to achieve. Thus it is the first thing to deal with in many cases. Many new prescription drugs can be useful in treating depression. That's another good reason to find a knowledgeable and compassionate physician to help you.

Weight loss and maintenance aren't easy, but the rewards make the effort worthwhile. As I've spoken with men and women over the years who have lost weight and kept it off, I have noted a particular pride and sense of satisfaction. That pride and satisfaction are well deserved. Go for it. This time, for sure, you'll succeed!

· 13 ·

DOES IT REALLY WORK? HERE'S PROOF!

Among my most cherished possessions, I treasure my file of letters I've received over the years from men and women who read my original book. Their success stories have inspired me to keep working. Let me share just a few of their comments:

> *I would like to tell you how much I enjoyed your book. It has been very informative for me. I had tried to bring my cholesterol down by diet but it only came down from 261 in January to 254 in April. Fortunately for me, my doctor recommended your book and the oat bran–niacin approach. In July my cholesterol had come down to 192. My triglycerides from 152 to 77, LDL from 170 to 122, HDL from 53 to 55. I feel great and together with an aerobic workout I don't need medication. I also lost 12 pounds. Thank you for putting your experience in print and allowing people such as myself to benefit from your findings.*
>
> *Sonia Z.*
> *Phoenix, AZ*

> *I followed your plan and in 2 months my total cholesterol went from 305 to 145 and my ratio fell from 5.7 to 2.69. Thank You!!!*
>
> *Linda B.*
> *Norman, OK*

> *According to my two recent blood tests, you have not overstated your promise of literally erasing heart disease from one's life. It was my lucky day when a friend brought me a copy of your book. Ten years have gone by that I have tried to reduce a cholesterol count of 280 by diet with no success. My internist never suggested niacin until I took your book into his office. I began your plan with his approval. I have found the success to be fantastic. After 2 blood tests cholesterol count was 188 in May and 166 in August. This all occurred since reading your book in March. Another plus is today I no longer need the blood pressure pills.*
>
> *Pauline K.*
> *Philadelphia, PA*

I'm particularly pleased when my readers tell me that they learned about my book through their doctors. While at first the medical community was skeptical, it has come to recognize the value of my approach and its benefits for their patients. Many physicians, in fact, subscribe to my *Diet-Heart Newsletter* to keep themselves informed so they can pass the information along to their patients.

Through the years I've revised my program, added new foods and supplements, and made it more effective and easy to follow. Fortunately, my newsletter subscribers have learned about those developments every step of the way for the past several years. I've enjoyed their feedback as I've suggested such products as SeQuester and the combined regimen of immediate- and sustained-release niacin. The program slowly evolved and eventually became the revolutionary approach I believe can eradicate heart disease. It was time to put it all together in a new book to share with the world.

Just as I did in 1985, I realized the importance of carefully testing the program in a clinical setting. I turned to my friend and physician Dr. Charles Keenan of Santa Monica for help. He invited patients to participate in the 1995 study. We met at Dr. Keenan's office every Monday evening for several weeks. One time we'd talk about heart-healthy shopping and nutrition label reading. Other times the topic would be restaurants, stress reduction, the importance of exercise, or weight control. In other words, I presented the information that subsequently became the book you're now reading. In a very real way, then, you have become a part of my world, and I welcome you!

I provided everyone with a notebook and asked them to keep a log of the foods they ate, the exercise they got, and the aspects of the program they were following. As I explained, this not only would help me learn but also would help keep them focused and show their regular progress. I definitely suggest that you also keep some sort of diary. Jot down the foods and beverages you eat and drink and then see if you can calculate the number of grams of fat you're consuming on a daily basis. Record your exercise activities and see how much you progress over the coming weeks. Note the supplements you take. It'll help keep you on track.

Our Santa Monica study took place over an eleven-week period. Participants represented a real cross-section of typical American men and women. We had schoolteachers, a lawyer, office workers, retirees, a professional golfer, and even an NBA Hall of Fame former basketball player. It was a wonderful experience, and we quickly became friends, almost like a large family.

The participants received oat products from the Quaker Oats Company, including ready-to-eat oat bran cereal, hot oat bran from which either cereal or muffins could be prepared, and oatmeal. We passed out canisters of Pro-Fibe, the new soluble fiber product detailed in chapter 7. KCD Inc. provided supplies of SeQuester. Endurance products of Tigard, Oregon, supplied niacin, vitamin/mineral supplements, and antioxidants. Samples of Spice 'n' Slice sausage mixes let the group experiment with those useful products. Participants were able to purchase ultra-low-fat beef products at reduced cost, thanks to combining orders and thus cutting shipping costs. Phytosterol was not available at the time of our study, so we could not include it.

Dr. Keenan's office staff took blood samples for testing cholesterol and chemistries at the beginning, at the end of five weeks, and at the conclusion of the study at eleven weeks. The findings are summarized in the table on page 182. Owing to personal and business conflicts, some of the participants were unable to complete the entire eleven-week program. A total of ten men and women did so and were compliant with the regimen. Not everyone did as well. Some admitted that their diets were not on target, and others forgot to take the pills as directed. As they say, you can lead a horse to water, but you can't make it drink.

As you'll see, however, even looking at the average improvement of the entire group, results were remarkable. Total cholesterol declined an average of 17 percent, and triglycerides fell by 38 percent. Far more spectacular were the results for those who followed the program to the fullest—the way I'm sure you're going to do. Look at these numbers and predict your own success: total cholesterol down by 28 percent, LDL down by 30 percent, and triglycerides down by 58 percent. Note that the improvements really indicate a slashing of heart disease risk.

Pay particular attention to the individual results: TB's total cholesterol fell from an original 242 to 167. JG's dropped from 249 to 196. EH from 283 to 197. BS's came from 267 down to 197. That's what can happen when you put your mind to it.

While weight loss was not the focus of the study, a satisfying loss of approximately one pound per week was reported by those who needed to reduce and who followed the program as directed. Five-pound weight losses were common, and one individual lost fifteen pounds.

Impressed by the results of our study, Dr. Keenan's brother Joseph at the University of Minnesota suggested that we submit it for presentation. The paper I wrote was accepted, and we presented it at the 2nd International Heart Health Conference in Barcelona, Spain, in May 1995.

THE PROGRAM AT A GLANCE

For years you've heard and read about the importance of cholesterol reduction as part of a total approach to preventing heart disease. Perhaps you've tried but failed, or maybe you slipped along the way and have now resolved to get the job done. This book contains the entire program that helped the participants in Santa Monica get their numbers under control. Now you can do it too. Here's the program at a glance.

1. Have your lipid profile tested at your doctor's office. Make sure you get measurements of all the components, including total cholesterol, LDL cholesterol, HDL cholesterol, triglycerides, and risk ratio. If you have a family history of heart disease you may wish to include a test for the Lp(a) risk factor. For details see page 52. Get the exact numbers from your doctor; don't settle for "everything's fine."

2. Start improving your diet with the information you'll get in part 4 of this book. Shoot for 20 percent fat, avoiding as much saturated fat as possible. Enjoy alcohol in moderation. Maintain a food diary to keep you focused.

3. Determine your healthy weight and make up your mind to achieve that weight. The low-fat diet will put you on the right track. Feed only the weight you want, not the pounds you want to lose.

4. Add plenty of soluble fiber to your diet. Don't limit yourself to just one kind. Combining the different types of soluble fiber from oat bran, dried beans and peas, barley, and suggested supplements will achieve the best results.

5. Block the absorption of fat and cholesterol with both SeQuester and phytosterols. Keep a supply conveniently located so you don't eat a meal containing fat and cholesterol without them.

6. Supplement your diet with a good spectrum of vitamins and minerals. Make sure you get plenty of the B vitamins to prevent the buildup of homocysteine in the blood.

7. Use antioxidants to stop LDL cholesterol oxidation. A daily regimen of vitamins C and E, beta-carotene, and selenium—the ACES of chapter 8—will help keep your arteries clear.

8. Get plenty of aerobic exercise regularly. Make physical activity a part of every day's routine by walking and choosing the stairs rather than an ele-

vator. Think of your heart as a loved "pet" you want to take for a walk every day!

9. Control your stress and make an effort to relax and enjoy life. Everyone has stress. It's how we deal with it that makes the difference. Work relaxation techniques into your daily routine.

10. Retest your cholesterol levels after about ninety days. You should see a great deal of progress. If normal, terrific. If the numbers are still off, talk with your doctor about adding niacin to your program.

11. Keep up to date with the latest developments in research and new products with the *Diet-Heart Newsletter.* Just send a self-addressed, stamped, business-size envelope to:

The Diet-Heart Newsletter
Post Office Box 2039
Venice, CA 90294

You'll receive a sample issue and subscription information.

INDIVIDUAL RESULTS OF STUDY (+ INDICATES COMPLIANT INDIVIDUALS)

	BASELINE				5 WEEKS				10 WEEKS			
SUBJECT	TC	TG	HDL	LDL	TC	TG	HDL	LDL	TC	TG	HDL	LDL
SB	258	137	96	180	276	131	68	187	288	184	63	195
+TB	242	246	52	187	187	111	46	123	167	112	42	107
+PC	391	*	37	*	329	*	34	*	303	239	46	218
+DD	218	270	32	142	207	92	36	156	185	97	39	130
+JG	249	116	35	126	221	86	39	168	196	140	45	128
+JH	304	92	38	248	343	113	30	294	210	89	39	156
+EH	283	265	56	174	201	66	44	144	197	60	43	144
BH	326	266	65	208	282	254	48	165	279	201	55	184
+DI	363	1,380	NA	*	296	996	41	*	207	370	39	108
EJ	247	*	30	*	235	440	29	*	266	673	33	*
JK	321	319	NA	215	300	282	38	216	309	260	42	225
+VM	242	612	26	*	209	393	25	121	203	318	28	124
AN	230	109	41	167	NA	103	30	158	220	119	38	158
LO	245	158	47	172	223	72	55	155				
SS	273	58	71	192	319	95	60	248	281	101	63	201
+BS	267	190	40	196	236	127	40	171	197	95	39	139
+GS	308	287	44	177	264	203	45	186	223	92	37	149
VW	270	204	36	201					233	129	35	177

*Levels of triglycerides too elevated to calculate LDL

RESULTS OF ALL PARTICIPANTS COMPLETING THE STUDY

	BASELINE	5 WEEKS	10 WEEKS	% CHANGE
TC	280 mg/dl	258 mg/dl	233 mg/dl	–17
HDL	47	41	43	– 9
LDL	181	175	160	–12
TG	294	222	185	–38

RESULTS OF COMPLIANT PARTICIPANTS (10) COMPLETING THE STUDY

	BASELINE	5 WEEKS	10 WEEKS	% CHANGE
TC	287 mg/dl	250 mg/dl	208 mg/dl	–28
HDL	40	38	40	0
LDL	178	170	126	–30
TG	384	243	161	–58

· 14 ·

The Diet-Heart Newsletter

Just wanted to let you know how much I enjoy your newsletter and all the wonderful information, recipes, and the "Shopping List" section.

PFT
Tustin, CA

There is no doubt in my mind whatsoever that the information you have provided in your newsletter has contributed measurably to prolonging my life. My most abundant and sincerest Thank You's!

EPS
Federal Way, WA

Of all the health-oriented newsletters, yours has been the most interesting and helpful. Thank you for writing it.

MFB
Racine, WI

The *Diet-Heart Newsletter* is my way of staying in touch with my readers and keeping them up-to-date on the very latest in research and new products. I answer my readers' questions and put current controversies into proper perspective. This is the best way to keep you informed and motivated.

I first reported on SeQuester, phytosterols, and other breakthroughs in the newsletter. Don't miss out on the next major development!

I'd love to send you a sample issue and subscription information absolutely free of charge. Just send me a self-addressed, stamped, business-size envelope.

The Diet-Heart Newsletter
Post Office Box 2039
Venice, California 90294

Part III

Cutting Through the Confusion

.

.

.

Cutting Through the Confusion

Once upon a time, it was easy to follow dietary advice: eat your meat, drink your milk, have some fruits and vegetables, and fill out the rest with breads and cereals. Then it started getting complicated. Suddenly food took on an evil overtone. Diet was linked with disease.

So you listened as best you could and hoped for the best. But nightly news broadcasts and newspaper articles muddied the water. One day this or that was good; the next day it was bad.

Should you switch back from margarine to butter? Is alcohol actually good for you? How about garlic? Or fish oil? Confused? Join the club.

I've spent the past decade and more keeping on top of every development, and many times I've rolled my eyes when reading a misinterpreted report in the mass media. I've spoke with the researchers who originated certain ideas to get a clearer perspective, and I've shared that information with readers of my newsletter and audiences who attend my presentations and seminars.

In this section I've put together the information I've found to cut through the confusion.

· 15 ·

Trans Fatty Acids: *The Fly in the Margarine*

There you were, happily spreading your morning toast with margarine when you read the headline trumpeting that butter was better after all. What's a weary, heart-healthy consumer to do? Get the facts.

Although margarine first appeared in the 1940s as an economical alternative to butter, more recently its health advantages were the selling points. Unlike butter, margarine contains no cholesterol and has less saturated fat, the two components that raise cholesterol levels in the blood. But research showed that margarine contains so-called trans fatty acids that may raise those levels as much as saturated fats.

Time to switch back to butter? Absolutely not. But before looking at prudent recommendations, let's learn more about those trans fats.

All fats and oils consist of a medley of saturated, polyunsaturated, and monounsaturated fatty acids. When the saturated fats prevail, the fat is relatively solid at room temperature. Unsaturated fats tend to remain liquid. So to make margarine from, say, corn oil, which is primarily polyunsaturated, manufacturers add hydrogen atoms that partially or completely "saturate" the molecule, thus solidifying the oil.

Hydrogenated fats have a longer shelf life and are more resistant to rancidity. They are also more amenable to manufacturing such products as cookies, crackers, and a myriad of others. Supermarket shelves are loaded with products whose labels indicate the presence of hydrogenated oils of many types.

As hydrogen atoms are added, fatty acids become more saturated. Polyunsaturates become monounsaturates. Both polys and monos become saturates. Fortunately, the saturates formed are principally stearic acid, which does not have a cholesterol-raising effect. But starting many years ago, food scientists noted a more subtle change that happens when fats are converted from their naturally occurring "cis" state to the trans configuration. The chemical details aren't important; suffice it to say that the molecule in the cis state has a bend in its shape, while trans fats are straight. Saturated fats are also straight rather than bent, and because straight molecules tend to pack together more densely, the resulting fat is more solid.

For a while that remained a laboratory curiosity, seldom noted outside the journals of food chemists. But then researchers learned that the trans fats raised cholesterol levels of laboratory animals. Then the evidence began piling up that the same thing happens in humans.

A Dutch study in 1990 demonstrated cholesterol raising, but it took thirty-three grams of trans fats a day to get the effect. In 1992, a USDA investigation determined that a diet with ten to twenty grams of trans fats would raise cholesterol levels as much as a diet high in saturated fats would raise them. The principal researcher, Dr. Joseph Judd, stated that one should assume that trans fats raise LDL cholesterol, gram for gram, as much as saturated fats.

Trans fats started making headlines in 1993 when results of the Nurses' Health Study were published. In that study, the eating habits of seventy thousand women were tracked for eight years. Those eating the most foods rich in trans fats were 50 percent more likely to develop coronary heart disease and to have heart attacks.

In 1994 Harvard researchers, working in cooperation with the USDA, reported that patients suffering heart attacks consumed significantly more trans fats, especially in margarine, than those who did not suffer MIs. Those whose diet was rich in trans fats were twice as likely to have heart attacks.

Then in 1995 an international study in *Lancet,* a British medical journal, showed that trans fats were far more dangerous when manufactured from polyunsaturates, such as corn oil, than when made from monounsaturates, such as canola oil. Of course most of the hydrogenated fats one encounters are from polyunsaturated oils, such as corn and soybean.

Looking at all the data regarding trans fats in the medical literature, most studies point an accusing finger at these new villains. In all fairness, however, not all studies find increased risk. Researchers today conclude that one should view trans fats with the same suspicion as saturated fats and should expect them to raise cholesterol levels just as much. Trans fats also lower HDL levels.

Of course, for those living on raw fruits and vegetables and bowls of rice, this poses no problem. But what about the rest of us who enjoy a balanced diet of mixed foods?

The logical and prudent approach is to avoid trans fatty acids as much as possible. Fortunately, that's not very difficult to do.

According to the latest (1994) USDA food consumption data, margarine is the top source of fat in the American diet, contributing more than 7 percent of the total fat intake. Shortening provides another 4 percent or more. For a person whose diet contains one hundred grams of fat daily, that means an intake of about twelve grams from margarine and shortening.

The next step is to determine how much trans fats are in margarines on the market. Margarine is measured in one-tablespoon servings. A serving of stick margarine contains 1.0 to 3.0 grams of trans fats. That's in addition to 1.0 to 2.0 grams of saturated fat. Soft, tub margarines provide anywhere from 0.0 to 2.5 grams of trans fats, and products in squeeze and spray bottles have virtually none. Those figures come from the National Association of Margarine Manufacturers.

By way of comparison, a one-tablespoon serving of butter contains 7.6 grams of saturated fat. Thus, even the worst stick margarines has fewer cholesterol-raising grams of fat than butter, and that's not considering its thirty-three milligrams of cholesterol. Butter is not better!

What about other foods? At this time, manufacturers are not required to list trans fats separately. If saturated, polyunsaturated, and monounsaturated fats are listed, one can subtract them from the total to determine the trans level, assuming that the ingredient list includes hydrogenated oils. As a rule of thumb, you can count on half the total fat listed as being a combination of saturated and trans. Vegetable shortenings have about 2.0 grams of trans fats per tablespoon.

The other major source of trans fats comes from fried fast foods. A four-ounce serving of french fries has from 2.41 to 3.43 grams. One doughnut contains from 0.44 to 3.19 grams. Again, you can count on half or more of the total fat used for frying in fast-food restaurants to be a combination of saturated and trans fats.

So how much trans fat does it take to damage our hearts? A fairly clear picture comes from the Nurses' Health Study. Those with the highest intake of trans fats, and thus most likely to develop heart disease, consumed an average of 5.7 grams daily. That compares with women who had the smallest amount in the diet, 2.4 grams daily.

Since the major source of total fat is margarine, and one can easily find brands that are low in both total fat and calories, one can avoid the trans fat trap there. I like to use the Promise Ulta Lowfat margarine as well as the I Can't Believe It's Not Butter spray margarine. Both are practically free of trans fats. In Italian restaurants and at home, I'll ask for some olive oil to use with my bread.

Selecting low-fat and nonfat products such as cookies and crackers automatically slashes trans intake. When it comes to fast foods, I personally limit french fries to an infrequent treat. Then again, I did those things way before any awareness of trans fats hit the world. While I do think that trans fats do have an adverse effect on cholesterol levels and should be limited accordingly, the bigger problem continues to be saturated fat.

· 16 ·

FISH AND FISH OIL: *Don't Let This One Get Away*

Remember the Eskimo paddling his kayak in the TV ad in the 1980s as the announcer told how fish oil protects against heart disease? Those ads are gone, thanks to the Food and Drug Administration's crackdown, but the interest in fish and fish oil continues. Research data and resulting media reports on fish oil have been conflicting, leaving you and others confused.

There's no doubt that Eskimos are protected from heart disease by way of their fatty diets. Most of that fat comes from seal and whale meat, both of which are rich in omega-3 fatty acids, a type of polyunsaturated fat. That same fat can be found in fattier fish such as salmon. The hastily drawn conclusion: Fish oil conveys heart protection.

Then the holes in that tenuous argument came to light. Adding fish oil by swallowing capsules actually raised levels of cholesterol in the blood. Beneficial effects weren't always seen. Was it the specific omega-3 fatty acid sold in capsules that conveyed protection or something else in the Eskimo's diet?

Things in nature are usually far more complex than those created in chemistry labs. The pills contain one, or maybe two, omega-3 fatty acids. For the record, those are eicosapentanoic acid (EPA) and docosahexanoic acid (DHA). However, fish have many, many other chemical compounds, some of which might activate the effect of the EPA and DHA. Moreover, there were questions of purity and potency of the capsules. Capsule sales waned, but research interest waxed. Today we have a much clearer picture of the roles of fish and fish oils.

FISH OIL AND CHOLESTEROL

No doubt the most discouraging news came in the late 1980s when data indicated that people taking fish oil capsules often saw rises in total cholesterol and especially in levels of the bad LDL cholesterol. Certainly no one wanted that. But such individuals consumed additional fat by way of those pills while continuing their intake of saturated fat. That's not the way the Eskimos do it.

A better way to judge the value of a diet including fish would be to compare diets rich in fish oil with those rich in saturated fats and polyunsaturated fats of plant origin. Dr. Edwin Bierman did just that at the University of Washington. Subjects with high cholesterol levels got diets enriched with butterfat and other saturated fats, salmon oil, or safflower oil. Compared with those on the saturated fat diet, those consuming fish oil reduced their total cholesterol by 34 percent and those getting safflower oil got a 26 percent reduction.

There was an additional bonus for the salmon oil group. While safflower oil had no effect on triglycerides, the fish oil brought levels down by 32 to 44 percent, depending on how high the counts were to begin with.

In a collaborative study between the Oregon Health Sciences University in Portland and the University of Tromso in Norway, researchers took a closer look at fish oil and blood lipids. When subjects replaced some of their saturated fat with fish oil, their total cholesterol levels fell. Results were best for those eating a diet with reduced total fat intake, though benefits were derived with both low-fat and high-fat diets.

You must view fish oil, whether taken in the form of capsules or food, as another source of fat in the diet. When this specialized form of polyunsaturated fat replaces saturated fat in the diet, both total and LDL cholesterol levels go down. When added to an already high-fat diet, those fish oils could make cholesterol counts go up.

FISH OIL AND HYPERTENSION

Can fish oil lower your blood pressure? That depends on how high it is to begin with. Researchers in Chicago and Boston gave individuals either fish oil or olive oil capsules totaling six to twelve grams. The individuals being studied had very mildly elevated hypertension, and the fish oil had no effect.

The data for thirty-one different studies, involving 1,356 patients, were analyzed in *Circulation* in 1993. In eight studies fish oil did not affect blood pressure in healthy subjects, those whose pressures were not significantly elevated. Nine studies showed a small but important drop in blood pressure for hypertensive patients. Their measurements dropped 3.4 and 2.0 mm Hg (millimeters of mercury) in systolic and diastolic readings, respectively.

FISH OIL AND BLOOD CLOTTING

Pinch or punch an Eskimo ever so lightly, and he or she will bruise easily. That's also the case with arthritis patients who take large amounts of aspirin. Both Eskimos and arthritis patients have lessened blood clotting ability. While bruises may not be desirable, reduced clotting may be the key to heart disease protection.

Dr. Manfred Steiner looked at the effects of fish oil on blood platelets, those cells involved with clotting, in patients at Brown University. The more platelets stick together, a process termed adhesion, the more clotting occurs. Three groups took 16, 32, or 48 fish oil capsules daily for three weeks. All three had reduced platelet adhesion, more so with those on higher doses.

I hasten to add two important facts. First, Dr. Steiner's patients had an abnormally high platelet adhesion rate to begin with. Second, those are mighty high fish oil intakes and resulted in side effects, including gastric disturbances and "fish breath."

The fact remains, however, that fish oil does reduce blood clotting, and that's important for people trying to prevent heart attacks. Remember, though, that Eskimos don't take fish oil capsules.

Even small increases in dietary fish oil can favorably influence blood clotting. In a study involving more than fifteen thousand people in four communities in the United States, researchers at the University of Minnesota found that increased intakes of fish oil correlated with lowered blood clotting tendencies. It's not an all or nothing matter. As with all the other aspects of the program I follow and advocate in this book, you can do a little of this and a little of that, making small, easy changes in lifestyle, to achieve, in total, enormously improved health and reduced risk of heart disease. We'll get to the specifics of my recommendations shortly.

FISH OIL AND FLEXIBILITY

Some doctors believe that fish oil can improve their arthritis patients' flexibility, "lubricating" those joints, as it were. It turns out that such improved flexibility also applies to the arteries supplying blood to the heart, turning back the clock on hardening of the arteries.

After giving patients fish oil capsules for six weeks, researchers at the University of Minnesota were delighted to see improved flexibility, which was measured by examining the arteries' ability to stretch in response to changes in blood pressure. Giving capsules of olive oil as control placebos had no such effect.

In this particular 1994 study there was no improvement in cholesterol levels, perhaps because the twenty patients studied had Type II non-insulin-dependent diabetes.

FISH OIL AND HEALTH

The vast majority of investigations have concluded that fish consumption lessens the incidence of heart disease and heart attacks and increases longevity. As a practical consideration, such studies could not always include fish oil capsules, since they covered many years.

One such long-term study involves hundreds of Dutch men in the Netherlands. Initial findings showed that those who consumed more than twenty grams of fish per day on average had a significant protection against heart attacks. Data published in 1994 show the same fish intake also protects against stroke. That's a little less than an ounce of fish daily.

Here in the United States, a long-term study called the Multiple Risk Factor Intervention Trial examined the data from 6,260 middle-aged men. Those men consuming an average of 664 mg of fish oil, either from fish itself or capsules, had a 40 percent lower risk of dying from cardiovascular disease, including both heart attacks and strokes. For men eating fatty fish at least twice a week or taking three 500 mg fish oil capsules daily in the two years following a heart attack, risk of death dropped by 29 percent.

Then a much-publicized study of health professionals supposedly concluded that eating fish didn't really influence the incidence of heart disease. As is often the case, the news media simply didn't get this one right.

During six years of follow-up of nearly forty-five thousand males, 1,543 "coronary events," including heart attacks, deaths, and bypasses and angioplasties, occurred. Statistical comparisons were made between and among those who ate fish or didn't, considering just how much they ate. One might have expected that those eating the most fish would have the fewest number of events, but that was not the case. However, the data underlined previously published data both here and abroad. Those eating any amount of fish, even very small amounts of fish, regularly had 26 percent less incidence of coronary events than those who ate no fish.

Headlines in 1995 blaring that fish offered no protection were wrong. Eating small amounts of fish does slash risk of coronary events. As is so often the case when the smoke clears and the ashes settle, more is not necessarily better. For those who have felt guilty about ordering anything other than fish for dinner, that should be good news, indeed.

In the case of fish and fish oil, more can actually be potentially dangerous. Some studies suggest that eating fish eight times a week or so may undermine the response of the immune system. Even Eskimos pay a price for their protection from heart attacks: their risk of hemorrhagic stroke—bleeding in the brain—increases owing to lessened clotting potential.

FISH AND FISH OIL IN PERSPECTIVE

There is absolutely no downside to eating a moderate amount of fish on a regular basis. No data show anything but benefits. Taking up to 1,000 mg (one gram) of fish oil as capsules daily poses no risk of even the most insignificant side effects. More might make you burp or give you GI upset.

I'm lucky. I actually enjoy fish and other seafood and frequently prefer it over other choices. To me, a piece of absolutely fresh salmon broiled to perfection ranks right up there with a prime steak. If you, too, love fish, read on. I'll deal with you fish haters in a moment.

Even discounting the accumulated data strongly suggesting a number of distinct benefits of fish, simply replacing a meal rich in saturated fat with a fish meal rich in omega-3 polyunsaturated fat makes a lot of sense. Just doing that will certainly influence your cholesterol levels and provide some other advantages as well.

As with oat bran, it's more than just substituting a healthy dish for a less healthy one. The fish oils we know, and possibly some fishy components we don't, might make your coronary arteries more flexible, lower your triglycerides, decrease your blood's tendency to clot when you least want it to, lower your blood pressure if it's way up there, and actually lessen your risk of heart disease and death. Not bad at all. Makes that salmon dish sound even more delicious.

Think about the irony of this. Contrary to other dietary advice, it's a good idea to seek the fattiest pieces of fish you can find. Picture that salmon slab dripping and smoking on the backyard barbecue grill. Savor that tuna belly sashime or sushi. Feel your mouth water as you prepare a herring or sardine snack. Yes, go for the fat!

While other types of fish are heart-healthy choices, especially when compared with meats high in saturated fat, the fatty fish have the edge. It's the omega-3 fatty acids you want, possibly along with yet-undiscovered beneficial nutrients.

FISH WITH THE MOST OMEGA-3 FATTY ACIDS (MORE THAN 1.0 GRAM)*

Anchovies	Mackerel	Sardines
Bluefish	Salmon	Tuna (fresh)
Herring	Sable	Whitefish

FISH WITH MODERATE OMEGA-3 FATTY ACIDS (0.5 TO 0.9 GRAMS)*

Oysters (Pacific)	Shark	Swordfish
Pompano	Smelt	
Trout	Striped bass	

FISH WITH LITTLE OMEGA-3 FATTY ACIDS (LESS THAN 0.5 GRAM)*

Carp	Grouper	Rockfish
Catfish	Mahi Mahi	Shellfish
Flounder	Pike	Snapper

**Per 3 1/2 ounce serving, raw*

Okay, so you don't like fish. Now what? Consider one of the plant sources of omega-3 polyunsaturated fatty acids, including canola and soybean oil, flaxseed and flaxseed oil, and linseed oil. Unfortunately, there's not as much as you'd find in fish (or seals if you have a harpoon handy), and the body will convert this source into only EPA, not DHA, which is also important. But it's better than nothing.

To put this advice into some perspective, canola oil, which is the richest form of the omega-3 fatty acid alpha-linolenic acid, provides 1.4 grams per tablespoon. Other sources supply far lesser, though still significant, amounts.

· 17 ·

I Love Coffee, I Love Tea

We Americans love to start the day with a steaming, aromatic cup of coffee. Call it java or joe, take it black or light with sugar, stop at one cup or have three or four, we really enjoy our daily boost. Even decaf drinkers find comfort in the hot, soothing yet stimulating beverage. So millions were jolted by the news that coffee drinking raised cholesterol levels.

The association of coffee with heart disease came from Scandinavia. Coffee drinkers, researchers said and newspapers blared, had higher levels of the bad LDL cholesterol and more risk of heart disease and attacks. Say it isn't true, coffee lovers begged. Maybe it's because the subjects smoked cigarettes or their diets were high in fat, anything but the coffee!

The controversy raged for three full years, with some studies confirming the early reports and others totally disagreeing. One article said ill effects could be attributed only to "full-octane" coffee, while another indicated that even decaf had problems. Maybe it was a matter of the particular beans used, and the more expensive arabica beans were favored for a while over the cheaper but more powerful robusta beans. Was it a matter of quantity, and, if so, how much was safe to drink? It went on and on, and I must admit I was growing tired of reporting one study after another in my *Diet-Heart Newsletter* (see page ____).

Then, finally, came the light at the end of the tunnel. That came in a report in the journal *Arteriosclerosis and Thrombosis* from researchers in the Netherlands. The culprit, it turned out, was not coffee itself but the way some folks make it—especially in Scandinavia where all the trouble started in the first place, where they boil and decant their brew.

The ninety-six-day trial involved sixty-four healthy subjects, thirty-three men and thirty-one women from an industrial town in the eastern Netherlands. During the first seventeen days, everyone drank six cups of boiled-and-filtered coffee daily. Then for the next seventy-nine days the men and women volunteers sipped six cups of either unfiltered boiled coffee, boiled-and-filtered coffee, or no coffee at all.

The results were dramatic and straightforward. For those drinking unfiltered boiled coffee, total and LDL cholesterol rose by an average of sixteen milligrams. That's a lot. But those consuming the filtered brew or not imbibing at all had no elevations.

The solution, after years of debate, was simply to pour the coffee through a filter. Of course that's something most Americans do anyway. The filter in our coffeemakers trap the fatty substances—termed cafestrol and kahweol in case you need to know—and we can toss them away with our worries and concerns.

But the Dutch researcher, Dr. Martijn Katan, continued with his research and published more of his findings in 1995. Not only could Scandinavian-style boiled coffee raise cholesterol counts, but other unfiltered brews did the same. Those consuming coffee sediment equal to the amount found in 1.5 liters of Turkish coffee saw a twenty-five milligram leap in cholesterol in three weeks. Other culprits were French press, espresso, and Greek coffees. No reports on what that amount of caffeine did to the volunteers' nerves.

The general consensus today in the medical community is that coffee and tea pose no real risk for those of us who enjoy them in moderation. Ah, there's that word again. Here moderation means about three cups daily, no more than five. To me, that's a lot of coffee, especially if it's not decaf. I'd personally be climbing the walls.

Most of the time I do drink decaf, since I find that I no longer need the caffeine lift I required before starting my program of regular and rigorous exercise. But that doesn't mean I don't enjoy a cup or two of high-test brew on leisurely weekends or to recharge my batteries after a long day when there's still a long evening to go.

Whatever your preference, bottoms up! Enjoy it with no guilt or worries.

AND THE GOOD NEWS ABOUT TEA . . .

. . . is that it can actually be good for you. Studies at the University of Scranton in Pennsylvania indicate that both black and green tea are packed with antioxidants that help keep the LDL cholesterol from clogging your arteries. Original work with tea drinking in Asia pointed to the superiority of green and oolong teas. But it appears that black teas are just as good.

Work published in the *British Medical Journal* in 1995 showed that Japanese men who drank the most tea had 5.5 percent lower total cholesterol, 12 percent less triglyceride, and 3 percent higher HDLs than men who did not drink tea.

What's so special about tea? Substances called flavonoids that are also present in fruits and vegetables act as antioxidants and give tea its heart-protecting qualities. Research in the Netherlands revealed that Dutch men who consumed the most flavonoids had less than one-third the number of fatal heart attacks compared with those whose intake was the lowest. Most of those healthful flavonoids came from tea. Apples and onions came in at second and third place in their diets. Red wine has also proven a good source of flavonoids, as has red grape juice.

It appears that we can make a toast to good health with a number of beverages. So, what'll it be, coffee or tea?

· 18 ·

A Spoonful of Sugar . . .

. . . does a lot more than make the medicine go down. Let's face it, we all enjoy some sugar in the foods we eat, and there is absolutely no reason to feel guilty! Sugar has gotten an undeservedly bad reputation, and it's about time that we clear matters up once and for all.

. . . doesn't make you fat. FDA researchers compared the sugar composition of moderate (13 teaspoons a day) and high (26 teaspoons a day) sugar users in 1992 and found no correlation with obesity. Each of those teaspoons is worth sixteen calories. Although sugar-sweetened soft drinks can pack ten teaspoons in a twelve-ounce can, and other snacks add those teaspoons up quickly, the real villain in overweight is fat, not sugar. Of course, overweight individuals will need to cut back on all sources of calories.

Does a Coca-Cola sweetened with NutraSweet taste just as good to you? Terrific, you can use the saved calories for something else. At home I drink Cokes with NutraSweet. But Diet Coke out of a machine at the movies is sweetened with saccharin, which I personally hate. So on those occasions I drink regular Coke.

The word *moderation* raises its head again with sugar. Just because a cake is labeled fat-free doesn't make it free of calories. If one were to replace a serving of cake (or any other dessert or snack for that matter) made with fat with a serving made without that fat, but typically with more sugar, one wouldn't gain weight. But don't eat the whole cake!

Study after study has shown the same thing: It's not the sugar but the fat that makes folks fat. Too many calories from any source will put on the pounds if you don't burn them off. A gram of fat provides nine calories, while a gram of sugar gives you only four. Eating sugar-free chocolates is the ultimate in self-deception. When you want that piece of chocolate, select the very best, and then enjoy just a taste.

. . . doesn't cause diabetes. It's only a problem if you already have the disease. Type I, insulin-dependent, diabetes is a genetic disorder in which the patient's pancreas doesn't produce enough insulin to adequately regulate sugar levels in the blood. Type II, non-insulin-dependent, diabetes also has a hereditary correlation but develops in middle age, usually in those who are overweight and sedentary. Frequently by returning to normal weight and getting into a regular, rigorous exercise program patients can completely eliminate the symptoms of Type II diabetes.

. . . doesn't made kids hyper. Despite the beliefs of mothers all over the country, there's just no scientific documentation of the link between sugar and hyperactivity (or with food dyes and additives). In research done at the University of Iowa, sixteen boys diagnosed with hyperactivity—more properly termed attention deficit hyperactive disorder, by the way—drank a sugary drink after lunch and then after a night of fasting. In neither instance did the boys show an association between sugar and the hyperactive behavior.

So why are moms so sure about the evils of sugar? Because they don't take into consideration the surroundings their kids are in when they eat or drink those sweet treats. Children are lots more hyper at parties and get-togethers—with or without the sugar. This is a myth that'll take years to go away, if ever.

. . . is not addictive. Sorry, chocoholics, it's not the sugar that's got you hooked. All of us get a craving for something sweet now and then.

. . . does not cause heart disease. Thanks to funding from the National Dairy Council (NDC), one researcher in England had his unfounded opinions trumpeted around the world. The NDC, of course, wanted to get attention away from the saturated fat and cholesterol in its products. The sugar theory has pretty much died down now, but every once in a while one still hears about the supposed link to coronary heart disease. Just not true.

So What's Wrong with Sugar?

It can cause dental caries, especially if left in contact with teeth over a prolonged period of time, as with chewing gum, sucked candies, or sipped sodas. Limit lengthy contact with the teeth and rinse the mouth afterward.

Sugar also has no particular nutritional value. But those "empty calories" can perk up candied yams and acorn squash. I think you'll love my recipe for those vegetables on page 304. When you bake, sugar provides indispensible bulk. Desserts just won't come out right without it.

Thanks to modern food technology, many fat-free dessert items can be found today. If you read the nutrition labeling and compare the regular and fat-free versions of this cake or that cookie, you'll find that the calorie counts won't be much different. Sugar, along with one or more of the fat substitutes such as maltodextrin, guar gum, carrageenan, or a host of others, largely replaces the fat. But it's the fat that causes the problems, not the sugar, so enjoy without guilt. If you see that you've gained a pound or two, why not increase the amount of exercise you do so you won't have to give up that extra piece of cake?

But Isn't Fructose Better?

Just exactly why some self-styled food purists consider fructose, fruit sugar, superior to sucrose, which comes from plants as well, mystifies me. Both substances, quite obviously, are "natural." Ironically, research has shown that fructose, especially in the form of high-fructose corn syrup, can actually cause a rise in LDL cholesterol levels. That was found true by the USDA in men who got 20 percent of their calories from fructose; the average intake in the United States is 10 to 14 percent of calories. If anything, sucrose is actually better for you than fructose, not the other way around. On the other hand, neither will be a problem (in moderation) as part of a balanced diet containing a wide variety of foods.

What About Pure Fruit Juice Concentrate?

This question was addressed in the *Berkeley Wellness Letter* of September 1993. It pointed out that using fruit juice concentrate as an ingredient does not make any product lower in calories than plain old cane sugar. Whether honey, brown sugar, raw sugar, table sugar, fruit sugar, grape sugar, turbinado sugar, or any other kind, sugar is sugar, and all of it is handled by the body in the same way. It's all converted to glucose in the body and used for energy.

The irony is that the popularity of juicers and extractors has led to weight gain in those who, trusting the healthfulness of their homemade fruit juices, don't realize how many calories those drinks contain. Another problem with juicers is that for the most part the fiber gets thrown down the drain.

· 19 ·

Take Sodium Advice with a Grain of Salt

About fifty million American adults have high blood pressure, a silent killer with no symptoms in nine out of ten cases. Hypertension is a major risk factor for cardiovascular disease, greatly increasing the chances of having a heart attack or stroke.

For many people, sodium restriction helps control hypertension. That's because salt and other sodium compounds are involved in a chemical sequence initiated in the kidneys that ends with the production of a substance that raises blood pressure.

For many years we've heard the unequivocal advice that all Americans should significantly reduce their salt and sodium consumption. There was little if any argument against these public recommendations, possibly because, unlike the dairy industry, the salt producers have no loud and well-financed voice. No one questioned the authorities and salt was labeled "the enemy." It got to where if one dared to reach for the salt shaker, he or she was likely to be castigated.

But as is the case for off-the-rack recommendations, one size does not fit all. Scientific facts have toppled public health theory. First, salt intake does not always lead to hypertension. Second, only a small percentage of people are sodium sensitive. Third, sodium restriction does not lower blood pressure for all people. Fourth, other minerals must be balanced. Fifth, severe sodium restriction may actually be harmful for some individuals. Let's look at these issues in some detail so we can come to logical conclusions.

The international Intersalt Study is the most comprehensive population study yet undertaken to get some answers. Researchers looked at blood pressures and sodium intake in people in thirty-two countries. The results revealed little link between sodium intake and hypertension in people around the world.

Yes, in populations where sodium consumption is extremely low—at a level where most of us would find the diet virtually inedible—blood pressure is low in the majority of persons. Yet that was true in only four out of fifty-two centers studied. In the other forty-eight centers where there was wide variation in sodium intake, there was little if any difference in blood pressure. These findings suggest that unless sodium is very severely limited, most persons will not see any improvement. Any drop in blood pressure, on average, will be clinically insignificant.

Yes, it is also true that where sodium intake is very high, there will be a notable increase in high blood pressure in the population when viewed as a trend, though not a statistically significant cause-and-effect relationship. Also, that trend is weak, requiring considerable manipulation of the numbers to make restriction advocates' point. In other words, one would have to view the entire population rather than individuals, since individuals will show virtually no response to salt.

Bear in mind that those data reflect averages. Even in a population where salt intake is very high, only some individuals will show a rise in blood pressure. The majority will have a normal blood pressure, even though they consume the same amount of salt.

Another study, published in the January 1990 issue of the *Archives of Internal Medicine,* also failed to show a strong sodium/hypertension link. For three years, 841 men and women were observed for the blood pressure–lowering effects of diet. Some restricted sodium alone; a second group cut back on calories; a third group reduced both sodium and calories; while a fourth group was put on a low-sodium, high-potassium diet. The group with the greatest drop in blood pressure was that which reduced calories. Those cutting back on sodium alone showed little difference.

It turns out that some people are salt sensitive and others are not. Some people who consume a lot of sodium have normal pressures while others whose intake is low have elevated numbers. Of those with currently existing hypertension, only 25 to 50 percent will benefit from sodium restriction, based on a large number of studies done all over the world. Of the general population, perhaps 10 to 25 percent of adults' blood pressures are influenced by sodium intake.

There's no longer any scientific question regarding salt sensitivity. It is very real. In fact, researchers are now trying to develop a test for such sensitivity so that physicians can know which patients need sodium restriction and which do not, rather than prescribing it for everyone. That test is still off in the future. We do know, however, that people who are older, heavier, and have less fiber in their diets are more likely to be salt sensitive, according to work done at Johns Hopkins University. We can't do much about aging, of course, but we can reduce weight and increase fiber consumption, both of which have been shown to be of more value in controlling hypertension than salt restriction anyway.

It may be possible that a low-salt diet can do more harm than good. Dr. Brent Egan, then at the Medical College of Wisconsin in Milwaukee, found that a low-salt diet will not reduce blood pressure in 50 percent of people with higher-than-normal pressures and in 80 percent of those with normal levels. In fact, for some people, salt restriction may actually result in higher blood pressure!

Even more disturbing was a study linking low sodium consumption with an increase in heart attack risk. Working with hypertensive men at the Albert Einstein College of Medicine in New York City, Dr. Michael Alderman detected an unexpectedly high incidence of heart attacks in those with low amounts of salt in their urine, reflecting their dietary restrictions. The study followed nearly two thousand men for almost four years. More than four times as many heart attacks occurred in men with the lowest amounts of sodium in their urine compared with men with the highest levels of urinary sodium.

Dr. Alderman also studied more than one thousand hypertensive women, but only nine of them suffered heart attacks during the study period, too small a number to draw any conclusions. Among the men there were forty-six heart attacks.

These data don't mean that everyone should rush out and start gobbling salt. The patients involved had significant hypertension and other factors to consider. But the findings do cast a big shadow on blanket recommendations that everyone severely restrict sodium consumption. Those recommending very low-sodium diets may be hurting people.

Dr. Egan has continued his research at the Medical University of South Carolina in Charleston. In one study, he worked with twelve lean and eighteen obese patients. Obese subjects had high blood pressure as well as elevated cholesterol levels, while lean individuals had normal counts. He placed both groups on a low-salt diet for seven days and then switched them to a high-salt diet. Both diets had the same amounts of calories and fat. The low-salt diets had no effect on lowering blood pressure, and the high-salt diets failed to raise blood pressure.

So what are doctors and their patients to do? Dr. Egan takes a very practical approach with his own patients. He has them monitor their blood pressures for a week before starting a low-salt diet in order to establish a baseline. Then they keep track of their pressures after cutting back on salt. If there is no reduction in blood pressure after one to two months, Dr. Egan tells them to discontinue salt restriction. After all, why follow a prescription that doesn't work?

What about people who currently have normal blood pressures? The old saying "If it ain't broke, don't fix it" probably applies. This is particularly true for adults rather than for children. Blood pressure increases with age, and if one hasn't developed hypertension by adulthood, it's unlikely that the amount of sodium currently in the diet will lead to future problems.

Still, as in all things, moderation should be the watchword. Some salt in our foods makes them taste better. That's especially important for those of us trying to follow a reasonably low-fat diet. Excessive salt consumption results in fluid retention that contributes to weight gain and places a greater burden on the kidneys, so it's not a matter of abandoning all reasonability. Moderate sodium intake.

So what's moderation? Dr. Egan aims for between six and ten grams of sodium a day for most individuals, depending on whether their blood pressures respond to limitations. To put that into perspective, there are about 2,400 milligrams (2.4 grams) of sodium in one teaspoon of salt. Dr. Suzanne Oparil, a hypertension researcher at the University of Alabama and president of the AHA from 1994 to 1995, suggests limits on salt and sodium intake only for those with high blood pressure.

Want to moderate your sodium consumption? The salt shaker is probably the worst place to start because it contributes only 15 percent of the average person's daily intake. Processed foods, on the other hand, are responsible for 75 percent of all sodium. The remaining 10 percent is naturally present in all sorts of foods. Cut back a bit on those processed foods, and you should be able to enjoy a moderate sprinkle of salt at the table without any problem, and that's where most of us enjoy it the most—and, of course, on the rim of the margarita glass!

Those arguing in defense of salt restriction return to the physiological mechanism by which sodium raises blood pressure. To prove that salt added to the diet leads to hypertension, Australian scientists working in Gabon, Africa, studied a colony of chimpanzees. Their natural diet consisted of fruits and vegetable matter. Half the chimps were given a liquid that provided up to fifteen grams of salt daily.

After twenty months on the salt-laced diet, seven of the thirteen chimps showed an average increase of thirty-three systolic blood pressure and ten diastolic. Normal adult pressure is 120/80, with the upper number showing pressure when the heart pumps blood (systolic) and the lower number indicating pressure when the heart rests (diastolic). Three chimps showed no increase, and three did not drink all the salty liquid. The researchers concluded that salt raises blood pressure in chimps, and since they're closely related to us, the same applies to humans.

But look at those data a bit more closely. Note that three of the chimps showed no change at all. Next consider the fact that Americans consume about ten grams of salt daily and weigh twice as much as chimpanzees, who were fed fifteen grams. That would be like tripling our average intake. Just because massive amounts of salt lead to an increase in blood pressure in chimps who had no tolerance to it, owing to the total lack of additional salt in their natural diet, doesn't mean that moderate use of salt is a bad thing for us.

Again, that word *moderate*. I'm not advocating a diet of pickles, salt, and soy sauce. I'm just saying that there's no good science to indicate the need for anything more than moderation in salt and sodium intake. Maybe ten grams daily is on the high side. But 2.5 grams is restrictive and unpalatable. Shoot for something in the middle, like about six grams daily.

If sodium isn't the horrible villain we've been led to believe, what can we do to control hypertension? After all, it is a major killer. Actually there are a number of things we can do before resorting to prescription drugs that are expensive and have significant side effects.

Dozens of investigators have found that lifestyle modifications can, in fact, control cases of mild to moderate hypertension and can significantly reduce the need for medications in severe cases. First, reduce weight to normal; that will result in dramatic improvements almost immediately. Next, get more exercise on a regular basis. Absolutely, positively quit smoking. Try to cut stress and to relax and enjoy life more. Limit alcohol to no more than one or two drinks daily, perhaps less if blood pressure is particularly high.

But it may be what people don't eat, rather than what they do, that contributes to hypertension. Dr. David McCarron of the Oregon Health Sciences University in Portland pioneered the research showing that insufficient calcium intake could be as important or more important than consuming too much sodium. Today, additional studies appear to corroborate his initial findings.

One cardiovascular benefit derived from calcium is a lessening of arterial pressure in those with high blood pressure. One study has shown a 23 percent decrease in hypertension risk in women taking an 800 mg calcium supplement daily.

In one of the largest studies of its kind, California researchers at UCLA found that every gram of calcium consumed per day lowered the risk of high blood pressure an average of 12 percent for the 6,634 men and women participating. Benefits are greater for certain individuals, Dr. James Dwyer reported. Those under forty have 25 percent less risk per gram of calcium. Lean men and women have 18 percent risk reduction. Those drinking less than one alcoholic beverage per day get a 16 percent cut in hypertension risk per calcium gram consumed. Those who were lean, under age forty, and moderate drinkers enjoyed the greatest risk reduction of all. For them, consuming at least one gram of calcium daily resulted in a 40 percent reduction in risk of high blood pressure.

Continuing his research, Dr. McCarron believes that one should seek a balance of minerals, including sodium, calcium, and potassium. Other investigators have come up with impressive data supporting the importance of magnesium as well.

One twelve-year study of California adults suggested that high potassium intake protects against stroke, the worst result of hypertension. For men, those with low potassium intakes had 2.6 times more stroke risk than those with high consumption of potassium-rich foods. For women, low intake multiplied risk by nearly five times.

In 1991, University of Pennsylvania researchers found that just ten days of potassium restriction resulted in rises in blood pressure, whether one had normal or elevated pressure to begin with. Scientists have also shown that potassium supplements can lower pressures in many hypertensive individuals. Interestingly, when people are restricting sodium, adding potassium has no beneficial effect.

But one needn't turn to supplements for potassium. Many foods are rich in the mineral. One medium banana has 450 milligrams, a potato packs 844 milligrams, and a teaspoon of salt substitute is loaded with potassium. See the table on page 209.

Dr. McCarron suggests that you don't forget magnesium either. It's the balance of all the minerals, he believes, that ensures good health. Dark green, leafy vegetables; nuts; soybeans; and whole grains are all good sources of magnesium.

It's going to take a long time for the world to catch up with the scientific realities regarding sodium and blood pressure. Many of those who have advocated sodium restriction for years are going to be reluctant to admit that maybe they were wrong. Others haven't kept up with scientific research. Since the dollars involved with salt sales are relatively low, it's not likely that anyone will trumpet that research via advertising and public relations.

So what do you do? If your blood pressure is normal, there's no need for restricting salt and sodium intake beyond normal moderation. If your doctor diagnoses hypertension, it's worth a trial to determine if limiting sodium consumption helps. If after a month or two of effort, there is no improvement, there's little if any reason to continue to limit your sodium. If your doctor questions that line of thinking, you might take the advice of Dr. Alderman in New York: "Concerned hypertension patients may want to ask their doctors for evidence that a low-salt diet is advantageous."

SOURCES OF POTASSIUM

FOOD	AMOUNT	POTASSIUM (MG)
Honeydew melon	1/4 melon	940
Potato (baked)	1 medium	844
Dried figs	5 whole	666
Prunes	10 medium	626
Dates	10 whole	541
Tomato puree	1/2 cup	525
Dried apricots	10 halves	482
Banana	1 medium	451
Winter squash	1/2 cup	445
Raisins	1/3 cup	375
Lima beans	1/2 cup	370
Cantaloupe	1/4 melon	341
Orange (navel)	1 medium	250
Strawberries	1 cup	247
SALT SUBSTITUTES	one tsp	
Morton lite salt		1,500
Morton salt substitute		2,800
No salt		2,500
No salt (seasoned)		1,330

· 20 ·

A Loaf of Bread, a Jug of Wine, and a Healthy Heart

Drinking alcoholic beverages has been one of life's pleasures for thousands of years. Throughout history, physicians have extolled alcohol's health benefits. Sumerian doctors prescribed beer, Egyptian physicians recommended beer or wine, and Greek healers used herb-infused wine as medicine. Today we have the scientific proof that drinking in moderation is actually good for most people.

In cultures around the world, the notion that a glass or two of wine is healthful is so obvious that it shouldn't take dozens of scientific studies to prove it. However, the puritan ethic repudiating pleasures of the flesh cast a negative light on drinking, especially in America, even to the point of denying the validity of initial research.

Rarely have scientific findings been so unequivocal. Typically one can find data to defend either side of a health issue. Studies on alcohol, however, have uniformly concluded that those who drink in moderation tend to live longer than those who don't imbibe.

But the naysayers weren't ready to throw in the towel. Surely, they said, those abstainers included former alcohol abusers who were already sickened by their excesses. Additional studies were done, eliminating all but lifelong teetotalers, and the conclusions were the same.

Some physicians have even said that if alcohol were a new invention, it would be hailed as a "wonder drug" and prescribed by doctors regularly. Many researchers feel that it should be prescribed for heart protection to patients without contraindications. As with all miracle drugs, however, some negatives must be considered. So let's put the risks and benefits into proper perspective.

ALCOHOL AND YOUR HEART

The first solid evidence of alcohol's heart-protecting benefits came from work done by Dr. Arthur Klatsky at Kaiser Permanente in California. In 1974 he found that abstainers suffered more heart attacks than drinkers. After that, the data piled up. In 1977 the Honolulu Heart Program demonstrated that those who had never drunk alcohol had twice the risk of heart disease as those who consumed alcohol in moderation.

Later, two long-term Harvard investigations proved the benefits of alcohol for both men and women. In one, physicians who drank alcoholic beverages had fewer cardiac events, including heart attacks and bypass surgeries. Their risk was cut by about 30 percent. In the other, women in the Nurses' Health Study who drank in moderation received protection from heart disease. Statistically speaking, average risk of death during the twelve-year period was rated as 1.0. Those women consuming one to three drinks weekly had a death risk of 0.83 when compared with nondrinkers. That is to say, they were significantly protected owing to their alcohol consumption. Women having more than three but fewer than eighteen drinks weekly had a 0.88 risk of death, but women consuming more than eighteen drinks per week increased their risk of death to 1.19.

Similar data have been collected around the world. Researchers in Finland, Britain, Australia, Japan, New Zealand, and elsewhere reached the conclusion that those who consume alcohol in moderation were likely to live longer than those who abstain. That decreased mortality is primarily attributed to cardiac protection. In Britain, physicians' drinking habits were correlated with their health for thirteen years. Researchers reported in the *British Medical Journal* in 1994 that men who had eight to fourteen drinks per week had the lowest mortality—30 percent lower than in nondrinkers. Mortality from CHD was lower for drinkers at all consumption levels and was lowest at fifteen to twenty-one drinks per week.

Alcohol provides its protection against heart disease primarily by raising HDL levels in the blood. The effect was first noted by Dr. Charles Hennekens of Harvard in 1987, who found that both HDL components went up. Dr. Hennekens and his associates continued the scientific pursuit of the alcohol/CHD link and published their findings in late 1993 in the *New England Journal of Medicine*. They confirmed that moderate alcohol intake slashed the risk of heart disease, in large part by boosting HDLs. Their statistics were based on total alcohol consumption, whether from wine, beer, or spirits. In all cases, HDL levels went up for drinkers. (HDL as measured in one's blood consists of two components, termed HDL_2 and HDL_3. Early critics of the theory that alcohol confers protection against heart disease felt that perhaps only one of those components was raised by alcohol, and that rises in total HDL counts did not really signal protection if the truly protective component was not increased.)

But increases in HDL levels explain only a certain amount of alcohol's protection against heart disease. Another focus recently has been on how alcohol affects clotting mechanisms in the blood. Clots are frequently responsible for initiating heart attacks by blocking the flow of blood through an artery already narrowed by atherosclerosis. The greater the tendency of blood to clot, the more the risk of MI.

It turns out that alcohol interferes with clotting in three ways. First, when blood platelets are particularly sticky, they tend to form clots more readily; alcohol makes those platelets less sticky. Second, a substance in blood known as fibrinogen facilitates clotting; alcohol breaks down that fibrinogen, reducing levels in the blood and thus preventing excessive clotting. Third, a natural clot-buster termed TPA (tissue plasminogen activator) increases in the blood of drinkers. Interestingly, doctors inject doses of TPA to dissolve clots of patients suffering a heart attack, thus reestablishing blood flow.

Little or no research has been done, however, on the main reason people drink in the first place: pleasure and relaxation. A cocktail before dinner or a glass or two of wine during that meal certainly are enjoyable. After the day's work and stress, it's nice to lean back and relax with a dry martini or a fine cabernet sauvignon. Stress is a significant risk factor for heart disease, and I can't think of many more pleasant ways to reduce that stress!

WHAT IS MODERATION?

While those described as moderate drinkers enjoy a longer, healthier life than those who totally abstain from alcohol, heavier drinkers lose that advantage. Plotting out the data, one comes up with what is referred to as a "J-shaped curve." Have one or two drinks a day, on average, and your risk of heart disease drops and your chances for long life increase. That's the bottom of the curve. As one imbibes in more than that moderate amount, the mortality rate owing to other causes affected by excessive alcohol intake goes up, overwhelming the cardiac protection.

In every study that I am aware of, moderation has been defined as one to two drinks daily on average. One drink would be a six-ounce glass of wine, a twelve-ounce can of beer, or a 1.5-ounce shot of spirits. Thus a standard twenty-six-ounce bottle of wine contains four to five servings.

The line between moderation and excess has been rather strictly drawn. Enjoy one or two drinks daily and reap the health benefits as well as the pleasures. Up your average to three or more a day, and while the protection against heart disease remains, risk of death from other causes increases, first canceling out the initial advantage over abstainers and then significantly cutting longevity. Thus the *J* shape of the curve.

The hazards of alcohol are very real. That's why doctors have, for the most part, been cautious about blanket recommendations. A certain percentage of those who drink will become alcoholics, and a significant number will drink heavily. We hear a lot about the so-called French Paradox and how the regular consumption of wine in France protects against CHD despite a high-fat diet. Seldom mentioned, however, is the extremely high rate of cirrhosis of the liver in that country. Excessive alcohol intake also leads to peptic ulcers, cancer of the liver, pancreatitis, hemorrhagic stroke, hypertension, damage to the heart muscle called cardiomyopathy, and a variety of oral cancers as well as colon cancer. Of course, alcohol also provides significant calories, contributing to obesity.

Women face additional dangers. While moderate consumption protected those participating in the Harvard Nurses' Health Study, that same amount of alcohol appeared to cause a 30 percent increase in the risk of breast cancer. Although that connection has not been positively confirmed, the possibility remains.

Alcohol has also been implicated in fetal alcohol syndrome, including low birth weight. No one has yet to determine how much liquor consumption might be involved with such negative effects to the infant, and the cautious advice remains for pregnant women to abstain. The odds of a young woman developing heart disease are relatively low, so the benefits of alcohol consumption may be outweighed by the potential of breast cancer. Conversely, a postmenopausal woman might cut her risk of having a heart attack with a glass or two of wine or a beverage of her choice.

Should You Drink Alcohol?

Every person is different and must be considered individually. If you have doubts, talk about your medical and family history with your doctor. A fifty-year-old man who drinks moderately and has a history of heart disease but no history of colon cancer, for example, might benefit in terms of CHD while not worrying about any potential increase in risk of cancer. For a young woman with a history of breast cancer in the family but no heart disease, on the other hand, alcohol might not be advisable.

Certainly there are individuals who should not drink, period. Those with a history of alcoholism are playing Russian roulette by trying to drink socially; for them, even one drink is too much. Established liver disease may lead your doctor to discourage your imbibing. Controlling blood pressure often requires eliminating alcohol or at least restricting it.

Despite those gloomy thoughts, however, most men and women can enjoy moderate alcohol consumption throughout their adult lives with no ill effects. And the protection against heart disease remains very real.

WHAT'LL YOU HAVE?

Initial research explored the health benefits or hazards of alcohol in general, rather than of a specific beverage. Most studies have focused on drinkers rather than on their drinks. The two largest studies done to date, with physicians and nurses, did not delineate the drink of choice. All types of alcohol have shown benefit, both by raising the levels of HDL and inhibiting blood clotting.

Do you prefer a beer with your meals or while watching a ballgame on TV? Johns Hopkins researchers have good news for you. Their study focused on beer drinkers and found the same benefits.

But certainly the lion's share of attention has focused on wine. Though the information had been in the medical literature for quite a while, the *60 Minutes* presentation of the French Paradox created a huge increase in sales of wine in general and red wine in particular.

Can red wine really wash away the ill effects of butter, cream, and pâté? No investigator doubts there's more to it than that. The French eat small portions of meats and sauces, along with lots of bread and many servings of fruits and vegetables. They eat three meals a day, with virtually no snacking in between. Some regions of France rely on a more healthful Mediterranean diet, with olive oil replacing the butter and cream. Obesity is far less common in France than in America. People exercise more there. Then there is that little factor known as heredity; some people simply have less genetic risk than others, and the French appear to be particularly lucky in that regard.

But does wine have an advantage over other alcoholic beverages? And, if so, is red better than white? In his continuing research, Dr. Klatsky at Kaiser Permanente in California compared drinkers of red and white wines and found no difference in health benefits. Both groups had the edge over those who didn't drink at all. However, he notes that wine drinkers tend to be more educated and more affluent than those who choose other beverages and that such individuals typically are more health conscious in general, smoking less and exercising more. Thus the lifestyles of wine drinkers may be more responsible for their better health than their drinking preferences.

That being said, there are a couple of theoretical advantages to red wine over other alcoholic drinks, including white wine. Owing to the production methods employed, red wine contains a substance called resveratrol, coming from the skins that are left on the grapes to impart the red color. The skins are removed when making white wine.

Resveratrol has a slight cholesterol-lowering ability. But one would have to drink a lot of red wine to get any such effect. Moreover, red grape juice is an even richer source of resveratrol than red wine. Odd that there hasn't been a big jump in sales of grape juice, no?

What else can one find in red wine? Well, it's a source of phenols, which are known to be antioxidants. Like other antioxidants, phenols can prevent oxidation of LDL cholesterol and limit its ability to damage arterial walls. (See chapter 8) Then again, one could get far more antioxidants in a glass of either carrot juice (beta-carotene) or orange juice (vitamin C).

Finally, red wines have more flavonoids than white wine or other alcoholic drinks. Those flavonoids have a strong anticlotting action in the blood, making platelets less sticky. Since clot formation frequently is the precipitating factor in heart attacks, that's worth noting, but all alcohol reduces clotting.

The amount of flavonoids in a glass or two of red wine pales in comparison with that found in fruits and vegetables, especially when eaten with skins intact. Remember that the French are big eaters of fruits and vegetables as well as being red wine drinkers. Moreover, a lot of the wine in France is white rather than red, yet the rate of heart disease is no different in the areas where people prefer one or the other. Finally, green teas enjoyed throughout the Orient are particularly rich sources of flavonoids.

So there you have it. While wine, especially the reds, has a theoretical advantage over other alcoholic beverages, those benefits are probably inconsequential. The principal protective mechanisms of alcohol are its ability to raise HDL levels and to inhibit clotting. Those mechanisms are shared by all alcoholic beverages. It's your choice. Enjoy the drink you prefer.

What do I drink? I enjoy an alcoholic beverage almost every day, always in the evening rather than during the day. One day my wife and I may sit down before dinner with a cocktail. It might be a Manhattan, an old fashioned, or a martini. Another day we'll have spicy food that calls for a cold beer, and the rest of the time we'll share a bottle of wine, either white or red, depending on the meal.

More important than what you drink is when you drink. The best time to tipple is during the evening meal. A big dinner, especially one rich in fat, raises the fat content of the blood significantly. Clotting factors also increase. Some say those are two good reasons why so many heart attacks occur in the late evening and early morning hours. Alcoholic beverages inhibit that clotting for many hours after the time you imbibe. The antioxidant properties of that glass of red wine, along with those fruits and vegetables, can limit the oxidation of LDL cholesterol at its highest level of the day.

Virtually every nation's toast while clinking glasses is an invocation of good health. And, with that thought, I lift my glass to you and say . . .

À santé! (French)

Na zdrowye! (Polish and Russian)

L'chaim! (Hebrew)

· 21 ·

GARLIC: *A Clove a Day Keeps Heart Disease Away*

Folklore has it that a necklace of garlic can keep vampires at bay. Now scientific evidence is piling up all over the world that a clove or two a day might help keep heart disease away. Perhaps coincidentally, garlic has long been a staple ingredient in the cuisines of the world that seem to enjoy protection from heart disease.

Folk medicine touts garlic as a cure for practically anything that ails you. But, of course, scientists didn't put much stock in such claims. That is, until proof began showing up. Since 1960, an astonishing one thousand papers have been published on garlic's benefits in terms of heart disease, cancer, and immunity and infectious diseases.

In 1993 researchers at the New York Medical College published their meta-analysis of garlic research, pooling the data from numerous studies. They concluded that the equivalent of one-half to one clove of garlic daily resulted, on average, in a 9 percent reduction in total cholesterol. Additionally, garlic appears to prevent excessive blood clotting and may also reduce blood pressure.

That same year, Russian scientists gave glowing reports on how garlic limited uptake of LDL cholesterol by atherosclerotic cells grown in laboratory dishes and how the bulb inhibited growth of those artery-clogging cells. Their work was done with garlic powder. We still need studies done with human subjects, not just isolated cells, to be sure of these benefits of garlic.

In June 1993, an article in the *American Journal of Medicine* described a double-blind study in which nineteen men and twenty-three women participated. Half took 300-milligram garlic tablets three times daily, while the other half got a placebo. After twelve weeks, total cholesterol came down from an average of 262 to 247 and LDL was reduced by 11 percent. Levels of the protective HDL were not affected.

In 1995, German investigators reported that total cholesterol dropped by 8 to 12 percent after taking 600 to 900 mg of garlic as tablets. They reiterated garlic's ability to reduce blood pressure and pointed out the additional benefit of reduced clotting.

Certainly that's all good news. Unfortunately, the studies didn't control for weight or fat consumption by the participants. No long-term investigations have determined whether garlic's effects continue for a year or more rather than for weeks or months. Finally, no good dosages studies have determined whether, as most people would naturally ask, If a little is good, is more better?

So where does that leave us? Actually, in a pretty good position. There is absolutely no downside to enjoying garlic as an ingredient in food or taking it as supplements. It would take a dozen or more raw cloves on an empty stomach to create any gastric upset. There are hundreds of delicious ways to add this member of the lily family to your diet. One of my favorites is to roast a whole head of garlic and squeeze the cloves onto bread for a wonderful spread at dinner.

Want to try it? Snip the tips off a head of garlic and remove the papery layers. Brush lightly with olive oil and wrap the head in aluminum foil. Bake one hour at 350°F. Allow to cool a bit and then squeeze the pungent, semiliquid garlic onto your bread. Taste it once, and I guarantee this delicacy will become a regular part of your diet.

Using garlic in cooking is easy. Place cloves on a cutting board and give them a smack with the flat side of a large knife or put the cloves under the knife and whack it with your hand. That'll crack the husk so it's simple to peel off. Then either crush the cloves with the same knife or mince to incorporate into recipes.

Still too much trouble? Reach for the bottle of garlic powder. Just one-third of a teaspoon contains as much garlic as you'd get from six Kwai tablets or four Kyolic tablets, according to the CSPI.

If you opt for a garlic supplement, don't take more than three 300-milligram tablets daily. We have pretty good evidence that that much probably will provide benefits, but there's no indication at this time that more would be better. The substance thought to be responsible for the heart-protecting effects of garlic is alliin, a precursor to alicin and diallyl disulfide, the sulfur compounds that give garlic its distinctive bite. Both Kwai and Kyolic have been used in studies, and one doesn't appear superior to the other. Watch the price. There's no reason to spend your money on costly garlic supplements when inexpensive brands such as KAL provide the punch for much less.

· 22 ·

Iron and Heart Disease: *A Rusty Proposition*

When a Finnish study linked iron with heart disease, national headlines sent another fear into the public's mind. Some manufacturers came up with vitamin/mineral supplements with no added iron. Unfortunately, as additional data became available, the information didn't get the attention needed to put the matter into perspective, so let's do that now.

The theory that high levels of iron in the blood increased the risk of heart disease was first proposed in 1981 by Dr. Jerome Sullivan in South Carolina. He noticed that women were protected against heart disease before menopause, but lost that protection when they stopped menstruating. Perhaps, he thought, regular blood loss led to iron loss and lower iron stores. He suggested that iron levels be measured and that men and postmenopausal women might gain the protection of premenopausal women by routinely contributing blood. The theory lost favor, however, when it was noted that postmenopausal women receiving hormone replacement therapy were no longer at risk of heart disease and that it was probably estrogen that protected the hearts of premenopausal women.

Then in 1992 the study from the University of Kuopio in Finland rocked the world of cardiology. Men with a high level of iron stored as ferritin were found to be at twice the risk of heart disease of those with lower counts. That paper resulted in a lot of follow-up research, but the subsequent findings did not back the initial Finnish theory.

In a 1993 study, Harvard researchers examined nearly five hundred physicians and the levels of ferritin in their blood. Dr. Meir Stampfer said the study was designed to be similar to the Finnish work. Those with high ferritin levels, more than two hundred micrograms per liter of blood, had no more risk of heart attack than those with lower measurements.

Another study that same year, also at Harvard, followed nearly 46,000 men for four years to see if iron intake, rather than measurements in the blood, might show a correlation. Data included both dietary iron and supplements. For the most part, neither was associated with heart disease, but the iron from meat, so-called heme iron, was linked with a larger number of heart attacks. Men in the top 20 percent of heme iron intake had a 43 percent increase in risk of MI when compared with men in the bottom 20 percent.

But the men at risk also had other contributing factors, especially elevated levels of total and LDL cholesterol. That was also true in the original Finnish study. Dr. Alberto Ascherio concluded that the heme iron may increase the damage produced by those other risk factors. For example, the iron may contribute to LDL oxidation and result in greater development of atherosclerosis.

At about the same time, the Finnish researchers reported that leisure-time exercise appears to reduce stored iron. The question, then, was whether one value of exercise is, perhaps, to deplete iron storage. But the idea of stored iron posing a link was still in dispute.

Nibbling away at the theory, investigators at Chicago's Loyola University studied the iron levels in the blood of four thousand men and women participating in a health and nutrition survey. Ironically, the higher the iron, the lower the risk of heart attack. However, stored iron, ferritin, was not measured.

If stored iron was the culprit, as the Finns and others maintained, then those with very high levels should be particularly at risk of heart attack. The disease known as hemochromatosis is characterized by abnormally high levels of stored iron. In fact, the principal Finnish iron researcher, Dr. Jukka Salonen, became interested in the concept because he, himself, has hemochromatosis.

So doctors at Baltimore's Johns Hopkins University turned to the hospital's autopsy registry and examined the records of more than 48,000 deaths over a one hundred-year period. They identified the files that noted an iron overload and compared the records in terms of the coronary arteries at death. Surprisingly, not only did iron overload not correlate with risk of heart disease, those with hemochromatosis actually had cleaner arteries than those with lower levels of stored iron.

In those with excessive levels of stored iron, the mineral infiltrates various organs of the body including the muscle of the heart, the myocardium. That factor does, indeed, link with development of cardiomyopathy, the degeneration of the heart muscle, but only in the extreme cases of hemochromatosis, a relatively rare disorder. One in 250 men has the gene for hemochromatosis.

In a further look at the autopsy data, the Hopkins researchers took cholesterol levels into consideration. They concluded that unless cholesterol levels were elevated, the link between iron levels and heart disease is weak. Of the patients with hemochromatosis, four had cholesterols over 240. The worst case was a man with a level of 329, and that patient did, indeed, have severe coronary disease. So, again, cholesterol levels appear to be more important than iron levels, although the Hopkins doctors concluded in late 1993 that it would still be possible for high iron storage to exaggerate the influence of cholesterol.

Another study, published in April 1994 in the *New England Journal of Medicine,* splashed more cold water on the iron theory. Evaluating more than 4,500 men and women, the researchers found no correlation between body iron stores and the risk of coronary heart disease.

At most, the risk of heart disease would appear to be increased only by high intake of heme iron. Other than for men with hemochromatosis, there's no need to worry about the iron in supplements, food product fortification, or other dietary sources. Bear in mind, however, that men and women over fifty years old don't need extra iron. But even with heme iron, the association is suggestive rather than conclusive. The point becomes moot in those following a heart-healthy diet who would automatically cut back on beef consumption. That doesn't mean eliminating beef, but rather reducing serving sizes and particularly fatty cuts. The correlation between heme iron and heart disease was seen only in those with the highest beef consumption. Ah, there's that word moderation again. The biggest risk iron poses might come from stepping on a rusty nail.

Part IV

Food As You Like It

· 23 ·

The Magic Kitchen

Imagine that one day you enter your kitchen and find that your favorite, day-to-day foods have been magically transformed. The fat and cholesterol have been sucked out, leaving only the fun and flavor.

No more choices to make, no more reason for guilt. Every food on the pantry shelf, in the freezer, or in the refrigerator has been metamorphosed from a coronary-disease-causing caterpillar into a healthful butterfly.

It's not likely that the food fairy will visit tonight, but you can make those dramatic changes in your kitchen. You'll then be able to eat virtually everything that you want, any time you want it. Dust off those old family recipes, the ones you thought you'd have to give up forever. Even if they call for cheese, butter, and cream poured over eggs, lobster, and red meat.

Transforming your kitchen starts in the supermarket. Foods that were previously off-limits have come back in heart-healthy versions. No more taboos on those cream soups we all loved to cook with because now the fat, cholesterol, and sodium contents have been slashed. I can't think of a single dish that I can't eat because I fear its effect on my cholesterol level or my waistline.

List the foods you need for the next few days or for the week. Then it's off to the supermarket. But instead of throwing items into your cart without a thought, make those decisions to buy or not to buy based on the Nutrition Facts label on each package.

For that next visit, plan to spend an extra twenty minutes. That'll give you the time to compare and contrast all the items on your list, brand by brand. Do that exercise for the next three shopping trips. After that, you'll start repeating the purchases you made on the first trip. No need to read those labels again. As time goes on, you'll know exactly what products to buy, and your kitchen will continuously metamorphose. The calories, fat, cholesterol, and sodium in your pantry will plunge, and you and your family will scarcely taste or notice the difference.

Throughout this chapter I've used brand names of products so you can go directly to the shelves and find them. I've pretty much covered the waterfront for products most often used in American kitchens. But it's impossible to list every one of the tens of thousands of food products on the market today, and more arrive on the shelves daily.

As you walk the aisles with your shopping cart, keep an eye peeled for new items. Take a moment to pick them up and read the labels. Think of label reading as a sort of hobby, finding new food treasures now and then, things that you would never have considered in the past. Who'd have thought, ten years ago, that you could buy fat-free potato chips or Crackerjacks? Who knows what's on the horizon in the coming months or even weeks?

READING THE LABELS

Of all the things you purchase, none gives you the advance information for an intelligent decision afforded by the current food labels. The revised Nutrition Facts format introduced in 1994 allows you to see just how much fat and how many calories a serving provides. The ingredients label shows you just where that fat and those calories come from.

Take a look at the sample Nutrition Facts on page 227. The most important facts are the servings per container, in this case four, and the total fat, three grams. Ask yourself whether you'll have just one serving or whether the entire container just might wind up being a serving! That's very often the case for dessert and snack foods. Not that there's anything wrong with that; just be honest with yourself.

You'll also find full ingredient labeling on all processed, packaged foods, including standardized foods such as mayonnaise, macaroni, and bread, which were previously exempt. Those nutrients are listed in descending order by weight.

By combining the information from the ingredient label with the Nutrition Facts, you'll know just what you're eating. For example, while you wouldn't mind consuming seven or eight grams of fat from, say, canola or olive oil, that amount of hydrogenated oil or tropical oil might well give you pause.

Fortunately, we can trust the labels to be quite accurate. The Food and Drug Administration (FDA) tested three hundred products in 1994 to see if information on food labels was on target. FDA found 94 percent of the labels correctly labeled fat content and 93 percent provided accurate caloric content. You can believe the labels on national brands rather implicitly. Regional brands are quite reliable. Local products, which seldom get FDA attention, might be

The New Food Label at a Glance

The new food label will carry an up-to-date, easier-to-use nutrition information guide, to be required on almost all packaged foods (compared to about 60 percent of products up till now). The guide will serve as a key to help in planning a healthy diet.*

Serving sizes are now more consistent across product lines, stated in both household and metric measures, and reflect the amounts people actually eat.

New title signals that the label contains the newly required information.

Calories from fat are now shown on the label to help consumers meet dietary guidelines that recommend people get no more than 30 percent of their calories from fat.

% Daily Value shows how a food fits into the overall daily diet.

The **list of nutrients** covers those most important to the health of today's consumers, most of whom need to worry about getting too much of certain items (fat, for example), rather than too few vitamins or minerals, as in the past.

Daily Values are also something new. Some are maximums, as with fat (65 grams or less); others are minimums, as with carbohydrate (300 grams or more). The daily values for a 2,000- and 2,500-calorie diet must be listed on the label of larger packages. Individuals should adjust the values to fit their own calorie intake.

The label of larger packages must now tell the number of calories per gram of fat, carbohydrate, and protein.

Nutrition Facts

Serving Size 1/2 cup (114g)
Servings Per Container 4

Amount Per Serving

Calories 90 — Calories from Fat 30

	% Daily Value*
Total Fat 3g	**5%**
Saturated Fat 0g	**0%**
Cholesterol 0mg	**0%**
Sodium 300mg	**13%**
Total Carbohydrate 13g	**4%**
Dietary Fiber 3g	**12%**
Sugars 3g	
Protein 3g	

Vitamin A	80%	•	Vitamin C	60%
Calcium	4%	•	Iron	4%

* Percent Daily Values are based on a 2,000 calorie diet. Your daily values may be higher or lower depending on your calorie needs:

	Calories	2,000	2,500
Total Fat	Less than	65g	80g
Sat Fat	Less than	20g	25g
Cholesterol	Less than	300mg	300mg
Sodium	Less than	2,400mg	2,400mg
Total Carbohydrate		300g	375g
Fiber		25g	30g

Calories per gram:
Fat 9 • Carbohydrate 4 • Protein 4

* This label is only a sample. Exact specifications are in the final rules.
Source: Food and Drug Administration 1993

off a bit. That's especially true for store brands. For example, I once found a caramel popcorn with almonds labeled as low fat, with just two grams of fat per serving and four servings per container. But the generous allowance of almonds boosted the fat content significantly. Did I buy the snack? Yes, and it was delicious, but I knew I had to calculate double the listed fat. I also knew that the fat, coming exclusively from the nuts, was the healthful monounsaturated type.

Most of the confusion in reading labels comes from the combining of the metric and English measurement systems. Let me make it easy for you. A 3½-ounce serving equals one-hundred grams. Obviously, 3 percent of 100 is 3, 17 percent of 100 is 17, and so forth. So if you were to see a label listing its product as 97% fat-free you know that 3 percent is fat. Three percent of 100 grams is, of course, three grams. Therefore, there are three grams of fat per 3½-ounce serving. Some food processers boast that their products are, say, "80% fat free." That claim might look good at first, but do your metric mathematics. That product contains twenty grams of fat per 3½ ounces. And, to put that into even a clearer perspective, the metric equivalent is twenty-eight grams per ounce.

If all this is new to you, it will take a little time to get used to processing the information. At first I spent quite a lot of time trying to decipher labels. Now the decision making is practically automatic. I'll give you a headstart by citing of the fat-gram content of some commonly consumed foods as we continue our shopping trip in this chapter.

LITTLE THINGS MEAN A LOT

For the most part, Americans are very well nourished. We get plenty of protein, and most of us get enough vitamins and minerals either through our foods or supplements. Our fiber intake has increased during the past decade of awareness. So let's not throw the baby out with the bathwater when we try to improve our nutrition status. There's no need to make any radical changes. Just a tweak here and there will do the trick.

Let's start that tweaking by learning just where the fat in our diets comes from. You're in for some surprises. The U.S. Department of Agriculture (USDA) reported its finding from the Continuous Survey for Food Intakes of Individuals conducted between 1989 and 1991 at a conference held in 1994. That survey identified the top sources of fat in our diets. Here's the list:

TOP SOURCES OF FAT

Food	*Percentage of Fat*
Margarine	7.13
Whole Milk	5.42
Shortening	4.14
Mayonnaise/Salad Dressing	3.25
American Cheese	3.21
Ground Beef, Regular	2.67
Low-fat Milk, 2%	2.33
Eggs	2.21
Butter	2.05
Total	32.41

Of course these figures refer to the consumption of the average American. You may already have started to cut back on fat, and the figures may not pertain in all cases to your personal current situation. But, again on average, most Americans get a total of 32.41 percent of their fat from these nine dietary sources. That's nearly one-third of total fat intake. In other words, by simply paying attention to modifying the fat intake from these food categories, one can get down to a healthy fat intake without changing anything else in the diet!

Let's look at those foods one by one. Margarine provides more than 7 percent of all the fat we consume. How can you cut that figure back? Rather than choosing a regular margarine with eleven grams of fat per tablespoon, pick a soft-tub type with only two to three grams. Instead of sautéing in margarine, spray the pan with vegetable oil spray and eliminate practically all the fat. Replace the margarine in baking recipes with Bateman's Baking Butter (see page 234) and cancel out all of that fat.

Whole milk contributes 5.42 percent of our dietary fat, and 2 percent low-fat milk—a real misnomer—comes across with another 2.33 percent. Gradually work your way down from whole, to 2 percent, to 1 percent, and then finally to skim and cancel all that fat.

The next category is a bit more tricky. Shortening supplies 4.14 percent of dietary fat for Americans. That's primarily from processed foods and fast foods, with some added at home in baking and cooking. While you can't eliminate all the shortening without suffering some really significant deprivation, you can certainly cut back by choosing low-fat items, as I'll point out throughout this section of the book.

Mayonnaise and salad dressings bring 3.25 percent of the fat to our tables. Supermarket shelves offer a wide selection of low-fat as well as fat-free "mayos" and dressings.

American cheese—not counting all the other varieties of cheese we eat—provides 3.21 percent of America's fat. Cheese has nine grams of fat per ounce. Hate the fat-free cheeses? How about compromising with the low-fat varieties that cut the fat in half but still have the flavor and melt you want.

Ground beef has up to 30 percent fat by weight. It's responsible for 2.67 percent of all the fat in the American diet. By following my suggestions on page 238, you can cut that fat down to a mere 5 percent by weight.

Eggs are better known for their cholesterol than for the fat, but each yolk has five grams. Counting both the whole eggs and the "invisible" eggs in baked and processed foods, eggs provide 2.21 percent of dietary fat. By using the egg substitutes for omelets, French toast, baking, and cooking—places where you won't taste the difference—you can eliminate all that fat. You'll also save forty-five calories per replaced egg. Save the whole eggs for breakfasts when you'll really enjoy them—and block the absorption of cholesterol with phytosterols.

Finally, butter supplies 2.05 percent of total fat eaten. Most of that fat is saturated. This is one food we can all do without, except for very special, infrequent treats.

You don't need a dietitian or a mathematician to modify your diet regarding those nine food items. It's really easy, and the results can be remarkable. Researchers from the University of Minnesota wanted to know just how much of a difference making only one such change would make.

In 1994 they gave a group of volunteers the same diet, containing 30 percent of its calories from fat, with either whole milk or skim. Everything else remained the same. Just the type of milk varied from one group to the other. After only six weeks, those drinking skim milk had a 6.8 percent lower total cholesterol level than those drinking whole milk. On average, both groups drank a little more than two glasses daily. That one change produced a nearly 7 percent difference. Little things do mean a lot!

Quite frankly, if you were to change only those nine foods, you'd already be well ahead of the game. That's especially true when you include SeQuester and the phytosterols in your program, blocking the fat and cholesterol from other foods. Now let's look more closely at our shopping list to see how we can fine-tune our choices.

THE PRODUCE SECTION

In the past, the benefits of fruits and vegetables were thought to come from their replacement of other, artery-clogging foods. Today we know that they have a positive advantage of providing not only antioxidants but also a rainbow of healthful substances we're only beginning to discover.

Meeting the recommendation of eating at least five servings of fruits and vegetables daily isn't as difficult as it may sound at first. Those servings, as determined by dietitians, are smaller than one normally would expect. For example, just fifteen small grapes constitute a serving. A large pear equals two servings, not one. A serving of juice is four ounces, not six or eight. In general, count one-half cup of fruit as one serving. The same holds for vegetables. Greens, including cabbage and spinach, provide one serving per cup. A typical salad has about two cups of greens.

Start with breakfast. Slice a banana into your cereal and enjoy a glass of juice. Depending on sizes, you've gotten two to four servings in right there. Add an apple or a salad to your lunch. Have a piece of fruit for an afternoon snack. At dinner, start with vegetable soup. Munch on raisins while watching TV in the evening.

For the most part, you can go bananas (no pun intended) in the produce section. Practically everything there is virtually fat free. And cholesterol, don't forget, comes only from animal foods. In fact, there are only three exceptions. One medium avocado contains about 30 grams of fat, though most of it is the more healthful monounsaturated variety. Moderation is the watchword. The same applies to olives, which have 0.5 to 1 gram each. Because of the brine, they're also high in sodium—so are pickles. The only real offender in the plant kingdom is the coconut. One ounce has nearly 10 grams of fat, most of it saturated. A cup of coconut cream, in case you were thinking about pina coladas, packs 52.5 grams out of the can and 83.2 grams made from scratch. Even the coconut milk contains a lot of fat; at least 50 grams per cup, which is more saturated than lard. Sorry about that if you're a coconut lover. If you like it that much, simply keep your consumption in moderation, making room for that fat by compensating in other foods.

Here's food for thought: Islanders eat coconut all the time and don't have heart attacks. That's because they typically eat little if any meat. It's all a matter of balance.

Spend a bit of extra time in the produce section looking for foods you may not have purchased before: baby carrots, daikon, bok choi, fresh black-eyed peas. Talk with your green grocer about the best ways to prepare them. Exotics such as cherimoya and Asian pears keep coming along. Why not try them?

THE DAIRY CASE

Remember that USDA food survey when buying dairy foods. Happily, we can now enjoy every single milk product with less, or even none, of the offending fat and cholesterol. As a bonus calories plummet as well.

Start with an eight-ounce glass of milk. Whole milk has 8 grams of fat and 33 mg of cholesterol. Switching to 2 percent low-fat milk brings them down to 5 grams and 18 mg, respectively. Then consider the next move to 1 percent low-fat milk with about 2.5 grams of fat and 10 mg of cholesterol. Eventually you may graduate to nonfat (skim) milk with just a trace of each. Make your changes a little at a time, and you won't notice much difference.

Whether for cooking, baking, or drinking, buttermilk offers a nice alternative. Look for the brand with the lowest fat content. Wonderful in pancakes!

Find nonfat chocolate milk in the dairy case or make your own by mixing two tablespoons of chocolate syrup with skim milk. It's nice for variety.

Unlike whole milk, and even low-fat milk, you can freeze skim milk. The caveat against freezing is because the butterfat separates when frozen milk thaws. Without fat in skim milk, there's no problem. In fact, the milk may taste even richer. Now you can store an extra quart in the freezer so you never run out.

After a while you'll actually prefer the clean, fresh taste of nonfat or at least 1 percent low-fat milk, but it just does not work in coffee. For that you need a creamer. Half-and-half provides 3.3 grams of largely saturated fat per ounce. Older nondairy creamers used tropical oils, but today's creamers are a delight. Most have one to two grams of fat per tablespoon, typically from soybean oil. "Lite" versions of Carnation and Mocha Mix have less than a gram per ounce. You can even get those brands fat free. Use them in recipes as well as in coffee.

For years, health advocates including myself suggested replacing sour cream with nonfat plain yogurt. Close, but no cigar. Imitation sour creams, on the other hand, were made with coconut oil. Now every supermarket sells nonfat sour cream. Quality varies tremendously from brand to brand, so you'll want to taste test more than one. On the West Coast, for example, Knudsen's is particularly good. Use it to make dips you may have been avoiding. Put a dollop on your baked potato with some chives or bring back those wonderful stroganoff recipes.

Standard cottage cheese has 4 percent milkfat, giving a four-ounce serving five grams of fat; 2 percent brands have two grams per half cup. Weight Watchers and others sell 1 percent cottage cheese, with just one gram of fat per serving. And if you opt for the fat-free types, try spooning in a bit of milk to make them creamy.

What a Difference a Gram Makes

Often just one gram of fat in a product makes it vastly superior to the fat-free versions. There's just no comparison between Borden's low-fat cheese slices with one gram of fat and the fat-free slices. The same applies to cheese shreds, which just won't melt on your pizza or tacos. Opt, instead, for low-fat shreds. What's a gram or two of fat over the course of the whole day? The idea is to improve your diet to a level you can happily live with, not to a point of deprivation that you'll most likely abandon after a month or two.

FATS, OILS, AND DRESSINGS

With all the talk about fats being bad and yet some oils supposedly being healthy, it's no wonder people are confused. Let's cut right to the bottom line. Yes, some fats and oils are better than others. Ultimately we want to keep the saturated fats—and the trans fats—in our diet as low as possible, and the total amount of fat in reasonable moderation. That's actually not so hard to do.

The chart on page 37 lists most of the commonly used oils in the American diet. You can easily see that saturated fat content varies enormously.

On the other hand, we know now that monounsaturated fats such as those found in olive oil and canola oil are among the healthiest. People in the Mediterranean have used olive oil extensively for thousands of years, and they have one of the best health records in the world. When it comes to taste, probably nothing compares with olive oil. A drizzle of extra-virgin oil sparks many an Italian dish, but sometimes we don't want the flavor of our oil to get in the way of other ingredients. That's the time for the bland-tasting canola oil, with even more monounsaturates than olive oil.

Yet neither of those oils holds up well to high heat. We also need oils that have what's called a high smoke point such as corn, safflower, or sunflower. All are low in saturates. Peanut oil has a high smoke point, can be heated to high temperatures for stir-frying, and gives a special flavor to those foods. Walnut oil mixed with equal parts of raspberry vinegar makes a wonderful dressing when sprinkled over greens such as radicchio, endive, oak leaf lettuce, and others; sesame oil provides an intense burst of flavor even when used in tiny quantities.

We can save an enormous amount of fat with a product that's been around for decades. In my kitchen I rarely prepare a meal without somehow using one of the vegetable oil sprays such as Pam. Be sure to toss a can of regular and butter flavor spray in your shopping cart.

To me, butter flavor Pam is indispensable. I even use it to "butter" a piece of toast before spreading on the marmalade or preserves. Spraying nonstick pans not only makes the pan "more nonsticky" but also provides a bit of flavor. A spray of Pam is just as effective as a tablespoon or two of oil to sauté onion, garlic, or sliced peppers.

NOTE: EVERY TIME YOU REPLACE ONE TABLESPOON OF OIL—ANY OIL—YOU SAVE FOURTEEN GRAMS OF FAT AND 120 CALORIES.

If you're a baker, the next item on the shopping list will save not only fat and calories but a lot of time as well. Many recipes instruct you to grease and flour the baking pan before adding the batter. Baker's Joy combines the oil and flour in a convenient spray. A simple spritz and you're done.

Remember that shortening makes a hefty contribution to the total fat consumed in the American diet. Bateman's Baking Butter, a newly developed fat replacement available to the public, can totally eliminate the shortening in all your baking. This wonderful new product replaces butter and other shortening on a one-to-one basis, whether measuring by weight or by volume. With every order of tubs of Baking Butter, you'll receive a pamphlet of recipes and tips for successful fat-free baking. We've tried Mrs. Bateman's fudge brownies, carrot cake, chocolate cake, chocolate chip cookies, cinnamon rolls, banana bread, and pie crust. Every recipe was a winner and had the family clamoring for more. While the pie crust still doesn't measure up to my mother-in-law's artery-clogging, lard-based crust, this one is the best fat-free crust I've found in years of searching. My only negative experience was using Baking Butter as suggested for sautéing as a replacement for oil; it just doesn't work, and you're better off staying with Pam. For baking you can't beat it. Order directly from the company by calling (800) 574-6822.

Now we come to another of my favorite products: Butter Buds. Frankly, I don't know what I'd do without this item. Made by Cumberland Products and distributed nationally, this is the first product of its kind. Molly McButter and others have come along since. But only Butter Buds comes in packets as well as in sprinkle containers and, for my purposes, that's essential.

Ironically, I find the originally intended use of Butter Buds to be completely unacceptable. According to the manufacturer, the packets are to be mixed with water to create a butter substitute. I find it terrible that way. The trick is to use the product in its concentrated form to provide the full blast of butter flavor. For example, when preparing acorn squash, directly replace butter or margarine with Butter Buds. As the vegetable cooks, the flavor permeates the food and you'd swear it was dripping with butter. The same goes for mashed potatoes.

But here's the real discovery, which I credit entirely to my wife Dawn. You can replace the butter or margarine called for in a variety of packaged products with Butter Buds and you can't tell the difference. If directions call for two tablespoons of butter or margarine, use one tablespoon of Butter Buds straight out of the packet. Just remember that two-to-one ratio, regardless of quantity required. Here are some examples of fabulous fat savings.

Kraft Macaroni and Cheese dinner is an all-American favorite. The fat per serving in the package is 2 grams. That's not bad at all. But that number jumps to 13 grams after preparing as directed. Instead of the ½ cup of margarine called for on the family size package, use ¼ cup of Butter Buds and skim rather than whole milk. You'll get all that wonderful, creamy, cheesy flavor with a tiny fraction of the fat.

How about those Noodle Roni products as side dishes for dinner? They save a lot of time, and the whole family loves them. But the price you pay in fat and calories is high. In both the angel hair pasta with herbs and the corkscrew pasta with four cheeses, fat and calories are listed at two grams and 130 calories as packaged. Once again, use one tablespoon of Butter Buds rather than margarine and skim milk instead of whole, and you'll have terrific fat savings.

Salad dressings and mayonnaise, you'll recall, contribute a lot of our dietary fat, according to the USDA survery. But you can virtually eliminate that fat with low-fat and nonfat products now on the market. Only trial and error will zero you in on the dressings you'll enjoy eating. It's a matter of taste. You might try making your own dressing with healthful olive oil.

When it comes to choosing a mayonnaise, shopping is a lot easier. Just pick up a jar of Best Foods Low-Fat Mayonnaise (Hellmann's on the East Coast and in the Midwest). It's the hands-down best of all. Just one gram of fat per tablespoon, but what a difference that single gram makes compared with the fat-free mayonnaises on the market. This brand is really delicious. Use it to make tartar sauce for fish, salad dressings, and every recipe that calls for mayo.

Butter Versus Margarine Is No Contest at All

While the caloric content is about the same for stick margarine and butter, of the latter's 11.4 grams of fat per tablespoon, 7.1 are saturated. Compare that with various brands of margarine:

Brand	Total fat (Grams)	Saturated fat (Grams)	Calories
Mazzola (stick)	11.0	2.0	100
Nucoa (stick)	11.0	2.0	100
Nucoa Smart Beat (tub)	3.0	1.0	25
Weight Watchers (tub)	6.0	1.0	50
I Can't Believe It's Not Butter (tub)	10.0	2.0	90
I Can't Believe It's Not Butter Lite (tub)	6.0	1.0	50
Promise Ultra (tub)	3.5	0	30

Two things become obvious on this chart and in your supermarket as you read labels. First, there's a lot less saturated fat in any kind of margarine compared with butter. Second, you can see tremendous variations from brand to brand. It's up to you to determine how much fat you want. Of course, taste comes into play, and you'll want to do a bit of experimenting to see how far you can cut the fat and still enjoy the flavor. You may even want to stock a couple of brands for different applications.

Soups, sauces, and gravies offer easy and tasty ways to cut fat. You can further slash the fat content of just about any soup or broth by putting the can in your freezer for a few minutes prior to opening. The fat will congeal on top, allowing you to skim it off. Fat will rise to the top to a certain extent even on the pantry shelf.

I like to use broths and bouillons in cooking. Try one to add extra flavor to rice or boiled potatoes. Today you can also find sodium-reduced broths in any market.

Dried soup mixes and ramens are convenient, but read the labels carefully. Most top ramen noodle soups deliver a whopping eighteen grams of fat. That's because they fry the noodles and then put more fat in the flavor packets. Look for low-fat versions such as Campbell's or drop some noodles or other pasta into chicken broth to make your own.

Experiment with a variety of gourmet soup mixes such as split pea, black bean, and many bean mixtures. You're in control of additional ingredients such as meat, broth, and salt. Putting more beans into your diet increases your daily consumption of both soluble and insoluble fibers.

Canned soups of all sorts come in reduced-fat versions. They're great with a sandwich. Stock some of the cream soups to use in a variety of recipes. Thinned out a bit and jazzed up with a few herbs or spices, those soups make wonderful sauces.

Simmer sauces make meal preparation a whole lot easier. Read the labels to choose low-fat varieties. Betty Crocker Recipe Sauce for chicken cacciatore has less than one gram of fat and 570 mg of sodium. Add an extra garlic clove or two and some bell pepper strips. I also like to add extra veggies. The teriyaki flavor, to which you can add beef, pork, or chicken, also has less than one gram of fat and 820 mg of sodium. I add fresh broccoli during the last five minutes of simmering.

Try Ragu Chicken Tonight sweet and sour simmer sauce with pork tenderloin chunks. I add some crushed garlic cloves, quartered onions, and bell pepper strips. This item is particularly healthful, with zero fat and just 280 mg of sodium. Ragu's honey mustard sauce is great with either chicken or pork, and I add some fresh green beans during the last ten minutes.

Serve the simmer sauce meals with rice or pasta. Total preparation time, including setting the table, is never more than thirty minutes. These are real life savers in a time crunch.

Sauces and gravies pose no fat challenges. You may not know it, but those packets of dried gravies in any flavors are virtually fat free. The ones in the jars have just a gram or two.

I keep a "library" of dried sauce and gravy mixes in my pantry. Mix the packet contents with water as directed or add with water to the skillet in which you prepare your meat to scrape up those little bits and pieces to provide a real "homemade" quality. Thinking of that gravy over a mound of mashed potatoes and a slab of meatloaf makes my mouth water. You too?

But how about some of those fancier sauces? Asparagus with hollandaise, broiled sea bass with béarnaise, beef bourguignonne—no problem, even for someone who's all thumbs in the kitchen or when there's no time to fuss. Just go to that library of sauce mixes in your pantry, and prepare the sauces with Butter Buds rather than butter or margarine.

MEATS, POULTRY, AND SEAFOOD

Despite the increasing popularity of vegetarianism, most Americans enjoy meats, poultry, and seafood of all sorts. The potential variety makes eating a lot more enjoyable. You can enjoy meat virtually every day if you wish and still keep your fat intake extremely low.

Beef and other red meats have gotten an undeserved bad rap because people have oversimplified healthy recommendations. Sure, some red meat is a major source of saturated fat and cholesterol, but other cuts are as low in fat as chicken breast without the skin.

According to statistics from the USDA, we eat more than 50 percent of all red meat in the form of ground beef. A quick look at the supermarket meat case reveals how that translates into a high-fat diet in this country.

By USDA standards, ground beef can contain no more than 30 percent fat. That means thirty grams of fat per 3½-ounces of raw meat. Lean ground beef has 22 percent fat, and ultralean ground beef has 15 percent. To put all this into perspective, skinless chicken breast has about four grams per 3½ ounces. See how beef got that bad image? But you can change all that.

Instead of picking up a package of preground beef, find a chunk of round steak or top sirloin. Ask the butcher to trim off the visible fat and then grind the meat. You'll have ground beef with a fat content of only five grams per serving. Stock your freezer with one-pound packages. You'll be able to make all your recipes with a dramatic slash in both fat and calories. With a mere five grams of fat, you can enjoy ground beef throughout the week, in spaghetti sauce, sloppy joe sandwiches, meatloaf, chili, tacos, and all your other favorites.

Just making this one change in your kitchen will instantly put you on the track to better health and weight control. It takes very little effort.

For those recipes calling for solid beef, whether steaks or roasts, choose USDA select. That's the leanest grade you can buy in the supermarket. You may be surprised at just how "skinny" beef can be. Here are the numbers for three-ounce servings after cooking and trimming.

Beef Cut	Calories	Total Fat	Saturated Fat	Cholesterol
Eye of round	143	4.2 g	1.5 g	59 mg
Top round	153	4.2 g	1.4 g	71 mg
Top sirloin	165	6.1 g	2.4 g	76 mg
Tenderloin	179	8.5 g	3.2 g	71 mg

Of course, other cuts are more "fat challenged," And you probably will want more than three ounces when eating steak. A fourteen-ounce slab of rib-eye steak packs forty-six grams of fat if you trim off the external fat. That number jumps to eighty-two grams if you don't trim!

So what's a real beef lover to do? Fortunately a few ranchers today appreciate the taste of a great steak and yet realize the importance of reducing fat. They're raising beef that is leaner yet as tender and flavorful as the old-fashioned kind.

One such source is Meucci Ranch beef. I've done a lot of research to find beef that I can recommend without reservations, and this is it. Fat content for all cuts is as low or lower than for skinless chicken breast or fish, as low as three grams and no more than five per 3½-ounce serving. As a side note, no steroids or hormones are used in raising this special beef, crossbred from a European breed called the Belgian Blue, which is known for its heavy muscling and low fat content. Moreover, the cholesterol level is one-third that of chicken breast. Thus, even an eleven-ounce hunk of steak has only nine grams of fat and the cholesterol of a 3½-ounce piece of chicken breast, about ninety milligrams.

Name a cut of beef, and Meucci Ranch can supply it: filet mignon, New York strip sirloins, T-bone steaks, ribeyes, top sirloins, beef ribs, sirloin tip roasts, rump roasts, and a so-called Belgium cut steak, which starts off as chuck or round steak and is crosscut for greatest tenderness. Celebrate St. Patrick's day with a corned beef brisket. Imagine chewing the last of the meat from a Porterhouse steak bone.

Prices are extremely reasonable, much less than those charged by other producers of "designer" beef. Expect to pay about the same as you do for choice beef in a butcher shop, and the prices include shipping directly to your door. Place your orders by calling (800) 484-5477, extension 2333 (BEEF). I'm sure that once you taste Meucci Ranch beef, you'll want to keep a supply of cuts in your freezer.

NOTE: BECAUSE MEUCCI BEEF IS SO LOW IN FAT, IT COOKS MUCH FASTER THAN ORDINARY BEEF. ENJOY IT RARE OR MEDIUM RARE. DON'T OVERCOOK.

Veal also offers an opportunity to enjoy red meat that's low in fat. Four ounces of cooked leg meat, for example, has less than six grams of fat. It's excellent for scallopini; try my recipe on page 287. For stews, ask your butcher for leg and shoulder meat cut into cubes; four cooked ounces provide less than five grams of fat. Also consider having your butcher grind some of that stew meat to blend with ground beef and pork (see page 238) for an outstanding meatloaf. I like to keep two or three ½-pound packages in my freezer for just that purpose.

NOTE: MUCH OF THE VEAL SOLD TODAY IS DESIGNATED AS "FREE RANGE" INDICATING THAT IT WAS NOT RAISED IN CONFINEMENT AS IN THE PAST. ASK YOUR BUTCHER IF YOU HAVE ETHICAL CONCERNS.

Pork is the big surprise in the meat case for those who have been misled into thinking that all pork is high in fat. Follow the old adage to "eat high on the hog." No, that doesn't mean expensive. Choose the cuts that come from the upper areas of the carcass: ham, loin, and tenderloin, rather than lower cuts such as bacon and ribs.

Ham steaks make an easy to prepare dinner. Many brands have as little as two or three grams of fat per 3½-ounces. Even if you double that serving size, the fat content remains very low.

Pork tenderloin truly is "the other white meat," with fat content similar to chicken breast without the skin. Count on only four grams per serving. You can use the tenderloin chunks as kabobs, in dishes that call for chicken breast, or prepared with one of the oven-fry mixes such as Shake 'n Bake—or try roasting a whole tenderloin.

Boneless, well-trimmed pork loin is also low in fat, about six grams per serving. Look, too, for butterfly chops. Roast an entire chunk. Don't forget to have some ground.

NOTE: MODERN PRODUCTION PRACTICES HAVE GREATLY REDUCED THE FAT IN PORK, AND THE ONCE PREVALENT SCOURGE OF TRICHINOSIS HAS BEEN VIRTUALLY ELIMINATED. IT IS NO LONGER NECESSARY TO OVERCOOK PORK TO KILL PARASITES. COOK TO AN INTERNAL TEMPERATURE OF 160 TO 165°F. IT'S OKAY IF THE JUICES RUN SLIGHTLY PINK.

Breeders have been developing leaner and leaner hogs to accomodate today's tastes. While certain cuts are now in the heart-healthy range, others have remained in the forbidden zone. Spareribs, for example, pack more than thirty grams of fat in 3½ cooked ounces of meat. After trimming all the fat off a cooked rib chop, one still is left with fifteen grams of fat in 3½ ounces.

Now the ultimate pork is available through Meucci Ranch, the same people who provide the ultra-low-fat beef. Carefully crossbred and fed, pork can return to the tables of those of us who want to stay heart smart. Imagine such treats as pork chops, filets, roasts, and even spareribs and baby back ribs with less than 3 percent fat. That equates to just three grams of fat per 3½-ounce serving, so you can eat a more realistic seven-ounce serving for no more than, and usually less than, six grams of fat. The phone number is the same as for the beef: (800) 484-5477, extension 2333.

Here's the way I like to prepare spareribs and baby back ribs. Place them in a large pot or Dutch oven and cover with water. Add two tablespoons of vinegar, a tablespoon of black peppercorns, four or five peeled and crushed garlic cloves, and a tablespoon of rosemary. Bring the water to a boil; then reduce the heat to a simmer and cover for fifteen to twenty minutes. Drain and slather the ribs with your favorite barbecue sauce and finish over the charcoal grill or under the broiler. That's a meal to prove to anyone that you can eat everything you want and still have your heart thank you for it!

Lamb offers the fewest low-fat choices, but one can still enjoy it now and then. Your best pick is the shank half of the leg, with 7.6 grams of fat per four ounces roasted.

The elegant rack of lamb normally has six ribs. Once you trim the fat and remove the bones, count on two three-ounce servings per pound and slightly over thirteen grams of fat per serving. That's more fat than my family and I normally want, but Dawn likes it as a once-a-year treat either for our anniversary or at Christmas. The point is that you can eat virtually any meat occasionally.

Game meats, on the other hand, can be enjoyed as often as you'd like or as often as they are available. Nature has made virtually all wild game very low in fat. I've listed some numbers for you in the following table, but for the most part you needn't be concerned about any game: it's all heart smart and calorie conscious.

Game Meat*	Calories	Total Fat	Saturated Fat	Cholesterol
Bison (buffalo)	162	2.7g	1.0 g	93 mg
Elk	166	2.2 g	0.8 g	83 mg
Rabbit (wild)	196	4.0 g	1.2 g	139 mg
Rabbit (domestic)	234	9.5 g	2.8 g	98 mg
Venison	179	3.6 g	1.4 g	127 mg

**4 ounces, cooked*

Now and then you'll see game in supermarkets but not often. Fortunately, a few companies ship mail orders taken by phone. Call or write for further information.

American Bison Meat Corporation
2330 Main Street
Ramona, CA 92065 (619) 789-3044

Best Butcher
PO Box 236
Rose Hill, KS 67133 (316) 776-0776

Black River Ranch
West 11282 Shiner Avenue
Withee, WI 54498 (800) 225-7457

Carabeef Ranch
Rout 1, Box 74
Sulphur Springs, AK 72768 (501) 822-3587

Texas Wild Game Cooperative
PO Box 530
Ingram, TX 78025 (800) 962-4263

Venison is becoming more popular on restaurant menus, and some supermarkets now carry it as well. The biggest supplier is Broadleaf Venison, which imports from New Zealand. Call (800) 336-3844 for a location near you or to place a mail order.

Poultry has long been recognized as a low-fat meat, and much has been written about it, so I won't go into detail. Suffice it to say that chicken or turkey breasts without the skin are lowest in fat. Dark meat has significantly more fat. See the table for details.

Just be careful in buying ground poultry, either chicken or turkey in bulk or burgers. Read the labels. Some products contain up to 15 percent fat; that's fifteen grams per 3½-ounce burger. Stick with ground white poultry or use ground beef as I've suggested.

Poultry*	Calories	Total Fat	Saturated Fat	Cholesterol
Chicken breast (skinless)	124	4 g	1 g	88 mg
Chicken (dark) (skinless)	160	8 g	2 g	92 mg
Turkey breast (skinless)	120	3 g	1 g	90 mg
Turkey (dark) (skinless)	160	8 g	2 g	93 mg
Duck (skinless)	188	9 g	3 g	84 mg
Duck (with skin)	368	32 g	8 g	84 mg

**4 ounces, raw*

In looking at the table, you can see that white meat has about half the fat of dark. Skin adds considerable fat; see the difference for duck as an example.

NOTE: FAT FROM CHICKEN BREASTS DOES NOT MIGRATE INTO THE MEAT DURING BROILING, ACCORDING TO RESEARCHERS AT THE UNIVERSITY OF MINNESOTA. REMOVE THE SKIN BEFORE EATING. HOWEVER, DO NOT STEW CHICKEN WITH SKIN ON, SINCE IT WILL ADD FAT TO THE SAUCE.

Perhaps you're looking for something completely and totally different to serve for a very special dinner. Put some African music, perhaps Paul Simon's "Graceland" album, on the stereo and offer your guests a variety of cuts of ostrich meat from Green Valley Meats in Kansas. Yams would be the perfect side dish, as they, too, originated in Africa. Appetizers could be ostrich sausage, with a main course of ostrich patties or medallions. As an alternative, consider outdoing Wolfgang Puck of Spago fame by preparing a pizza with spiced ground ostrich topping.

Ostrich is an up-and-coming product. Prices have been quite high, but Green Valley has tried to keep its prices as low as possible. Mention this book for a special offer. If you're looking for something out of the ordinary, this is it. Ostrich tastes like beef rather than like poultry, and its fat and cholesterol content are lower than chicken breast. Call (800) 556-2208 for further information or to place an order.

LUNCHEON MEATS AND SAUSAGES

Which luncheon meat is lower in fat: turkey ham or regular ham? Turkey? Sorry. Depending on the brand, turkey ham has up to three times as much fat, about six grams per 3½ ounces, as low-fat regular ham such as Danola or Healthy Choice with just two grams in the same serving size.

The same holds true for turkey pastrami as compared with low-fat pastrami made from beef round. In fact, as you start to read labels, you'll see that those turkey products aren't all they're cracked up to be. They're made with dark meat and skin.

For luncheon meats, shop at both the packaged section as well as in the service deli area in your supermarket. Look for products marked 95 percent lean. That means the average sandwich portion of two ounces of meat will have about two grams of fat.

In some supermarkets, the fat content of deli meats is clearly marked. In others, you'll have to ask which cuts are low in fat. Healthy Choice markets its thinly sliced rare roast beef nationally; it's 95 percent lean. Most meats, however, are distributed by local suppliers under a number of brands. Expect to find pastrami, corned beef, roast beef, Italian beef, turkey, and ham with as low as three grams of fat per 3½ ounces.

How can corned beef and pastrami be so low in fat? It's because they're made with beef round rather than the brisket. Sliced wafer-thin, they make excellent sandwiches.

For many years I avoided hot dogs entirely. The average frank has sixteen grams of fat, and most people find no problem in eating two. Chicken and turkey dogs don't improve the situation very much, with ten grams on average. Now, however, you could eat hot dogs every single day if you wanted to. Many frankfurters are 97 percent lean; that means one to two grams of fat each, about the same as the bun you wrap around them.

Healthy Choice also makes smoked sausage and Polish sausage links at the same fat level, a nice change of pace to put in a bun. Healthy Choice, and Hormel also, produce dinner-size links that are perfect for dinner in a hurry.

With very little effort, you can make low-fat sausages in your own kitchen. Spice 'n' Slice produces a variety of spice/curing agent blends that you can mix with ground turkey breast, lean pork or beef, or even ground venison if there's a hunter in the family. Each packet yields two pounds of sausage. Just mix the meat with the packet contents, add a bit of water, form into a cylinder, bake for an hour, and that's it. Flavors include bologna, pepperoni, salami, jerky, and both country-style and southern-style breakfast sausage. I mix in a bit of fennel seed with the breakfast sausage mix and ground beef to make pizza sausage that can't be distinguished from the pizza parlor offerings. The country-style sausage made with ground pork or turkey makes a terrific, easy dinner served with mashed potatoes, pork gravy, applesauce, and some vegetables.

You can order a sampler of the sausage mixes from the company by calling (602) 861-4094 or write for a descriptive brochure and catalog to Spice 'n' Slice, PO Box 26051, Phoenix, AZ, 85068-6051. Mention this book and you'll get a special deal.

Breakfast side meats on your shopping list might include ham, Canadian bacon, and turkey bacon. Now and then you might want to splurge on regular bacon, with thirteen grams of fat in a rasher of three slices, by preceding the breakfast with two SeQuester tablets.

For something different, try slicing rounds of Polish or smoked sausage and frying them in a nonstick pan sprayed with Pam. Delicious.

Healthy Choice breakfast links and patties, made with turkey and pork, are delicious, with just 1.5 grams of fat per serving. Look for them in the frozen foods section.

While turkey bacon, especially Jennie-O, can slash the fat at breakfast or for BLT sandwiches, there's nothing quite like the real thing. But the thirteen grams of fat found in three strips of pork bacon has kept most of us away from that flavorful favorite. Today you can get bacon with half the fat of ordinary bacon, and after cooking it will be even less than that. This wonderful bacon is produced by Meucci Ranch, so you might want to order a pound or so of it when you place your order for other dinner meats.

FISH AND SEAFOOD

As a blanket statement, you just can't go wrong in the seafood section of the supermarket. If you're a fish lover, you just can't miss.

For openers, fish have a special protective factor against heart disease. Even eating as little as two fish meals weekly provides that protection. That's probably because of a unique complex of fatty acids, especially the omega-3 fatty acid, which is said to be responsible at least in part for the fact that Eskimos virtually never suffer from heart disease. In fact, this is the one time that more is better when it comes to fat.

While the general consensus from those who research fish oil is that taking supplements probably does little good and might even do harm, doctors and investigators agree that fatty acids in fish consumed as part of an otherwise low-fat diet are healthy. Put in practical terms, that means we can seek out the fattiest and tastiest salmon and enjoy that fat with no guilt.

Here's a breakdown of the omega-3 fatty acid content (in grams) of 3½-ounce servings of fish:

Sardines (Norway)	5.1	Bluefish	1.2
Sockeye salmon	2.7	Mackerel (Pacific)	1.1
Mackerel (Atlantic)	2.5	Striped Bass	0.8
King Salmon	1.9	Yellowfin tuna	0.6
Herring	1.7	Pollock	0.5
Lake trout	1.4	Brook trout	0.4
Albacore tuna	1.3	Yellow perch	0.3
Halibut	1.3	Catfish	0.2

Some people still avoid shellfish, thinking they're high in cholesterol. That's because older testing methods gave erroneous measurements, including not only cholesterol but also harmless plant sterols in the totals published. Today we know that virtually all shellfish can be enjoyed regularly. Not only are shellfish actually lower in cholesterol, for the most part, than the meat of land animals, they're also extremely low in fat and calories. The following chart paints a bright picture.

Shellfish*	Calories	Fat	Cholesterol
Abalone	195	0.7 g	85 mg
Clams	74	1.0 g	34 mg
Crayfish	90	1.1 g	139 mg
Mussels	86	2.2 g	28 mg
Oysters	69	2.5 g	55 mg
Scallops	88	0.8 g	33 mg
Alaska crab	84	0.6 g	42 mg
Maine lobster	90	0.9 g	95 mg
Rock lobster (spiny)	112	1.5 g	70 mg
Shrimp	106	1.7 g	152 mg

**3½ ounces, raw*

But wait, you might say, what about those crayfish and shrimp? Isn't that a lot of cholesterol? Not really.

First, we now know that fat is the greater villain; the role of cholesterol is quite secondary. Second, even if you were to double the serving size, which would be quite a lot of these shellfish, the total would still be within the day's limits according to AHA recommendations. Third, 3½ ounces of either shellfish go a long way in a dinner. It takes the meat of eight medium-sized crayfish to equal just one ounce! That's twenty-eight crayfish to peel in one 3½-ounce serving. For shrimp, 3½ ounces is fourteen large ones. That should be plenty for most people, especially as part of an entire dinner.

What about those imitation shellfish? They're called surimi, made from ground pollock and other cold-water fish and formed into shrimp, crab, and lobster shapes and flakes. Surimi are definitely healthy choices. Four ounces provide only 113 calories, 1 gram of fat, and 34 mg cholesterol. Use them in salads and sandwiches or mixed with vegetables in a stir-fry.

Today you can even enjoy crispy breaded fish fillets in the frozen foods section. Look for Mrs. Paul's Healthy Treasures and Van de Kamp's Crisp & Healthy 97% Fat Free Fish Fillets with two four-ounce fillets per package, each with only three grams of fat, 170 calories, and 290 mg of sodium. They heat up beautifully for sandwiches or dinner entrees.

Are there any exceptions in the healthy world of fish and seafood? Well, yes, just two. And these won't be problems for most shoppers. One ounce of caviar delivers 50 calories, 3 grams of fat, and 90 mg cholesterol. Then again, few of us can afford to load our shopping carts with caviar and eat it by the pound! The only other exception is squid, with 104 calories, 1.6 grams of fat, and 265 mg of cholesterol. If you enjoy calamari, calamar, squid, or whatever you call it, keep the servings small, perhaps mixing a bit with other shellfish in a fish soup or pasta del mare. Or block the cholesterol with phytosterols.

NOTE: A DASH OF HOT SAUCE SUCH AS TABASCO HAS BEEN SHOWN TO KILL DANGEROUS BACTERIA FOUND IN RAW OYSTERS IN FIVE MINUTES, ACCORDING TO RESEARCHERS AT LOUISIANA STATE UNIVERSITY.

EGGS AND EGG SUBSTITUTES

Nutritionists consider egg protein as the gold standard of quality. Unfortunately, eggs also supply the lion's share of cholesterol in the American diet as well as quite a bit of fat. Each large egg contains somewhat over 220 mg of cholesterol and five grams of fat, all of it in the yolk.

Of course you can precede an egg meal with the appropriate amount of phytosterols and SeQuester and block the absorption of both the cholesterol and the fat. That's your choice. I enjoy eggs on a regular basis, thanks to those two. But there are other times when the egg substitutes fill the bill quite nicely.

Most egg substitutes on the market today are free of both cholesterol and fat, which also means a significant reduction in calories. Prices are reasonable.

Since egg substitutes are pasteurized, they pose no threat of salmonellosis, which is present in raw eggs. That makes them the perfect choice for making extra-rich milk shakes and holiday egg nog. Use them, too, in place of a coddled egg, for making a Caesar salad.

Egg substitutes are very convenient for baking and you really can't tell the difference in taste in the final product. They're terrific in omelets and also for making French toast. Which brand to select? That's a matter of taste, so try a few to see which you and your family like best.

A special brand of whole eggs has stirred up considerable controversy in nutrition and medical circles. Eggland's Best eggs are said to have no effect on raising cholesterol levels. Because of such claims, the FDA has limited sale of the product.

Eggland's Best eggs are high in iodine due to the feed fed to laying hens. That iodine supposedly blocks cholesterol absorption. The FDA has doubted that claim and has questioned the safety of potentially large iodine increases in the diet. The company says that volunteers fed the eggs did not experience a rise in serum cholesterol. We don't know whether those men and women would have reacted differently to ordinary eggs, since not everyone is sensitive to dietary cholesterol in the first place. Further studies on safety and efficacy are needed.

BEANS, PEAS, NUTS, AND NUT BUTTERS

Like eggs, this category of foods belongs in the meat group because beans, peas, nuts, and nut butters contain significant amounts of protein.

Dried beans and peas have almost no fat, no cholesterol, and contribute lots of fiber. Like oat bran, much of that fiber is soluble, which lowers cholesterol levels in the blood. That's true for all the dozens of kinds available. For free information and recipes, write to the California Dry Bean Advisory Board, 531-D North Alta Avenue, Dinuba, CA 93618.

Nuts were in the news when researchers found that people who regularly munched them had fewer heart attacks than people who didn't. That was true for walnuts and peanuts in two studies in which subjects replaced other foods such as meats with the nuts for a net reduction in saturated fat. Keep in mind that most calories in nuts come from fat. The following chart gives an overview of just how much. There's no reason to eliminate nuts; just enjoy them in moderation, one at a time rather than by the handful.

*Nuts**	*Calories*	*Fat*
Almonds	166–179	14–15 g
Brazil	186	18.8 g
Cashew	163	13.0 g
Filbert/hazelnut	188	18.8 g
Peanuts	164	13.9 g
Pecans	187	18.0 g

**One ounce, dry roasted (oil adds 1 gram per ounce)*

Nut butters should also be enjoyed in moderation because of their significant fat and calorie content. Again, moderate, not eliminate. A peanut butter sandwich now and then, fine. An hour-long session with an open jar and a spoon in front of the TV, no. Here are the numbers for two tablespoons:

Almond butter: 190 calories and eighteen grams of fat

Cashew butter: 190 calories and fifteen grams of fat

Peanut butter: 188 calories and sixteen grams of fat

Reduced-fat peanut butters have appeared on the market. They typically have 25 percent less fat. That means twelve grams of fat per two tablespoons rather than sixteen.

BREADS, CEREALS, PASTAS, AND NOODLES

What could be be healthier than this category of foods, which provides fiber and complex carbohydrates? Well, as a matter of fact nutrition guidelines such as the USDA nutrition pyramid call for us to increase our consumption of these foods, fruits, and vegetables. But we still need to pay attention to product labels, since fat content can sometimes be higher than we want. Cholesterol isn't a problem.

Bread, traditionally made with flour, water, salt, and yeast, has less than one gram of fat per slice. Shortenings added, however, can increase the total. The following chart will give you an overview but look at the labels of your selections in the supermarket until you become familiar with the best choices. (Data for one slice, approximately one ounce.)

Bread	Calories	Fat
French	70–80	1 g
Grain	60–80	1 g
Italian	45–70	0.5–1 g
Pita	65–75	0.5–1 g
Pumpernickel	70–80	1 g
Raisin	60–70	1–2 g
Rye	70–80	1 g
Wheat	70–90	1–2 g
White	40–80	1 g

Fiber content of bread is lower than you might expect, with most brands and flavors providing one gram or less. Look at the ingredient listing for whole wheat or other whole grains to jack the fiber up to about two grams or so.

Bread crumbs have less than one gram of fat per serving, usually considered two tablespoons. Despite the addition of oil to flavored crumbs such as Progresso Italian, fat content remains at that low level.

Dinner rolls and sandwich rolls can be a major source of hidden fat in the diet. Croissants may not be a surprise at seven to fourteen grams of fat each, since you probably realize that they are made with butter. Unless you're already reading those labels, though, you may not know that ordinary dinner roll can pack up to five grams apiece; and most of us eat more than one at a meal. The following chart provides an overview; find the lowest fat brands in your own supermarket.

	Calories	Fat
BROWN-AND-SERVE DINNER ROLLS		
Pepperidge Farm	50	1.0 g
Bread du Jour *(Italian)*	80	1.0 g
Bread du Jour *(French)*	230	2.0 g
Wonder *(Buttermilk)*	80	2.0 g
READY-TO-EAT DINNER ROLLS		
Pepperidge Farm *(Party)*	51	1.2 g
Roman Meal	69	1.2 g
Home Pride *(White)*	80	2.0 g
REFRIGERATED DINNER ROLLS		
Pillsbury *(Butterflake)*	140	5.0 g
Pillsbury *(Crescent)*	100	6.0 g
Parkerhouse	85	1.5 g
SANDWICH ROLLS		
Hamburger *(Wonder)*	120	2.0 g
Hamburger *(Wonder Light)*	80	1.0 g
Hoagie *(Wonder)*	400	7.0 g
Hoagie *(Pepperidge Farm)*	210	5.0 g
Hoagie *(French Roll)*	100	1.0–2.0 g
Hot Dog *(Pepperidge Farm)*	140	3.0 g
Hot Dog *(Wonder Light)*	80	1.0 g
Kaiser	150–180	3.0 g
"SCRATCH" BISCUITS		
Bisquick *(Original)* *(with 2% milk)*	110	4.0 g
Bisquick *(Original)* *(with skim milk)*	90	3.0 g
Bisquick *(Reduced Fat)* *(with skim milk)*	90	2.0 g
Goldrush	70	1.0 g

BREAKFAST CEREALS

Some like 'em hot, some like 'em cold, but however you like your breakfast cereals, they're a great way to start the day. Yes, it's definitely true that you shouldn't skip this important meal. In fact, the bigger the breakfast the better.

Slice in some bananas or peaches. Drop in some berries. Serve with a glass of juice. Pour in some skim or 1 percent low-fat milk. Still hungry? Add a wedge of melon or a piece of whole wheat toast.

After all these years, I still start most days with a big bowl of oat bran cereal. My favorite is the Quaker Oat Bran cold cereal in the big red box. If you can't find it in your supermarket, ask the manager to stock it. This ready-to-eat cereal has as much oat bran fiber as the original hot oat bran. A bowl supplies all the soluble fiber you need daily.

In selecting a cereal, be sure to read both the ingredient and the nutrition-facts labels to find out where the fat, if any, is coming from. For example, pure oat bran has no added ingredients of any kind, just the bran of the oat grain. Yet the label tells you that each ounce contains two grams of fat. That's because the grain itself has a small amount of fat. Conversely, a cereal may have quite a lot of partially hydrogenated oils.

Looking at the chart that follows, you might not think that a gram or two or three of fat per serving is any big deal. But a serving is one ounce, and most people easily eat two, three or even more ounces of cereal. (Again, consider also the source of that fat, whether from the grain itself, perhaps slivered almonds or other nuts, or added hydrogenated oils.)

Cereals can be, and should be, a major source of fiber in the diet, along with fruits and vegetables. Some are a major disappointment in that arena, while others really deliver. Do take a special notice of the granolas, which may be lower in fiber than you'd expect, as well as being high in fat.

Not surprisingly, the enterprising managers of supermarkets place cereals with kid appeal at kids' eye level, while adult cereals are on the upper shelves. Both sugar and fat are considerable in many, if not most, children's cereal products.

Of the two, veto a cereal choice on fat rather than on sugar. While a cereal might be 50 percent sugar, and not very acceptable for breakfast, as a snack it compares very nicely with candy, which is 100 percent sugar.

Do you enjoy hot cereals? Other than the instant varieties, most have no added sugar or other ingredients. If just taste is your goal, take your pick. But you might be surprised that not all the hot cereals provide the fiber you might expect. Cream of Wheat, for example, has virtually no fiber. Wheatena, on the other hand, packs four grams into every ounce. Scan these one-ounce servings for an idea of the variety.

Cereal/Brand	*Calories*	*Fat*	*Fiber*
READY TO EAT			
Amaranth Flakes *(Health Valley)*	100	3.0 g	2.7 g
All Bran	70	1.0 g	10.0 g
Bran Buds	70	1.0 g	8.0 g
Raisin Bran	120	1.0 g	5.0 g
Corn Flakes	100	0 g	1.0 g
Corn Flakes *(Frosted)*	110	0 g	tr*
Nutri-Grain	100	1.0 g	3.0 g
Fruit Loops	110	0 g	1.0 g
Grape Nuts	100	1.0 g	3.0 g
Honey Graham Oh!s	122	3.2 g	tr*
Quaker 100% Natural	127	5.5 g	2.0 g
Special K	110	0 g	1.0 g
Alpha Bits	110	1.0 g	tr*
Quaker Oat Bran	100	2.0 g	4.0 g
Fruity Pebbles	110	1.0 g	tr*
Granola *(Post)*	127	4.1 g	1.0 g
Granola *(Nature Valley)*	126	4.9 g	1.0 g
Granola *(Kellogg's Reduced Fat)*	110	2.0 g	2.0 g
HOT CEREALS			
Oat Bran	100	2.0 g	4–6 g
Oatmeal	100	2.0 g	2–3 g
Multi-Grain	100	1–2 g	4–7 g
Wheat *(Quaker Whole)*	92	0.6 g	2.2 g
(Cream of Wheat)	100	0 g	1 g

**trace*

PANCAKE AND WAFFLE MIXES AND FROZEN

Whether you're making them from scratch or from mixes or simply heating frozen brands, you can save an enormous amount of fat and cholesterol with pancakes and waffles. Take the time to read some labels in the supermarket, taste test some of the low-fat brands, and from that point forward your kitchen will produce delicious, healthful breakfasts without having to think about the matter any further.

On one end of the spectrum, Hungry Jack blueberry pancake mix delivers a whopping fifteen grams of fat per serving. At the other end, you can find brands that have as little as one gram. While some brands are made with egg yolks, others have no cholesterol. Here are some examples of great products:

- Goldrush pancake and waffle mix makes some of the most delicious breakfasts I've ever eaten. Just one gram of fat per serving, and that fat comes from lecithin rather than hydrogenated oils. To locate a retail outlet, you can call the Cal-Gar Corporation, makers of Goldrush products, at (800) 729-5428. They'll also send you a case of their products at wholesale plus freight if you mention this book, just so you can become familiar with them.
- Lunds Swedish Pancake mix contains no oil or eggs. You can add egg substitute rather than the whole egg called for in the directions. These are the thin, delicate pancakes most of us enjoy only in fine restaurants. Now you can have them any time in your own home. To help you find them, call Noon Hour Foods in Chicago at (312) 782-1177.
- Bisquick Reduced Fat mix helps you slash fat for pancakes, waffles, and biscuits. How much? Three pancakes made with regular Bisquick and 2 percent milk have twelve grams of fat. The same serving made with the reduced-fat Bisquick and skim milk brings that number down to four grams of fat and zero cholesterol.
- Aunt Jemima Lite Buttermilk Complete lowers the fat even more. Three four-inch pancakes have two grams of fat and ten milligrams of cholesterol.

If you have a taste for blueberry pancakes, avoid mixes that include "blueberries." Those blueberries are actually imitations made with hydrogenated oils. Instead, add either fresh, frozen, or canned blueberries of your own. They taste better also.

Although it takes just a minute or two to blend a pancake mix with milk and egg substitute, you may opt to have a container of frozen batter in your freezer. A quick review shows the winner to be Aunt Jemima with two grams of fat per serving; Downyflake has nine grams, Swanson's Budget Breakfast has twelve grams. The downside of premade batter is that it's made with whole eggs, contributing about thirty milligrams of cholesterol.

Frozen waffles allow for breakfast in a hurry. The cholesterol content of all brands is minimal, indicating that just a tiny bit of egg goes into each. Fat varies widely. Two Roman Meal waffles have 14 grams; Downyflake oat bran waffles have 13 grams for the same size serving; Aunt Jemima comes in at just over 11 grams, and two of her oat bran waffles have less than 6 grams; Eggo Common Sense oat bran waffles have 8 grams for two. In general, waffles have significantly more fat than pancakes in order to make them crisp, but you can easily stock your freezer with the lowest fat brands possible.

CRACKERS

When I got serious about watching my fat intake, reading the labels on cracker boxes was one of my more unpleasant surprises. Just one-half ounce of crackers had two, three, or more grams of fat. To put that into perspective, one-half ounce of saltines is five crackers. Much of the added fat a decade ago came from animal fat and/or tropical oils.

Things are a lot healthier today. Nabisco SnackWells with zero fat and zero cholesterol are available in both wheat and cracked pepper flavors. The cheese-flavor crackers are reduced in fat with one gram in eighteen pieces; compare that with Cheez-Its with four grams in twelve pieces.

Do you enjoy Carr's English soda crackers? Their snap and crunch makes them longtime favorites of many. But the label reveals animal fat as an ingredient. Happily, you can get the same taste and crunchiness from Hearts crackers made by Valley Lahvosh. The only fat comes from the wheat itself, making them virtually fat free.

Soup and oyster crackers have undergone a more healthful transformation as well. No more animal fats. Choose either Oysterettes or Sunshine brand, with just one gram of fat in sixteen to eighteen pieces.

PASTA AND NOODLES

Nothing could be easier than picking a healthy pasta. Virtually all brands are 100 percent fat free and cholesterol free and made with wheat flour (duram or semolina) and water as they have been for centuries. It is said that there are more than six hundred varieties and shapes of pasta and that each has its own flavor and characteristics.

Fresh pasta contains whole eggs, adding a significant amount of cholesterol. Look for the brands that use only egg whites, eliminating that downside, or swallow some phytosterols before you eat to block the cholesterol absorption.

Noodles were invented long ago by the Chinese, who remain heavy consumers. With one exception, Chinese noodles are virtually fat free; look for cellophane or long rice noodles. The exception is chow mein noodles, fried in oil, with nearly nine grams of fat per ounce.

The Japanese noodles—soba, somen, and udon—are similarly free of fat, with just a trace per ounce. But top ramen noodles are fried, with about seventeen grams of fat per serving.

Egg noodles have well over four hundred milligrams of cholesterol per one-pound package, typically enough to serve four. You can eliminate the cholesterol with a number of brands that eliminate the yolk, using only egg whites.

TORTILLAS

While corn tortillas have no fat or cholesterol, flour tortillas have both, as they're often made with lard. Look for brands which replace that lard with soybean oil.

DESSERTS AND SNACKS

Scarcely a week goes by that a new fat-free dessert or snack doesn't hit the shelves. There's not much point in my naming them, since practically anything you like comes in a fat-free version.

Unfortunately, fat-free doesn't mean calorie-free, and a lot of people have gained weight by thinking these products could do no wrong. Again, as always, read the labels and compare the fat-free sweets with regular versions. The calories are just about the same, simply replacing the fat with sugars. There's nothing wrong with these goodies, but be realistic. If a package lists eight servings with one hundred calories each, and you routinely eat half the package, you're downing four hundred calories. 'Nuff said.

The surprises are in the packages that don't tout their fat-free status.

Puddings made by Knorr, Jell-O, and Royal contain no fat when made with skim milk. Flan produced by any of those three companies contains no eggs and is fat free. Knorr makes wonderful soufflé mixes that are a breeze to prepare. The chocolate flavor has one gram of fat per serving, and the lemon has less than a gram. Both are made with egg whites and have no cholesterol. Directions call for adding water and sugar.

Nothing conjures dietary decadence as strongly as does a hot fudge sundae. For me, it recalls childhood memories of family treats. Today you can make yourself this spectacular indulgence with practically no fat. Start with fat-free ice cream. I prefer Dreyer's (on the West Coast) or Edy's (on the East Coast) because I can form a hard ball with an ice cream dipper the way my Dad taught me to do at his drug store soda fountain. That hard ball stands up to the sauce better than a soft serving. Microwave some nonfat hot fudge made by either Mrs. Richardson's or Smucker's and drizzle it over the ice cream. Top with a spritz of ReddiWhip Lite and a maraschino cherry. Fantastic!

Potato chips, caramel corn, Crackerjacks, and all your favorite snacks come in fat-free versions. Try a few of them to see which you like best.

You know you're going to snack in the evening. Everyone does it. So why not plan to make at least some of those snacks a healthy part of your total nutrition profile for the day? Here are some suggestions.

- Take grapes off the stems, rinse, and sprinkle them lightly with sugar. Then freeze. They make a delightfully different, cooling treat for late-night TV viewing.
- Slice apples or cut into wedges on a platter, then drizzle with Smucker's fat-free caramel sauce. Tastes just like the old-fashioned taffy apples.
- Dip raspberries, one at a time, into a little glass of Chambord raspberry liqueur. If you prefer, make it orange slices into dark Jamaican rum.
- Cut chunks of honeydew melon and serve with a dipping sauce made with half honey and half freshly squeezed lime juice.
- Peel and freeze bananas. Serve with chocolate syrup.

The Food and Drug Administration approved the artificial fat olestra made by Procter and Gamble in late 1995. The first approval was for use in snack foods such as potato chips and crackers. National distribution will increase, initially as P&G's own brand and later by other companies purchasing olestra from them.

Consumer taste panels have found the products to be as tasty as full-fat varieties, and my family and I fully agree. We think they're delicious! They're far better than baked fat-free snacks.

Olestra is a unique, man-made fat substitute produced from sucrose (table sugar) and vegetable oil. Chemical manipulation renders the molecules incapable of digestive breakdown, and olestra passes through the digestive tract without being absorbed. Thus olestra contributes no calories and no fat to the diet.

Unlike other fat substitutes, olestra stands up to high heat and thus can be used for deep-frying snacks. Future applications might be for commercial fast-food production or for home use. Olestra looks and feels exactly like ordinary oils.

Procter and Gamble has conducted animal and human studies with olestra for the past twenty-five years. Many highly respected scientists and physicians have reviewed the data and concluded that olestra is safe for human consumption, at least when used in moderation. When one considers that a tiny, one-ounce bag of potato chips packs ten grams of fat and olestra chips have none, the health benefits could be significant.

So what's the fly in the ointment? Some critics, notably the CSPI, have labeled olestra as unsafe. They lost their bid to block FDA approval, but have continued to proclaim dire warnings. Let's look at those allegations.

First, CSPI and other critics say that olestra causes digestive distress. Actually, the number of symptoms reported during testing was no different from that reported from ordinary snacks. Virtually all foods can cause upsets at one time or another. Those of us who eat a lot of fiber can testify to that. Second, CSPI warns of potential cancer. Even in animal studies using huge amounts of olestra, no such cancers were detected. Third, critics claim that olestra interferes with absorption of fat-soluble vitamins A, E, K, and beta-carotene. In truth, many foods interact with nutrients, and, again, fiber has some effect on nutrient absorption. To counterbalance any such losses, Procter and Gamble will fortify its products with those nutrients. For people already consuming those vitamins in supplements for their antioxidant effects, olestra's influence is negligible.

To borrow a line from Procter and Gamble, olestra is a substitute for fat, not for common sense. Enjoy olestra snacks in moderation, perhaps a few bags of chips per week. I seriously doubt you'll have any problems, and you'll probably find the chips to be a tasty treat.

I see olestra as the tip of the iceberg, a promise of things to come. We'll no doubt see other fat substitutes coming down the pike, as well as new applications for them in the foods we want to enjoy.

SHOPPING AS A HOBBY AND A WAY OF LIFE

You have your tastes and I have mine. I've tried to give you an overview of the many, many foods available in supermarkets today. Needless to say, I couldn't list each and every item sold nationally, not to mention those that may be sold only locally.

After three trips to the supermarket, you'll be well on your way to having your own version of the Magic Kitchen. As time permits on trips thereafter, take a moment to read the label when you spot a new product. It's really nice to find nonfat and low-fat versions of foods you always thought were off-limits. After a while I'll bet that you'll find food shopping becomes more enjoyable—especially when you view it as a hobby and a way of life.

Extend your explorations beyond your local supermarket. Visit specialty shops, fish markets, farmers markets, and ethnic food stores. Make food shopping a priority.

I've provided a number of charts to familiarize you with fat and other nutrient information for various foods. I can also recommend two books that are encyclopedic listings of tens of thousands of foods: *The Corinne T. Netzer Encyclopedia of Food Values* (Dell, 1993) and *The Complete & Up-To-Date Fat Book* by Karen J. Bellerson (Avery paperback, 1993).

· 24 ·

Lunch with a Punch, Not a Paunch

What do you think about lunch? Do you view it as fun or just fuel? In France, Greece, and other countries, lunch constitutes the biggest meal of the day. In Spain, after that midday meal it's siesta time. But here in America we don't often have the luxury of such scheduling. More typically it's a matter of getting fed.

That attitude, unfortunately, leads a lot of us into trouble. We don't take the time to plan midday meals, and when the needle on our fuel gauge reads nearly empty and our cells are screaming for food, we'll settle for anything. That usually means high fat content. We also fall into a rut, eating the same things over and over.

In the next few pages, I'd like you to think about the options you have but probably haven't considered. Whether at home or in the workplace, lunch can be enjoyable and healthful, with tremendous variety. Sandwiches needn't be boring.

Readers of Lawrence Saunders's novels are familiar with detective Francis X. Delaney's love of interesting sandwiches. The descriptions are mouthwatering, and one could gain five pounds just by reading *The First Deadly Sin*. Though I've never met the man, I'm sure that Saunders really loves food.

Lunches needn't be elaborate, but some planning makes for interest. Variety, they say, is the spice of life. The Japanese never know what to expect when they open their lunch boxes at noon; they often contain a bit of this, a taste of that.

Nothing could be simpler than the renowned European ploughman's lunch. A chunk of bread, a piece of meat and/or cheese, and a piece of fruit—all to be washed down by a glass of wine. Little effort in preparation and heavy on the enjoyment quotient.

Both the Japanese lunch box and the ploughman's lunch demonstrate something that every child instinctively knows and wants. It's better to have a number of different foods rather than a lot of just one thing. I'd rather have a small sandwich with an assortment of bits and pieces of other foods than a larger sandwich. A little container of cottage cheese; a baggie with a few sticks of carrots, celery, olives, and radishes; a mini-tub of nonfat chocolate pudding; and a pop-top can of sliced peaches or fruit cocktail. Use your imagination. Keep your eye out for such things in the supermarket.

Unlike children who would opt to have only those finger foods with no major "centerpiece," most adults want a main course for lunch. That usually will take the form of sandwiches. The trick here is to assure variety without resorting to high-fat cold cuts. Happily, today that's no problem.

AN ODE TO THE EARL OF SANDWICH

The good earl was a gambling man who didn't want to take time away from the gaming tables, even to eat. The answer was a piece of meat held in bread with one hand. Today we can't get away from our desks, and we reach for that same sandwich. You can have a low-fat version of your favorties: ham, corned beef, roast beef, chicken, turkey, even pastrami.

How about that ethnic favorite, lox and cream cheese on a bagel? The bagel is virtually fat free. Lox, being smoked salmon, contains the kind of fat that protects against rather than induces heart disease. There are at least three brands of nonfat cream cheese, including Philly, the granddad of them all. Include a slice of fresh Bermuda onion, a slice of tomato, and a few black Greek olives, and you've got a feast.

As the Earl of Sandwich knew, you could make a meal of anything put between two slices of bread or in the middle of a bun or roll. The most unlikely leftovers can make an absolutely terrific sandwich. Sliced meatballs or meatloaf. A few spoonfuls of chili in a bun. Some stew, with the pieces cut very small—not bad cold, but even better if you have a microwave oven handy at work.

To me, a submarine is the ultimate sandwich because it has such variety. Start with a crusty French roll and fill it up. One essential meat is bologna and at least three companies make it 97 percent fat free: Oscar Mayer, Healthy Choice, and Hormel. (Those three also produce a wide variety of other low-fat products as well; try them all.) Put in all the kinds of meats you want, plus a slice or two of cheese. Then pack in a fistful of lettuce, sliced onion, tomato, peppers, and olives. You can sprinkle on some nonfat Italian dressing in advance, but to keep it fresher put the dressing in a little container so the bread doesn't get soggy.

What about something far more mundane: the peanut butter and jelly sandwich? Sure, peanut butter is relatively high in fat, with seventeen grams in two tablespoons, but as part of the total food intake, that fat shouldn't be a problem. Of course, peanut butter has no cholesterol and has more unsaturated than saturated fat. Enjoy it! Have one as part of the regular rotation.

Maybe it's only popular in the Midwest where I grew up, but a cream cheese and jelly sandwich ranked right up there with the classic PB&J. I must admit that for years, I avoided these treats because of my commitment to heart health. When nonfat cream cheese came into the market, I immediately made a sandwich and enjoyed it with all sorts of conjured childhood memories. My own children, however, looked at me as though I was enjoying roadkill! Here in California, I guess, cream cheese sandwiches are not big sellers. But give it a try, and I think you'll have another lunch item to add to the list.

Speaking of cream cheese, it makes a great spread instead of butter or margarine on many other kinds of sandwiches. Try it with bologna, roast beef, turkey, and just about anything. Spread it also on bagels, muffins, and toast. For maximum enjoyment, allow the cream cheese to come to room temperature rather than eating it straight out of the refrigerator.

LUNCH IN A CRUNCH

Okay, you forgot to take along a lunch and there's no time to go out and no one to send out for food. Your work schedule is murder, but you're getting a hunger headache. The unfortunate solution too often is a quick trip down the hall to the candy and snack machine. Lunch becomes a chocolate bar and a bag of chips. Zero nutrition, zero satisfaction, and maximum fat.

You need a survival plan, a contingency for office fare. If you take just a bit of time to organize your "lunch in a crunch" strategies, you'll be the envy of your workplace and your body will thank you for it.

The bottom line, simply enough, is to have the supplies and foods available at all times to eat an enjoyable, healthful meal no matter what disaster befalls you at work. Keep a box in your office or locker or file it in the *F* drawer for food. You'll need knives, forks, and spoons; a larger knife for cutting and a spoon for serving; then some napkins and a can opener; and finally plastic glasses, cups, plates, and bowls.

For just a few dollars, you can buy an immersion heating element in a drugstore or discount market. Use it to heat water for coffee, tea, or soup. If you want to get fancy, you could buy a hot plate and a small pot to heat up foods. Ideally, of course, it would be nice to have a small refrigerator and a microwave.

You'll want a supply of coffee, tea, herbal teas, dried or canned soups, soft drinks, and fruit juices. A nice cup of cocoa with a marshmallow in the afternoon can provide a touch of comfort to take the edge off your daily stress.

Stock up on foods that won't spoil. Here's a handy checklist:

- Cans of soups, stews, and chili. Many are microwavable. Others can be heated up with your heating coil in a glass or ceramic cup or bowl. Look for Campbell's Healthy Request.
- Shelf-top meals that don't require refrigeration. Hormel makes a number of these that are low in fat. Its spaghetti and meat sauce contain just five grams of fat and only twenty mg of cholesterol. It's a very satisfying meal.
- The Campbell's low-fat ramen in individual-serving cups is almost as good as the high-fat regular ramen. As with all such products, simply add boiling water to the cup. Total fat is two grams. If you read the ingredients in small print, you'll see that some of that fat comes from palm oil. Obviously, it would be better if Campbell's used a less saturated fat, but at two grams it becomes more a philosophic argument than a real concern.
- Minicans of tuna, salmon, chicken, and turkey chunks. Eat right out of the can or make a quicky sandwich or enjoy with crackers. (SnackWells wheat or cracked pepper crackers.)
- Breakfast cereals in miniboxes. In a pinch, you can eat them by the handful. The boxes also open into disposable "bowls" into which you can pour milk.
- Carnation Instant Breakfast. Not a gourmet treat but a speedy meal you can gulp down.
- Nutrition Bars. Find these in sporting goods stores, as they're a favorite with outdoorsmen. Each bar packs about 230 calories with just a gram or two of fat, and provides complete nutrition.
- Snacks. Rather than surrendering your need for a bite in the afternoon to the standard machine fare, stock your own: bags of dried fruit; boxes of raisins; trailmix, known as "gorp" in some circles; Hostess Lights cupcakes and Twinkies; nonfat chips and cookies.
- Fresh fruit. Rotate supplies of apples, pears, bananas, oranges, tangerines, and such to keep them fresh. Take leftovers home on Fridays and bring in a new supply on Mondays.

- Individual servings of applesauce, sliced fruits and fruit cocktail, nonfat puddings, and whatever else catches your fancy in the supermarket.
- Condiments. Salt and pepper. Those little packets of mustard, ketchup, and relish you find in the bottom of the bag when you buy fast foods, and the soy sauce, sweet and sour sauce, and Asian mustard that comes when you get Chinese takeout food.

BROWN BAG SALAD BARS

While the standard salad of iceberg lettuce and a slice of radish is about as nutritious as a glass of water, and the dressing you dump on can turn it into absolute junk food, a fine salad can be an excellent meal by anyone's guidelines. If you have a refrigerator at work to keep the salad cool, or you're willing to carry a little cooler (the size designed for a six-pack), a salad might become another part of your regular lunch rotation—or eat it on a roll as a salad sandwich.

Pack your salad in a plastic container with a good seal. Make it a complete meal: cauliflower and broccoli flowerets; sliced or cherry tomatoes; a handful of dark green, leafy vegetables such as spinach; bits of celery, radish, and cucumber; shreds of cheddar cheese; grated carrots; diced beets; and julienne strips of ham or turkey or both. Don't forget a little container of nonfat or low-fat salad dressing and some crackers.

Today's salad bars also feature soups. That's another meal that's easy to brown-bag to work. All you really need is a wide-neck Thermos bottle to keep your soup, stew, or chili nice and hot until lunch time. Bring some bread or crackers, a spoon, a napkin, and you're all set. All it takes is planning.

EATING OUT FOR LUNCH

"Power lunch"—that used to mean a couple of martinis followed by a steak dinner and a bottle of red wine. Fortunately, those days seem to be gone forever. We're all more aware of the health implications of such indulgences. Interestingly, surveys have shown that top executives judge employees and people with whom they're negotiating by the kind of meals they order. The power lunch of today that gets the nod of approval—and often the sale or the deal—is health smart, low in fat, and devoid of alcohol.

Whether you're trying to impress someone or merely trying to take care of the only body you'll ever own, restaurants today provide a wide spectrum of choices. You can be heart smart in fast-food places, French bistros, and every eatery in between. See a full discussion of dining out on page ____.

MEANWHILE, BACK IN THE KITCHEN . . .

Obviously, your choices become significantly broader when eating at home rather than at work, but even so you don't want to burn out on anything. You might consider adopting my own rule of thumb: Don't eat anything at home that you could take along with you to work. Keep the simpler sandwiches in the brown bag.

Backward Breakfasts

Maybe you don't have time to fix yourself a nice, hot breakfast before rushing off to work. Perhaps you're not even up to it in the morning when you're at home. Why not have that breakfast for lunch?

Consider an omelet or a steaming bowl of oatmeal with all the trimmings of fruit, brown sugar, and slivered almonds or perhaps a breakfast sandwich served on an English muffin.

Instant Pizza

Okay, the easiest thing to do is to pick up the phone to have a pizza ordered, but it'll still take at least thirty minutes to get there, and you'll have to tip the delivery boy. Not to mention the price of the pizza itself. Here's a way you can have minipizzas on your plate in just a few minutes using ingredients you've probably already got in your refrigerator.

Start with split English muffins. Spread on a tablespoon of Ragu or other pizza sauce. Sprinkle on some low-fat mozzarella cheese; either Healthy Choice or Frigo Truly Light—both have a mere two to three grams of fat per ounce. Top with sliced black olives, strips of ham or Canadian bacon, or rounds of Healthy Choice smoked sausage or Polish sausage. You might even have some pizza sausage in the freezer from a time when you made pizza for dinner (see page 299). Then just bake on a cookie pan in a 400° F. oven for ten minutes or so.

French Dip and Italian Beef Sandwiches

While cold roast beef sandwiches may be fine for brown-bagging it, you can have a real taste treat at home. Use low-fat thinly sliced roast beef found in the deli section; Healthy Choice is 97 percent fat free, and other brands come close. Heat up some au jus gravy from any of the packaged dry mixes on the market; I find Lawry's to be one of the best tasting. All are virtually free of fat. While the au jus is heating, split a French roll, spray with a bit of butter flavor Pam, and toast lightly in the oven or in a countertop toaster oven. Dip the beef into the au jus just long enough to heat, not so long as to cook the beef further. Pile the beef on the roll and ladle on extra au jus to taste; some people like to make their bread really soggy, while others prefer to dip the sandwich bite by bite in a little dish of the au jus.

For a variation, convert the French dip into an Italian beef sandwich. Add one teaspoon of Italian seasoning to the au jus. Sauté slices of bell pepper until tender in a nonstick pan sprayed with Pam and then add to the au jus. Pile both the beef and peppers on the roll and enjoy, perhaps with a salad and nonfat Italian dressing.

Monte Cristo Sandwiches

I avoid Monte Cristo sandwiches in restaurants because they're dipped in egg batter and then deep fried. But I can easily achieve the same wonderful tastes at home far more healthfully. It's more of an effort than I want to spend if I'm eating alone but worth it when cooking for the entire family, especially if the meal is a late lunch or early dinner.

Start with large slices of fresh white bread of bakery quality, rather than soft packaged bread, though the latter will do in a pinch. Mix two ounces of egg substitute, one ounce of skim milk, and one-fourth teaspoon of vanilla extract for each sandwich in a large wide bowl. Dip one side of each slice of bread into the egg mixture. On the undipped side of the bread place two ounces of low-fat sliced ham (Danola is my own favorite) and a slice of low-fat Swiss or Monterey Jack cheese and cover with a second slice of bread to make the sandwich. Grill on a nonstick electric griddle set at 400° F or a frying pan till golden brown. Dust with powdered sugar.

An option that some people (myself included) like, but that others (such as Dawn), absolutely hate, is to spread the inside of the bread with one or two teaspoons of raspberry jam or preserves. The combination of flavors is really quite good.

Meatball Sandwiches

This one is a complete no-brainer. The next time you make spaghetti and meatballs for dinner, double the recipe for the meatballs and freeze with plenty of pasta sauce. When you have a taste for a meatball sandwich, simply thaw and heat the meatballs and sauce in the microwave. Slice a crusty roll about halfway through, put in the meatballs and sauce, and sprinkle with grated Parmesan cheese.

Because I first enjoyed meatball sandwiches in an Italian neighborhood in Chicago, I like to have a little dish of *giardinara* on the side. For the uninitiated, that's a delightful combination of vegetables, including carrots, celery, and cauliflower, marinated in a rather sour vinegar. You'll find it in jars in most supermarkets anywhere in the country.

Sloppy Joes

Here's another example of how you can enjoy red meat as often as you'd like, with no more fat than you'd expect in chicken breast. For 95 percent fat-free ground beef, use round steak that the butcher trims before grinding.

I've experimented with a number of recipes, including one that was a family favorite for years. In fact, for years my brother and I felt that our Aunt Sylvia's sloppy joe recipe was the best ever. Then one day Tom and I were talking, and we tiptoed around the subject for a while before admitting that we no longer bothered with all the chopping and mixing. The bottom line is that the best sloppy joe comes from mixing the ground beef with Hunt's Manwich. Two veteran sloppy joe lovers had simultaneously and independently come to the same conclusion. Try it yourself. Freeze whatever is left over for a sandwich a month or so later.

Hamburgers and Cheeseburgers

As they say in police movies, you can do this the easy way or the hard way, your choice. The easy way is to simply keep a supply of low-fat hamburger patties you mail order from Meucci Ranch in your freezer. Then just thaw one out, fry it on a nonstick pan, put it on a bun with whatever trimmings you like, and you're done.

The hard way is to prepare the patties yourself. (Not a whole lot of work, really.) Some prefer their hamburgers as plain ground beef, while others like seasonings and chopped this and that. If you're one of the former, that's that. If you like some flavorings in your patties, to each pound of ground beef add one-fourth cup each of finely minced onion, bell pepper, celery, and carrot along with two tablespoons of minced parsley and salt and pepper to taste. Form into patties. Again, freeze the patties you don't use (or double the recipe) so you can have a supply on hand when you don't have the time to mess.

Some people tell me that nonfat cheese slices won't melt on a hamburger. No problem. Just tent the cheese-topped hamburgers with aluminum foil for one minute.

Now, to me a hamburger or cheeseburger isn't complete without a pile of grilled onions. Thinly slice a good onion, separate into rings, and slowly sauté in a nonstick pan sprayed with butter flavor Pam. Just don't rush it. In fact, making the onions should be the first step in preparing your meal to give the onions plenty of time to cook.

Like the taste of a Big Mac? Select poppy seed buns in the market and flavor the cheeseburger with Thousand Island dressing. You don't have any on hand? Make your own by mixing one-half cup of low-fat mayo, two tablespoons of ketchup, and one teaspoon of sweet pickle relish.

Hot Dogs, Sausages, and Bologna Sandwiches

Now that we have hot dogs, smoked sausage, and Polish sausage with just 3 percent fat—one or two grams of fat per link—you can enjoy these as often as you'd like. Boil, broil, or microwave. Top them however you like. For something a bit different, try splitting the sausages lengthwise and frying them in a nonstick pan. While I normally like mustard on hot dogs, ketchup seems to be better when they're fried.

That brings us to an old Chicago favorite of every kid on my block—

fried bologna. (Though we all called it "baloney" back then.) Try it. Just spray a nonstick pan, fry a couple of slices per sandwich, and serve on either white or rye bread. Fried bologna is also good with a slice of low-fat American cheese melted over it; to get the cheese to melt, use a frying pan cover or tent with aluminum foil.

Grilled Cheese Sandwiches

The first time I ever tried to make a grilled cheese sandwich with low-fat cheese, the bread got hard as a rock and burned and the cheese remained unscathed. I thought that cheese could withstand nuclear war. Then I came up with a method that works perfectly.

Put a couple of slices of cheese between two slices of bread on a microwave-safe dish and nuke the sandwich for about thirty seconds. The cheese will melt beautifully into the bread. Spray both sides with butter flavor Pam until the bread's nice and yellow. Toast on a nonstick pan until golden brown.

Now, you're not going to believe how good this sandwich tastes. It's a whole experience. You pick it up, and there's a slight feel of oil from the Pam on your fingers. Bite into it, and you'll hear the crunch as your teeth sink into the soft bread and then the melted cheese. Food scientists refer to all this in terms of "organoleptic qualities," which is to say that you're enjoying the sandwich with all your senses, harkening back to memories of delicious grilled cheese sandwiches past.

Again, this is a personal preference based on family tradition, but I like to have grilled cheese sandwiches with a mug of steaming cream of tomato soup. Campbell's Healthy Request has only a couple grams of fat if you make it with skim milk.

For variety, add a slice of ham to the cheese sandwich—or a slice or two of tomato or a smear of jelly or preserves.

Tuna and Salmon Salad Sandwiches

Actually, all it takes to make a tuna or salmon salad sandwich is the fish mixed with some mayonnaise. Okay, some people like to add chopped celery and onion. If you want a really good sandwich, try a recipe I came up with while still in college. Back then, mayo had eleven grams of fat per tablespoon.

Happily, today you can get it fat free and use all you want. Now, this recipe may sound a bit strange when you read it, but everyone who's ever tried it thinks it's terrific.

1 can tuna or salmon (6½ or 7½ ounces)
¼ cup finely chopped apples
¼ cup finely chopped celery
1 green onion minced
6 pimiento-stuffed green olives, sliced
1 tbsp lime juice
Tabasco sauce to taste (3 drops or more)
Low-fat mayonnaise (Best Foods/Hellmann's)

Loosely mix all ingredients, using your fingers rather than a spoon so you don't "homogenize" the salad into a paste. Add enough mayo to hold it together. Serve on toasted bread.

Bacon, Lettuce, and Tomato Sandwiches

Three strips of bacon, a rasher, contain about thirteen grams of fat. Add a tablespoon of regular mayo, and you're up to twenty-four grams. I used to eat two sandwiches at a time. That's as much fat as I eat in a whole day now! But I can once again enjoy a BLT.

Turkey bacon has the same terrific flavor but only two to 2.5 grams of fat per strip. A rasher for a sandwich has six to seven grams. Of course the mayo these days has little fat. (No problem with the lettuce and tomato, of course.)

Serve your BLT with a handful of Louise's nonfat potato chips and a bowl of Campbell's Healthy Request soup. The whole luncheon comes out to less than ten grams.

Wait, you say, turkey bacon can't possibly taste as good as pork belly bacon. Actually, you'll be surprised at just how good it really is. Those imitation soy-based "bacon" products, no, but the turkey bacon, yes. If you want to go halfway on this one, make equal portions of turkey bacon and pork bacon. Average fat content for three strips, then, will be nine to ten grams. Still not bad at all now and then. Or order some bacon from Meucci Ranch.

By the way, if you have any of that turkey bacon left over, store it either in the refrigerator or the freezer and pull it out when you want to enjoy a bacon cheeseburger.

Australian Sausage Rolls

There's no question that you can eat virtually everything you want for lunch and still keep the fat content way down. I think most American favorites are here in this chapter, but just for fun, here's a recipe for the Australian lunch preference that I developed when I was working in the Land Down Under.

1 small onion, minced
1 garlic clove, crushed
2 tsp fresh parsley, minced
2 tsp chives, minced
2 tsp marjoram, minced
salt and pepper to taste
4 sheets phyllo pastry
1 pound lean ground beef
2 slices bread, crumbed

Add onion and garlic to ground beef, breadcrumbs, salt, and pepper. Add parsley, chives, and marjoram. Mix thoroughly. Divide into four portions and roll into sausage shapes. Spray one sheet of phyllo dough at a time with butter flavor Pam and wrap the "sausages." Place on a cookie pan sprayed with Pam. Bake at 400° F for thirty minutes or until a light golden brown. I like them with a bit of ketchup. G'Day, Mate!

· 25 ·

Dinner with the Kowalskis

I really wish you could have joined my family and me for dinner last night. We had beef sauerbraten, potato pancakes, red cabbage, and applesauce. The rich, brown sauce was so delicious we all used chunks of bread to soak up every last drop, even though Ms. Manners would frown on that. What a comforting meal!

The fact is, we eat like that all the time. An invitation to dinner with the Kowalskis doesn't mean tasteless food eaten because it's "good for you." We eat food because it tastes good. The food we eat just happens to be good for us because I've learned how to perform magic on the dishes we all enjoy: pork chops, pizza, chicken à la king, meatloaf, mashed potatoes, and gravy. Every-night it's another great meal.

No, I don't spend my entire life in the kitchen. Neither does Dawn. Both of us are extremely busy with our careers and the children and other aspects of our lifestyle. We don't have time to spend hours and hours on elaborate preparations.

I remember paging through a vegetarian magazine given to me by a friend who is a strict vegan. "Look at those delicious recipes," he said. They did sound good, but they called for fifteen to thirty ingredients per dish and entailed three or four preparation and cooking steps. A meal would require a number of those dishes. I had the same response to a recent book that detailed all sorts of fancy, fat-reduced recipes, which I probably couldn't get my kids to eat anyway. Besides I'd need a personal chef to do the preparations.

At the end of the day, I want the food on the table without a lot of hassle, and I definitely want that warm, fuzzy feeling a hot all-American meal can provide. I love the food smells that fill the house. They turn a house into a home, I think. I love to watch my family devour every last bite with gusto, knowing that they're well cared for, and I love the feeling of satisfaction only that kind of food can provide. Sorry, but steamed vegetables and rice don't do the trick for me.

I think all those rewards are worth the effort. Especially since not that much effort is required. It all comes down to some planning and organization.

A report from Tufts University stated that about 47 percent of Americans don't decide what to make for dinner until they're on their way home from work. Eleven percent of them choose the evening meal only after they're in the kitchen, ready to cook.

Imagine what that's like. In fact, you probably don't have to imagine it: you live that way, at least some of the time. You open the refrigerator door, staring blankly, wondering what you can throw together that'll keep everyone satisfied. It all needs to be done quickly, too, because the whole family's hungry. You, personally, are starving and more than a little tired. "Hey kids," you yell, "what do you want for dinner?" No one knows.

It's no different if you're living alone or with only one other person. Getting no answers from the cluttered interior of the refrigerator, you decide to forget the whole thing and call for a pizza. Again. No matter what your family circumstances, I have a better idea.

You don't have to turn into a Mrs. Cleaver feeding Ward, Wally, and the Beaver. Welcome to the 1990s—two-income families, more activities and demands, less cooking time. No problem. If you could open that refrigerator door and find the ingredients you needed to toss together, put in a pot, and set the timer, cooking a hearty meal wouldn't be a chore.

For us planning for the week starts on Sunday mornings. That's the day for chores around the house: fix the broken hinge, take out the garbage, do the week's laundry—a typical, not very glamorous scenario. While Dawn's doing the wash and sorting out clothes and such, I make up a list of meals for the week, an actual menu. Some real quickies and some that'll take a bit more time. No particular order or assigned days for what meals. That'll be dictated by the way the week goes. Things happen, as you well know.

Starting with Sunday evening's dinner, I map out what we'll be eating for the next several days. For each given day I select a main dish; starch in the form of potatoes, rice, or pasta; some vegetables, and bread. Then I add what I need to the shopping list hanging on the side of the refrigerator, held by a magnet next to a report or a test one of the kids is proud of and wants the world to see. Then it's off to do the shopping. An hour or so later I've got everything I need to feed the family for the week. No surprises, no last minute panic, and no rush.

The master list gets coordinated with the calendar. If Tuesday evening is open house at Jenny's school, then maybe dinner will come out of the freezer.

All this planning is doable. You'll not only improve your eating habits but cut down on chaos as well. You'll all be happier for it. After a while planning becomes a habit, and you'll wonder why you ever got flustered by the demands of dinnertime.

You and your family no doubt have your favorite dishes. Start making a list of all those dishes. As you discover new recipes, add those to the list. Virtually all recipes can now be prepared using the techniques and ingredients detailed in this book. Whether an old-fashioned recipe handed down for generations or one clipped out of today's newspaper food section, practically nothing is off-limits anymore.

To get you started, let me tell you about some of the Kowalskis' favorites. I have a regular rotation that I use so that I never really have to think too hard about what to serve. Assuming you eat at home five days of the week, if you have a list of sixty meal suggestions, you won't eat the same meal twice in three months unless you want to. I've provided thirty of my own, with ideas for substitutions that could easily double that number. Now all you'll have to do is make your list for the week, get the necessary ingredients into the pantry and refrigerator, and you'll be set to go.

Now and then, when my schedule works out that way, I like to not only shop ahead but also chop ahead. We've all seen those TV chefs whipping through their recipes with gleeful ease because they have everything premeasured and ready to go. Sure, it'd be great to have an assistant do the same for us, but we mere mortals have to do it for ourselves.

Doing a stir-fry is fast and simple. There's nothing to whisking those chopped veggies and slivers of meat and chicken and seafood in the wok while a pot of rice cooks in the steamer or on the stove. It's all the chopping that takes the time. If I'm doing a shish kebab recipe on a given evening, I'll often prepare everything for both that meal and the stir-fry at once. Only one mess to clean. I keep my ingredients in plastic bags in the refrigerator ready to go into the wok the next evening.

I happen to be a big advocate of training children to cook. It gives them a feeling of independence and pride in their skills and prepares them to go off on their own some day. (I think parents' job from the moment of birth is to provide the care and education and nurturing to enable the children to leave home.) There's no reason why the kids can't help out with meal preparation. Mine have been doing so since they were big enough to see over the top of the counter. Let them peel potatoes, cut carrots, slice onions, skin the chicken, and on and on.

Or how about working as a couple? It'll give you two time that you prob-

A MONTH OF DINNER SUGGESTIONS FROM US TO YOU

1. *Sauerbraten and potato pancakes*
2. *Chicken cacciatore and spaghetti*
3. *Pork patties and mashed potatoes*
4. *Smoked pork chop with yams and peas*
5. *Chicken yakitori and rice*
6. *Swedish meatballs with noodles and carrots*
7. *Roast salmon with peppercorn sauce*
8. *Rich 'n' creamy fettucine*
9. *Sweet 'n' sour pork with rice*
10. *Spaghetti and meatballs*
11. *Turkey sandwiches and mashed potatoes*
12. *Chili mac*
13. *Roast pork tenderloin*
14. *Veal scallopini and angel hair pasta*
15. *Mexican fiesta*
16. *Barbecue chicken and roasted potatoes*
17. *Manicotti with three cheeses*
18. *Chicken à la king*
19. *Meatloaf with mashed potatoes and gravy*
20. *Lobster Newburg*
21. *Oven-fried chicken*
22. *Cheeseburgers*
23. *Pesto pasta and minestrone soup*
24. *Pepper steak*
25. *Roast turkey*
26. *Rare, juicy steaks*
27. *Pizza*
28. *Chinese stir-fry*
29. *Shepherd's pie*
30. *Skewered shrimp and scallops*

ably never have to talk about things—not a bad way to catch up on the day's happenings. Working together cuts prep time in half and makes that time a whole lot more enjoyable. Do it a few times, and you'll find yourselves working as a well-oiled machine.

In writing this chapter, I thought about breaking my little collection of meal ideas into the usual cookbook categories: pork, chicken, turkey, beef, pasta, and so forth. But I decided to mix and match those ideas on a day-by-day basis just the way I do in my own home. Maybe you'd like to simply follow the ideas in order, one day at a time, for your own family. I'll start with the meal we had last night, the sauerbraten, and go on to the chicken cacciatore I've got planned for tonight. This should give both of us an appetite!

DAY 1: SAUERBRATEN AND POTATO PANCAKES

I have quite a cookbook collection, including one on German cuisine from the famous Luchow's restaurant in New York City. Its recipe calls for preparations that include marinating the meat for three days. Give me a break! My total preparation time was about thirty minutes.

For the sauerbraten I used a chunk of Meucci Ranch beef chuck steak. If you haven't ordered a supply of that ultra-low-fat beef, you can use round steak instead. I sliced the meat into one-inch slices about the size of my palm and browned them in a tablespoon of canola oil in a heavy aluminum pot. Removing the browned meat, I poured in two cups of water and a packet of Knorr's sauerbraten mix. After bringing the liquid to a boil, I returned the beef to the pot, reduced the heat, and simmered for 1½ hours. It was Sunday, so I got things started while Dawn and the kids were out shopping at a January clearance sale. By the time they returned, the house was filled with the perfume of the simmering sauce.

Potato pancakes add a special touch to German foods. The commercial mixes made with dried potatoes aren't very good. Fortunately, making them from scratch isn't that much work and I've developed a terrific low-fat version.

While the sauerbraten beef was browning, I grated four large, peeled potatoes, about two pounds, into a large mixing bowl. Next I sprinkled on a teaspoon of salt and mixed well. The salt encourages the potatoes to "weep." I then finely minced a small onion, coming to about ⅓ cup, and measured out three tablespoons of flour and two ounces of egg substitute.

The trick with potato pancakes is to get the moisture out. I put the grated potatoes into a cotton towel and squeezed out the water; you'll be surprised how much comes out. Then I mixed all the ingredients together.

When my family returned and we were ready for dinner, I fried the potato pancakes on a hot griddle sprayed with butter flavor Pam. The recipe makes eight cakes or "latkes" as they're sometimes called. Figure on about six minutes of cooking time.

The meal was served with applesauce and red cabbage. I find that commercially prepared red cabbage in jars is about as good as I can make from scratch. Of course, there was plenty of bread to sop up the last of the wonderful sauce.

DAY 2: CHICKEN CACCIATORE AND SPAGHETTI

This was a Monday evening meal, following a particularly frantic day. There was very little time for food preparation, and a quickie meal was in order. Instead of making the cacciatore from scratch, I used one of the Ragu Chicken Tonight simmer sauces but with a few extras.

Chicken Cacciatore

1 pound boneless, skinless chicken breasts
1 jar Ragu Chicken Cacciatore simmer sauce
1 tbsp canola oil
3 large garlic cloves, crushed
1 small onion, chopped
1 bell pepper, cut in eighths

Brown chicken breasts in a large, heavy skillet with the canola oil. While the breasts brown, prepare the garlic, onion, and pepper. Add the garlic and onion midway through the browning. Then pour in the simmer sauce. Simmer for twenty minutes, add the pepper, and simmer another ten minutes.

That evening I cooked a pound of spaghetti, following the instructions on the package, and a pot of fresh black-eyed peas.

A loaf of crusty Italian bread and a nice chianti finished off the meal. Total preparation time was twenty minutes by the clock, and dinner was on the table in forty minutes.

There was enough left over for Dawn to take with her for lunch at the school where she teaches English the next day. I always make more pasta than we can eat at one time, since leftovers are terrific for lunch.

DAY 3: PORK SAUSAGE PATTIES AND MASHED POTATOES

Anyone from America's heartland will recognize this midweek meal. My mother used pork links, but those are extremely high in fat. My approach is very low in fat and high in flavor.

Pork Sausage Patties

2 pounds fresh ground pork loin or tenderloin
1 package Spice 'n' Slice Country Breakfast Sausage mix
1 tsp sage

I hope you've ordered a selection of Spice 'n' Slice mixes. Just mix the package with the sage and then mix in with the two pounds of ground pork sausage. Form into patties. I use half the patties for the evening's meal and freeze the other half for future breakfasts. Fry the patties in a nonstick skillet sprayed with Pam.

Mashed Potatoes

4 medium russet potatoes, peeled and quartered
1 tsp salt (optional)
1 packet Butter Buds
8 oz evaporated skim milk

Bring potatoes to boil in salted water, reduce heat to a low boil, and cook for about twenty minutes or until potatoes are fork tender. Drain. With an electric hand mixer, crush potatoes well before adding Butter Buds and skim milk. (You can use ordinary skim milk instead of the canned evaporated milk, but the latter provides a richer, creamier result.) You'll be amazed that these potatoes taste as though they were made with butter and cream.

As options for mashed potatoes, you can use nonfat sour cream and two tablespoons prepared horseradish, or try mashing in a few crushed cloves of garlic. I always make enough mashed potatoes to freeze a container or two for future meals.

For gravy, use any of the dry pork gravy mixes in the supermarket. They're all practically devoid of fat. Serve with a vegetable of your choice and applesauce (which, for us, was left over from Sunday's sauerbraten meal).

DAY 4: SMOKED PORK CHOPS AND YAMS WITH PEAS

Here's an excellent example of a meal that you can put on the table faster than you can have a pizza delivered. Hormel packages smoked pork chops that are 94 percent lean; if you cut off the small rind, the yield will be 96 percent lean. Heat in a pan sprayed with Pam. Then pour in a splash of coffee to produce "red eye" gravy if you wish.

You have two choices for the yams. One is to simply open a can of yams, heat, and serve. The other is to pop a few fresh ones (pierced so they don't explode) into either the microwave oven for ten minutes or a standard oven at 400° F for forty minutes. Roasted yams or sweet potatoes are absolutely delicious. Try a dollop of nonfat sour cream, a sprinkle of Butter Buds, or both.

Green peas go particularly well with the chops and yams. Canned peas aren't very tasty and are loaded with salt. Opt for the frozen peas instead. You get to decide just how much salt, if any, you add to the water.

I like to have some good rye bread with this meal, though my children prefer white bread.

OPTION: REPLACE THE SMOKED PORK CHOPS WITH HAM STEAKS; THE FAT CONTENT IS ABOUT THE SAME.

DAY 5: YAKITORI CHICKEN AND RICE

My children have the job of cleaning off the table and washing the dishes after dinner. They love this meal because there's so little to clean up after eating one of their favorites.

Yakitori Chicken (Skewered Teriyaki with Vegetables)

1 pound boneless, skinless chicken breasts, in cubes
1 cup beef broth
1 tbsp soy sauce
1 tbsp brown sugar
1 tbsp saki or dry sherry
2 tbsp finely sliced or grated fresh ginger (2 tsp dry)
2 bell peppers, cut in eighths
1 medium onion, cut in quarters

8 large mushrooms
2 cups pineapple (fresh or canned)

Mix the soy sauce, brown sugar, saki or sherry, and ginger in a large plastic bag. Place chicken, vegetables, and pineapple in the marinade and marinate in the refrigerator for two to three hours. Alternate foods in skewers and broil indoors or grill outdoors.

Rice

We stock at least three kinds of rice at all times: short grain, long grain, and basmati. All taste different. Try them all. Invest in a rice cooker; they're very inexpensive and ensure the rice will come out properly cooked every time. Depending on how hungry the family is on a given evening, I'll make from one to two cups of rice with equal amounts of water. If you like drier rice, use less water; if you like it a bit sticky, use more. With an electric rice cooker, you simply put the rice and water together, cover, push a button, and it's done in about twenty minutes.

DAY 6: SWEDISH MEATBALLS AND NOODLES WITH CARROTS

The list of ingredients may look daunting for this recipe, but the actual preparation is simple and takes little time, making it possible to do this meal midweek on a day that you're not completely frazzled. You might also think about doubling the recipe to freeze the extra uncooked meatballs for an evening when you don't have time to fuss, but you'd like a nice, comforting meal.

Swedish Meatballs

1½ pounds lean ground beef (or ½ pound each ground beef, veal, and pork)
1½ slices white bread with crusts trimmed off
2 oz egg substitute
½ tsp vinegar
½ cup skim milk
1 medium onion, minced
¼ tsp nutmeg
½ cup fresh dill, minced, salt and pepper to taste

1 cup nonfat sour cream
¼ cup dry sherry
½ cup beef broth
2 tbsp oil

Soak bread in skim milk and work together with your fingers or a spoon until you have mush. Add egg substitute, vinegar, nutmeg, half the minced dill (¼ cup), and salt and pepper and mix. Now add the meat and minced onion and blend well. Form into walnut-sized meatballs. (This is the time to freeze half of them for another time.) Fry in a large skillet with the oil, or you may prefer to spray a nonstick pan with Pam to avoid the oil entirely.

While the meatballs are frying, mix the remaining dill with the sour cream in one container (I use a measuring cup) and the sherry and beef broth in another. This is the time to start cooking the noodles and carrots to be served along with the meatballs. Remove the fried meatballs and pour the sherry/broth mixture into the hot pan to deglaze it, with the ensuing sizzle making a gravy as you scrape the bits off the bottom of the pan. Return the meatballs to that sauce and warm through. Finally, add the dill/sour cream and blend. (Make sure that the meatballs and sauce are only warm, not hot, so the sour cream doesn't crack.)

Noodles

While you might prefer mashed potatoes, Swedish meatballs are traditionally served with egg noodles. If cholesterol isn't a concern, you can use traditional noodles. If you're trying to limit your cholesterol intake, use cholesterol-free noodles; at least two brands are in the markets. Fould's No-Yolks noodles are available in three widths, but I think a better product is Creamette Yolk-Free Ribbons. Both brands are very low in sodium, and you might want to salt the water even if you don't normally do so to spark the flavor. Or use regular egg noodles and block the cholesterol with phytosterols.

DAY 7: ROAST SALMON AND PEPPERCORN SAUCE

I'm not going to include a lot of fish and seafood recipes in this book, simply because they are naturally low in fat and don't require any special shopping or cooking techniques. By all means, include fish and seafood in your weekly meal plans. I give you this recipe because it's a simple preparation you might not have considered, along with a sauce that's really intended to accompany beef rather than fish. Give it a try.

Roasting has to be the easiest, most foolproof method of cooking fish. You can use an indoor oven at high (450°) heat or the indirect heat method over charcoal outdoors. Plan on six ounces of salmon fillet per person; ask for thick slices. Preheat the oven, place fillets on the wire rack of a broiling/roasting pan, and roast for eight minutes. Older recommendations of ten-minute cooking times are outdated, since longer cooking time dries the fish out, and it loses the juiciness and flavor.

The sauce couldn't be simpler. I buy the Knorr Green Peppercorn sauce mix, prepare it according to package instructions, and add one tablespoon of drained capers. The sauce is practically fat free, with about one gram per serving, and really complements the richness of salmon.

This sort of elegant meal calls for a special vegetable, such as asparagus; wild rice or a long-grain/wild rice blend; a loaf of crusty French bread; and a bottle of red wine. Pinot Noir goes particularly well with it.

Here's another example of a meal that would impress any guest, much less your family, and yet takes mere minutes to prepare. From start to finish, you shouldn't spend more than thirty minutes in the kitchen.

DAY 8: RICH 'N' CREAMY FETTUCINE

Who says creamy, rich sauces have to be loaded with fat and cholesterol? This recipe proves you can have it all!

5 garlic cloves, crushed
3 slices of onion, chopped
2 tbsp olive oil
8 oz egg substitute
5 tbsp fat-free Parmesan cheese
½ cup fresh basil, chopped
½ cup fresh parsley, chopped
1 pound fettucine
salt and pepper to taste

Sauté onion and garlic in olive oil until onion is tender and transparent. Do not brown garlic. Mix egg substitute with basil, parsley, and Parmesan cheese. Combine the two mixtures in the largest mixing bowl you have in the kitchen and add salt and pepper to taste. I add 1 teaspoon of salt and a few twists of freshly ground pepper.

Prepare fettucine according to package directions. Drain fettucine and *immediately* put wet, hot pasta in the large mixing bowl over the egg/cheese/onion/garlic/basil/parsley mixture and toss thoroughly. The hot, wet pasta will cook the eggs and melt the cheese, creating a rich, creamy sauce.

Enjoy with a nice salad that includes lots of veggies, such as broccoli, carrots, bell peppers, and such, both raw and cooked leftovers, and one of the fat-free Italian dressings. Try an Italian white wine such as Pinot Grigio.

DAY 9: SWEET 'N' SOUR PORK WITH RICE

Dawn was never fond of sweet 'n' sour dishes of any sort until I sparked the dish with some garlic. That little touch makes all the difference in this easy-to-prepare midweek meal.

1 pound pork tenderloin, fat trimmed, cubed
1 tbsp canola oil
3 large garlic cloves
1 jar Ragu Chicken Tonight simmer sauce
1 bell pepper, cut in eighths
1 large head broccoli, cut in flowerets
8 large mushrooms, cut in quarters

Heat canola oil in large, heavy skillet or pot that comes with a cover. Brown tenderloin cubes. Add crushed garlic during the last minutes of browning meat. Pour in simmer sauce and simmer twenty minutes. Add peppers, broccoli, and mushrooms and simmer ten more minutes. If you like your vegetables very crisp, delay adding them until the last five minutes of simmering. Serve with mounds of steaming rice.

DAY 10: SPAGHETTI AND MEATBALLS

It's a rare American family that doesn't count this meal as one of its favorites. Ordinarily made with ground beef that's too high in fat, your recipe or mine should use a ground beef that's just 5 percent fat. Just have your butcher trim the visible fat off round steak, sirloin, or London broil before grinding. I prefer to fry my steak in a little oil, though you can cut the fat even more in a nonstick pan sprayed with Pam. Make your own sauce from scratch or choose one of the many commercial sauces on the market. Dawn and I like the Classico sauce with black olives and mushrooms or the tomato basil. Ross likes Ragu and Jenny prefers Prego, so we alternate. You can also reduce the sodium content significantly by opting for Healthy Choice sauces.

Italian Meatballs

1 pound lean ground beef
¼ cup finely chopped onion
¼ cup finely chopped green bell pepper
3 large garlic cloves, minced
1 tsp Italian seasoning
1 tsp salt (optional)
½ tsp freshly ground black pepper

Combine all ingredients and form into walnut-sized balls. Fry in either a tablespoon of canola oil or in a nonstick pan sprayed with Pam.

Spaghetti

Spaghetti is just one of literally hundreds of different pasta shapes and sizes. It's the middle of the long pastas we generically call "spaghetti" in terms of thickness. For variety, try all the sizes from capellini to spaghettini to linguini. The thinner the pasta, the shorter the cooking time and the more important it is to have the pasta moving freely in sufficient boiling water to cook properly and to avoid the pasta's clumping. Don't overcook.

Along with your spaghetti and meatballs, enjoy a crisp salad for starters and a vegetable side dish, perhaps either green beans or green peas to provide a color contrast.

Italians think Americans are strange for eating bread with pasta, preferring one or the other, but most of us like a loaf of bread on the side—and, of course, a red wine.

Manga!

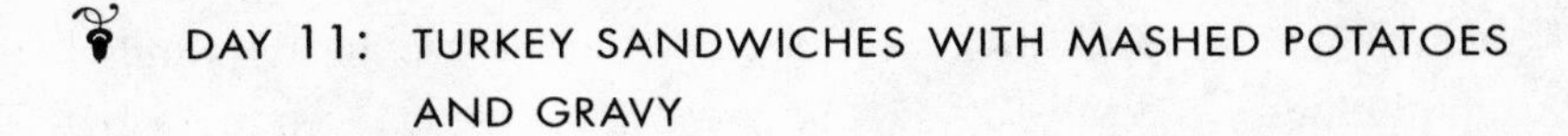

DAY 11: TURKEY SANDWICHES WITH MASHED POTATOES AND GRAVY

Every roadside diner along the whole length of Route 66 has this hot, open-faced sandwich on the menu. It's an American favorite, and fortunately, it's no problem to prepare.

Start with Tyson, Butterball, Foster Farms, or other brand of preroast turkey breast. You'll find it vacuum sealed in the poultry section. Cut into slices one-fourth- to one-half-inch thick.

In a large, high-sided frying pan, prepare one of the commercial dry turkey gravy mixes. All are virtually fat free. My favorite is Durkee, though that's sometimes more difficult to find. You may opt for Pepperidge Farms homestyle turkey gravy in a jar; it's 98 percent fat free. Add turkey slices, mix well with gravy, cover, and simmer to heat turkey through.

Serve on slices of bread substantial enough to hold up to the gravy, not a soft sandwich bread such as Wonder. I like to use sourdough bread.

Depending on the amount of time you have that day, you can make mashed potatoes according to the recipe on page 278 or you can pull out a container of frozen potatoes. Peas and carrots make a colorful side dish, and don't forget the cranberry sauce.

DAY 12: CHILI MAC

Speaking of roadside diners, when's the last time you had a hot bowl of chili? That'll take the chill off, whether you're coming in from shoveling the snow or from skiing down the slopes. Again, we can slash the fat with 95 percent lean ground beef.

I've tried quite a number of chili recipes, including those said to have won awards at this contest or that chili cook-off. When it comes down to it, the commercial mixes are just as good or at least darned close. Pick your brand.

The real trick is in picking the beans and such that you add to the meat and mix. Hands down, I think the best on the market are S&W Chili Beans, followed by Hunts. Truly those beans make a huge difference.

Start by sautéing a small onion, finely chopped, in a skillet sprayed with Pam. When the onions are tender and translucent, add the beef and brown it. Then add a packet of chili mix, two cans of S&W Chili Beans, and one can (16 oz) of drained and chopped tomatoes. Bring to a boil, reduce heat, and simmer fifteen minutes.

While that chili simmers, cook a box of Creamette's elbow macaroni according to package directions. Next, set out dishes of chopped onion, low-fat cheddar cheese shreds, and Sunshine Oyster Crackers. Serve the chili in bowls over the macaroni. Let everyone serve himself the side dishes.

If you think about it for a minute, you have a completely balanced meal in a bowl: pasta, meat, vegetables, dairy, and bread. Wash it down with an appropriate glass of cold beer.

Save that little bit of chili that might be left over to spread on a hotdog for lunch. The leftover onions and cheese shreds will be perfect on top of that chili dog—or do you call them Coney Island dogs? Or just Coneys? Anything you call 'em, those are tasty sandwiches.

DAY 13: ROAST PORK TENDERLOIN

Lean pork tenderloins can be enjoyed in a number of ways, some of which are included in this chapter. One of the easiest and yet most elegant preparations is to simply roast a whole tenderloin. Plan on four or five ounces per person.

First, as always, trim off the visible fat from the outside. I like the Hormel tenderloins, since they're well trimmed to begin with. Then peel and cut garlic cloves into little wedges you'll drive into holes stabbed into the tenderloin along its length. How many cloves you insert depends on how much you like garlic. Garlic lovers won't think six or seven cloves per pound is too much. Finally, thinly slice a medium-sized onion and separate into rings with which you'll smother the roast. Put the meat on the wire rack of a roaster/broiler pan and roast at 350° F for about thirty minutes or until the meat thermometer registers 160° F. Transfer the roast to a serving platter and carve into slices at the table. Let everyone take some onions to put on top.

As is true for all roasts, practically any side dishes will go along perfectly with a pork tenderloin. You might like a baked potato; if so, put it into the oven forty minutes before the roast. A baked sweet potato will take just a little longer than the meat.

For a vegetable, consider either the green bean casserole or the acorn squash with brown sugar on page 304. If you don't have the time to fiddle around, some sliced beets out of the can will do just fine.

DAY 14: VEAL SCALLOPINI AND ANGEL HAIR PASTA

Okay, you have the choice of a dish that takes practically no time and tastes very good, or one that'll definitely require work and is spectacular. Maybe you can do both, on different days with different schedules.

For your first option, when you've no time to cook, opt for using Lawry's Weekday Gourmet Veal Marsala Sauce. Find it along with a number of other Lawry flavors in any supermarket. Each packet of sauce contains enough for twelve ounces of meat. Combine the fact that veal is very expensive with the potential of filling up on the pasta and side dishes, and those twelve ounces of meat will probably be enough for four people. As one alternative, you can substitute turkey cutlets for the veal, perhaps increasing the amount of meat.

Preparation is a simple matter of flattening the cutlets, sautéing them in a bit of olive oil (rather than the butter or margarine recommended on the package), and pouring the sauce over the meat. Serve with angel hair pasta, sprinkled with a drizzle of extra-virgin olive oil, and fresh black-eyed peas or another vegetable.

Your other option takes far more work and is best left for special occasions. Dawn discovered this recipe in the *Chicago Sun-Times,* which in turn attributed it to a man in Seattle. When she cooks a really fine meal, this is the recipe I ask Dawn to do for me. Do it once, and you'll be hooked. I think it's better than any I've ever tasted.

As with the easier approach above, serve with angel hair and black-eyed peas, both drizzled with olive oil, and of course, a particularly good bottle of red wine you've been saving.

Dawn's Veal Scallopini Marsala

Butter Flavor Pam
1 tbsp onion, finely chopped
1 tbsp carrot, finely chopped
1 tbsp celery leaves, finely chopped
½ tsp thyme (dried)
1 bay leaf
2 tbsp parsley, finely minced
2 tbsp flour
1 cup beef bouillon

1 tbsp tomato paste
1 pound veal sliced for scallopini

Spray nonstick skillet with Pam; sauté onion, carrot, celery leaves, thyme, bay leaf, and parsley over very low heat until vegetables begin to brown, about five minutes. Sprinkle on and blend in the flour. Add the bouillon and stir frequently over medium heat until the mixture boils and thickens. Stir in the tomato paste and simmer for five minutes. Put sauce mixture through a strainer and set aside.

1 cup flour
1 tsp thyme oregano, salt, pepper,
1 tsp oregano
1 tsp salt
Pam
1 tsp pepper
1 tsp grated Parmesan
8 large mushrooms, thinly sliced
2 large garlic cloves, crushed
2 tbsp Italian parsley (or regular parsley), minced
1 cup Marsala wine

Combine the flour and herbs and then dredge veal slices. Spray pan with Pam and sauté veal about two minutes per side. Don't worry about browning it. Spray the same pan with more Pam and sauté the mushrooms and garlic until the garlic is tender. Stir in the reserved sauce till warmed, then add the Marsala. Return the veal to the pan and heat through and serve. It's worth the effort!

DAY 15: MEXICAN FIESTA

Distinctively delicious, Mexican food traditionally is rich in saturated fats: lard in the refried beans, flour tortillas, and main dishes; butterfat in the sour cream and cheeses; and the high-fat beef. Only recently have some Mexican restaurants begun to advertise lower fat dishes done without lard. But for years my family and I have enjoyed these south-of-the-border treats in our own healthful versions. Today it's easier than ever to go as low in fat as you want.

Start with the refried beans. Look for cans labeled as vegetarian, made with soybean oil or totally fat free. Spark the flavor with a splash of hot sauce blended in when you warm the beans. Mix in some shreds of cheese and sprinkle some on top.

Whether a dish calls for cheddar cheese or Monterey Jack, you can pick either nonfat or low-fat versions. Buy shreds or shred your own at home. Use one of the nonfat sour creams.

Cooking instructions for all brands of Spanish rice call for butter or margarine. Use half that amount of Butter Buds instead. For example, replace two tablespoons of butter of margarine with one tablespoon of Butter Buds. You won't be able to tell the difference.

If your menu calls for tacos, enchiladas, or burritos use 95 percent lean ground beef from your butcher. For beef fajitas, choose either a London broil sliced thinly or the ultra-low-fat fajitas beef from Meucci Ranch.

Premade taco shells are deep fried, a major source of fat. Make your own easily in the oven. Start with corn tortillas. Spray with Pam on both sides. Fold in half and stuff with a paper napkin to keep the U-shape. Place on a cookie sheet and bake about ten minutes at 400° F.

Use any leftover tortillas to make chips. Just cut them into quarters, spray with Pam, salt lightly if you prefer, and toast in the oven on another cookie sheet in the same 400° F oven. I think they taste better than the fat-free tortilla chips you find in supermarkets. Serve those chips with a bowl of salsa at the beginning of the meal, or make a sour cream dip with Hidden Valley Fiesta dip mix.

You'll spot a number of mixes for making tacos, enchiladas, burritos, and fajitas along with other packaged gravy mixes. For the most part, simply follow package instructions, using the ingredients we've just discussed.

Part of the fun of the Mexican meal is putting it all together at the table. Instead of making everything for your family, put the fixings out for them. Picture the table covered with bowls of taco shells and spiced ground meat, warm flour (low fat) tortillas, shredded cheese, sour cream, refried beans, shredded lettuce, tomato wedges, and onion rings. Don't forget bottles of Mexican hot sauces, or mild ones for the timid.

Now for the beverages of choice. Although food scientists have found that cold milk is best at relieving the burning in the mouth from chilis and peppers, I'll stick with my *cervezas,* bottles of ice-cold beer! *Mucho Gusto!*

DAY 16: BARBECUE CHICKEN AND BROASTED POTATOES

When I serve this meal to guests, they often ask how I get the chicken so tender, yet completely cooked, while the sauce isn't blackened. The trick is in simmering the chicken parts prior to barbecuing either indoors or out. As a side benefit, the skin comes right off even from parts that otherwise would be difficult to skin, such as the wings and drumsticks.

For each person, count on one-half breast, one drumstick, and one wing or two "drumettes," which are the two halves of the wing without the tip. Place the chicken in a large pot along with three bay leaves, a tablespoon of whole black peppercorns, and four crushed garlic cloves. Add enough water to cover the chicken. Bring to a boil, reduce heat, and simmer covered for twenty minutes. Drain and allow to cool before removing the skin. Reserve "soup."

Do you have your own barbecue sauce, treasured by your family and handed down for generations? If not, pick one of the commercial brands. We like Bullseye brand hickory flavor. Healthy Choice makes a barbecue sauce with reduced sodium. Whatever the sauce, slather it on generously and allow the annointed chicken parts to drink it in for a while in the refrigerator if you're making the dish in advance.

When you're ready for dinner, grill or broil only long enough to heat the chicken through and darken the sauce. Baste a couple of times with extra sauce while cooking. Don't forget that the chicken is cooked, so don't overdo it.

Now for the potatoes. Depending on sizes of appetites, prepare one potato, small, medium, or large, per person. Cut unpeeled into wedges and simmer fifteen minutes in the chicken soup you reserved after draining the chicken. Don't fully cook the potatoes. Drain and place the potatoes on a cookie sheet. Spray lightly with Pam and sprinkle with salt and pepper to taste and with finely minced fresh parsley. Roast in a 400° F oven for about thirty minutes, until crisp on the outside and tender on the inside.

Because this is finger food, we continue the concept by serving raw vegetables and dip rather than the usual cooked veggies. Prepare a nice, big bowl of carrot sticks, celery, and broccoli flowerets to dip into your choice of dip made with nonfat sour cream.

As a final touch, make some homemade cornbread. Try Gold Rush cornbread mix; call the company to find a local supplier or to have some sent directly to you. Read the details on the company and its products on page 254.

What you have here is one messy but delicious meal, and fingers are going to get very sticky. In addition to the usual napkin, give everyone an extra, wet one in a bowl next to the plate.

DAY 17: MANICOTTI

I've always loved cheese-stuffed pasta dishes such as manicotti, but the fat content is exceptionally high. These days I opt for a low-fat menu selection in Italian restaurants, reserving my taste for manicotti and similar dishes for meals at home. I found this recipe, which I modified appropriately, on a box of Ronzoni manicotti, and I think it's as good as any I've tasted. The first time I served the dish, my family went nuts over it. I'm sure you will also.

Cheese-Filled Manicotti

1 package (8 oz) manicotti
1 container (15 oz) Frigo Truly Light fat-free ricotta cheese
2 cups low-fat shredded mozzarella cheese
½ cup grated fat-free or low-fat Parmesan cheese
2 oz egg substitute
1 tbsp chopped parsley
¼ tsp salt
¼ tsp pepper
⅛ tsp nutmeg
2 cups pasta sauce of your choice

Prepare pasta according to package directions; drain, rinse in cold water, and keep moist until ready for stuffing. While pasta cooks, mix ricotta cheese, 1½ cups of the mozzarella cheese, ¼ cup of Parmesan cheese, egg substitute, parsley, salt, pepper, and nutmeg. Spoon mixture into pasta, about ⅓ cup per shell. Spray 13-x-9-inch baking pan with Pam and arrange filled manicotti in single layer. Pour pasta sauce over shells. Sprinkle with remaining mozzarella and Parmesan cheeses. Bake at 350° F for fifteen minutes or until hot and bubbling with cheese melted.

OPTION: MAKE TWO SERVINGS, BAKE ONE AND FREEZE THE OTHER FOR UP TO TWO MONTHS. THAW IN MICROWAVE AND BAKE AS USUAL, OR BAKE FROZEN FOR ABOUT NINETY MINUTES.

Serve with green peas or beans, a loaf of Italian bread, and a nice bottle of chianti. Really hungry? Start with a salad or a bowl of minestrone soup.

DAY 18: CHICKEN À LA KING

When I was growing up in Chicago, my parents took us to a restaurant downtown where I came to love chicken à la king. I always ordered it with a glass of chocolate milk, and I still enjoy that, though for me it's a matter of bringing back pleasant memories. When we finished everything on our plates, my brother and I went to the "treasure chest" where we could select a little prize for being good eaters. You won't need to reward the family for polishing their plates when you serve this recipe.

1 pound cooked chicken breast meat, cubed
1 can (10¾ ounce) Campbell's Healthy Request Cream of Celery soup
1 can (10¾ ounce) Campbell's Healthy Request Cream of Chicken soup
8 oz low-salt (Swanson's or other) chicken broth
4 oz Carnation Fat-Free Non-Dairy Creamer
1 tbsp paprika
2 tsp tarragon (dried)
16 oz package frozen peas and carrots

To cook the chicken, simmer breasts in water for twenty minutes or microwave fifteen minutes on high. Cube chicken or tear into large shreds. While chicken cooks, mix all ingredients except peas and carrots in a large bowl. Prepare peas and carrots according to package directions. Bring soup mixture to a low boil in a large, high-sided frying pan or pot, add chicken and return to bubbling; finally add peas and carrots. Serve with mashed potatoes.

OPTION: You can use this recipe to make terrific chicken potpie. Look for low-fat frozen crusts or use filo pastry sheets sprayed, one sheet at a time, with butter flavor Pam. Bake at 400° F for fifteen minutes or until golden brown.

DAY 19: MEATLOAF, MASHED POTATOES, AND GRAVY

Meatloaf happens to be one of my favorite dishes, right up there with steak and lobster. I worked out this recipe many years ago, then modified it to lower the fat content. It tastes just as good as ever. You could use just beef, rather than a combination of meats, but the taste will be different and, I think, not as good. Have your butcher prepare the ground veal and pork from well-trimmed veal round and pork loin.

1 pound lean ground beef
½ pound lean ground veal
½ pound lean ground pork
½ green bell pepper, finely chopped
3 slices onion, finely chopped
4 large stuffed green olives, chopped
1 cup bread crumbs
3½ tbsp ketchup
2 oz egg substitute
1½ tbsp Worcestershire sauce
¼ tsp sage
¼ tsp pepper
¼ tsp marjoram
¼ tsp celery salt
½ tsp salt (optional)
2 large garlic cloves, minced
½ tsp Dijon mustard
1 package dry brown gravy mix
1 cup water

Combine ground meats well. Then blend in bell pepper, onion, olives, and bread crumbs. Separately mix remaining ingredients and then add that mix to the meat mixture. Form into loaf shape, place on wire rack of roaster/broiler pan, and bake in a 350° F oven for 90 minutes or until meat thermometer registers 165°.

Combine meatloaf drippings with one package of dry brown gravy mix of your choice and one cup of water, bring to a boil, reduce heat, and simmer fifteen minutes. Serve with mashed potatoes and the vegetable of your choice.

DAY 20: LOBSTER NEWBURG

If one single dish conjures up a cardiologist's nightmare, it's Lobster Newburg. According to James Beard, it was named for an American named Wenburg and the name degenerated. Beard's version of this elegant dish calls for butter, heavy cream, and egg yolks. Needless to say, mine calls for a bit of substitution. Fortunately, earlier estimates of lobster's cholesterol content were greatly exaggerated, and of course, there's virtually zero fat in this shellfish.

Unless you just struck oil in your backyard, you probably don't include live lobsters in your weekly food budget. But you can find frozen lobsters rather reasonably priced in outlet sources. Here in California, I shop for mine at Trader Joe's, where I buy slipper lobsters for about the price I'd pay for, say, pork tenderloin. One pound easily satisfies four people, as this is a rich-tasting dish.

If using frozen lobster, thaw and soak in a brine made of two cups water and three tablespoon salt. This process "refreshes" the lobster and removes any fishy odor and flavor. Then place lobster in a pot of boiling water. When water returns to a boil, reduce heat and simmer just five minutes, no more. Drain and cool, then cut lobster into chunks. Now you're ready to do the recipe.

Lobster Newburg

1 pound cooked lobster chunks
2 tbsp olive oil
¼ cup brandy
½ cup Carnation Fat-Free Non-Dairy Creamer
4 oz egg substitute
freshly ground black pepper to taste

Sauté lobster in olive oil until hot, no more than five minutes. Add brandy and light, tipping the pan back and forth to ensure continued burning until the alcohol is consumed. Mix creamer and egg substitute in a skillet and simmer over very low heat; mixture will thicken slightly after about three minutes. Add lobster to the cream sauce and heat through. Season with pepper. Serve with rice and a medley of baby vegetables. This meal calls for one of your good white wines. Light the candles and enjoy.

DAY 21: OVEN-FRIED CHICKEN

Don't you get tired of having your chicken broiled all the time? Don't you miss the crunch of fried chicken? No problem. Consider using either Shake 'n Bake or Oven Fry mixes to make your chicken. Both add just two grams of fat per serving. Boxes contain two packets of mix and plastic bags for coating the chicken; each packet contains enough for four servings of chicken. For four eaters, I make two chicken breasts (for one half per person), four drumsticks, and four wings. Remove the skin from the chicken, moisten with water, and toss with coating mix in a plastic bag.

Serve with either broasted or mashed potatoes. Heat some chicken gravy for the spuds. For an extra Southern touch, make some cornbread and black-eyed peas.

OPTION: TRY THE SHAKE 'N BAKE OR OVEN FRY COATINGS FOR PORK CHOPS AS WELL. (THE EXTRA CRISPY TYPES HAVE EXTRA FAT.) SELECT BONELESS LOIN CHOPS AND TRIM THE RIND OF FAT PRIOR TO COATING.

 DAY 22: CHEESEBURGERS AND TRIMMINGS

Be it ever so humble, there's nothing like a good cheeseburger. Start with extra-lean beef. Make four patties per pound. Season to taste with salt and pepper prior to grilling on a large skillet or electric griddle sprayed with Pam. Cook three minutes per side. About halfway through cooking the second side, put on a slice or two of low-fat cheese and tent with aluminum foil or skillet cover. Serve on a sesame seed roll with the trimmings you enjoy: lettuce, tomato slices, raw or grilled onion rings, pickles, and condiments.

Put out bowls of fat-free potato chips and vegetarian baked beans. If corn is in season, this is the time to enjoy it on the cob.

For those onions, slice thinly and separate into rings. Grill over a low heat in a large nonstick pan liberally sprayed with Pam. Sprinkle with a bit of paprika. Let the onions cook for the entire preparation time, about thirty minutes, to slowly turn them golden brown and slightly crispy here and there.

No doubt the beverage of choice for this meal will have to be a chocolate milk shake or malt. For each shake add six ounces of skim milk, one dip of Dreyer's or Edy's fat-free ice cream (vanilla or chocolate for a double-chocolate shake), two tablespoons of chocolate syrup, and if preferred, one tablespoon of Carnation malted milk mix into a blender; swirl until smooth and serve into large glasses topped with a "head" of Reddi-Wip Lite whipped topping.

So much for steamed vegetables and rice!

DAY 23: PESTO PASTA AND MINESTRONE SOUP

I give Dawn full credit for this pesto recipe, which has lots of flavor even though she greatly reduced the fat content. It goes well with pastas of all sorts, but we usually have pesto with spirals (rotini) or shells. Consider the pasta as the main course, with side dishes of vegetables and a crusty bread. Or enjoy your vegetables in the minestrone soup.

Pesto

2 cups basil, trimmed of stems, loosely packed
¼ cup pine nuts (pignoli or pinons)
¾ cup nonfat or reduced-fat Parmesan cheese, grated
3 large garlic cloves
¼ cup olive oil

Put all ingredients except olive oil into blender and pulse until well mulched. Scrape down sides as necessary. Add olive oil a little at a time, pulsing to blend. Add to hot, drained but still wet, pasta and toss to coat evenly.

OPTION: MAKE A DOUBLE RECIPE THE WAY DAWN DOES AND FREEZE HALF FOR ANOTHER TIME. YOU CAN ALSO CHIP OFF A BIT OF THE FROZEN PESTO NOW AND THEN FOR A MARVELOUS SEASONING FOR SOUPS.

Minestrone Soup

There are as many variations on minestrone soup as there are chefs to prepare it. This one comes from a good friend of mine, Christian Chavanne, who grew up in the South of France. He's now the executive chef at the yacht club in Corpus Christi, Texas. His recipe serves four, so you might want to double it for the freezer.

2 tsp olive oil
1 medium onion, minced
1 scallion, chopped
1 medium carrot, peeled and diced
2 quarts low-salt chicken broth
¾ cup cooked or canned and drained white beans
2 small zucchini, diced
2 large ripe tomatoes, seeded and diced

1 tbsp tomato paste
½ small head of cabbage, finely chopped
½ tsp Italian seasoning
1 bay leaf
½ package (10 oz) frozen spinach
1 tbsp salt (optional)
½ tsp ground black pepper (freshly ground is best)
4 oz elbow macaroni (such as Creamette)
½ cup frozen green peas
2 tbsp fresh parsley, chopped
2 tbsp fresh basil, chopped

Sauté onion and scallion in olive oil in a large saucepan for three minutes. Add carrots and sauté another three minutes. Add broth, zucchini, tomatoes, tomato paste, cabbage, Italian seasoning, bay leaf, spinach, salt, and pepper. Bring to a boil, lower heat, and simmer one hour. Add pasta, peas, parsley, and basil; simmer an additional ten minutes. Serve with a sprinkle of grated Parmesan cheese if you wish and a twist or two of freshly ground black pepper.

DAY 24: HELEN'S PEPPER STEAK

This isn't pepper steak by ordinary definitions. It's more like a stroganoff with bell peppers. But my Mom always called it pepper steak. Unfortunately, I had to give it up for a few years until nonfat sour cream and reduced-fat cream of tomato soup came on the market. The lowest fat version will call for Meucci Ranch chuck steak, but you can also use round steak trimmed of visible fat. Mark my words: If you make this recipe once, it will become a family favorite—or my mom's name isn't Helen!

1 pound low-fat beef cut into ½-inch strips
1 tbsp canola oil
1 packet dried onion soup mix
¼ cup water
2 large green bell peppers cut into strips
1 bay leaf
1 can (10¾ ounce) Campbell's Healthy Request Cream of Tomato soup
2 tbsp nonfat sour cream

In a heavy skillet that has a cover, brown meat in oil. Add dried onion soup mix and water, stir, cover, and simmer one hour or until tender. Add bay leaf, tomato soup, and a little more water if needed. Simmer fifteen minutes. Add green pepper strips and simmer a final fifteen minutes. Remove from heat and allow to cool down a bit before adding the sour cream so it doesn't crack. Serve with noodles.

DAY 25: ROAST TURKEY AND ALL THE TRIMMINGS

Who says we have to wait until Thanksgiving to enjoy this festive treat? Why not have it a few times a year? There's nothing to it.

Start with a turkey breast, rather than the whole turkey. The breast is lowest in fat and easiest to carve, eliminating the mess that surrounds a full bird. During the summer, roast it over charcoal. In colder times, roast the turkey in the oven. Try using a plastic cooking bag; it keeps the breast nice and juicy.

Either way, roast some sweet potatoes or yams at the same time. Pierce them to prevent explosion, wrap with aluminum foil, and cook about forty-five minutes or until fork tender.

Stove Top stuffing is the way to go unless you want to go to the bother of making your own from scratch. In neither case should you stuff the bird, since that allows the fat to drip into the dressing, turning it into one giant fat ball. Read the Stove Top label, and you'll see that a one-half-cup serving has three grams of fat as packaged and nine grams as prepared after you add the butter or margarine the directions call for. You can cut that additional fat entirely by simply replacing the butter or margarine with Butter Buds; instead of two tablespoons of margarine, use one tablespoon Butter Buds. Otherwise, follow the instructions exactly. You'll get all the taste, and you won't miss the fat.

You'll want cranberry sauce, of course. And plan on a green vegetable to balance the color as well as the nutrition. Let us all give thanks for our low-fat abundance!

DAY 26: RARE, JUICY STEAKS

I'll make this one brief, since there's only one way to enjoy a filet mignon, New York strip sirloin, or ribeye with less fat than you'd get from a chicken breast without the skin or even a piece of white fish. Meucci Ranch will be happy to ship its steaks right to your door.

Because these steaks are so low in fat, they don't char when you cook them. To get that effect, simply rub in a bit of olive oil or spray some Pam on both sides. The fat burns off when cooking and sizzles that meat just like we like it. The low-fat content means the steaks cook a lot faster, so figure on no more than three minutes per side to get a rare or medium-rare steak.

To me, steak automatically calls for a baked potato. I top mine with a sprinkle of Butter Buds, a dollop of nonfat sour cream, and perhaps some chopped chives. Let the Butter Buds melt into the potato before putting on the sour cream.

For a vegetable, corn on the cob fills the bill like no other. If it's not in season, perhaps some carrots will suffice. Along with the steaks, pop tomato halves topped with some low-fat or nonfat Parmesan cheese into the oven. Broil to cook the tomato and brown and melt the cheese. Mighty good!

DAY 27: PIZZA

America discovered pizza in the 1950s, and we haven't stopped devouring those pies since. In fact, pizza consistently tops the foods ordered outside the home. Sure, the ones delivered to your door are good, but you can make your own and save both fat and money. Start by making the crusts.

Pizza Crust

¾ cup plus 4 tsp warm water
1 tsp granulated sugar
1 pkg dried active yeast
2¾ cups all-purpose flour
1 tsp salt
2 tbsp cornmeal

Mix water, sugar, and yeast in a small bowl. Stir often until it starts to froth (about five minutes). Preheat oven to 425° F. In a large bowl, mix flour and salt. Add yeast mixture and knead by hand for five minutes. (If you have a mixer with a dough hook, mix on low for five minutes or until dough is elastic.) Place the dough into a bowl covered with a damp cloth and let rise for thirty minutes at room temperature.

Divide the dough into four equal portions. Roll each into a ball and knead one more minute per ball. Let rise another ten minutes.

Roll out onto a floured surface and sprinkle equal amounts of cornmeal on the top of two baking sheets. Place each dough round on the sheet and brush with bit of olive oil.

For the sauce, use either Ragu or other commercial brands, or buy a little container at a local pizza parlor on the way home from work. Spread that sauce evenly over the four crusts. Now it's up to you to decide what you like on yours. The advantage of four separate crusts is that you can make them all differently, depending on everyone's tastes. Here are some choices:

bell peppers	Canadian bacon or ham
sliced tomatoes	pineapple
black or green olives	anchovies
onions	jalapeño peppers

Do you like sausage? So do I. I keep a supply of pizza sausage in my freezer so I'll have it handy. To make pizza sausage, mix one pound of lean ground beef with one half package of Spice 'n' Slice Southern Style Breakfast Sausage mix and one teaspoon of fennel. Pinch off into little dabs to be spotted all over the pizza. I freeze the sausage in two-ounce portions, enough for one small pizza along with other toppings.

Or do you prefer pepperoni? Then order a supply of the Spice 'n' Slice pepperoni sausage mix. Just mix the package of spices and curing agents with two pounds of lean ground beef or other meat, form into a cylinder, and bake one hour. Let cool and slice into thin rounds for your pizza. Freeze the rest for future use.

Of course, you need cheese. Even the federal government won't call it a pizza if it doesn't have cheese. Just ask Wolfgang "Spago" Puck, who tried to call his cheeseless designer creations "pizza." You get to choose how much fat you're willing to pile on by the kind of cheese you select.

Of course, there's nonfat mozzarella, made by Alpine Lace and Healthy Choice, either in ready-to-use shreds or blocks you can grate, but that cheese doesn't melt too well. You can improve the melt by putting the cheese *under* the tomato sauce, by combining the sauce and cheese, or by spraying the cheese with a bit of Pam before baking.

Regular mozzarella cheese has about six grams of fat per ounce. Part-skim mozzarella brings that down to four grams. Now at least two brands,

Frigo Truly Light and Sargento Light, lower the fat content to 2.5 grams per ounce. Putting three ounces of such cheese on your pizza lifts the total fat to 7.5 grams. There's very little other fat in that meal, so that number might be totally acceptable to you. Surely there is a big difference in taste, melt, and "mouth-feel" with the low-fat rather than the nonfat cheese.

OPTION: MOST OF THE WORK IN A PIZZA COMES FROM MAKING THE CRUST. ALTHOUGH THE CRUST PRODUCED WITH MY RECIPE IS REALLY EXCELLENT AND WORTH THE EFFORT, IN A TIME CRUNCH YOU MIGHT OPT TO BUY A READY-MADE CRUST IN A SUPERMARKET. CONTADINA IS ONE BRAND. ANOTHER POSSIBILITY IS TO ASK THE LOCAL PIZZA PARLOR TO SELL YOU THE CRUST AS WELL AS THE SAUCE FOR YOU TO PUT TOGETHER AT HOME.

 DAY 28: CHINESE STIR-FRY

A typical Chinese take-out meal for four can easily top twenty dollars. With that figure in mind, it won't take long for you to recoup an investment in a good electric wok with a nonstick surface. I prefer electric over the kind that goes over the stove-top heating element, either gas or electric, because of the far superior temperature control. In addition to Chinese stir-fry, you'll be able to make other foods, including Mexican fajitas, with ease. You won't go wrong with a wok purchase.

What to stir-fry? What do you like? You can stir-fry all the meats, seafood, and vegetables you prefer. There's something therapeutic about working with a good chef's knife and cutting board to prepare ingredients such as these:

- lean beef cuts
- pork tenderloin
- fish of all sorts
- shrimp, crab, and scallops
- fresh vegetables including broccoli, carrots, bean sprouts, snow peas, celery, spinach, cabbage, bok choi, bell peppers, onion, asparagus, and mushrooms
- dried mushrooms
- canned vegetables, including baby ears of corn, water chestnuts, mushrooms, and bamboo shoots

A glance at the Chinese/Asian section of your supermarket will get your imagination and tastebuds working. You'll find packets of seasonings to create a spectrum of flavors from sweet and sour to black bean to garlic and ginger to spicy Szechwan.

Though the stir-fry process might seem intimidating at first, you'll find it is one of the simplest and actually foolproof cooking techniques. Heat the wok and add some peanut or corn oil, perhaps with a dash of sesame oil for additional flavor. This is one time not to use canola oil, since it smokes at high temperatures. Then toss in your chopped vegetables, stir with the oil for just two or three minutes, and they're done. Remove the veggies and fry up your meats, fish, or chicken. Mix them together, add your seasonings, and you're set to eat. Serve with plenty of steamed rice.

DAY 29: SHEPHERD'S PIE

Traveling in Australia with me while I was on a media tour with one of my books, my family fell in love with what's originally a British dish called shepherd's pie. This is a mixture of minced lamb with peas and carrots, topped with mashed potatoes as the "crust," and baked. Of course, as served in a restaurant, that Australian pie was extremely high in fat. So I came up with a healthier version.

1 pound low-fat ground beef
1 tbsp canola oil
½ cup chopped onions
1 tbsp paprika
1 tsp onion powder
1 tsp garlic powder
1 tsp white pepper
1 tsp salt (optional)
1 bay leaf
4 oz water

Heat canola oil in skillet. Brown beef together with onions. Add remaining ingredients. Bring to bubble and simmer for five minutes.

Spray a 9-x-9-inch casserole dish with Pam. Spread meat mixture and top with mashed potatoes. Bake in 400°F oven for twenty minutes. Serve with a salad and crusty bread. G'Day, Mate!

DAY 30: SKEWERED SHRIMP 'N' SCALLOPS

You can make this recipe with any fish or seafood combination you wish. Skewer the veggies separately, since they take longer to cook than either shrimp or scallops.

Marinade

½ cup chicken broth
1 tbsp lime juice
1 tbsp lemon juice
1 tbsp orange juice
1 tbsp cider vinegar
2 tbsp canola oil
3 tbsp finely chopped parsley
3 cloves garlic, minced
½ tsp salt
½ tsp white pepper

Skewering Foods

½ pound scallops
½ pound shrimp
1 green pepper, cut in eight pieces
1 large sweet onion (Bermuda, Maui, Vidalia)
2 pounds small red potatoes (approximately 8 potatoes)

Peel and devein shrimp. Rinse scallops. Mix marinade ingredients into large plastic food storage bag. Place seafood and vegetables in marinade, seal, and refrigerate two to three hours. Skewer the shrimp, scallops, and veggies separately. Broil or grill until shrimp and scallops lose their transparency; do not overcook these delicate foods. Vegetables will take about ten minutes; seafood about four minutes. Serves four.

DON'T FORGET THE VEGETABLES

We're only beginning to discover the underlying benefits of eating plenty of fruits and vegetables every day. Many people turn their noses up at vegetables, relegating them to garnish on the plate rather than a major part of the meal. I think that's because we're used to dull, boring preparations. Steamed vegetables with a squirt of lemon juice might be all right now and then, but a little creativity is long overdue.

I'll bet that squash probably isn't one of your family's favorites, but try acorn squash my way. Cut it in half, scoop out the seeds, and pierce repeatedly with a fork. Then sprinkle both halves with brown sugar and Butter Buds. Microwave on high for fifteen minutes. You'll have a delicious side dish in no time.

Go back to some of the old-fashioned recipes in those old Betty Crocker and Fannie Farmer cookbooks. Generally, they call for butter, cream, and cream soups, but you can easily substitute low-fat ingredients. Do you remember that 1950s favorite, green-bean casserole? The original recipe was packed with ninety grams of fat coming from cream of mushroom soup, half-and-half, and canned French-fried onions. Today you can use Campbell's Healthy Request Cream of Mushroom Soup, evaporated skim milk, and low-fat or nonfat potato chips to make a wonderful 1990s rendition.

Green Bean Casserole

1 9 oz package frozen green beans (don't thaw)
1 10¾ ounce can Campbell's Healthy Request Cream of Mushroom Soup
1 cup evaporated skim milk
½ tsp onion powder
¼ tsp garlic powder
¼ tsp salt
¼ tsp pepper
½ cup crushed low-fat or nonfat potato chips

Preheat oven to 425°F. Put green beans into a two-quart baking dish. Stir together remaining ingredients except the potato chips and pour over beans. Bake for fifteen minutes or till bubbling. Top with crumbled potato chips.

How much fat is in this updated version? Just five grams from the soup for the entire recipe. Obviously, the beans, skim milk, and seasonings add no fat at all, and the potato chips will have either no fat or just a gram or two.

BE YOUR OWN DIETITIAN

I asked Barbara Crouse, R.N., to do the nutrition analyses for the recipes in these chapters. She's the dietitian at the Heart Institute of the Desert in Rancho Mirage, California, where I act on a consulting basis as director of lifestyle modification. As you've seen, these recipes are quite low in fat. Barbara was kind enough to put them through her computer, but I've been cooking and enjoying those foods for years, not knowing exactly how many grams of fat, milligrams of cholesterol, or calories were in them.

But I knew that they were quite healthy because I've learned to "eyeball" a recipe and make a pretty accurate general assessment. If an original recipe calls for cheddar cheese, I use low fat instead. Rather than nine grams of fat per ounce of cheese, I get just three. If I use three ounces of cheese in the recipe, the total fat grams from cheese will be nine. The meat or poultry or pork will provide another three to six fat grams per ounce, using the kinds that I've suggested for you as well. All oils have fourteen grams of fat per tablespoon, so I calculate accordingly. Then I consult the nutrition facts labels to see how much fat comes from whatever products I'm using that day. Add it all up, divide by four for my family, and there it is. Nothing to it.

Well, there you have it: a month's supply of low-fat recipes, assuming that you want to cook or have time to do so, thirty days in a row. More realistically, you'll probably go out for food once or twice a week, and you'll intersperse these ideas with food favorites of your own.

I've included only three seafood menus, and only one of those is for a fish dinner. As discussed earlier, those who consume fish a couple of times weekly are better protected against heart disease, but since fish preparation is relatively straightforward, I'll leave that to you. Just be sure not to overcook fish. It should still be quite moist in the center, rather than dry and flaky.

With all these things considered, you'll have the next two months of food decisions covered. During those eight weeks, you'll also want to follow some or all of the recommendations I've made throughout the book in terms of exercise and the use of phytosterols and SeQuester to block the absorption of cholesterol and fat, respectively. You'll also want to discuss the potential use of niacin with your physician if your cholesterol level is signficantly elevated. It's all part of the revolution to eradicate heart disease now and into the twenty-first century. *Bon apetit!*

NUTRITIONAL ANALYSIS OF RECIPES

RECIPE (PAGE)	CALORIES	FAT (GRAMS)	SATURATED FAT (MG)	CHOLESTEROL (MG)	SODIUM
LUNCH					
Monte Cristo Sandwich (266)	432	7.2	1.7	37	1,187
Sloppy Joe (267)	302	7.0	2.3	72	638
Cheeseburger (268)	400	7.1	1.8	72	594
Grilled Cheese (269)	252	5.9	4.1	29	522
Tuna Salad Sandwich (269)	291	5.6	1.0	39	968
BLT Sandwich (270)	222	3.7	0.4	45	792
Australian Sausage Roll (271)	257	7.0	2.1	72	140
DINNER					
Sauerbraten (276)	257	10.0	2.8	76	475
Potato Pancakes (276)	124	0.5	0.1	0	286
Chicken Cacciatore (277)	349	14.0	2.7	96	601
Pork Sausage Patties (278)	144	4.2	1.4	81	725
Yakitori Chicken (279)	323	9.0	2.5	96	171
Swedish Meatballs (280)	650	10.0	1.7	72	224
Roast Salmon & Sauce (281)	223	6.7	1.0	88	505
Fettucine (282)	375	8.0	1.7	3	138
Sweet 'n' Sour Pork (283)	294	9.5	1.7	81	604
Italian Meatballs (284)	185	5.7	2.0	77	590
Turkey Sandwiches (285)	268	4.5	0.9	48	1,951
Chili Mac (285)	625	8.5	2.0	72	1,413
Roast Pork Tenderloin (286)	144	4.0	1.4	80	58
Veal Scallopini (287)	167	5.5	2.1	89	301
Barbecue Chicken (290)	380	10.0	2.2	138	375
Manicotti (291)	588	17.0	8.0	70	1,295
Chicken à la King (292)	451	12.0	4.0	111	804
Meatloaf, Mashed Potatoes, & Gravy (292)	335	11.3	3.7	110	460
Lobster Newburg (293)	217	8.5	1.2	82	487
Cheeseburger (295)	400	7.1	1.8	72	594
Pesto Pasta (296)	561	20.0	2.8	2	59
Minestrone Soup (296)	280	4.5	0.8	0	670
Pepper Steak (297)	676	12.3	2.7	77	1,175
Roast Turkey/Trimmings (298)	332	8.4	1.8	119	570
Skewered Shrimp 'n' Scallops (303)	362	4.0	0.5	106	323

ALL ANALYSIS REFLECTS 1/4 OF RECIPE

· 26 ·

Dining Smart for Your Heart

Eating out has become an American way of life. We consume about half of our meals in restaurants, dining out on average nearly four times a week. Today, restaurants aren't always a luxury; for dual income families, there's just less time to cook.

American restaurants offer more variety than any others in the world. Yet some critics complain that dining out is a health threat. Bunk. It's a matter of making wise selections. Condemning restaurants because they serve high-fat dishes is like attacking bakeries because they sell doughnuts as well as bread.

HAVE IT YOUR WAY!

Many people are intimidated by servers in restaurants. They fear asking a question or making a request. Ironically, the server in American restaurants is the best in the world. Take advantage of that. Remember that you're the one leaving the tip.

The server is there to answer your questions, bring special requests to the chef, and make certain that everything brought to your table is up to expectations.

You have a right to know how the chef's special is prepared. Ask about the sauce. Is it cream-based? Is the fish sautéed in butter? Get specific about it. Once a server promised that the fish was sautéed only in olive oil, but the dish arrived with the fish swimming in butter. "The chef does not sauté in butter," the server explained, "he *finishes* with butter!"

My wife Dawn came up with a terrific shortcut. I simply tell the server that I don't eat dairy foods and ask what dishes either have none or can be made without butter or cream.

If the salmon comes with a cream sauce and the halibut has a black olive and garlic creation, ask to have the sauces switched. If no sauces meet your needs, request a special concoction. You will be surprised at how often you can create your own masterpiece.

It's best to know something about a restaurant in advance. One of the best ways to do that will also save you a lot of money. A Connecticut-based company publishes a bargain-seeker's book titled *Entertainment '96* (or whatever the year) that offers two-for-one meals. The book provides the menus for restaurants in a given city along with prices you can expect to pay. You receive one complimentary dinner or lunch when a second of greater or equal value is purchased, from fine dining to fast food. Books are available from November 1 through August 31. More than one hundred cities from Akron to Winnipeg are served in the United States and Canada. The price of the book is a pittance in comparison to what you'll save in the course of the year. Give the company a call at (800) 374-4464 to place your order.

'ROUND THE WORLD CUISINE

You can find healthful, delicious foods in every country in the world. Here in America we can enjoy all those cuisines right in our own backyards. It just takes a bit of knowledge about those foods to make the wisest choices.

Italian restaurants remain America's eating-out favorites in survey after survey. Whether decorated with the stereotyped red-and-white checked tablecloths and a dripping candle in a chianti bottle or the trendy trappings of more modern incarnations, Italian restaurants offer delicious foods both old and new.

Start with a marvelous bowl of soup. Minestrone combines the best of Italian cookery with its beans and vegetables, and every chef prepares it in a distinctive way. Try an order of "pasta fazool," as the old-timers would call *pasta e fagioli*, a combination of beans and macaroni in a soothing broth.

Antipasta salad comes dressed with a splash of olive oil and vinegar, just as it's been for decades. Then on to the main course.

No true Italian could consider a meal complete without pasta. Hundreds of shapes and configurations give the same basic blend of flour and water totally different tastes and textures.

For sauce, choose a classic tomato with basil blend, a marinara, or the spicy *putanesca* named for the "working girls" whose charms beckoned more effectively when the bellies of prospective customers were filled with food and drink. Not familiar with *putanesca* sauce? It's made with olives, capers, tomatoes, anchovies, and hot peppers in any number of combinations.

Purists need no bread, believing that pasta should suffice. Others enjoy the crunch of a crusty Italian bread, dipped perhaps into the last of the sauce. You can also enjoy your bread as *bruschetta,* slightly toasted with garlic and olive oil, topped with tomatoes and fresh basil. It's the original Italian open-face sandwich.

Actually, pizza is a variation on that same theme. The first pizza was *margherita,* a very simple combination of crust, tomatoes, basil, and olive oil. Of course, any menu today will list at least a dozen variations. Most come with cheese, and that's where the fat lurks.

Virtually any pizza can be made without cheese, however, and many of the earliest were designed with none at all. Next, one could ask the chef to put on half the normal amount, thus cutting the fat in half. Third, and my personal approach, is to take my own cheese along. Frigo Truly Lite mozzarella has just 2.5 grams of fat per ounce, as compared with 6 to 7 grams in ordinary mozzarella. Dawn keeps it in her purse when we go out for pizza and hands it to the server when we place our orders. Don't be shy about doing things your way.

Italians love fish and seafood of all sorts, and you'll see *pesce della casa,* or fish of the house, on every menu. Try grilled whole snapper stuffed with lemon, garlic, and herbs and wrapped in grape leaves; salmon fillet on a bed of garlicky, wilted spinach; or tuna with a piquant sauce of capers, anchovies, hot pepper, parsley, and olive oil.

Then, too, there are the chicken and veal dishes to consider. Chicken with Marsala wine, mushrooms, and shallots, or done with dried tomato, mushroom, rosemary, garlic, and white wine. How about a classic veal piccata with thinly pounded medallions of meat gently sautéed in extra-virgin olive oil with lemon, capers, and garlic?

Whatever your choice, Italian wine accompanies the meal beautifully: a crisp, white pinot grigio or a dark red chianti classico. Enjoy the beverage that has been linked with good health for centuries. *Salut!*

A bit of food history worth noting: Olive oil has always been revered in Italy, a part of the culture for millennia. When butter was first introduced by invaders from the northern countries, Italians considered it barbaric. For years thereafter, only the poorest peasants who could not afford good olive oil ate butter.

French restaurants actually owe a huge debt of gratitude to Italy. While many consider French cuisine the ultimate, its roots are Italian. When Catherine de Medici left her homeland to marry into the French royalty to bind the two countries, she brought with her more than a dozen of the best Italian chefs. Even today, similarities remain. There's no reason to assume that French restaurants are off-limits to those seeking healthy fare.

From the harbor at Marseilles comes the incomparable dish known as bouillabaise, morsels of fish and shellfish simmered in a fragrant saffron broth. Along with crusty bread and a bottle of wine, it's an incredibly satisfying meal. Sample the delights of Provence. This is one of the purest expressions of food flavors, carefully balancing, for example, a delicate piece of fish with olive oil, white wine, and herbs. Ask your server what specialties of Provence the chef takes greatest pride in creating and let him prepare your repast accordingly.

But maybe you've come for lunch and don't want a large meal. Perhaps a salade nicoise will be perfect for you, with its flakes of tuna, intense tiny black olives, anchovy fillets, green beans, slices of potato, cucumber, onion, and peppers, mixed with lettuce, radishes, and parsley. Too early for wine? Try a bottle of mineral water. Close your eyes as you sip and imagine it bubbling up from the rocks and into a crystal pool in the mountains of France.

What sorts of entrées might you expect on the heart-healthy side of a French menu? Rabbit in mustard sauce, venison, chicken breast with wine and artichoke, sea bass with bell pepper sauce, or sautéed veal and herbs. The only thing that limits most of us will be the prices!

Chinese food spans the entire spectrum of take-out chop suey to Chinois cuisine, a blending of Chinese and French. All the way along that spectrum are entirely different eating experiences. Cantonese is the most bland, the kind we remember from our childhoods. Mandarin, Hunan, and Szechwan have more exciting flavors.

When in a Chinese restaurant, eat as the Chinese do. Instead of a platter of chicken with a few vegetables and a tiny bowl of rice, they eat a huge bowl of rice, lots and lots of vegetables, and a bit of chicken or meats. Oil has always been considered a sign of wealth and luxury in China, so Chinese hosts will try to serve their guests as much as possible. Instead of being the honored guest, try to eat in a more authentic manner. Simply ask that the chef use as little oil as possible. Since each dish is individually prepared, that will pose no problem. You'll find that your food tastes a lot better with less oil than you may be used to, yielding clearer flavors and allowing you to taste the individual ingredients.

The media hype over Chinese food being "bad" for you came from choosing the highest fat dishes. There are dozens of perfectly healthy choices on any Chinese menu.

Soups make an excellent start. Each bowl tastes fresh because it's made to order. The chef starts with a chicken broth to which he adds various items, so you can tailor the soup to meet exactly your preferences. I always ask for more mushrooms to replace the pork.

Then it's on to the main courses. Chinese servers will do virtually anything to make the meal exactly the way you want it to be. You can custom design your meal to meet your precise tastes and desires. You might find ingredients from two or three dishes that you'd like to have combined with the sauce from yet a fourth listing. No problem.

Ask questions. Don't wait till the dish gets to your table to learn that the sweet-and-pungent chicken is fried twice: once battered and deep-fried and then stir-fried along with the sauce. That's the kind of dish that has gotten Chinese food a bad name.

The Chinese are not renowned for desserts. A bowl of chilled lichee nuts, a unique fruit, or a dish of sliced oranges ends the meal nicely. Fortune cookies are a lot of fun and low in fat as well. We trade our high-fat almond cookies for extra fortune cookies.

Thai food at first appears similar to Chinese, but the flavors are distinctive. Start with the hot and sour shrimp soup or the Thai fish and seafood chowder. You'll love the special tang and the underlying taste of cilantro. Many dishes are marinated in coconut milk, which, unfortunately, will leave some saturated fat in its wake. We limit ourselves to one such dish to be shared by the family.

Thai curries are very different from the Indian offerings and much lower in fat. Remember that the Thai love their food really hot and spicy; order accordingly. Put out the fire with Thai beer, a rich brew with a creamy head and full flavor.

You'll spot a number of fish dishes on the menu, either poached or steamed with aromatic blends of spices, including lemongrass. Expect the freshest fish possible, freshness being practically a fetish for all Asian chefs.

Look for a long list of distinctive Thai noodle dishes: delicate glassy noodles; spaghetti-sized rice noodles; flat, broad, filling, and satisfying noodles—all with names you'll want to leave to the server to pronounce.

No Thai dishes are served with vegetables. Order those separately from a typically extensive selection: stir-fried green beans with chilis, greens with garlic and oyster sauce, spinach with fish sauce, and others.

Other Asian cuisines offer their own remarkable tastes. If you're lucky enough to live where Philippine, Indonesian, and Korean restaurants spring up, look to them for wonderfully healthy and delicious variety. Japanese restaurants are more common and offer a wide selection of low-fat dishes. It's no coincidence that the Asian countries have the lowest rates of heart disease in the world.

Middle Eastern restaurants provide a fine change of pace. Staple foods from country to country and from restaurant to restaurant are hummus (chick peas with garlic and sesame seed oil) and baba ghanousch (eggplant dip). Eat them with pita bread as appetizers. Skewers of meats and vegetables come with the fragrant basmati rice.

South-of-the-border cuisine has been a problem for the health-minded diner. But just as Chinese restaurants have forsaken MSG, Mexican eateries are getting rid of the lard and offering healthier choices. Look for restaurants that advertise the lighter approach.

You'll also find more restaurants serving Southwestern foods. Fajitas are common: tortillas stuffed with chicken along with green peppers, onions, and mushrooms. So are more creative dishes such as grilled salmon in corn husks with green chile pesto and roasted pepper and corn salsa.

Even in more traditional Mexican restaurants, you can find foods that are low in fat. Opt for chicken enchiladas with red ranchero sauce or fish done with tomatoes, capers, and chilis. If the place still makes its refried beans with lard, ask for black beans instead. You might even consider bringing along your own low-fat cheese.

DINING OUT FOR BREAKFAST

It's no problem to find restaurants to help you break your fast without breaking your resolve to keep the fat and calories low. As a frequent traveler, I'm delighted that most of the major hotel chains list low-fat breakfasts on their menus. Hyatt, for example, makes an egg fritatta with egg substitute and a glaze of low-fat cheese, filled with green peppers and onions. The hotel even lists the number of grams of fat and milligrams of cholesterol and sodium in heart-healthy dishes for their heart-smart clientele.

That kind of service isn't limited to fancy restaurants. Denny's was one of the first family chains to offer egg substitutes. You can order any of their omelets, scrambled eggs, or French toast. Since they don't carry low-fat cheese (yet) I bring a little plastic bag of shreds with me for the chef to use in my meal. I then order my hash browns done with as little oil as possible; the flavor of the potatoes is a lot better that way. An order of ham is just right for two persons to split, or you might spot Canadian bacon. Either provides a mere fraction of the fat in bacon or sausage.

When you find a place that doesn't carry egg substitutes, simply ask the chef to use egg whites for the omelet. If you haven't tried that yet, you'll be delighted at the light flavor.

Is there a good deli in your neighborhood? Enjoy a platter of lox and bagels, with some Bermuda onion, tomatoes, and black olives. Soon we'll see nonfat cream cheese on the menu. Until then, bring a little from home. You'll make the people around you jealous they didn't think of it.

McDonald's pioneered the concept of fast-food breakfast with its Egg McMuffin. That chain also makes low-fat breakfasting easy to do. Its apple bran muffin has zero fat, and Cheerios and Wheaties are also on the menu. How about some pancakes with maple syrup? Without the margarine a stack has only four grams of fat and ten milligrams of cholesterol. But what about that Egg McMuffin? It contains eleven grams of fat and about two hundred milligrams of cholesterol. You might want to swallow a couple of SeQuester and phytosterol tablets with your orange juice.

Wherever you happen to be, at home or away, delicious, heart-smart breakfasts aren't hard to find. A fruit platter is a great way to start the day; it's something most of us aren't likely to put together for ourselves early in the morning. The same holds for good, old-fashioned oatmeal served with the works: strawberries, bananas, raisins, and some slivered almonds. I like mine with brown sugar. In the mood for a waffle? Depending on the restaurant, count on anywhere from eight to twelve grams of fat. That's really not bad, compared with fourteen grams or so for the typical blueberry muffin. If you prefer pancakes, figure on about two grams per cake.

A large percentage of the fat in any breakfast comes from the butter or margarine you add at the table. You'd be amazed at how quickly that habit can be broken. Instead of reflexively spreading it on your toast, pancakes, waffles, and muffins, try some honey or jelly or preserves. Can't go cold turkey? Use half the amount you've gotten used to, and gradually cut back. One pat of margarine or butter (one teaspoon) has four grams of fat; every tablespoon has twelve. Multiply that by the number of times you use it at the table every day, and you'll see how it adds up. Cut back, and you'll have more fat grams to enjoy in other foods both at breakfast and throughout the day.

FAST FOOD WITHOUT GUILT

The obvious advantage to fast food is that it's fast. But there's more to it than that. Fast food tastes good to us, as it does to people around the world.

McDonald's didn't build a global empire just because they could put a sandwich in a bag in a couple of minutes. Unfortunately, fast food usually means fat food, but you can get the taste and convenience without paying that fat tax. Some suggestions:

- McDonald's McLean Deluxe is a quarter-pound burger with lettuce, pickle, and tomato on a sesame seed bun and only eleven grams of fat. Wash it down with a vanilla or chocolate shake for just five to six grams more.
- Burger King's BK Broiler is a whopper of a chicken breast sandwich. Skip the BK sauce and opt for the barbecue sauce instead to cut out a lot of fat.
- Wendy's regular hamburger has nine grams of fat. A much larger grilled chicken sandwich with a nice sauce on a good bun has the same fat allowance. If you're extra hungry, go for the baked potato or the salad bar.
- Subway's submarine sandwiches are made to your order, with tuna, lean roast beef, turkey, or a crab/seafood blend (my favorite), and all the veggies they can pile on. Hold the mayo and oil.
- Regional sandwich shops include Au Bon Pain with great soups to go with your sandwich made on a terrific selection of breads. Blimpie makes a nice sandwich on pita bread and your choice of meats. D'Angelo adds steak and chicken stir-fry to the usual meat offerings, at eleven and four grams of fat, respectively.
- Arby's roast beef sandwiches rely on paper-thin, sliced beef round that is naturally low in fat. The regular has eighteen grams, juniors come in at eleven, and French dips have fifteen grams. Cut the fat further by replacing the beef with turkey breast.
- Jack-in-the-Box Teriyaki Bowls are a nice change of pace—lots of rice topped with chicken teriyaki and a few carrots and broccoli at a mere 1.5 grams of fat. Also try the chicken fajita pita with chicken, grilled onions, lettuce and tomatoes, and cheddar cheese on pita bread. Total fat content comes to eight grams, even with the cheese.
- Kentucky Fried Chicken's Rotisserie Gold is my hands-down favorite for a chicken dinner on the run. The marinade flavor goes all the way down to the bone, and the chicken's moist and juicy. Get the white-meat, quarter-section meal with mashed potatoes and coleslaw all for fourteen grams of fat. An ear of corn adds only two grams more. Just stay away from the biscuits or cornbread; one packs twelve grams of fat. Ask for an extra side dish instead.
- Chick-fil-A has about five hundred outlets in thirty-two states serving up one of the best chicken sandwiches I've ever tasted. The original Chick-fil-A sandwich is a skinless breast with a unique pressure-cooker/deep-frier prepa-

ration. The result is all the flavor you want and expect from a fried sandwich but with a very reasonable 8.5 grams of fat and only 360 calories. Taste this one to believe it, and order the lemonade. Call (404) 765-8000 for locations.

- Long John Silver's deep-fried fish and chips are astronomically high in fat, as are the fish sandwiches at other fast-food outlets. But for a mere two grams of fat, you can order the light portion baked fish with paprika; you'll get two pieces of fish with rice pilaf and a small salad. Opt for the lemon crumb fish, and the fat goes up to four grams. Want a hush puppy or two to go with that? Each has two grams of fat. Need even more food? Start with seafood chowder at six grams or the gumbo at eight grams.
- Taco Bell's Border Light menu includes tacos, burritos, and salads with half the usual fat. The chain uses low-fat cheeses and nonfat sour cream. If you like Mexican food, this is the place to indulge that taste.

There's no doubt in my mind that very soon many if not most restaurants will offer low-fat cheeses and nonfat sour cream. Remember that it wasn't too long ago that if you wanted decaf coffee, you had to settle for instant Sanka. The more the demand, the greater will be the supply.

- Pollo Loco and other similarly named outlets serve marinated chicken grilled over open flames. Most have gotten rid of the lard in their tortillas and refried beans. Ask to be sure.

ROOM FOR DESSERT?

American love licking ice cream cones, frozen custards, and frozen yogurts. One of our first treats as infants is often a messy ice cream cone, and Dad's right there to photograph the whole spectacle.

For years, the goal seemed to be to design the ice cream with the highest amount of butterfat. Now virtually all companies offer wonderful low-fat and nonfat alternatives.

Baskin-Robbins 31 Flavors has an extensive menu. Choose from fat-free daiquiri ices; fat-free yogurts in a dizzying array of flavors; soft-serve sorbet; fat-free frozen dessert made with Simplesse fat substitute; and sugar-free, low-fat frozen desserts with just one or two grams of fat per serving. When you want something other than a cone to lick, try the Sundae Bars with flavors such as light chocolate with caramel ribbon.

Remember the soft-serve stands of yesterday? They're still around, but now their products reflect our current tastes. Carvel has Thinny-Thin in various flavors with zero fat. Dairy Queen's regular vanilla cone has been trimmed down to seven grams of fat; small cones have four grams. If you want to dump the fat entirely, you can do so with frozen yogurts. TCBY has three grams per four-ounce serving. Colombo offers both nonfat and low-fat versions, and their Breezer is a soft-serve dessert with no fat, no dairy, no lactose, and no salt.

This is Bliss is amazingly good and yet it is dairy free, fat free, lactose free, cholesterol free, preservative free, sucrose free, and also free of artificial sweeteners. Their flavors are wonderful. This is Bliss is worth looking for, so call the company at (800) 892-5283 to find a location in your area.

SITTING DOWN WITH THE FAMILY

What happens when you want more than fast food but don't want to spend a lot of money for a dinner away from home? This niche has been filled by a number of local, regional, and national restaurant chains as well as by individually owned establishments. Here, too, you can enjoy a nice, low-fat meal without spending a fortune to do it.

America's family restaurants blend a wide variety of foods aimed at pleasing as many people as possible. This is one-stop shopping for stir-fry dishes, fajitas, salad bars, pasta and other Italian favorites, and basic cuisine such as roast beef and mashed potatoes. Above all, never forget that you can have whatever you want: Ignore any cautions against asking for substitutions. The competition, especially at major chains, has gotten fierce, and no one wants to lose your patronage. That fettucine primavera on the menu may be made with a cream sauce, but almost certainly you can get yours with a tomato sauce instead.

Frequently diners complain that portions are too large. One option is to order just one entrée, split it between two persons, and round the meal off with soups, salads, and appetizers. Another approach is to ask for a doggie bag immediately and put half away for a meal at home another day. Third, look for advertised early bird or sunset specials; often the portions are slightly smaller and the price tag is half the usual tariff.

Can't make up your mind about a dinner? How about having what we call in our family a "backward breakfast," which means having breakfast for dinner. Many of us can't fit going out to breakfast into our busy schedules. An Ultimate Omelet at Denny's, for example, is a really big meal and makes a wonderful dinner at a reasonable price. Have it stuffed with tomatoes, bell peppers, onions, and diced ham, along with hash browns made with very little oil and an English muffin. How about a stack of pancakes and a juicy ham steak?

Sometimes I enjoy a hot sandwich, backed up by a steaming bowl of soup, for dinner. One of my favorites is a French dip. The au jus served with that dish is virtually free of fat, but the beef isn't always as lean as I can prepare at home. When I eat out, I ask that the chef to convert the French dip to a turkey dip, which uses thinly sliced turkey breast rather than the beef.

Remember that au jus for other occasions as well. It's a great alternative to thick, heavy sauces and adds a flash of flavor to foods you might not otherwise think about. Splash some on a baked potato. Ask for a little dish of it to go with a swordfish steak. It sparks otherwise bland vegetables.

Quite a few of the national chains have introduced special "lite" menus. Look for entrées including grilled shrimp, citrus chicken, baked fish with tomato sauce, London broil, and stir-fries of all sorts. Bennigan's, Chili's, Denny's, and the Ground Round all have such menus. Houlihan's offers mesa salmon grille, blackened chicken quesadilla, and sizzling fajitas. TGI Friday has completely revamped its menu and now presents a wide array of healthy alternatives, including a turkey burger made with ground breast meat rather than the usual blend of white and dark meat. At Baker's Square look for orange roughy with rice pilaf and honey mustard chicken. Big Boy restaurants have come a long way since the days of double-burgers. Try their cajun cod and breast of chicken with mozzarella dinners, both with just twelve grams of fat. Country Kitchen has its Right Choice selections, including old-fashioned calico bean soup, barbecued pork sandwich, herb grilled chicken, and the all-American hot sandwiches (roast beef, meatloaf, or turkey). All have less than four hundred calories, 100 mg of cholesterol, and 1,000 mg of sodium. They're serving more than breakfast at IHOP these days; look for ham steak and London broil dinners. Shoney's has introduced LightSide meals, which all have less than five hundred calories: charbroiled shrimp, lasagna, spaghetti, baked fish, charbroiled chicken, and beef patty. They come with a garden salad.

Become more aware of the restaurant options in your area. Look through the entertainment section of your newspaper for advertised specials. When out shopping, drop into restaurants to check their menus for future meals.

Local chapters of the AHA publish brochures titled *Dining Out To Your Heart's Content,* which list restaurants offering heart-healthy selections. Call information to get the phone number of the AHA office near you.

NUTRITION LABELING IN RESTAURANTS?

A few restaurants, especially in hotels catering to businesspeople, list the fat, calories, cholesterol, and sodium in their food. Most fast-food restaurants make nutrition information available on request. Other restaurants put those little red hearts next to menu selections, but you can't always be sure just what they mean. The FDA has indicated it would like to see restaurants provide nutrition analyses, but that could be years from now.

In the meantime, one can make a pretty good educated guess about the nutrition status of a menu item. While you can't be expected to memorize lists of information or to carry charts and tables around with you, you can develop a sense of judgment based on just a few figures. Chicken breast, for example, has four grams of fat per 3½-ounce serving without the skin; leave on the skin, and the fat jumps to fourteen grams. Now double those numbers for entrée-sized servings in restaurants. An ounce of cheddar cheese has nine grams and mozzarella has six. When ordering a pizza you can specify just how many ounces of cheese you want on it, and thus you'll know exactly how many grams of fat you'll get. The numbers for commonly eaten foods are discussed throughout this book. It's a good idea to familiarize yourself with at least ballpark estimates.

WHETHER BY SEA, WHETHER BY AIR

You're flying at thirty-five thousand feet above the earth, and the flight attendent asks whether you'd like the cheese-laden glob of lasagna or the mystery meat with bacon grease, both of which have been sitting in the heater for the past two hours. You actually want neither, but now you're starving and it's not very convenient to step out for an alternative meal. You get the meal, enjoy it little or not at all; then you feel guilty and angry at the same time, since for that fat indulgence you could have dined exquisitely at a three-star French restaurant with all the stops pulled.

Make a vow: Never again! There's no reason to put up with that kind of food on virtually any airline in the skies today. Well, okay, maybe with the exception of Russia's Aeroflot. All you have to do is contact the airline, or have your travel agent do so, at least twenty-four hours prior to the flight to get a meal more to your liking.

Airlines don't really advertise their special meals. That's because they cost a lot more money than the standard fare, largely because they have to be specially prepared and call for more expensive ingredients. You can be sure that the person next to you will be green with envy when your special meal arrives and he or she has to settle for the usual.

All the airlines have a low-fat, low-cholesterol meal, whether for breakfast, lunch, or dinner. You can even ask what that meal will be. One time when I made a request at Air New Zealand, the agent actually asked me what I'd like. I was happy to tell her, and that's just what I got: a nice piece of broiled fish, some vegetables, a salad, and rolls served with margarine. When flying in the morning, I request an egg-substitute omelet, and often I get it. Otherwise you might have to settle for cereal and skim milk.

For something different, try either the vegetarian meal or a fruit platter. Both tend to be particularly fresh and beautifully presented. American Airlines has a very nice cold seafood platter, and all the airlines offer a seafood alternative. American is also the only airline from which you can order an Oriental stir-fry.

Here's a list of the airlines. Make a copy for your Rolodex or phone directory.

Air Canada	(800) 422-6362
Alaska Airlines	(800) 426-0333
American West	(800) 235-9292
American Airlines	(800) 433-7300
Continental	(800) 525-0280
Delta	(800) 221-1212
Northwest	(800) 225-2525
Southwest	(800) 435-9792
TWA	(800) 221-2000
United	(800) 241-6522
USAir	(800) 428-4322

But what if you forgot, and you're now at the airport with twenty minutes before departure? Take a walk through the terminal and visit the deli, restaurant, or other food outlets to see what you might take onto the plane with you. Depending on the city, you'll be disappointed or delighted. Sometimes you'll have to settle for a turkey breast sandwich—although an hour later that may well seem like a meal fit for the gods! Other times you'll find wonderful regional favorites. Dallas has a marvelous seafood bar. In San Francisco you can order a delicious sandwich on their incomparable sourdough bread. Bagels and lox to go is a great choice at many delis.

Just as we've come to expect the worst in foods in the air, so we demand the very best when we have a chance to go on a cruise. Certainly this might be just the time to toss caution to the winds and pig out completely. I've known people who deliberately lose five pounds in the weeks prior to a cruise so they can enjoy gaining it back during that marvelous week at sea. Ultimately, it's all a matter of balance and moderation taken not over just a week or even a month but a lifetime.

But let's say that you want to enjoy that cruise, eat all sorts of marvelous foods, and still keep fat and calories in control. Many of the cruise lines now cater to such desires, but none does it so well as Commodore. In addition to the standard menu, Commodore prints a special menu from which you can choose one meal or the entire week's selections. Commodore calls it the Lite Cuisine Menu.

Ask your travel agent to help you find cruise lines, as well as other vacation choices, that offer heart-healthy meals.

No matter where in the world you happen to be, at home or far away, remember to balance energy in with energy out. Stay active. You can always keep exercise in your lifestyle. There's just no reason not to get some exercise regardless of where you are or what you're doing. Thirty minutes of brisk walking per day is really all you need to maintain your metabolism and your cardiovascular health. Actually there's no better way to see a new city than by foot.

GO AHEAD AND SPLURGE!

As you can see, it's quite easy to eat out in restaurants and still enjoy a wide variety of foods that are both delicious and heart smart. But there are times when you want the prime rib even though salmon is on the menu. Maybe it's your wedding anniversary. Maybe you're at a restaurant noted for their desserts. Go for it!

I really believe that people who never give in to the urge to splurge eventually become so obsessed with food that they become neurotic about it. It's no surprise, then, that after a period of time they completely abandon all efforts at moderation. That's particularly true, in my experience, with those trying to follow an ultrastrict deprivation lifestyle.

Modify the old maxim "all things in moderation" to "all things in moderation including moderation"! Now and then, let yourself go! Give yourself permission to enjoy yourself, to relish every single bite without any guilt.

As a parent, you wouldn't allow your child to have ice cream and candy instead of nutritious foods at every meal, but you certainly do allow those treats now and then. Give that child within you the permission to indulge—not every day, not in every restaurant, not for every occasion including Groundhog Day. But when you really feel like doing so, break loose.

I have a simple rule of thumb. On those indulgent occasions, I don't even think about how many grams of fat I might consume. I assume it's high, and that's that.

If I did that every day, I'd gain weight and my coronary arteries would soon clog. I couldn't swallow enough SeQuester tablets to block all the fat in those splurges. Normally I shoot for about fifty to fifty-five grams of fat daily. So to make up for the extra grams on that special day, I cut back by ten grams per day for the next few days. Taken over time, I really haven't blown it at all.

Now, that's not just idle speculation. Dr. Margo Denke at the Health Sciences Center of the University of Texas in Dallas has spent years studying exactly that kind of calculation. Having worked with hundreds of men and women, she is convinced that healthy eating is a matter of choices made over the long haul, not just what you eat—or don't eat—for a day or so. She agrees with me that tallying and balancing those fat grams is the best way to go.

Interestingly, as time goes on, you'll find that the urge to splurge strikes less frequently, and you'll find those indulgences less and less satisfying. Tastes change. Mine have, and so will yours. That doesn't mean I don't enjoy food. I love it! But now, for example, I eat my bread without butter, just as the Europeans have done for years, and love it that way. Drawn butter actually spoils the taste of lobster for me.

There are so many wonderful foods out there to be enjoyed. Expand your horizons. Try new ethnic foods. Ask the server for suggestions. Remember that most of the world's population routinely eats a low-fat diet without thinking about it.

Keep a kind of running score in your memory. Remember a particularly good sandwich you had here, a breakfast that was healthy and enjoyable there, a dinner that was right on the mark at yet another place. Soon there'll be so many places, with so many excellent selections, that your restaurant dining will be truly à la heart.

References

CHOLESTEROL

Corti, M.C. et al. HDL cholesterol predicts coronary heart disease mortality in older persons. *Journal of the American Medical Association.* 1995: volume 274, number 7, pages 539–544.

Denke, M.A. Review of human studies evaluating individual dietary responsiveness in patients with hypercholesterolemia. *American Journal of Clinical Nutrition.* 1995: volume 62, pages 471S–477S.

Falk, E. et al. Coronary plaque disruption. *Circulation.* 1995: volume 92, pages 657–671.

Goode, G.K. and Heagerty, A.M. In vitro responses of human peripheral small arteries in hypercholesterolemia and effects of therapy. *Circulation.* 1995: volume 91, pages 2898–2903.

Gotto, A.M. Lipid lowering, regression, and coronary events. *Circulation.* 1995: volume 92, pages 646–656.

Iribarren, C. et al. Serum total cholesterol and mortality. *Journal of the American Medical Association.* 1995: volume 273, number 24, pages 1926–1932.

LaRosa, J.C. and Cleeman, J.I. Cholesterol lowering as a treatment for established coronary heart disease. *Circulation.* 1992: volume 85, number 3, pages 1229–1235.

Law, M.R. et al. By how much and how quickly does reduction in serum cholesterol concentration lower risk of ischaemic heart disease? *British Medical Journal.* 1994: volume 308, pages 367–372.

Pearson, T. et al. Optimal risk factor management in the patient after coronary revascularization. *Circulation.* 1994: volume 90, number 6, pages 3125–3133.

Quinn, T.G. et al. Development of new coronary atherosclerotic lesions during a four-year multifactor risk reduction program: the Stanford Coronary Risk Intervention Project (SCRIP). *Journal of the American College of Cardiology.* 1994: October 24, pages 900–908.

Wannamethee, G. et al. Low serum cholesterol concentrations and mortality in middle-aged British men. *British Medical Journal.* 1995: volume 311, pages 409–413.

HOMOCYSTEINE

Genest, J. et al. High levels of amino acid may influence heart disease risk. American Heart Association 67th Scientific Sessions. November 1994.

Kittmer, S. et al. Plasma homocysteine and risk of cerebral infarction. American Heart Association 35th Annual Conference on Cardiovascular Disease Epidemiology and Prevention. April 1995.

Robinson, K. et al. High plasma homocysteine is a risk factor for CHD in men, women, and the elderly and is linked to vitamin B deficiency. American Heart Association 35th Annual Conference on Cardiovascular Disease Epidemiology and Prevention. April 1995.

Selhub, J. et al. Association between plasma homocysteine concentrations and extracranial carotid-artery stenosis. *New England Journal of Medicine.* 1995: volume 332, pages 286–291.

Stampfer, M.J. and Malinow, R.M. Can lowering homocysteine levels reduce cardiovascular risk? *New England Journal of Medicine.* 1995: volume 332, pages 328–329.

Williams, R.R. et al. Higher plasma homocysteine and increased susceptibility to adverse effects of low folate in early familial coronary artery disease. Arteriosclerosis, Thrombosis, and Vascular Biology. 1995: volume 15, pages 1314–1320.

LIPOPROTEIN(A)

Maher, V. H. G. et al. Effects of lowering elevated LDL cholesterol on the cardiovascular risk of lipoprotein(a). *Journal of the American Medical Association.* 1995: volume 274, pages 1771–1774.

Rader, D.J. and Brewer, H. Lipoprotein(a). Clinical approach to a unique atherogenic lipoprotein. *Journal of the American Medical Association.* 1992: volume 267, number 8, pages 1109–1111.

Ridker, P.M. et al. Plasma concentration of lipoprotein(a) and the risk of future stroke. *Journal of the American Medical Association.* 1995: volume 273, number 16, pages 1269–1273.

Schaefer, E.J. et al. Lipoprotein(a) levels and risk of coronary heart disease in men. *Journal of the American Medical Association.* 1994: volume 271, number 13, pages 999–1003.

Terres, W. et al. Rapid angiographic progression of coronary artery disease in patients with elevated lipoprotein(a). *Circulation.* 1995: volume 91, pages 948–950.

Thompson, G.R. et al. Familial hypercholesterolaemia regression study: a randomised trial of low-density-lipoprotein apheresis. *Lancet.* 1995: volume 345, number 8953, pages 811–816.

TRIGLYCERIDES AND HDL LEVELS

Drexel, H. et al. Plasma triglycerides and three lipoprotein cholesterol fractions are independent predictors of the extent of coronary atherosclerosis. *Circulation.* 1994: volume 90, pages 2230–2235.

Miller, M. et al. Long-term predictors of subsequent cardiovascular events with coronary artery disease and "desirable" levels of plasma total cholesterol. *Circulation.* 1992: volume 86, pages 1165–1170.

NIH Consensus Conference. Triglyceride, high-density lipoprotein, and coronary heart disease. *Journal of the American Medical Association.* 1993: volume 269, number 4, pages 505–510.

Vega, G.I. and Grundy, S.M. Lipoprotein responses to treatment with lovastatin, gemfibrozil, and nicotinic acid in normolipidemic patients with hypoalphalipoproteinemia. *Archives of Internal Medicine.* 1994: volume 154, pages 73–82.

SMALL,DENSE LDL

Slyper, A.H. Low-density lipoprotein density and atherosclerosis. *Journal of the American Medical Association.* 1994: volume 272, number 4, pages 305–308.

FIBRINOGEN

Anderson, J.W. et al. Prospective, randomized, controlled comparison of the effects of low-fat and low-fat plus high-fiber diets on serum lipid concentrations. *American Journal of Clinical Nutrition.* 1992: volume 56, pages 887–894.

Anderson, J.W. et al. Cholesterol-lowering effects of psyllium-enriched cereal as an adjunct to a prudent diet in the treatment of mild to moderate hypercholesterolemia. *American Journal of Clinical Nutrition.* 1992: volume 56, pages 93–98.

Brumback, R.A. Oat products: lowering of lipids, education of public. *Journal of the American Medical Association.* 1992: volume 268, pages 2649–2650.

Cerda, J.J. et al. Inhibition of atherosclerosis by dietary pectin. *Circulation.* 1994: volume 89, pages 1247–1253.

Davidson, M.H. et al. The hypocholesterolemic effects of beta-glucan in oatmeal and oat bran. *Journal of the American Medical Association.* 1991: volume 265, pages 1833–1839.

Hunninghake, D.B. et al. Hypocholesterolemic effects of a dietary fiber supplement. *American Journal of Clinical Nutrition.* 1994: volume 59, pages 1050–1054.

Keenan, J.M. et al. Randomized, controlled, crossover trial of oat bran in hypercholesterolemic subjects. *Journal of Family Practice.* 1991: volume 33, pages 600–608.

Kelley, M.J. et al. Oat bran lowers total and low-density lipoprotein cholesterol but not lipoprotein(a) in exercising adults with borderline hypercholesterolemia. *Journal of the American Dietetic Association.* 1994: volume 94, number 12, pages 1419–1421.

Koval, G.M. Dietary oat fiber sources and blood lipids. *Journal of the American Medical Association.* 1992: volume 268, page 985.

Montalescot, G. et al. Fibrinogen after coronary angioplasty as a risk factor for restenosis. *Circulation.* 1995: volume 92, pages 31–38.

Ridker, P.M. et al. Plasma concentration of cross-linked fibrin degradation product (D-dimer) and the risk of future myocardial infarction among apparently healthy men. *Circulation.* 1994: volume 90, pages 2236–2240.

PHYTOSTEROLS

Brown, K.M. et al. Vitamin E supplementation suppresses indexes of lipid peroxidation and platelet counts. *American Journal of Clinical Nutrition.* 1994: volume 60, pages 383–387.

Day, C.E. *The Cholesterol Connection.* 1987: Artery Press, Fulton, Michigan.

Denke, M.A. Lack of efficacy of low-dose sitostanol therapy as an adjunct to a cholesterol-lowering diet in men with moderate hypercholesterolemia. *American Journal of Clinical Nutrition.* 1995: volume 61, pages 392–396.

Lees, A.M. et al. Plant sterols as cholesterol lowering agents. *Atherosclerosis.* 1977: volume 28, pages 325–328.

Mattson, F.H. et al. Optimizing the effect of plant sterols on cholesterol absorption in man. *American Journal of Clinical Nutrition.* 1982: volume 35, pages 697–700.

Miettinen, T.A. et al. Reduction of serum cholesterol with sitostanol-ester margarine in a mildly hypercholesterolemic population. *New England Journal of Medicine.* 1995: volume 333, pages 1308–1312.

Slota, T. et al. Comparison of cholesterol and beta-sitosterol. *Gut.* 1995: volume 24, pages 653–658.

ANTIOXIDANTS

Campbell, D. et al. Selenium and vitamin E status. *British Journal of Nutrition.* 1989: volume 62, pages 221–227.

Gey, K.F. et al. Inverse correlation between plasma vitamin E and mortality from ischaemic heart disease. *American Journal of Clinical Nutrition.* 1991: volume 53, pages 326S–334S.

Hallfrisch, J. et al. High plasma vitamin C associated with high plasma HDL and HDL2 cholesterol. *American Journal of Clinical Nutrition.* 1994: volume 60, pages 100–105.

Hodis, H.N. et al. Serial coronary angiographic evidence that antioxidant vitamin intake reduces progression of coronary artery atherosclerosis. *Journal of the American Medical Association.* 1995: volume 273, number 23, pages 1849– 1854.

Jialal, I. and Grundy, S.M. Effect of dietary supplementation with alpha-tocopherol on the oxidative modification of low density lipoprotein. *Journal of Lipid Research.* 1992: volume 33, pages 899–906.

Morris, D.L. et al. Serum carotenoids and coronary heart disease. *Journal of the American Medical Association.* 1994: volume 272, number 18, pages 1439–1441.

Riemersma, R.A. et al. Risk of angina pectoris and plasma concentrations of vitamins A, C, and E and carotene. *Lancet.* 1991: volume 337, pages 1–5.

Rimm, E.B. et al. Vitamin E consumption and the risk of coronary heart disease in men. *New England Journal of Medicine.* 1993: volume 20, pages 1450–1456.

Stampfer, M. J. et al. Vitamin E consumption and the risk of coronary heart disease in women. *New England Journal of Medicine.* 1993: volume 20, pages 1444– 1449.

NIACIN

Berge, K.G. and Canner, R.L. Coronary drug project: experience with niacin. *European Journal of Clinical Pharmacology.* 1991: volume 40, pages S49–S51.

Brown, G. et al. Regression of coronary artery disease as a result of intensive lipid-lowering therapy. *New England Journal of Medicine.* 1990: volume 323, number 19, pages 1289–1298.

Carlson, L.A. et al. Pronounced lowering of serum levels of lipoprotein Lp(a) in hyperlipidaemic subjects treated with nicotinic acid. *Journal of Internal Medicine.* 1989: volume 226, pages 271–276.

Davignon, J. et al. Comparative efficacy and safety of pravastatin, nicotinic acid and the two combined in patients with hypercholesterolemia. *American Journal of Cardiology.* 1994: volume 73, pages 339–345.

Droad, J.M. et al. Nicotinic acid for the treatment of hyperlipoproteinemia. *Journal of Clinical Pharmacology.* 1991: volume 31, pages 641–650.

Hoffer, A. Niacin reaction (letter to the editor). *Journal of Family Practice.* 1992: volume 34, page 677.

Keenan, J.M. et al. Niacin revisited. A randomized, controlled trial of wax-matrix sustained-release niacin in hypercholesterolemia. *Archives of Internal Medicine.* 1991: volume 151, pages 1424–1432.

Kreisberg, R.A. Niacin: a therapeutic dilemma. *American Journal of Medicine.* 1994: volume 97, pages 313–316.

Lavie, C.J. Marked benefit with sustained-release niacin therapy in patients with "isolated" very low levels of high-density lipoprotein cholesterol and coronary artery disease. *American Journal of Cardiology.* 1992: volume 69, pages 1082–1085.

Luria, M.H. Atherosclerosis: the importance of HDL cholesterol and prostacyclin: a role for niacin therapy. *Medical Hypotheses.* 1989: volume 32, pages 21–28.

McKenney, J.M. et al. A comparison of the efficacy and toxic effects of sustained vs immediate-release niacin in hypercholesterolemic patients. *Journal of the American Medical Association.* 1994: volume 271, number 9, pages 672–677.

Squires, R.W. et al. Low-dose, time-release nicotinic acid: effects in selected patients with low concentrations of high-density lipoprotein cholesterol. *Proceedings of the Mayo Clinic.* 1992: volume 67, pages 855–860.

ALCOHOL

Fuchs, C.S. et al. Alcohol consumption and mortality among women. *New England Journal of Medicine.* 1995: volume 332, number 19, pages 1245–1250.

Gaziano, J.M. et al. Moderate alcohol intake . . . and decreased risk of myocardial infarction. *New England Journal of Medicine.* 1993: volume 329, number 25, pages 1829–1834.

Jackson, R. et al. Alcohol consumption and risk of coronary heart disease. *British Medical Journal.* 1991: volume 303, pages 211–216.

Klatsky, A.I. et al. Risk of cardiovascular mortality in alcohol drinkers, ex-drinkers, and nondrinkers. *American Journal of Cardiology.* 1990: volume 66, pages 1237–1242.

Rimm, E.B. et al. Prospective study of alcohol consumption and risk of coronary disease in men. *Lancet.* 1991: volume 338, pages 464–468.

COFFEE

Urgen, R. et al. Effects of cafestol and kahwool from coffee grounds on serum lipids and serum liver enzymes in humans. *American Journal of Clinical Nutrition.* 1995: volume 61, pages 149–154.

EGGS

Barr, S.L. et al. Reducing total dietary fat without reducing saturated fatty acids does not significantly lower total plasma cholesterol concentrations in normal males. *American Journal of Clinical Nutrition.* 1992: volume 55, pages 675–681.

Ginsberg, H.N. et al. A dose-response study of the effects of dietary cholesterol on fasting and postprandial lipid and lipoprotein metabolism in healthy young men. *Arteriosclerosis, Thrombosis, and Vascular Biology.* 1994: volume 14, pages 576–586.

Lehtimaki, T. et al. Cholesterol-rich diet induced changes in plasma lipids. *Annals of Medicine.* 1992: volume 24, pages 61–66.

McCombs, R.J. et al. Attenuated hypercholesterolemic response to a high-cholesterol diet in subjects heterozygous for the apolipoprotein A-IV-2 allele. *New England Journal of Medicine.* 1994: volume 331, pages 706–710.

FATS

Gardner, C.D. and Kraemer, H.C. Mono-versus polyunsaturated dietary fat and serum lipids: a meta-analysis. American Heart Association Scientific Sessions. November 1994.

Mata, P. et al. Effect of saturated, monounsaturated and polyunsaturated n-6 and n-3 fatty acid-rich diets on the susceptibility of LDL to oxidative modification. American Heart Association Scientific Sessions. November 1994.

Nash, D. Grapeseed oil and HDL and LDL cholesterol. American College of Cardiology Annual Meeting. March 1993.

Uusitupa, M. et al. Effects of two high-fat diets with different fatty acid compositions on glucose and lipid metabolism in healthy young women. *American Journal of Clinical Nutrition.* 1994: volume 59, pages 1310–1316.

FISH OILS

Ascherio, A. et al. Dietary intake of marine n-3 fatty acids, fish intake, and the risk of coronary disease among men. *New England Journal of Medicine.* 1995: volume 332, number 15, pages 977–982.

McVeigh, G.E. et al. Fish oil improves arterial compliance in non-insulin-dependent diabetes mellitus. *Arteriosclerosis, Thrombosis, and Vascular Biology.* 1994: volume 14, pages 1425–1429.

Morris, M.C. et al. Does fish oil lower blood pressure? *Circulation.* 1993: volume 88, pages 523–533.

Nordoy, A. et al. Individual effects of dietary saturated fatty acids and fish oil on plasma lipids and lipoproteins in normal men. *American Journal of Clinical Nutrition.* 1993: volume 57, pages 634–639.

Praskash, C. et al. Decreased systemic thromboxane A2 biosynthesis in normal human subjects fed a salmon-rich diet. *American Journal of Clinical Nutrition.* 1994: volume 60, pages 369–373.

GARLIC

Jain, A.K. et al. Can garlic reduce levels of serum lipids? *American Journal of Medicine.* 1993: volume 94, pages 632–635.

Orekov, A.N. et al. Direct antiatherosclerotic and antiatherogenic effects of garlic. *Cardiovascular Drugs and Therapy: Abstracts of the 5th International Symposium on Cardiovascular Pharmacotherapy.* 1993: volume 7, page 428S.

Warshafsky, S. et al. Effect of garlic on total serum cholesterol. *Annals of Internal Medicine.* 1993: volume 119, pages 599–605.

IRON

Ascherio, A. and Willett, W.C. Are body iron stores related to the risk of coronary heart disease? *New England Journal of Medicine.* 1994: volume 330, number 16, pages 1151–1153.

Miller, M. and Hutchins G.M. Hemochromatosis, multiorgan hemosiderosis, and coronary artery disease. *Journal of the American Medical Association.* 1994: volume 272, pages 231–233.

Sempos, C.T. Body iron stores and the risk of coronary heart disease. *New England Journal of Medicine.* 1994: volume 330, pages 1119–1124.

NUTS

Fraser, G.E. et al. A possible protective effect of nut consumption on risk of coronary heart disease. *Archives of Internal Medicine.* 1992: volume 152, pages 1416–1424.

Sabate, J. et al. Effects of walnuts on serum lipid levels and blood pressure in normal men. *New England Journal of Medicine.* 1993: volume 328, pages 603–607.

SODIUM

Bullock, C. Don't throw your salt-shakers away, says S.C. researcher. *Heartstyle* (American Heart Association). 1994: page 4.

Goldfinger, S.E. An elemental finding. *Harvard Health Letter.* May, 1992. page 5.

Klag, M.J. et al. Salt sensitivity and risk of subsequent hypertension. *Circulation.* 1993: volume 88, page I–612.

Krishna, G.G. and Kapoor, S.C. Potassium depletion exacerbates essential hypertension. *Annals of Internal Medicine.* 1991: volume 115, pages 77–83.

TRANS FATTY ACIDS

American Heart Association Nutrition Committee Advisory. *Trans Fatty Acids.* April 1, 1994.

Expert Panel on Trans Fatty Acids and Coronary Heart Disease. Trans fatty acids and coronary heart disease risk. Kris-Etherton P. M., ed. *American Journal of Clinical Nutrition* (supplement). 1995: volume 62, pages 655S–708S.

Litin, L., and Sacks, F. Transfatty acid content of common foods. *New England Journal of Medicine.* 1993: volume 329, pages 1969–1970.

Russell, R.M. Nutrition. *Journal of the American Medical Association.* 1995: volume 273, number 21, pages 1699–1700.

Willett, W.C. et al. Intake of trans fatty acids and risk of coronary heart disease in women. *Lancet.* 1993: volume 341, pages 581–585.

Index

(Page numbers in **boldface** refer to recipes)